FINANCIAL MARKET RATES AND FLOWS

FINANCIAL MARKET RATES AND FLOWS

SIXTH EDITION

❖ ❖ ❖

JAMES C. VAN HORNE

STANFORD UNIVERSITY

Prentice
Hall

UPPER SADDLE RIVER, NEW JERSEY

Library of Congress Cataloging-in-Publication Data

Van Horne, James C.
    Financial market rates and flows / James C. Van Horne—6th ed.
       p. cm.
    Includes bibliographical references and index.
    ISBN 0-13-018044-0
      1. Interest rates.   2. Flow of funds.   3. Capital market.   4. Hedging (finance)
    I. Title.
    HB539.V35 2000
    332.8—dc21   99-089729

VP/Editorial Director: James C. Boyd
Editor-in-Chief: P.J. Boardman
Senior Editor: Maureen L. Riopelle
Managing Editor: Gladys Soto
Editorial Assistant: Cheryl Clayton
Senior Marketing Manager: Lori Braumberger
Director of Production: Michael Weinstein
Production Manager: Gail Steier de Acevedo
Production Coordinator: Kelly Warsak
Permissions Coordinator: Suzanne Grappi
Manufacturing Buyer: Natacha St. Hill Moore
Senior Manufacturing and Prepress Manager: Vincent Scelta
Cover Design: Bruce Kenselaar
Composition: BookMasters, Inc.

10 9 8 7 6 5 4 3 2 1
ISBN 0-13-018044-0

PRENTICE HALL FINANCE SERIES

Personal Finance
Keown, *Personal Finance: Turning Money into Wealth*
Winger/Frasca, *Personal Finance: An Integrated Planning Approach*
Trivoli, *Personal Portfolio Management: Fundamentals and Strategies*

Investments
Alexander/Sharpe/Bailey, *Fundamentals of Investments*
Fabozzi, *Investment Management*
Fischer/Jordan, *Security Analysis and Portfolio Management*
Haugen, *Modern Investment Theory*
Taggart, *Quantitative Analysis for Investment Management*
Winger/Frasca, *Investments*
Haugen, *The New Finance*
Haugen, *The Beast on Wall Street*
Haugen, *The Inefficient Stock Market*
Sharpe/Alexander/Bailey, *Investments*

Portfolio Analysis
Fischer/Jordan, *Security Analysis and Portfolio Management*
Haugen, *Modern Investment Theory*

Options/Futures/Derivatives
Hull, *Introduction to Futures and Options Markets*
Hull, *Options, Futures, and Other Derivatives*

Risk Management/Financial Engineering
Hull, *Risk Management and Financial Engineering*
Mason/Merton/Perold/Tufano, *Cases in Financial Engineering*

Fixed Income Securities
Van Horne, *Financial Market Rates and Flows*
Handa, *FinCoach: Fixed Income* (software)

Bond Markets
Fabozzi, *Bond Markets, Analysis and Strategies*
Van Horne, *Financial Market Rates and Flows*

Capital Markets
Fabozzi/Modigliani, *Capital Markets: Institutions and Instruments*
Van Horne, *Financial Market Rates and Flows*

Corporate Finance, Survey of Finance, & Financial Economics
Bodie/Merton, *Finance*
Gallagher/Andrew, *Financial Management: Principles and Practices*
Haugen, *The New Finance: Case Against Efficient Markets*
Shapiro/Balbiret, *Modern Corporate Finance: A Multidisciplinary Approach to Value Creation*
Keown/Martin/Petty/Scott, *Basic Financial Management*
Keown/Martin/Petty/Scott, *Foundations of Finance: The Logic and Practice of Financial Management*
Emery/Finnerty/Stowe, *Principles of Financial Management*
Emery/Finnerty, *Corporate Financial Management*
Van Horne, *Financial Management and Policy*
Van Horne/Wachowicz, *Fundamentals of Financial Management*

International Finance
Baker, *International Finance: Management, Markets, and Institutions*
Grabbe, *International Financial Markets*
Rivera-Batiz/Rivera-Batiz, *International Finance and Open Economy Macroeconomics*

Capital Budgeting
Aggarwal, *Capital Budgeting Under Uncertainty*
Bierman/Smidt, *The Capital Budgeting Decision*

Mergers/Acquisitions/Takeovers
Hill/Sartoris, *Short Term Financial Management*
Weston/Chung/Siu, *Takeovers, Restructuring and Corporate Governance*

Short-Term Finance
Hill/Sartoris, *Short Term Financial Management*

Taxes and Corporate Financial Decision Making
Scholes/Wolfson, *Taxes and Business Strategy: A Global Planning Approach*

Insurance
Black/Skipper, *Life and Health Insurance*
Dorfman, *Introduction to Risk Management and Insurance*
Rejda, *Social Insurance and Economic Security*

Financial Markets and Institutions
Arshadi/Karels, *Modern Financial Intermediaries and Markets*
Dietrich, *Financial Services and Financial Institutions*
Fabozzi/Modigliani/Ferri/Jones, *Foundations of Financial Markets and Institutions*
Kaufman, *The U.S. Financial Systems*
Van Horne, *Financial Market Rates and Flows*

Commercial Banking
Dietrich, *Financial Services and Financial Institutions*
Sinkey, *Commercial Bank Financial Management*
Arshadi/Karels, *Modern Financial Intermediaries and Markets*

Entrepreneurial Finance
Adelman/Marks, *Entrepreneurial Finance*
Vaughn, *Financial Planning for the Entrepreneur*

Cases in Finance
May/May/Andrew, *Effective Writing: A Handbook for Finance People*

Financial Statement Analysis
Fraser/Ormiston, *Understanding Financial Statements*

Finance Center
For downloadable supplements and much more . . . visit us at www/prenhall.com/financecenter

CONTENTS

This book continues to be about interest rates, how they behave with changing market conditions, and how risk can be managed. We are concerned not only with primary securities, like Treasury and corporate bonds, but with derivative securities, like forward and futures contracts, debt options, swaps involving interest rates, credit and currencies, and mortgage derivatives. We will see also that embedded options in a bond or mortgage-backed security, like call and prepayment options, can be valued and option-adjusted spreads can be determined. Finally, our concern is with the management of a fixed-income portfolio and the tradeoff between risk and expected return.

Throughout, a rich body of theory is examined, as are the empirical evidence and practice that bear on the theory. The first half of the book is devoted to the foundations for understanding interest-rate behavior: market equilibration, funds flows between financial markets, mathematics of bond and money-market yields, inflation, maturity, coupon rate, default risk, and bond price volatility. The remaining chapters use these foundations to explore a variety of derivative securities and their uses, the influence of taxes on interest-rate differentials, and the social allocation of capital. The institutional backdrop is presented in conjunction with concepts, risk, and practice—not as separate chapters. I believe this approach is more lively than the chapter-by-chapter institutional descriptions seen in most books.

Because of the rapid change in interest-rate practice and theory, this edition represents another substantial revision. By chapter, the important changes follow. All data in **chapter 2** on the flow of funds have been updated, and a new section is added on the total debt outstanding for various major sectors of the economy. **Chapter 3,** Foundations for Interest Rates, has been streamlined and cut back in places. The empirical parts of **chapter 5,** Inflation and Returns, have been substantially reworked, and the section on inflation-indexed bonds and Treasury TIPS is largely new. Significant changes appear in **chapter 6,** The Term Structure of Interest Rates; these changes deal with modeling the term structure, as well as with relevant empirical work. Bond portfolio management, with respect to duration and convexity, has been strengthened in **chapter 7,** and the arbitrage efficiency between zero-coupon and coupon bonds is illustrated with an actual situation.

Perhaps the greatest changes occur in **chapter 8,** Default and Liquidity Risk. A new section is included on liquidity, and substantial changes have been made in the treatment of credit ratings, default losses and migration patterns, quality yield spreads over time, high-yield debt, and yield spreads with respect to maturity. The chapter also has been resequenced. **Chapter 9,** the first of several derivative securities chapters, contains a new section on forward contracts. In addition, implied repo rates are explained. **Chapter 10,** Derivative Securities: Options, includes a new treatment of interest-rate cap, floor, and collar valuations using "caplets" and "floorlets." A new section on interest-rate corridors also has been developed. **Chapter 11,** Derivative Securities: Interest-rate and Credit Swaps, contains an entirely new section on credit derivatives,

an important market that is continually developing. Also in this chapter is a new section on pricing an interest-rate swap, and an example is presented. The chapter has
been reorganized in other ways as well, and the treatment of secondary market values
is expanded.

Chapter 12, Embedded Options and Option-Adjusted Spreads, includes a new section on putable bonds and their valuation. The section on empirical evidence bearing
on the call feature has been largely reworked. **Chapter 13** on mortgage securities has
been completely rewritten to reflect important changes in mortgage-backed securities.
Overhauls of the treatment of mortgage derivatives, modeling prepayments, and to-be-
announced (TBA) pricing are evident. **Chapter 14,** Controlling Currency Risk, has new
sections on the Euro currency, on foreign-bond portfolio management, and on emerging market debt. Finally in **chapter 15,** The Influence of Taxes, the treatment of municipal bonds has been substantially reworked to explain better the nature of the market
and the valuation of municipals in relation to taxable bonds. Throughout, the book has
been thoroughly reviewed and updated. Only the more substantive changes are mentioned here.

Financial Market Rates and Flows can be used as a foundation text or as a supple-
ment for courses in fixed-income securities, money and banking, money and capital
markets, investments, financial risk management, and financial institutions. In addition,
it is useful to those in the financial community, in business, and in government who are
concerned with investing in or issuing fixed-income securities.

James C. Van Horne
Palo Alto, California

THE FUNCTION OF FINANCIAL MARKETS

In this book, the underlying structure of financial markets is examined, as is the price mechanism, which brings about a balance between supply and demand. Our purpose is not to describe specific money or capital markets or the institutions involved in these markets; this information is available elsewhere. Rather, this book provides a basis for understanding and analyzing interest rates and funds movements in financial markets. The instruments studied are financial assets. Unlike real, or tangible, assets, a **financial asset** is a paper claim on some other economic unit. It does not provide its owner with the physical services that a real asset does. Instead, financial assets are held as a store of value and for the return that they are expected to provide.

SAVINGS-INVESTMENT FOUNDATION

Financial assets exist in an economy because the savings of various economic units (current income less current expenditures) during a period of time differ from their investment in real assets. In this regard, an economic unit can be (1) a household or partnership, (2) a nonprofit organization, (3) a corporation (financial or nonfinancial), or (4) a government (federal, state, or local). For a number of reasons, most economic units do not balance the amount they invest during an interval of time with the amount they save. These reasons include the present income of the economic unit, expected future income, costs of goods and services, personal tastes, age, health, education, family composition, and current interest rates.

Assume for the moment a closed economy in which no foreign transactions occur. If savings equal investment for all economic units in that economy over all periods of time, there would be no external financing and no financial assets. In other words, each economic unit would be self-sufficient; current expenditures and investment in real assets would be paid for out of current income. A financial asset is created only when the investment of an economic unit in real assets exceeds its savings, and it finances this excess by borrowing, issuing equity securities, or issuing money (if the economic unit happens to be a monetary institution).[1] Of course, in order for an economic unit to finance, another economic unit or other units in the economy must be willing to lend. This interaction of the borrower with the lender determines interest rates. For identification, economic units whose current savings exceed their investment in real assets are called **savings-surplus units.** Economic units whose investment in real assets exceeds their current savings are labeled **savings-deficit units.**[2] In the economy as a whole, funds are provided by the savings-surplus units to the savings-deficit units. This exchange of funds is evidenced by pieces of paper representing financial assets to the holders and financial liabilities to the issuers.

If an economic unit holds existing financial assets, it is able to cover the excess of its investments in real assets over savings by means other than issuing financial liabilities. It simply can sell some of the financial assets it holds. Thus, as long as an economic unit holds financial assets, it does not have to increase its financial liabilities by an amount equal to its excess of investment over savings. The purchase and sale of existing financial assets occur in the **secondary market.** Transactions in this market do not increase the total stock of financial assets outstanding. It is possible, although unlikely, for a substantial number of savings-deficit units to exist in an economy over a period of time and for little change to occur in the total financial assets outstanding. For this to happen, however, savings-deficit units must have sufficient financial assets to cover the excess of their investment in real assets over savings and, of course, must be willing to sell these assets.

EFFICIENCY OF FINANCIAL MARKETS

The purpose of financial markets is to allocate savings efficiently in an economy during a period of time—a day, a week, a month, or a quarter—to parties who use funds for investment in real assets or for consumption. In this section, we regard financial markets in a broad sense as including all institutions and procedures for bringing buyers and sellers of financial instruments together, no matter what the nature of the financial instrument. If those economic units that saved were the same as those that engaged in capital formation, an economy could prosper without financial markets. In modern economies, however, a balance is *not* achieved. The more diverse the pattern of desired savings and investment among economic units, the greater the need for efficient financial markets to channel savings to ultimate users. Their job is to allocate savings from savings-surplus economic units to savings-deficit units so that the highest level of want satisfaction can be achieved. These parties should be brought together, either directly or indirectly, at the least possible cost and with the least inconvenience.

---

[1] A financial asset may be created for the purpose of financing consumption in excess of current income. Although it is possible for investment in real assets for a period to be zero, that investment would still exceed the negative savings of the economic unit.

[2] These labels correspond to those given by Raymond W. Goldsmith, *The Flow of Capital Funds in the Postwar Economy* (New York: National Bureau of Economic Research, 1965).

STAGES OF EFFICIENCY

Efficient financial markets are essential to assure adequate capital formation and economic growth in a modern economy. To appreciate this statement, imagine an economy without financial assets other than money.[3] In such an economy, each economic unit could invest in real assets only to the extent that it saved. Without financial assets, then, an economic unit would be greatly constrained in its investment behavior. If it wanted to invest in real assets, it would have to save to do so. If the amount required for investment were large in relation to current savings, the economic unit simply would have to postpone investment until it had accumulated sufficient savings. Moreover, these savings would have to be accumulated as money balances, there being no alternatives. Because of the absence of financing, many worthwhile investment opportunities would have to be postponed or abandoned by economic units lacking sufficient savings.[4]

In such a system, savings in the economy would not be channeled to the most promising investment opportunities; accordingly, capital would be less than optimally allocated. Those economic units that lacked promising investment opportunities would have no alternative except to accumulate money balances. Likewise, economic units with promising opportunities might not be able to accumulate sufficient savings rapidly enough to undertake the projects. Consequently, inferior investments might be undertaken by some economic units, while very promising investment opportunities would be postponed or abandoned by others. Capital is misallocated in such a system, and total investment tends to be low relative to what it might be with financial assets. In this situation, growth in the economy is restrained, if not stagnant, and the level of economic want satisfaction is far from optimal.

The preceding discussion has been confined to the private sector of the economy. With money, however, the federal government is able to finance its purchases of goods and services by printing money. If the federal government increases the supply of money in keeping with increases in the demand for money by other economic units, purchases of goods and services by the government increase. To the extent that the federal government centralizes investment and channels it into promising opportunities, capital formation in the economy is efficient. However, if the government is a cumbersome bureaucracy that is unresponsive to market conditions, government decisions are unlikely to result in efficient capital formation.

FINANCIAL ASSETS

We turn now to the situation in which an economy has financial assets as well as money, but no financial institutions. With financial assets, investment in real assets by an economic unit is no longer constrained by the amount of its savings. If the economic unit wants to invest more than it saves, it can do so by reducing the amount of its money balances, by selling financial assets, or by increasing its financial liabilities. When an economic unit increases its financial liabilities, it issues a **primary security.** For this to be done, however, another economic unit or other units in the economy must be willing to

---

[3] In a barter economy, without money or financial assets, each economic unit must be in balance with respect to savings and investment. It must invest in real assets in an amount equal to its savings. No economic unit could invest more than it saved.

[4] The development of this section draws on John G. Gurley and Edward S. Shaw, *Money in a Theory of Finance* (Washington, DC: The Brookings Institution, 1960).

purchase it. In a developing economy, these transactions between borrower and lender usually take the form of direct loans. The ability of economic units to finance an excess of investment over savings greatly improves the allocation of savings in a society. Many of the problems cited earlier are eliminated. Individual economic units no longer need to postpone promising investment opportunities for lack of accumulated savings. Moreover, savings-surplus units have an outlet other than money balances for their savings— an outlet that provides an expected return.

Still, there are degrees of efficiency. A system of direct loans may not be sufficient to assemble and "package" large blocks of savings for investment in large projects. To the extent that a single savings-surplus economic unit cannot service the capital needs of a savings-deficit unit, the latter must turn to additional savings-surplus units. If the need for funds is large, users may have considerable difficulty in locating pockets of available savings and in negotiating multiple loans. For one thing, their information network is limited. Consequently, ultimate savers and investors need to be brought together in a more efficient manner than through direct loans between the two parties.

To service this need, various loan brokers may come into existence to find savers and bring them together with economic units needing funds. Because brokers are specialists who are continually in the business of matching the need for funds with the supply, they are usually able to perform more efficiently and at a lower cost than are the individual economic units themselves. One improvement is that they are able to divide a primary security of a certain amount into smaller amounts more compatible with the preferences of savings-surplus economic units. As a result, savers are able to hold their savings in a diversified portfolio of primary securities; this feature encourages savers to invest in financial assets. The resulting increased attractiveness of primary securities improves the flow of savings from savers to users of funds. In addition to performing the brokerage function involved in selling securities, investment bankers may underwrite an issue of primary securities. By underwriting, investment bankers bear the risk of selling the issue. They buy the primary securities from the borrower and resell them to savers. Because they pay the borrower for the security issue, the latter does not bear the risk of not being able to sell the securities. This guaranteed purchase makes it easier than otherwise for savings-deficit economic units to finance their excess of investment in real assets over savings.

Another innovation that enhances the efficiency of the flow of savings in an economy is the development of secondary markets, where existing securities can be either bought or sold. With a viable secondary market, a savings-surplus economic unit achieves flexibility when it purchases a primary security. Should it need to sell the security in the future, it will be able to do so because the security is marketable. The existence of secondary markets encourages more risk taking on the part of savings-surplus economic units. If, in the future, they want to invest more than they save, they know that they will be able to sell financial assets as one means of covering the excess. This flexibility encourages savings-surplus economic units to make their savings available to others rather than to hold them as money balances. In addition, the secondary market gives valuable pricing information to the primary market. The prices and yields reflected in this market provide a rational basis for borrowing and lending decisions in the primary market and for pricing new loans. The mechanism by which savings-surplus economic units come into equilibrium with savings-deficit units is known as the **price discovery process.**

All of the things discussed in this section contribute to the efficiency of the flow of savings from ultimate savers to ultimate users through primary securities. As a result, capital allocation is more efficient: Savings are more readily channeled to the most promising investments.

THE ROLE OF FINANCIAL INTERMEDIARIES

Up until now, we have considered only the direct flow of savings from savers to users. However, the flow can be indirect if financial intermediaries are in the economy. Financial intermediaries include depository institutions, insurance companies, pension funds, and mutual funds. These institutions purchase primary securities and, in turn, issue their own securities. Thus, they come between ultimate borrowers and ultimate lenders. In essence, they transform direct claims—primary securities—into indirect claims—**indirect securities,** which differ in form from direct claims. For example, primary securities that a bank acquires include business loans, consumer loans, and mortgages; the indirect claims issued are demand deposit accounts, savings accounts, and certificates of deposit. A life insurance company, on the other hand, purchases mortgages and bonds, and issues life insurance policies.

Financial intermediaries transform funds in such a way as to make them more attractive. On one hand, the indirect security issued to ultimate lenders is more attractive than is a direct, or primary, security. In particular, these indirect claims are well suited to the small saver. On the other hand, the ultimate borrower is able to sell its primary securities to a financial intermediary on more attractive terms than it could if the securities were sold directly to ultimate lenders. Financial intermediaries provide a variety of services and economies that make the transformation of claims attractive.

1. *Transaction costs.* Because financial intermediaries are continually in the business of purchasing primary securities and selling indirect securities, economies of scale not available to the borrower or to the individual saver are possible. As a result, transactions costs and costs associated with locating potential borrowers and savers are lowered.
2. *Information production.* The financial intermediary is able to develop information on the ultimate borrower in a more efficient manner than the saver. Moreover, the intermediary may be able to reduce the moral hazard problem of unreliable information. Another possible advantage is that intermediaries can protect the confidentiality of information.
3. *Divisibility and flexibility.* A financial intermediary is able to pool the savings of many individual savers to purchase primary securities of varying sizes. In particular, the intermediary is able to tap small pockets of savings for ultimate investment in real assets. The offering of indirect securities of varying denominations may make financial intermediaries more attractive to the saver. Moreover, borrowers have more flexibility in dealing with a financial intermediary than with a large number of lenders and are able to obtain terms better suited to their needs.
4. *Diversification and risk.* By purchasing a number of different primary securities, the financial intermediary is able to spread risk. If these securities are less than perfectly correlated with each other, the intermediary is able to reduce the risk associated with fluctuations in value of principal. The benefits of reduced risk are passed on to the indirect security holders. As a result, the indirect security provides a higher degree of liquidity to the saver than does

a like commitment to a single primary security. To the extent individuals are unable, because of size or for other reasons, to achieve adequate diversification on their own, the financial intermediation process is beneficial.

5. *Maturity.* A financial intermediary is able to transform a primary security of a certain maturity into indirect securities of different maturities. As a result, the maturities of the primary and the indirect securities may be more attractive to the ultimate borrower and lender than they would be if the loan were direct.

6. *Expertise and convenience.* The financial intermediary is an expert in making purchases of primary securities and in so doing eliminates the inconvenience to the saver of making direct purchases. For example, not many individuals are familiar with the intricacies of making a mortgage loan; they have neither the time nor the inclination to learn.

Financial intermediaries tailor the denomination and type of indirect securities they issue to the desires of savers. Their purpose, of course, is to make a profit by purchasing primary securities yielding more than the return they must pay on the indirect securities issued and on operations. In so doing, they must channel funds from the ultimate lender to the ultimate borrower at a lower cost and/or with more convenience than is possible through a direct purchase of primary securities by the ultimate lender. Otherwise, they have no reason to exist.

To illustrate this notion, suppose that without financial intermediaries the rate of interest to a borrower would be 9 percent. In addition, the borrower must incur the indirect costs of searching for lenders and arranging for the loan. Suppose that these costs approximate 1 percent per annum. Therefore, the effective cost of borrowing via the direct loan is 10 percent. The rate of interest to the lender, of course, is 9 percent. However, search costs are incurred by the lender. In addition, the amount of funds the lender has available may not correspond to the amount that the potential borrower wishes to obtain. As a result, it may be necessary to pool the funds of several potential lenders, and this involves time and energy. Also, there is the cost of administering the loan and attending to the numerous details involved. The amount that some individuals are required to lend may be so great, relative to their total financial assets, that it precludes adequate diversification. Such lenders must be compensated for the greater risk. Finally, the lumpiness of the loan may result in pockets of unusable funds. For example, an individual may have $2,700 to lend, but the loan amount is only $2,500. As a result, $200 is idle.

Suppose that all these costs correspond to an annual interest rate of 4 percent. When this is deducted from the gross interest rate of 9 percent, the "net" interest rate to the lender becomes 6 percent. Thus, we have the following:

Borrower:	
Total cost to borrower	10%
Less search costs	1%
Interest rate charged	9%
Lender:	
Gross interest rate received	9%
Less costs of search, administration, pooling, and diversification constraints	4%
Net interest return	5%

Therefore, the differential between the total cost to the borrower and the net return to the lender is 10 percent less 5 percent, which equals 5 percent.

Suppose now that financial intermediation is possible, and that a deposit-type intermediary stands ready to accept longer-term deposits at a 6 percent rate with no inconvenience to the saver. The intermediary also will lend to the borrower in question at an 8 percent rate. The 2 percent spread between the two rates covers the expenses of the intermediary and provides it with a profit. We see then that the ultimate borrower is able to borrow at a lower effective rate—9 percent (including search cost) as opposed to 10 percent. Moreover, the net return to the lender is higher—6 percent as opposed to 5 percent.

Thus, financial intermediaries may make financial markets more efficient. By transforming primary securities into indirect securities, they are able to lower the cost to the ultimate borrower and provide a security better suited to the ultimate lender. The yield differential, as represented by the difference in yield between the borrower's cost and the net yield to the saver on an equivalent loan, is narrowed by their presence. One of the marks of efficient financial markets is that when opportunities for profit exist or arise, financial intermediaries and other financial innovations come into being to exploit the opportunity. By entering the market, they tend to narrow the differential, as defined earlier. Thus, they facilitate the movement of savings from ultimate savers to ultimate borrowers at a lower cost and with less inconvenience.

With the introduction of financial intermediaries, we have four main sectors in an economy: households, nonfinancial business firms, governments, and financial institutions, including the monetary authority. These four sectors form a matrix of claims against one another. This matrix is illustrated in Figure 1-1, which shows hypothetical balance sheets for each sector. Financial assets of each sector include money as well as primary securities. Households, of course, are the ultimate owners of all business enterprises, whether they are nonfinancial corporations or private financial institutions. The figure illustrates the distinct role of financial intermediaries. Their assets are predominantly financial assets; they hold a relatively small amount of real assets. On the right-hand side of the balance sheet, financial liabilities are predominant. Financial institutions, then, are engaged in transforming direct claims into indirect claims that have a wider appeal. The relationships of financial to real assets and of financial liabilities to net worth distinguish them from other economic units.

DISINTERMEDIATION AND SECURITIZATION

However, economic units will use intermediaries only if the marginal benefit from doing so equals or exceeds the marginal cost. If, due to changing conditions, this ceases to occur, there will be a reversion toward direct loans and security issues. This reversal process is known as **disintermediation.** In other words, when financial intermediation no longer makes the financial markets more efficient in an operational sense (e.g., less cost and/or inconvenience), disintermediation occurs. Thus, financial market efficiency does not necessarily improve with more stages of intermediation.

One manifestation of the disintermediation phenomenon is securitization. **Securitization** involves taking an illiquid financial asset, such as a mortgage or a car loan, packaging it into a pool of like assets, and then issuing marketable securities backed by the asset pool. The motivation is economic; in those situations where it occurs, less cost is involved than with intermediation through depository institutions. Securitization works

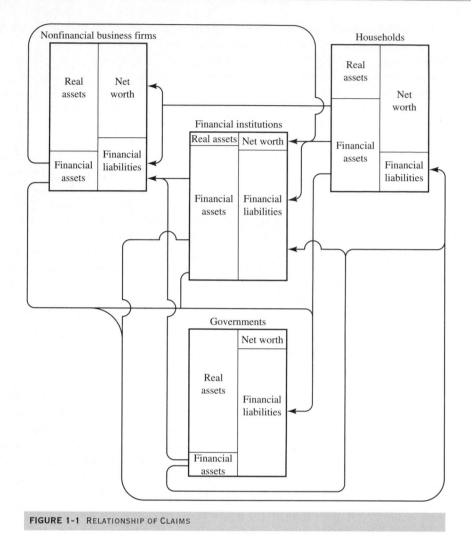

FIGURE 1-1 RELATIONSHIP OF CLAIMS

to the benefit of investment banks but to the detriment of depository institutions. All this is in keeping with the drive for efficiency, which is rooted in the profit motive. More is said about the securitization of assets in chapter 13.

COUNTRY EFFICIENCY

The more varied the vehicles are within a country, and among countries, by which savings can flow from ultimate savers to ultimate users of funds, the more efficient the financial markets of an economy usually are. More developed financial markets offer greater choices for the saver in putting savings to work and greater financing opportunities for the borrower. The utility of both is increased. With efficient financial markets, then, sharp differences can occur between the pattern of savings and the pattern of investment for economic units in an economy. The result is a higher level of capital formation, growth, and want satisfaction.

Finance, then, is a facilitator for efficiently channeling savings. Whether or not finance works well in this task is a function of several things. Perhaps the most important incentive is the overall macro policies of a country. People who save must have confidence in what they will have in the future. In turn, this is affected dramatically by the perceived integrity of the currency. The ability to realize future goods and services upon conversion depends on likely future inflation and on capital and exchange rate controls. Getting inflation under reasonable control has a salutary effect on the financial markets of a country. The telltale sign of whether a country is successful in establishing confidence is not so much whether foreigners come into that country's financial markets, but whether individuals in the country bring their money back for domestic investment.

Apart from this key strategy of macro policy, other more specific strategies exist for a country in developing its financial market efficiency. These include tax policy, regulatory policies with respect to both domestic and foreign investment, the privatization of state-owned enterprises, and accounting rules and regulations. All these policy variables influence the efficiency of a country's financial markets and, as a result, how well it does in promoting savings and in channeling them to productive investment opportunities.

FINANCIAL INNOVATION

Financial innovation comes about to exploit profit opportunities arising from **operational inefficiencies** of the type described earlier. A second foundation for innovation is the drive for **complete markets.** A complete market exists when time-state contingencies in the world are spanned by a set of financial instruments. Simply put, this means that the supply of instruments available with particular features is sufficient to satisfy the desires of investors. In contrast, an incomplete market exists when there is an unfilled desire for a particular type of instrument by an investor clientele. If the market is incomplete, it benefits a financial institution or direct borrower to exploit the opportunity by tailoring an instrument to the unfilled desires of investors, whether those desires have to do with maturity, coupon rate, protection, call feature, cash-flow characteristics, or the like.

In reality, there are simply too many time-state contingencies in the world for financial markets to be truly complete. It is a question of moving toward completeness, not eliminating incompleteness. Moreover, inefficiency and incompleteness are interrelated. Imperfections will often make the market less complete as well as less efficient. Therefore, it is a matter of degree by which the financial markets become more efficient and more complete through financial innovation.

A third reason for financial innovation is to **reduce the disparity of information** between capital raisers and capital suppliers. Asymmetrical information among parties leads to agency costs. The parties undertake costly monitoring and bonding devices to protect themselves against each other. To the extent that the features of a financial innovation better align the objectives of the various parties and, as a result, conflicts of interest are lessened, agency costs can be reduced. All of these reasons—achieving operational efficiencies, completing markets, and reducing agency costs—add value in the sense of financial markets better performing their function of channeling savings in society.

THE CATALYST FOR CHANGE

In steady-state equilibrium, the financial markets would be highly efficient, though not perfectly so because of certain remaining imperfections. In addition, they would be reasonably complete in the sense of there being little or no unfilled desires of investors. In steady-state competition, the financial instruments that should have been provided and the operational efficiencies that should have been achieved will already have happened. Finally, the design of the instruments is such that agency costs are minimized. The result is no financial innovation. Steady state occurs.

For financial innovation to occur, there must be changes in the environment, such as (1) tax law changes, (2) technological advances, (3) changing interest-rate and currency levels as well as volatility, (4) changes in the level of economic activity, and (5) regulatory change. With a change in one or more of these factors, the equilibrium is upset. Profit opportunities arise, and new financial products and processes are introduced to exploit the opportunity.

When tax laws change, the equilibrium structure of risk versus after-tax return is altered. As a result, new financial products often emerge, as do revisions in existing products. New technology in computer-based information and funds transfers prompts changes in the delivery of financial services. These changes tend to be process changes directed to making the market more efficient operationally. To remain competitive, efficiency is crucial, and those that do not adapt to new technology are quickly left behind. To survive, a financial intermediary must be cost effective in processing transactions.

Rapidly changing inflation and fluctuating nominal and real rates of interest provoke the introduction of new financial instruments. Volatile foreign exchange rates have a similar effect. In all three cases, increased volatility prompts the introduction of products that do a more effective job of shifting risk. Changes in economic activity also foster financial innovation. In periods of economic prosperity, the focus tends to be on growth, and the thrust of new product development is on achieving this objective. In a sharp recession, the focus shifts to risk-reducing devices.

Last is the change in environment caused by changes in regulations. In the United States, dramatic deregulation of the financial services industry occurred beginning in the late 1970s. Banking, insurance, securities firms, mortgages, payments mechanisms, and many other aspects of financial services were deregulated. Geographic and product differentiation, once the hallmarks of the financial services industry, are now difficult to sustain. Barriers to entry were largely dismantled and competition heightened, followed by a lower average pricing of services. In this atmosphere, financial innovation flourished.

Whatever the nature of the catalyst, financial innovations occur in response to profit opportunities. In competitive markets, the profitability of a financial innovation to its original promoter may decline over time. This would be the case if the promoter fully exploited its first-mover advantage and charged a high price. The profitability associated with an innovation does not go unnoticed. Others enter the marketplace with a like product or process. As this occurs, the profit margins of promoters erode and consumers of financial services increasingly benefit from the financial innovation.

Another introduction strategy is for the promoter not to charge the highest price possible, based on its temporary monopolistic position. With this strategy—nongouging, if you will—the promoter hopes to capture a large market share of subsequent business. The idea is to achieve a quantity advantage, based on being the innovator.[5] This strategy is particularly compelling when the period between the product/process innovation and the onslaught of imitators is short.

TYPES OF INNOVATIONS

A financial innovation may be either a new product, such as zero-coupon bonds, or a new process, such as a new delivery system for funds transfers. With financial innovation, seldom do we observe something entirely new. Rather, innovation typically involves modification of an existing idea—either a product or a process. The dramatic technological breakthroughs that occur in the product markets usually are not found in the financial markets.

During the last 10 years, thousands of financial innovations have occurred. The majority are in the product area and, more specifically, involve fixed-income securities (debt and preferred-stock instruments). Technological advances promote process changes more than they do product changes. Electronic funds transfers, automatic teller machines, point-of-sale terminals, credit card data processing, and telecommunications all have changed dramatically the way financial products are provided and priced.

In summary, financial innovation has lowered the cost of financial intermediation, widened the choice of financial instruments in which to invest and which to issue, and lowered the cost of inconvenience in some cases. As long as the economic and political environment is changing, financial innovation will continue to flourish.

THE IMPLICATIONS OF SAVINGS

Having outlined the reason for financial assets in an economy and traced through the efficiency of financial markets and financial innovation, we now consider the implications of savings, individually and collectively, for economic units. Recall that savings represent current income less current consumption.

For the *individual,* savings represent expenditures foregone out of current income, and they may be the result of a number of acts. One of the most familiar is spending less than one's discretionary income, with the difference going into a savings account. The buildup in a savings account, in itself, does not represent an act of savings but, rather, is the result of it. Other aspects of savings for the individual are less familiar. For example, savings may be the result of repayment of principal in a mortgage payment. Another means by which net worth may be increased is through contributions, either voluntary or involuntary, to a pension plan. In addition, an individual may save through the payment of a premium on a life insurance policy.

For the *corporation, net* savings represent earnings retained during the period being studied—that is, profits after taxes and after the payment of dividends on preferred and common stock. *Gross* savings for corporations include capital-consumption

---

[5] For empirical support of this strategy, see Peter Tufano, "Financial Innovation and First-Mover Advantages," *Journal of Financial Economics* 25 (December 1989): 213–40.

allowances (mainly depreciation) in addition to retained earnings. Finally, savings for a *government* unit represent a budget surplus, and dissavings, a budget deficit.

For a given period of time, the total uses of funds by an economic unit must equal its total sources. Thus,[6]

$$RA + MT + L + E = S + D + IM + B + IE \qquad \text{(1-1)}$$

where

$RA =$ gross change in real assets
$MT =$ change in money held
$L =$ lending (change in fixed-income securities held)
$E =$ equity investment (change in equity securities held)
$S =$ net savings
$D =$ capital-consumption allowance
$IM =$ issuance of money
$B =$ borrowing
$IE =$ issuance of equity securities

All the symbols represent net flows over a period of time, and they can be positive or negative. Depending on the type of economic unit involved, however, some of the variables may not be applicable. As only monetary institutions can issue money, IM is applicable only to the central bank and commercial banks. Similarly, only corporations can issue equity securities, so IE applies only to them. For the economic unit, the total uses of funds on the left side of the equation must equal total sources on the right side.

For purposes of financial-market analysis, net savings for the economic unit usually are defined as

$$S = (MT + L + E) - (IM + B + IE) + (RA - D) \qquad \text{(1-2)}$$

gross savings	financing	net savings
through		through
financial assets		real assets

net savings through
financial assets

For the economy as a whole, *ex post* savings for a given period of time must equal *ex post* investment in real assets for that period. Consequently,

$$\sum_j S = \sum_j (RA - D) \qquad \text{(1-3)}$$

where j is the jth economic unit in the economy and the capital Greek sigma is the summation of all these units. Thus, changes in financial assets for a period cancel out when summed for all economic units in the economy.

$$\sum_j (MT + L + E) - \sum_j (IM + B + IE) = 0 \qquad \text{(1-4)}$$

---

[6] For simplicity, we assume a closed economy with no foreign transactions.

As a result, savings for the economy as a whole must correspond to the increase in net real assets in that economy. There is no such thing as savings through financial assets for the economy as a whole. However, individual economic units can save through financial assets, and this is the process we wish to study. The fact that financial assets wash out when they are totaled for all economic units in the economy is a recognizable identity. It is the interaction between the issuers of financial claims and the potential holders of those claims that is important. Also, we must recognize that desired, or *ex ante,* savings for the economy as a whole need not equal *ex ante* investment. The equilibrating process has implications not only for interest rates in general but also for the interactions among individual economic units.

DEGREES OF MONEYNESS

All financial instruments arising from savings flows have a common denominator in that they are expressed in terms of money—the accepted medium of exchange. Money, the most liquid of assets, is the measure against which various types of financial instruments are compared as to their degree of substitution. In this regard, **liquidity** may be defined as the ability to realize value in money. As such, it has two dimensions: (1) the length of time and transaction cost required to convert the asset into money, and (2) the certainty of the price realized. The latter represents the stability of the ratio of exchange between the asset and money—in other words, the degree of fluctuation in market price. The two factors are interrelated. If an asset must be converted into money in a short period of time, there may be more uncertainty as to the price realized than if there were a reasonable time period in which to sell the asset.

Financial markets tend to be efficient relative to other markets. As the good involved is a claim, evidenced by a piece of paper, it is transportable at little cost and is not subject to physical deterioration. Moreover, it can be defined and classified easily. For many financial markets, information is readily available, and geographical boundaries are not a problem. By their very nature, then, financial markets are efficient when compared with the full spectrum of markets.

Frequently, these markets are classified according to the final maturity of the particular instrument involved. On one hand, **money markets** usually are regarded as including financial assets that are short term, are highly marketable, and, accordingly, possess low risk and a high degree of liquidity. These assets are traded in highly impersonal markets, where funds move on the basis of price and risk alone. Examples of money markets include the markets for short-term government securities, Eurodollars, bankers' acceptances, and commercial paper. **Capital markets,** on the other hand, include instruments with longer terms to maturity. These markets are more diverse than money markets. Examples include markets for government, corporate, and municipal bonds; corporate stocks; and mortgages. The maturity boundary that divides the money and capital markets is rather arbitrary. Some regard it as one year, while others maintain that it is five years. Because the foundation for their existence is the same, we have not concerned ourselves in this chapter with the breakdown between the two markets.

Another classification scheme has to do with whether a financial instrument is a **primary** or a **derivative** security. A primary instrument is an underlying security like a fixed-income security, a common stock, or a currency. A derivative security derives its value from a primary instrument. In other words, it derives its pricing from prices of the associated primary instrument. Futures, forward, options, and swap markets are examples of derivative markets. As we shall see, they enable market participants to control risk more effectively.

INTEREST RATES AND ARBITRAGE EFFICIENCY

Our concern in this book is with the flow of savings from ultimate savers to ultimate users of funds. The allocation, or channeling, of savings in an economy is accomplished primarily through interest rates. Economic units with the most promising investment opportunities will pay more for the use of funds on a risk-adjusted return basis than those with less promising opportunities. To the extent that the former bid funds away from the latter, savings tend to be channeled to the most efficient uses. Interest rates adjust continually to bring changing supply and demand into balance.

A fundamental underlying phenomenon in the market equilibration process is arbitrage. Arbitrage simply means finding two things that are essentially the same, buying the cheaper, and selling the more expensive. Suppose there exist two risk-free bonds: Bond 1 is priced at $1,000 and pays $100 at the end of year 1 and $1,100 at the end of year 2; Bond 2 costs $800 and pays $1,000 at the end of year 2. Presently you own eight of Bond 1. If you continue to hold them, you will receive $800 at the end of year 1. If a risk-free party were to pay you 10 percent for the use of these funds from the end of year 1 to the end of year 2, the $800 would grow to $880. The total amount of funds you would have at the end of year 2 would be $880 plus (8 × $1,100), or $9,680. For Bond 2, $8,000 invested today would grow to $10,000 at the end of year 2. Clearly, you should sell your holdings in Bond 1 for $8,000 and invest in Bond 2.

As others recognize this arbitrage opportunity, they will do the same. Selling Bond 1, of course, exerts downward pressure on its price, while buying Bond 2 brings upward pressure on its price. Arbitrage actions will continue until the two bonds provide the same funds at the end of year 2. The simple, but powerful, notion here is that security prices adjust as market participants search for arbitrage profits. When such opportunities have been exhausted, security prices are said to be in equilibrium. In this context, a definition of market efficiency is the absence of arbitrage opportunities, which have been eliminated by arbitragers. Throughout this book, arbitrage will be seen as a force guiding the behavior of security prices and, hence, of relative interest rates.

❖ SUMMARY

A financial asset is a claim against some economic unit in an economy. It is held for the return it provides and as a store of value—reasons that differentiate it from a real asset. Financial assets and markets exist because during a period of time, some economic units save more than they invest in real assets, while other economic units invest more than they save. To cover an excess of investment over savings for a period, an economic unit can reduce its holdings of existing financial assets, increase its financial liabilities, or undertake some combination of the two. When it increases its financial liabilities, a new financial instrument is created in the economy. The existence of financial markets permits investment for economic units to differ from their savings.

The purpose of financial markets is to allocate savings efficiently in an economy to ultimate users of funds. For the economy as a whole, *ex post* investment must equal *ex post* savings. However, this is not true for individual economic units; they can have considerable divergence between savings and investment for a particular period of time. The more vibrant the financial markets in an economy are, the more efficient the allocation of savings is to the most promising investment opportunities, and the greater the capital formation is in that economy.

The various stages of financial market efficiency range from a barter economy to one that embraces a wide variety of financial intermediaries. A financial intermediary transforms the direct claim of the ultimate borrower into an indirect claim, which is sold to ultimate lenders. Intermediaries channel savings from ultimate savers to ultimate lenders at a lower cost and with less inconvenience than is possible on a direct basis. Otherwise, a reversion to direct loans and security issuance occurs, such as the securitization-of-asset movement.

Innovation serves to cleanse the financial markets. The foundations for financial innovation are to make the markets more efficient operationally and more complete in the sense of providing the financial instruments in demand. Changing tax laws, technology, inflation and interest rates, economic activity, and regulations prompt new financial products and processes.

All financial flows occur in terms of money, the most liquid of assets. Liquidity may be defined as the ability to realize value in money. In the chapters that follow, we investigate in depth both the flow of savings and the price mechanism—namely, interest rates—which bring about a balance between supply and demand in the various financial markets. Our concern is with both the level of interest rates and the differentials between interest rates for different financial instruments. In this regard, arbitrage is a guiding force by which financial markets equilibrate and interest rates are determined.

❖ SELECTED REFERENCES

Allen, Linda, *Capital Markets and Institutions: A Global View.* New York: John Wiley & Sons, 1997.

Bodie, Zvi, and Robert C. Merton, *Finance.* Upper Saddle River, NJ: Prentice Hall, 2000.

Leland, Hayne E., and David H. Pyle, "Informational Asymmetries, Financial Structure, and Financial Intermediation." *Journal of Finance* 32 (May 1977): 371–88.

Pyle, David H., "On the Theory of Financial Intermediation." *Journal of Finance* 26 (June 1971): 737–47.

Ritter, Lawrence S., William L. Silber, and Gregory F. Udell, *Principles of Money, Banking and Financial Markets,* 10th ed. Reading, MA: Addison-Wesley, 2000.

Van Horne, James C., "An Inquiry into Recent Financial Innovation." *Kredit und Kapital* 19 (December 1986): 453–71.

———, "Of Financial Innovations and Excesses." *Journal of Finance* 40 (July 1985): 621–31.

Varian, Hal R., "The Arbitrage Principle in Financial Economics." *Economic Perspectives* 1 (Fall 1987): 55–72.

2

THE FLOW-OF-FUNDS SYSTEM

An indispensable tool of financial-market analysts is the flow-of-funds framework. This framework enables them to analyze the movement of savings through the economy in a highly structured, consistent, and comprehensive manner. Analysts are able not only to evaluate the complex interdependence of financial claims throughout the economy but also to identify various pressure points in the system. The insight gained from studying these pressure points is valuable when it comes to analyzing possible changes in market rates of interest. In addition, the flow-of-funds framework makes possible an analysis of the interaction between the financial and the real segments of the economy.

The flow of funds is a system of social accounting. Its foundation was Morris A. Copeland's celebrated work in 1952.[1] The Board of Governors of the Federal Reserve System first began to publish data on the flow of funds in 1955 and published a revised and quarterly presentation of data in 1959. Since 1959, quarterly data have been published regularly by the Federal Reserve System. Flow-of-funds accounts are a companion to national-income accounts. Whereas the national-income accounting system deals with goods and services, or the real side of the economy, flow-of-funds data provide information on the financial side. For example, national-income accounts provide data on the amount of savings, but they give no information on how savings are used. The process by which funds flow from savings to investment is omitted. One must turn to flow-of-funds data to obtain this information. In this chapter, we discuss the structure of the flow-of-funds accounting system, examine the interrelationship of sources and uses of funds for various sectors in the economy, and, finally, investigate the uses of this information.

THE STRUCTURE OF THE SYSTEM

Flow-of-funds data for an economy are derived for a specific period of time by (1) preparing source-of-funds and use-of-funds statements for each sector in the economy,

---

[1] Morris A. Copeland, *A Study of Moneyflows in the United States* (New York: National Bureau of Economic Research, 1952).

(2) totaling the sources and uses for all sectors, and (3) presenting the information in a flow-of-funds matrix for the entire economy. The time span studied usually is either a quarter of a year or a full year.

SECTORING

The starting point in any flow-of-funds accounting system is the division of the economy into a workable number of sectors; the idea is to lump together those economic units with similar behavior. Because funds movements through sectors are being analyzed, economic units in a sector must be relatively homogeneous decision-making units if the analysis is to be meaningful. For this reason, sectors are defined along institutional lines according to the similarity of their asset and liability structures. The number of sectors used depends on the purpose of the analysis, the availability of data, and the cost involved in collecting the data. The maximum possible number of sectors, of course, is the total number of economic units in the economy; in the United States, this would be more than 100 million. The minimum number is two, for there can be no flow of funds with only one sector—the economy as a whole.

If too few sectors exist, significant relationships among various groups of economic units are likely to be hidden. On the other hand, if too many sectors exist, the analysis of the interaction among sectors becomes cumbersome. Here, the problem is that important relationships, although not hidden, may be overlooked. The number of sectors finally employed usually represents a compromise. In the sectoring of the economy, it is absolutely necessary that all economic units be included. Moreover, if foreign transactions are considered, a sector must be included for the rest of the world.

The four main sectors used in the U.S. flow-of-funds system are households, governments, business enterprises, and financial institutions. For reporting purposes, the Federal Reserve has subdivided some of these sectors, breaking them down into the following categories:

1. Households and nonprofit organizations.
2. Nonfinancial business (subsectors: farm, nonfarm, noncorporate, and corporate).
3. Governments (subsectors: state and local governments, U.S. government, federally sponsored credit agencies, and mortgage pools).
4. Banking system (subsectors: monetary authorities and commercial banks).
5. Nonbank finance (subsectors: savings institutions, credit unions, insurance companies, private pension funds, state and local government retirement funds, finance companies, mortgage companies, real estate investment trusts, mutual funds, money market funds, issuers of asset-backed securities, bank trusts and estates, and security brokers and dealers).
6. Rest of world.

The last sector comprises all residents and governments outside the United States. Essentially, it serves to net together all external inflows and outflows so that the flow-of-funds system can be brought into balance. As the Federal Reserve is the principal source of flow-of-funds data, the analyst must settle for this breakdown of the economy.

SOURCE-AND-USE STATEMENTS

Once the economy has been divided into sectors, the next step is to prepare a source-and-use-of-funds statement for each sector. The starting point here is a balance sheet for each sector at the beginning of the period being studied.

Sector A January 1, 200X	
Assets	*Liabilities and Net Worth*
Money	Financial liabilities
Other financial assets	
Real assets	Net worth
Total assets	Total liabilities and net worth

Most of the assets in the preceding balance sheet are reported at their market values. Recognize that the presence of financial assets on the balance sheet for one sector means that financial liabilities of the same amount appear on the balance sheets of other sectors in the economy. In other words, financial assets represent claims against an economic unit in another sector and, consequently, must be shown as a liability on that party's balance sheet. In contrast, real assets appear on only one balance sheet, namely that of the owner.

Also, we must recognize that financial assets and liabilities among economic units in a particular sector are netted out. The financial asset figure for the sector includes only claims against economic units in other sectors. By the same token, the financial liability figure includes only claims held by economic units in other sectors against economic units in the sector being studied. As long as at least one economic unit in a sector holds a financial claim against another economic unit in that sector, the financial asset figure and the financial liability figure shown on the balance sheet for the sector will be less than the sum of financial assets and the sum of financial liabilities for all economic units in that sector. This statement does not hold for real assets, however. Because a real asset appears on the balance sheet of only the economic unit that owns it, the real asset figure shown on the balance sheet for a sector is the sum of real assets for all economic units in the sector.

By definition, a balance sheet shows the stock of assets, liabilities, and net worth of a sector at a moment in time. By taking the change that occurs in stocks between two balance sheets at different points in time, expressed as Δ, we obtain the net flows for the sector over the time span. These net flows can be expressed in a source-and-use-of-funds statement for the sector.

Sector A Sources and Uses of Funds, 200X	
Uses	*Sources*
ΔMoney	ΔFinancial liabilities
ΔOther financial assets	
ΔReal assets	ΔNet worth
ΔTotal assets	ΔTotal liabilities and net worth

For the period, the net change in total assets for a sector must equal the net change in total liabilities and net worth. The change in net worth represents savings for the period—that is, the difference between current income and current expenditures. Positive savings imply an increase in total assets, a decrease in total liabilities, or both. A savings-deficit sector, with investment in real assets greater than its savings, must reduce its money holdings, sell other financial assets, increase its liabilities, or perform some combination of these actions. Conversely, a savings-surplus sector must show an increase in its holdings of financial assets (including money), a reduction in its financial liabilities, or some combination.

THE PREPARATION OF A MATRIX AND ITS USE

Once source-and-use-of-funds statements have been prepared for all sectors, these statements can be combined into a matrix for the entire economy. A hypothetical example of such a matrix is shown in Table 2-1. In the table, a closed economy consisting of four sections—households, business firms, financial institutions, and governments—is assumed. No foreign transactions are assumed to occur. We see that the matrix forms an interlocking system of flow of funds for the period. For each sector, the total uses of funds equal the total sources. Because the system is self-contained, the total uses of funds for all sectors must equal the total sources for these sectors. More importantly, total savings for all sectors during the period must equal the total increase in real assets for that period. Likewise, the total change in financial assets, including money, must equal the total change in financial liabilities. Again, we see that financial assets and financial liabilities cancel each other for the economy as a whole.

The value of the matrix is that it allows analysis of the flow of funds through various sectors of the economy in a manner similar to that of an input-output analysis. For the individual sector, savings need not equal investment in real assets, and the change in financial assets need not equal the change in financial liabilities. For example, business firms represent a savings-deficit sector in Table 2-1. For this sector, the excess of investment in real assets over savings was financed by an increase in financial liabilities in excess of the increase in financial assets. The existence of this savings-deficit sector means that one or more savings-surplus sectors must be in the economy for the period being studied. When we study the matrix, we see that households, financial institutions, and governments are savings-surplus sectors and finance the business sector on a net basis. Historically, households have been a substantial savings-surplus sector, but this has waned in the United States in recent years. In other economies, however, the household savings-surplus sector tends to be substantial. While financial institutions save, the amount is relatively small. This sector acts mostly as a financial intermediary; it increases its financial assets by issuing financial liabilities to finance the increase in financial assets. Because the sector contains commercial banks and the monetary authorities, it provides money to other sectors in the economy. The $5 source of money for this sector represents an increase in demand deposits and currency held by the public and governments as claims against commercial banks and the monetary authorities. Therefore, the total increase in money held by households, business firms, and governments must equal the increase in money-balance claims against the financial institutions sector.

Collectively, federal, state, and local governments ran a budget surplus for the period illustrated in Table 2-1. Although governments make substantial expenditures for

TABLE 2-1   Matrix of Flow of Funds of Entire Economy, 200X

	House-holds		Business Firms		Financial Institutions		Govern-ments		All Sectors	
	Uses	Sources	Uses	Sources	Uses	Sources	Uses	Sources	Uses	Sources
Net worth (savings)		88		77		4		10		179
Real assets (investments)	82		96		1				179	
Money	2		2			5	1		5	5
Other financial assets	37		18		60		17		132	
Financial liabilities		33		39		52		8		132
	121	121	116	116	61	61	18	18	316	316

real assets, their expenditures are not shown because of the lack of reliable estimates. Unfortunately, this rather important effect must be omitted from any analysis. A budget deficit for the governments sector must be financed by an increase in financial liabilities in excess of the increase in financial assets. The matrix in Table 2-1 illustrates the fundamental aspects of flow of funds in an economy over a period of time.

Certain information is destroyed in the final presentation of the results. As mentioned earlier, the change in financial assets and liabilities for a sector reflects changes that occur only with other sectors. No information is given about financial transactions among economic units in a given sector. Financial claims among these economic units simply cancel out. As a result, we do not know how much net financing occurs within the sector. The need for this information decreases, of course, as the number of sectors used in the flow-of-funds system increases.

Another problem is that the flow of funds for a period represents the net rather than the gross flow between two points in time. For example, the change in financial assets for a sector is simply beginning financial assets less ending financial assets. During the period, there may have been numerous changes in claims against economic units in other sectors. However, no information is given about the magnitude of these changes. For example, financial institutions may purchase $250 billion in mortgages over the period, while principal payments on existing mortgages held and the sale of existing mortgages amount to $140 billion. The net change in mortgages reported in flow-of-funds data for the financial institutions sector is $110 billion. Although it may be revealing to know the gross funds flow over time, we are constrained to the information available—namely, the net flow between the two dates. These shortcomings, together with the problem of appropriate sectoring of the economy discussed previously, should be recognized when interpreting the published data. In certain cases, they may have an important influence on the conclusions reached.

FEDERAL RESERVE FLOW-OF-FUNDS DATA

The basic source of data on the flow of funds is the Federal Reserve System. Each quarter, the *Flow of Funds Accounts* is published; it contains extensive data on net funds flows. This publication is available upon request to the Board of Governors of the Federal Reserve System, Washington, DC 20551.

An example of the type of information provided by the Federal Reserve is shown in Table 2-2. Here the household sector is illustrated. The gross savings for this sector are shown in row 9. For 1998, they were $985.5 billion. This figure should be compared with capital expenditures, row 11, to determine whether the sector was a savings-surplus or savings-deficit sector. We see that it was a savings-deficit sector, and this was for the first time since these data began to be compiled. The same thing occurred for the first two quarters of 1999. Recently then, the household sector has had negative savings, which has implications for real rates of interest (see chapter 5).

The difference between gross savings and capital expenditures should be reflected in a buildup of financial assets, row 16, less the net increase in financial liabilities, row 39. For 1998, gross savings minus capital expenditures were −$100.1 billion, a negative figure. The buildup in financial assets (row 16) less the net increase in financial liabilities (row 39) is labeled net financial investment, and it is shown in row 15 to be −$17.2 billion. Obviously negative $100.1 billion and negative $17.2 billion are not equal as they should be in concept. The discrepancy of −$82.9 billion is shown in the last row, 50. Although the flow of funds is an interlocking accounting system, which should balance, discrepancies unfortunately occur. These are due to inconsistencies in timing, valuation, classification, coverage, and statistical errors in data collection. As a result, we must work with this shortcoming and allow for errors and discrepancies in balancing.

With the information in Table 2-2, together with that for other sectors, we are able to construct a matrix of actual funds flows for a period of time. This construction is illustrated in Table 2-3 for 1998. As reflected in the table, households, nonfinancial business and nonbank finance were savings-deficit sectors. Nonbank finance is an aggregation of such institutions as savings institutions, credit unions, finance companies, life insurance companies, and real estate investment trusts (REITs). The last largely accounts for this overall sector being a savings-deficit one, as it invests in real estate to a far greater extent than its gross savings. Governments (state, local and federal) were substantial savings-surplus sectors. As discussed before, gross savings here are after-capital expenditures, which are not reported. The other substantial savings-surplus sector is the rest of the world. In this sector, all foreign economic units are lumped together. The sector records transactions between economic units in foreign countries and economic units in the United States. We see that in 1998 it provided large capital flows to the United States. In a sense, we "imported" savings from other parts of the world to finance the excess of domestic investment over domestic savings. This dependence coupled with low private domestic savings is a matter of concern to some.

CREDIT FLOWS

In addition to the information provided on ultimate sources and uses of funds, the Federal Reserve provides a wealth of information on the specific financial instruments through which savings flow. The information is of particular interest to capital market analysis. It tells what sectors finance with what types of instruments and what sectors hold these instruments. To illustrate the usefulness of this information, we examine three sectors in more detail—households, nonfinancial business, and commercial banks.

TABLE 2-2 Flow of Funds for Household Sector, 1994–1999II; Seasonally adjusted annual rate (billions of $)

		1994	1995	1996	1997	1998	—1999—	
							Q1	Q2
1	Personal income	5757.9	6072.0	6425.4	6784.1	7126.3	7349.3	7442.3
2	− Personal taxes and nontaxes	739.1	795.0	890.5	989.0	1098.2	1144.1	1162.7
3	= Disposable personal income	5018.9	5276.9	5534.8	5795.2	6028.1	6205.2	6279.6
4	− Personal outlays	4842.1	5097.3	5376.3	5674.1	6000.4	6250.7	6358.8
5	**= Personal savings, NIPA (2)**	**176.8**	**179.6**	**158.6**	**121.1**	**27.7**	**−45.5**	**−79.2**
6	+ Govt. insurance and pension reserves	93.0	84.3	116.1	118.4	103.6	94.6	99.5
7	+ Net investment in consumer durables	123.3	136.3	155.4	169.2	197.6	229.1	235.7
8	+ Consumption of fixed capital	565.6	588.2	605.0	627.6	656.5	675.3	683.8
9	**= Gross savings**	**958.7**	**988.5**	**1035.1**	**1036.4**	**985.5**	**953.5**	**939.8**
10	**Gross investment**	**1055.7**	**997.0**	**989.1**	**986.8**	**1068.4**	**875.9**	**990.0**
11	**Capital expenditures**	**860.5**	**889.8**	**949.7**	**994.6**	**1085.6**	**1170.5**	**1204.1**
12	Residential construction	249.1	244.9	269.0	278.0	314.6	351.3	370.8
13	Consumer durable goods	579.6	611.0	643.3	673.1	724.7	771.2	784.6
14	Nonprofit plant and equipment	31.9	33.8	37.4	43.6	46.4	48.0	48.7
15	**Net financial investment**	**195.2**	**107.2**	**39.4**	**−7.9**	**−17.2**	**−294.6**	**−214.0**
16	**Net acquisition of financial assets**	**515.1**	**471.1**	**416.4**	**362.8**	**481.2**	**287.5**	**378.1**
17	Foreign deposits	3.1	4.6	12.4	6.3	−0.3	8.2	7.3
18	Checkable deposits and currency	−29.8	−58.7	−59.1	−0.5	4.0	−25.8	−120.4
19	Time and savings deposits	−12.2	164.5	165.0	170.2	185.5	−136.2	121.8
20	Money market fund shares	13.4	97.9	56.1	82.9	149.8	72.0	32.3
21	Credit market instruments	268.0	5.5	61.4	−86.2	−37.0	244.9	255.1
22	Open market paper	1.2	1.3	7.4	3.6	4.2	4.7	5.3
23	U.S. government securities	297.3	−40.6	29.2	−192.6	−103.5	−207.2	268.3
24	Treasury	169.0	−41.9	−66.4	−203.6	−68.5	−406.6	190.7
25	Savings bonds	8.0	5.1	2.0	−0.5	0.1	−0.0	0.0
26	Other	161.0	−46.9	−68.4	−203.1	−68.6	−406.6	190.7
27	Agency	128.3	1.2	95.6	11.0	−35.0	199.5	77.5
28	Municipal securities	−50.2	−43.5	−22.2	29.4	31.1	81.2	10.6
29	Corporate and foreign bonds	30.5	95.0	49.3	76.1	33.1	368.9	−29.3
30	Mortgages	−10.7	−6.7	−2.3	−2.7	−1.8	−2.7	0.2
31	Corporate equities (3)	−175.8	−216.0	−327.3	−571.1	−542.1	−413.9	−587.9
32	Mutual fund shares	67.4	94.7	180.8	259.0	261.3	219.0	201.6
33	Security credit	6.7	18.6	35.3	52.6	64.1	−68.7	13.8
34	Life insurance reserves	35.5	45.8	44.5	54.3	53.3	40.8	65.9
35	Pension fund reserves	254.7	235.1	246.9	304.0	290.2	284.3	316.4
36	Investment in bank personal trusts	17.8	4.0	−8.6	75.0	55.7	64.1	53.0
37	Equity in noncorporate business	53.6	60.3	−0.6	6.1	−18.6	−2.5	12.3
38	Miscellaneous assets	12.8	14.8	9.7	10.3	15.3	1.2	6.8
39	**Net increase in liabilities**	**319.9**	**363.8**	**377.0**	**370.7**	**498.3**	**582.2**	**592.2**
40	Credit market instruments	316.3	350.3	351.7	325.5	470.3	553.3	511.0
41	Home mortgages	174.6	176.3	238.7	229.4	358.2	405.2	414.5
42	Consumer credit	124.9	138.9	88.8	52.5	67.6	126.6	53.2
43	Municipal securities	3.6	0.7	6.6	10.0	12.0	7.0	9.0
44	Bank loans n.e.c.	13.4	17.4	0.6	8.1	6.3	−14.7	0.1
45	Other loans and advances	7.1	26.6	12.4	18.1	13.3	10.8	14.0
46	Commercial mortgages	−7.4	−9.6	4.7	7.4	12.9	18.4	20.3
47	Security credit	−1.1	3.5	15.8	36.8	23.8	22.6	72.0
48	Trade payables	4.2	9.3	8.7	8.1	5.7	1.4	8.6
49	Deferred and unpaid life insurance premiums	0.5	0.7	0.8	0.3	−1.4	4.9	0.5
50	Discrepancy	−97.0	−8.5	45.9	49.6	−82.9	77.6	−50.2

Source: Flow of Funds Accounts of the U.S., Federal Reserve System.

TABLE 2-3	Matrix of Flow of Funds for 1998 (billions of $)				
Sector	Gross Savings	Capital Expenditures	Gross Investment	Net Financial Investment	Sector Discrepancy
Households	985	1,086	1,068	−17	−83
Nonfinancial Business	823	851	803	−48	20
State and Local Government	174		213	36	−39
Federal Government	100		74	16	26
Monetary Authorities and Commercial Banks	49	14	−8	−22	57
Nonbank Finance	50	88	105	17	−55
Rest of World	212		210	210	2
	2,393	2,039	2,465	192	−72

Source: Flow of Funds Accounts of the U.S., Federal Reserve System.

The information for households is in Table 2-2, whereas the data for the other two sectors are shown in Tables 2-4 and 2-5, respectively.

For households, we find that home mortgages (row 41) were the most important liability issued followed by consumer-credit borrowing (row 42). Turning to Table 2-5, we see in row 16 that banks were large acquirers of mortgages, but were a net liquidator of consumer credit (row 17). The largest purchaser of mortgages was federally related mortgage pools (not shown), which accounted for $192.6 billion during 1998.

The principal means by which businesses finance themselves, as shown in Table 2-4, are corporate bonds (row 30), bank loans (row 31), other loans and advances (row 32), mortgages (row 33), trade payables (row 35), and miscellaneous liabilities (row 37). During 1998, net equity financing was negative, as share repurchase and other retirements exceeded new issues by $267 billion. Turning to Table 2-2 for the household sector, row 29 tells us that this sector was a significant purchaser of corporate bonds on a net basis. Households reduced substantially their direct holdings of corporate equities, (row 31). They increasingly became indirect holders through pension funds and mutual funds. Table 2-5 for the commercial banking sector shows that bank loans (row 15) were substantial, and the majority of these were to business firms. This sector also was a moderate investor in corporate bonds (row 12).

IMPLICATIONS OF ANALYSIS

The analysis of the interlocking nature of financial claims can be extended to all the sectors and subsectors included in the information provided by the Federal Reserve. We have illustrated such an analysis for only three sectors. A more penetrating analysis would involve tracing each financial liability to find what sectors had acquired it as a financial asset. While flow-of-funds data will not permit analysis of the behavior of individual economic units or small groups of economic units, they enable one to evaluate economic units that are reasonably homogeneous in their behavior, as well as to trace the interaction of the financial system and the real system of the economy in a systematic and consistent manner. They tell the financial-market analyst how various sectors financed the excess of their investment in real assets over savings and how these sectors changed their holdings of financial assets. The flow-of-funds framework provides a

TABLE 2-4   Flow of Funds for Nonfinancial Business Sector, 1994–1999II; Seasonally adjusted annual rate (billions of $)

		1994	1995	1996	1997	1998	—1999—	
							Q1	Q2
1	Income before taxes	924.1	997.8	1075.0	1133.8	1144.4	1185.2	1219.5
2	**Gross savings**	**671.2**	**721.6**	**754.1**	**794.7**	**823.0**	**856.0**	**847.6**
3	**Gross investment**	**676.2**	**728.7**	**731.9**	**756.0**	**803.4**	**806.2**	**897.0**
4	**Capital expenditures**	**639.6**	**695.7**	**739.8**	**804.8**	**851.4**	**891.6**	**941.6**
5	Fixed investment	578.4	657.4	704.2	730.3	789.7	852.4	931.2
6	Residential construction	29.7	37.1	38.4	38.6	43.5	47.6	48.9
7	Plant and equipment	548.7	620.3	665.8	691.7	746.2	804.8	882.3
8	Change in inventories	61.2	30.7	32.1	67.4	59.3	39.5	12.4
9	Access rights from federal government	0	7.6	3.5	7.1	2.4	−0.3	−2.0
10	**Net financial investment**	**36.6**	**32.9**	**−7.9**	**−48.8**	**−48.0**	**−85.4**	**−44.6**
11	**Net acquisition of financial assets**	**352.2**	**514.8**	**490.6**	**381.7**	**436.2**	**710.1**	**485.4**
12	Foreign deposits	1.1	1.6	10.5	−6.3	8.3	15.9	16.1
13	Checkable deposits and currency	24.1	36.1	45.3	−1.7	36.5	104.6	53.6
14	Time and savings deposits	1.6	−15.8	11.4	11.4	8.0	16.3	23.6
15	Money market fund shares	7.5	25.7	10.4	25.1	46.5	26.8	24.7
16	Security RPs	−0.3	0.3	1.5	0.6	−1.1	2.5	2.2
17	Credit market instruments	18.3	−4.1	−5.1	−2.8	−2.6	10.4	39.5
18	Commercial paper	−0.6	1.3	11.4	3.8	−8.1	16.7	10.6
19	U.S. government securities	3.5	11.4	3.3	−9.1	5.7	−29.1	32.7
20	Municipal securities	2.0	−19.9	−5.8	5.1	7.3	−10.2	6.7
21	Mortgages	4.0	4.7	−6.7	−3.7	−3.4	−3.4	−3.4
22	Consumer credit	9.4	−1.6	−7.3	1.2	−4.1	36.3	−7.1
23	Mutual fund shares	2.1	4.6	3.3	−8.2	7.3	8.0	7.9
24	Trade receivables	85.9	90.3	104.3	53.3	26.3	88.7	85.1
25	Miscellaneous assets	212.0	376.2	309.1	310.3	306.9	436.9	232.7
26	**Net increase in liabilities**	**315.5**	**481.9**	**498.5**	**430.4**	**484.2**	**795.5**	**530.0**
27	Credit market instruments	150.0	277.2	253.2	380.6	524.5	682.6	431.1
28	Commercial paper	21.4	18.1	−0.9	13.7	24.4	64.4	3.4
29	Municipal securities	6.8	3.1	3.1	4.2	5.8	6.6	3.5
30	Corporate bonds	23.3	91.1	116.3	150.5	218.7	274.0	260.8
31	Bank loans n.e.c.	61.8	86.3	69.9	98.4	102.0	84.7	21.8
32	Other loans and advances	26.8	40.2	20.8	52.2	59.8	103.1	−19.4
33	Mortgages	9.8	38.4	44.1	61.6	113.9	149.8	161.0
34	Corporate equities	−44.9	−58.3	−69.5	−114.4	−267.0	−65.7	−354.0
35	Trade payables	85.8	88.1	71.5	75.7	−0.5	154.2	59.1
36	Taxes payable	0.4	1.3	11.1	11.3	7.8	−15.4	22.2
37	Miscellaneous liabilities	58.1	127.8	244.2	89.0	243.7	56.3	369.7
38	Proprietors' net investment	66.3	45.8	−12.1	−11.7	−24.3	−16.6	1.9
39	Discrepancy	−5.0	−7.1	22.1	38.7	19.6	49.8	−49.4

Source: Flow of Funds Accounts of the U.S., Federal Reserve System.

TABLE 2-5 Flow of Funds for Commercial Banking Sector, 1994–1999II; Seasonally adjusted annual rate (billions of $)

		1994	1995	1996	1997	1998	—1999—	
							Q1	Q2
1	**Gross savings**	**26.5**	**32.6**	**31.9**	**42.8**	**46.8**	**58.0**	**55.4**
2	**Fixed nonresidential investment**	**13.2**	**13.3**	**12.3**	**12.8**	**14.1**	**14.6**	**15.0**
3	**Net acquisition of financial assets**	**231.3**	**335.7**	**216.6**	**457.3**	**443.7**	**100.0**	**314.4**
4	Vault cash	5.5	2.4	4.6	−0.2	−2.9	18.1	5.0
5	Reserves at Federal Reserve	−3.5	−1.1	−4.6	6.8	−4.6	3.0	−2.1
6	Checkable deposits and currency	0.4	0.2	−0.2	−0.1	0.6	−1.5	−1.4
7	Total bank credit	156.8	273.4	189.9	350.0	335.8	33.0	141.3
8	U.S. government securities	−26.2	27.0	11.3	83.8	35.4	46.0	2.3
9	Treasury	−31.8	−11.7	−16.9	8.3	−56.1	2.0	−8.2
10	Agency	5.5	38.7	28.2	75.5	91.4	44.0	10.6
11	Municipal securities	−1.6	−4.2	0.9	2.4	8.2	10.1	4.1
12	Corporate and foreign bonds	4.3	8.4	1.4	27.8	38.0	−66.4	94.0
13	Total loans	183.7	239.8	174.2	234.7	253.4	42.4	43.6
14	Open maket paper	−1.5	−0.1	0.8	−0.8	−0.2	−0.7	−0.5
15	Bank loans n.e.c.	62.9	114.7	92.1	128.2	145.0	62.1	38.0
16	Mortgages	64.9	77.5	55.2	99.9	91.7	15.8	78.4
17	Consumer credit	63.1	43.2	24.8	−14.2	−3.6	6.1	−75.7
18	Security credit	−5.7	4.6	1.3	21.7	20.5	−40.8	3.5
19	Corporate equities	−1.4	2.1	1.8	0.6	1.3	1.6	−3.7
20	Mutual fund shares	−1.9	0.3	0.3	0.8	−0.4	−0.8	1.0
21	Customers' liability on acceptances	−2.4	−0.6	1.0	−2.8	−9.3	−4.0	−5.6
22	Miscellaneous assets	74.4	61.4	25.9	103.5	124.1	51.5	177.1
23	**Net increase in liabilities**	**255.1**	**300.6**	**203.7**	**490.5**	**467.5**	**59.8**	**310.5**
24	Net interbank liabilities	88.5	8.7	−51.2	−25.8	−26.0	28.5	65.2
25	To monetary authority	−1.5	0.7	4.1	−1.6	−1.1	−9.2	4.5
26	To domestic banks	−2.7	−3.1	−3.3	−19.9	3.4	58.7	−1.7
27	To foreign banks	92.7	11.1	−52.0	−4.3	−28.3	−21.0	62.4
28	Checkable deposits	−31.7	−45.9	−34.6	−19.8	−33.4	−2.7	−35.5
29	Federal government	−18.9	−4.7	9.7	−0.9	−14.6	30.3	45.5
30	Rest of the world	1.9	0.8	2.6	4.6	−2.0	5.1	27.8
31	Private domestic	−14.7	−42.0	−46.9	−23.5	−16.8	−38.1	−108.8
32	Small time and savings deposits	−1.0	113.9	123.1	148.3	183.7	−6.4	119.4
33	Large times deposits	21.3	54.8	105.3	107.9	72.3	−10.0	28.9
34	Federal funds and security RPs (net)	78.1	30.4	41.0	89.0	87.0	112.1	27.3
35	Credit market instruments	20.1	22.5	13.0	46.1	72.9	31.1	61.6
36	Open market paper	3.1	−2.2	2.9	3.3	−1.5	−1.1	6.3
37	Corporate bonds	7.7	18.5	7.8	23.7	27.6	35.2	−4.8
38	Other loans and advances	9.3	6.2	2.3	19.1	46.9	−3.0	60.1
39	Corporate equity issues	−3.3	−8.7	−14.3	−27.7	−12.7	−14.7	−22.2
40	Taxes payable	0.7	0.9	1.2	1.4	1.7	1.8	1.9
41	Miscellaneous liabilities	82.4	124.0	20.1	171.2	122.1	−79.8	63.7
42	Discrepancy	37.2	−15.9	6.7	63.2	56.5	3.2	36.6

Source: Flow of Funds Accounts of the U.S., Federal Reserve System.

structured, interlocking means by which to analyze what has happened in the capital markets. The interrelation of sources and uses among sectors enables the analyst to trace the movement of funds through various sectors of the economy for the period of time under review.

Given the breakdown of financial assets and liabilities provided by the Federal Reserve, a fairly detailed analysis of certain types of financial instruments and markets is possible. While data are individually presented for longer-term capital instruments, money market instruments—such as Treasury bills, commercial paper, bankers' acceptances, and negotiable certificates of deposit—are scattered among several broader categories. As a result, we are unable to trace through supply and demand patterns for a specific money market instrument.

For a capital market instrument, however, we are able to evaluate which sectors are important in the market and the magnitude of their purchases. When this analysis is extended over time, one is able to evaluate the degree of pressure in the various markets. Pressure arises whenever a traditional source of financing curtails its investment in the financial instrument. By comparing estimates of supply and demand, analysts obtain insight into strains in the system. Given likely strains, it may be possible to interpret their effect on interest rates for a particular type of instrument relative to interest rates in general. As we shall see later, this depends on the presence of market segmentation effects.

Thus, the flow-of-funds framework provides a basis for analyzing financial markets. The discipline of the interlocking matrix results in a more rigorous, consistent, and comprehensive evaluation than is possible on a market-by-market basis.

DEBT OUTSTANDING

The Federal Reserve System, in its flow-of-funds publications, provides data on the amount of debt outstanding by sector. These data are shown in Table 2-6 for the years 1961 through 1999II. The total outstanding at the time of this writing was $24.5 trillion, a staggering sum indeed. The table shows that federal government debt escalated rapidly until the mid-1990s, but has declined most recently. Home mortgages, corporate bonds, and domestic finance also have shown substantial increases. This table serves as a reference for the various markets we investigate throughout this book. It can be updated with the quarterly publication of these data by the Federal Reserve System.

❖ SUMMARY

The flow of funds is a system of social accounting that permits financial-market analysts to evaluate the flow of savings through various sectors of the economy. A sector consists of a grouping of economic units that are relatively homogeneous in their behavior. By combining source-and-use-of-funds statements for all sectors, we may obtain a matrix for the entire economy. This matrix shows the interlocking nature of financial assets and liabilities among various sectors. It enables us to analyze savings-deficit sectors and the means by which they finance the excess of their investment in real assets over savings, together with the behavior of savings-surplus sectors and the way they invest in financial assets.

TABLE 2-6 Debt Outstanding by Sector 1961–1999II (billions of $)

				Domestic Nonfinancial Sectors							
				Nonfederal							
				Households			Business				
	Total	Federal Government	Total Nonfederal	Total	Home Mortgage	Consumer Credit	Total	Corporate	State and Local Governments	Domestic Financial Sectors	Foreign
1961	767.7	243.2	524.6	224.0	145.7	63.4	222.7	160.2	77.8	34.9	25.5
1962	820.6	250.0	570.5	245.1	159.1	69.3	241.6	171.4	83.8	39.4	27.5
1963	876.0	253.8	622.1	270.9	174.8	77.9	262.0	183.0	89.2	46.6	30.8
1964	939.9	259.9	680.0	299.1	191.1	87.4	285.3	197.8	95.6	53.0	35.0
1965	1007.1	261.5	745.6	326.6	207.3	97.5	315.7	218.7	103.2	61.9	37.5
1966	1074.6	265.1	809.5	348.4	219.8	103.4	351.1	244.1	110.0	72.9	39.5
1967	1150.6	278.1	872.6	366.9	232.3	108.6	388.3	270.8	117.4	73.6	43.3
1968	1242.7	290.6	952.1	397.4	247.4	119.3	428.6	299.9	126.1	84.0	46.1
1969	1332.0	287.4	1044.6	426.8	262.7	129.2	479.5	335.3	138.3	111.5	49.2
1970	1422.3	299.5	1122.8	445.3	274.2	133.7	527.2	367.4	150.3	127.8	52.1
1971	1557.5	324.4	1233.1	487.1	297.2	149.2	579.2	395.6	166.7	138.9	56.6
1972	1713.5	339.4	1374.1	544.5	332.5	168.8	649.0	433.0	180.7	162.8	61.1
1973	1898.0	346.3	1551.7	614.1	371.4	193.0	742.8	497.0	194.8	209.8	67.4
1974	2072.3	358.2	1714.1	663.5	402.5	201.9	842.4	554.6	208.2	258.3	81.2
1975	2264.7	443.9	1820.8	715.3	439.9	207.0	886.2	575.2	219.4	260.4	95.6
1976	2508.3	513.1	1995.3	802.3	500.3	229.0	955.2	614.3	237.8	283.9	116.0
1977	2829.6	569.4	2260.2	934.6	590.8	264.4	1069.5	687.6	256.2	337.8	129.4
1978	3214.5	621.9	2592.6	1094.1	697.3	310.4	1203.0	761.6	295.6	412.5	157.6
1979	3606.5	657.7	2948.9	1258.5	809.1	353.1	1368.2	845.4	322.2	504.9	172.9
1980	3957.9	735.0	3222.9	1374.1	904.6	355.4	1504.3	911.6	344.4	578.1	197.2

TABLE 2-6 (cont.)

Domestic Nonfinancial Sectors

	Total	Federal Government	Total Nonfederal	Nonfederal — Households Total	Home Mortgage	Consumer Credit	Nonfederal — Business Total	Corporate	State and Local Governments	Domestic Financial Sectors	Foreign
1981	4366.4	820.5	3545.9	1480.8	971.9	373.1	1693.0	1028.6	372.1	682.4	210.7
1982	4788.3	981.8	3806.5	1547.7	1002.4	390.3	1845.0	1117.9	413.8	778.1	210.4
1983	5364.9	1167.0	4197.9	1706.2	1090.5	440.3	2030.6	1228.8	461.1	882.8	227.7
1984	6151.2	1364.2	4787.0	1918.4	1217.9	521.0	2355.0	1434.8	513.6	1052.4	235.5
1985	7132.7	1589.9	5542.8	2235.9	1407.7	603.8	2629.0	1612.4	677.9	1258.3	236.7
1986	7973.1	1805.9	6167.2	2489.0	1600.0	658.2	2926.1	1832.9	752.1	1593.6	238.3
1987	8675.0	1949.8	6725.3	2743.3	1816.0	688.6	3140.9	2004.5	841.0	1896.5	245.1
1988	9457.6	2104.9	7352.8	3011.3	2021.5	732.0	3446.5	2214.2	895.0	2145.8	252.4
1989	10161.0	2251.2	7909.8	3280.8	2220.7	793.3	3683.8	2397.0	945.1	2399.3	262.3
1990	10843.4	2498.1	8345.3	3554.3	2461.2	805.1	3798.7	2515.3	992.3	2615.8	286.0
1991	11305.2	2776.4	8528.8	3723.0	2619.2	794.5	3728.2	2463.2	1077.7	2786.7	301.2
1992	11832.6	3080.3	8752.2	3893.3	2762.2	800.6	3757.2	2506.6	1101.8	3046.3	316.0
1993	12431.8	3336.5	9095.4	4108.0	2892.6	859.0	3819.4	2563.0	1167.9	3346.1	385.8
1994	13013.9	3492.3	9521.6	4427.0	3070.2	983.9	3972.9	2708.9	1121.7	3822.2	370.3
1995	13734.3	3636.7	10097.6	4782.2	3251.4	1122.8	4245.2	2947.7	1070.2	4278.8	441.4
1996	14477.4	3781.8	10695.6	5105.1	3461.4	1211.6	4527.1	3141.0	1063.4	4827.7	518.7
1997	15261.1	3804.9	11456.3	5433.3	3693.2	1264.1	4903.5	3433.8	1119.5	5446.8	570.1
1998	16283.6	3752.2	12531.4	5903.6	4051.5	1331.7	5428.0	3852.2	1199.8	6515.6	603.7
1999—Q1	16597.4	3733.4	12863.9	6042.3	4152.8	1363.4	5600.0	3997.1	1221.6	6819.6	608.0
Q2	16813.8	3705.4	13108.4	6170.0	4256.5	1376.7	5707.8	4076.0	1230.6	7073.1	597.2

Source: Flow of Funds Accounts of the U.S., Federal Reserve System.

Subject to certain limitations, the flow-of-funds data give the financial-market analyst rich insights. By tracing through the sources of funds for investment in a particular financial instrument, one gains information about strains in the financial system and about interest rates. Analysts can gain insight not only from a study of flows that have occurred in the past but from using the rigorous flow-of-funds framework to make forecasts of the future. Finally, the Federal Reserve System provides information on the total debt outstanding by sector.

❖ SELECTED REFERENCES

Cohen, Jacob, *The Flow of Funds in Theory and Practice*. Norwell, MA: Kluwer Academic Publishers, 1987.

Copeland, Morris A., *A Study of Moneyflows in the United States*. New York: National Bureau of Economic Research, 1952.

The Flow-of-Funds Approach to Social Accounting. New York: National Bureau of Economic Research, 1962.

Goldsmith, Raymond W., *The Flow of Capital Funds in the Postwar Economy,* chapter 2. New York: National Bureau of Economic Research, 1965.

Introduction to the Flow of Funds. Washington, DC: Board of Governors of the Federal Reserve System, February 1975.

FOUNDATIONS FOR INTEREST RATES

As we showed in chapter 1, the function of financial markets is to facilitate the flow of savings from savings-surplus economic units to savings-deficit ones. The allocation of these savings occurs primarily on the basis of price, expressed by interest rates. Economic units in need of funds must outbid others for their use, holding risk constant. Although the allocation process is affected by capital rationing and government restrictions, interest rates are the primary mechanism whereby supply and demand are brought into balance for a particular financial instrument across financial markets. In this chapter, we analyze how the price mechanism works to bring the supply of a financial instrument into balance with its demand. In subsequent chapters, the focus is on explaining relative returns or return differentials among various financial instruments.

THE INTEREST RATE IN AN
EXCHANGE ECONOMY

Interest rates in financial markets are determined by a complex interaction of supply-and-demand forces. In order to understand these forces, we will simplify the problem by looking at it in varying degrees of abstraction. Essentially, we will focus on the choice of individual economic units between consumption and investment. In market equilibrium, of course, a balance must exist between investment and savings, or forgoing of consumption. We begin by looking at the consumption-savings phenomenon for the individual and then consider the equilibrating process among individuals. We assume initially a world of certainty and analyze the determination of the rate of interest in such a world—namely, the riskless rate. Following this presentation, we will consider the determination of interest rates when risk exists.

THE INDIVIDUAL CHOICE

Consider an individual with a two-point time horizon—now and one year from now. Moreover, suppose the individual is concerned only with a single commodity—call it corn. Although the example could be extended to a "basket" of consumption commodities, for ease of comprehension we simplify and consider only one commodity. The initial question is this: What is the individual's preference for present consumption vis-à-vis future consumption? The answer can be visualized with the help of Figure 3-1. Along the horizontal axis we have *present consumption,* whereas along the vertical we have consumption at time 1, or *future consumption.* The curves depict the individual's trade-off between present and future consumption and are called **indifference curves.** Along a curve, an individual is indifferent with regard to present or future consumption. To part with present consumption—that is, to save—the individual must be promised increasing amounts of future consumption, C_1. Each curve upward and to the right represents a higher level of satisfaction or utility. The object then is to strive for the highest indifference curve, because it represents the highest level of present and future want satisfaction. The indifference curves give us the **preference function** of the individual.

Imagine now a situation where individuals can produce corn, but no exchange occurs—that is, they cannot exchange the commodity they produce for something else or for corn in the future. The corn just harvested can either be consumed now or saved for the next planting. Suppose the production opportunity situation for the individual is depicted by the curve $X'X$ in Figure 3-2. Point X on the horizontal axis represents the individual's present endowment of corn—the harvest just past; it can be entirely consumed and nothing saved for next year's planting. In that case, consumption at time 1 will be zero. Alternatively, part or all of the present endowment can be saved as seed corn for next year's planting. In our world of certainty, we know the yield of corn at time 1, given an amount of seed corn held over at time 0. If all corn is held over as seed corn, consumption at time 1 will be X'. The $X'X$ curve shows the combinations of present and future consumption that are possible. Starting with the present endowment of X, note that each increment of corn saved for seed increases future consumption but at a decreasing rate. In other words, production increases but at a diminishing rate as more seed is planted in a given plot of land.

The optimum present consumption, and hence the savings of the individual, is represented by the point of tangency of the production opportunity curve with the highest indifference curve. This is depicted in Figure 3-2 by X^*. Given this equilibrium point, the individual would consume C_0^* of corn presently and withhold $X - C_0^*$ for seed. This would result in future production and consumption of C_1^*.

OPTIMUM WITH EXCHANGE

What happens if exchange is a possibility? By exchange we mean opportunities for the exchange of present and future claims to consumption—in this case, to corn—with other economic units. In general, this possibility allows the individual economic unit to obtain a higher level of present and future want satisfaction.[1] Suppose the market exchange opportunities are depicted by the diagonal lines shown in Figure 3-3. The slope of these lines describes the exchange ratio between present and future consumption. The graph shows that to obtain a number of units of present consumption, the individual must give up an even greater number of units of future consumption. This implies a

---

[1] The approach presented was formulated many years ago by Irving Fisher, *The Theory of Interest* (New York: The Macmillan Co., 1930).

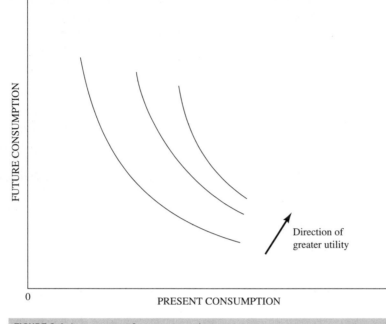

FUTURE CONSUMPTION

Direction of
greater utility

0   PRESENT CONSUMPTION

FIGURE 3-1 INDIFFERENCE CURVES FOR AN INDIVIDUAL

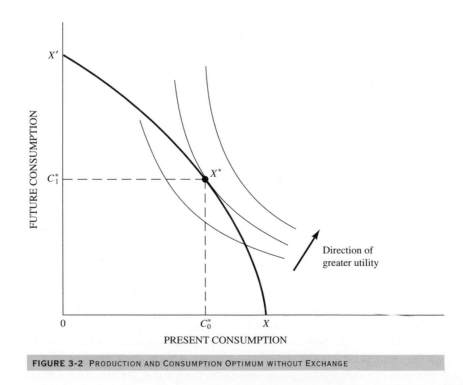

X'

FUTURE CONSUMPTION

C_1^*

X^*

Direction of
greater utility

0   C_0^* X

PRESENT CONSUMPTION

FIGURE 3-2 PRODUCTION AND CONSUMPTION OPTIMUM WITHOUT EXCHANGE

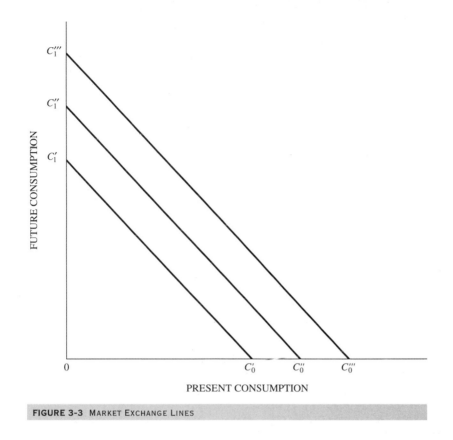

FIGURE 3-3 MARKET EXCHANGE LINES

preference in the market for present consumption vis-à-vis future consumption. The ratio of exchange for the first line and, because they are parallel, for all other lines, is

$$\frac{C_1'}{C_0'} = 1 + r \qquad \text{(3-1)}$$

Thus, r represents the rate of interest for the sacrifice of current consumption for future consumption. At this rate, trading in the market is possible between present and future consumption claims. While the interest rate is positive in this case, it need not be. Time preferences could favor future consumption vis-à-vis present consumption. In this case, the slope of the lines in Figure 3-3 would be less than 45 degrees and a negative interest rate would prevail.

Each line in the figure represents a level of endowment of present and future consumption: the further upward and to the right, the higher the level of endowment. The endowment can be thought of as a constraint in that it limits the opportunities for consumption. If the initial endowment in present consumption were C_0'', for example, only opportunities along the line $C_0'' C_1''$ would be possible. If C_0'' were consumed now, nothing would be exchanged for future consumption. At the other extreme, all of C_0'' could be exchanged for C_1'' of future consumption. Any combination between these two extremes is possible and connotes some exchange of present consumption for future consumption at an exchange ratio of $1 + r$. This corresponds to *lending*. In contrast, if one's endowment were entirely in a claim to future consumption, any exchange of future for present consumption would occur at an exchange ratio of $1/(1 + r)$. This corresponds to *borrowing*. Thus, the initial endowment can be in terms of present consumption claims, future consumption claims, or, as is likely, some combination of the two.

COMBINED EFFECT

Having analyzed separately the productive optimum in the absence of exchange and the exchange of present and future consumption claims (borrowing–lending) in the absence of production opportunities, we wish now to consider both simultaneously. For the individual economic unit, the derivation of production and consumption optimums is similar to the example in Figure 3-4. The productive opportunity set is denoted by the curve $X'X$, as it was in Figure 3-2. However, in this case the production optimum is not determined by the point of tangency of the production opportunity curve with the highest indifference curve. The situation is altered by the possibility of exchange. Optimal behavior by the individual is determined by the point of tangency between the production opportunity curve and the highest market exchange line. We see that this is point X^* in Figure 3-4.

Having determined a production optimum, individuals then would undertake borrowing or lending along the market exchange line, C_1C_0, until a point of tangency with the highest indifference curve is reached. We see in the figure that this is at point C^*, which is below and to the right of X^*, the production optimum. This means that individuals would exchange future consumption claims for present ones. In other words, in-

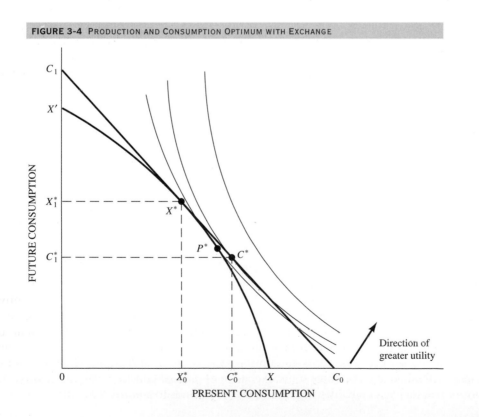

FIGURE 3-4 PRODUCTION AND CONSUMPTION OPTIMUM WITH EXCHANGE

dividuals would borrow. If the point of tangency were above X^* and to the left, individuals would have to lend to obtain an optimal balancing of present and future consumption claims.

To recapitulate, the individual should seek the productive opportunity along curve $X'X$ where a point of tangency exists between this curve and the highest market exchange ratio line. This is point X^*, and it implies that $X - X_0^*$ units of corn (along the horizontal axis) will be withheld as seed corn. It also implies X_1^* of future production on the vertical axis. Given a productive optimum of X^*, the individual then would borrow against future production in order to obtain the highest level of present and future want satisfaction. This is attained at C^*. It represents borrowing in the sense of giving up $X_1^* - C_1^*$ of claim to future consumption (vertical axis) for $C_0^* - X_0^*$ of additional present consumption (horizontal axis). Thus, the individual would move upward and to the left along line $X'X$ to point X^* and then downward and to the right along line C_1C_0 until point C^* was reached.

Note that the overall level of want satisfaction of C^* with production *and* exchange opportunities is higher than that obtained with production opportunities alone. The latter optimum would occur at P^*, where the productive opportunity curve is tangent with an indifference curve. With exchange opportunities, a higher level of want satisfaction is usually possible.

Also, we should emphasize that with production *and* exchange opportunities, determination of the production optimum, point X^* in Figure 3-4, is independent of the individual's utility preferences. This is illustrated in Figure 3-5, where we draw another set of indifference curves. The lower set of indifference curves depicts borrowing to obtain C^*, whereas the upper set depicts lending to obtain C^{**}. In both cases, determination of the productive optimum is distinct from the utility preferences of the individual. Put another way, the individual's utility preferences can change, but this will not affect the production optimum. This condition is known as the **separation theorem.** It derives from our underlying assumption that the individual can both borrow and lend at the market rate r. Under such circumstances the intertemporal production decision is based solely on the point of tangency of the productive opportunity curve with the highest market exchange line.

MARKET EQUILIBRIUM

Up until now we have assumed a given value for the slope of the market exchange line—that is, the rate of interest. In effect, the individual has been viewed as a price taker with the exchange ratio as the price. However, the market comprises many individuals, and the equilibrium rate of interest is determined by their interaction. For borrowing to occur, for example, one or more individuals must be willing to lend at an agreed-upon exchange ratio. To illustrate, suppose the production-consumption optimum for individual 1 is that shown in Figure 3-4. The figure suggests that the individual wants to exchange $X_1^* - C_1^*$ in future consumption claims for $C_0^* - X_0^*$ of present consumption.

Suppose the market has only one other individual, whose productive-consumptive equilibrium is illustrated in Figure 3-6. The slope of the market exchange line is the same as that in Figure 3-4. The productive optimum for this individual is X^* and, given his or her utility preference, this individual would strive to lend $X_0^* - C_0^*$ of present consumption claims for $C_1^* - X_1^*$ of future consumption claims. However, the amount the second individual desires to lend at the prevailing rate of interest is less than what the first individual desires to borrow. This creates a disequilibrium situation.

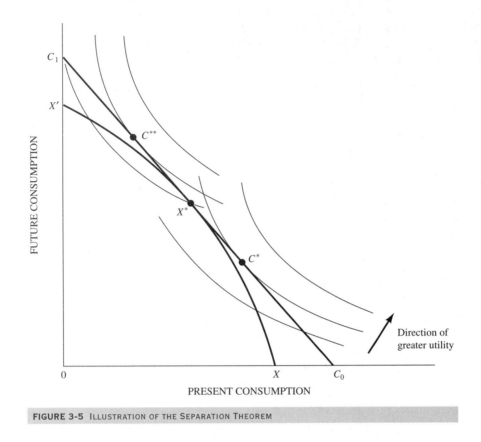

FIGURE 3-5 ILLUSTRATION OF THE SEPARATION THEOREM

The forces in this situation work in the direction of a higher rate of interest—thus, there is a greater slope to the market exchange line. With a greater slope, the second individual's productive optimum will be downward and to the right. This is depicted in the lower panel of Figure 3-7. Instead of X^* being the optimum production opportunity, given a market exchange line of $C_1 C_0$, X^{**} becomes the optimum, with a market exchange line of $C_1' C_0'$. Moreover, the individual is able to attain a higher indifference curve in lending owing to the greater slope of the market exchange line. The import of this is that at the new rate of interest, the individual is willing to lend more than before, $X_0^{**} - C_0^{**}$ as opposed to $X_0^* - C_0^*$.

The shift in slope of the market exchange line also affects the behavior of the first individual. His or her production optimum also shifts downward and to the right, as shown in the upper panel of Figure 3-7. Moreover, because of the higher rate of interest, this individual is able to achieve only a lower indifference curve. The overall effect is a dramatic lessening in his or her desire to borrow for current consumption, $C_0^{**} - X_0^{**}$ as opposed to $C_0^* - X_0^*$ before. In fact, the first individual wishes to borrow much less than the second individual desires to lend at the higher interest rate. Therefore, a lower rate of interest is in order. The interest rate, or slope of the market exchange line, will continue to adjust until the amount the first individual wishes to borrow equals the amount the second individual desires to lend.

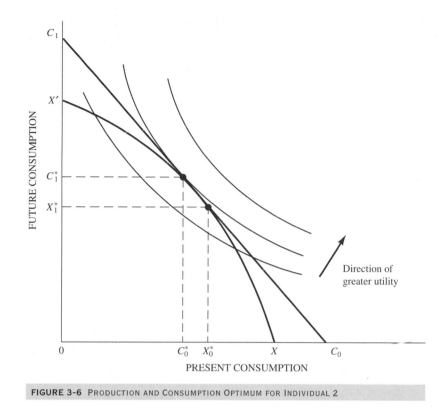

FIGURE 3-6 PRODUCTION AND CONSUMPTION OPTIMUM FOR INDIVIDUAL 2

Obviously, the "market" comprises more than two individuals. However, the equilibrating process works as illustrated when we have multiple economic units. As the rate of interest changes, some individuals will want to borrow more or less, while others will want to lend less or more. In fact, as the interest rate rises, some economic units previously wanting to borrow will want to lend; as the interest rate declines, some economic units will wish to borrow although they wanted to lend before. This relationship can be visualized by shifting the slope of the market exchange lines in Figure 3-7. Market equilibrium is achieved when desired lending equals desired borrowing across all economic units. In the context of chapter 1, lending corresponds to saving, or the refraining from current consumption, whereas borrowing corresponds to investment, or dissavings.

Market equilibrium then is determined by the forces of supply and demand for current consumption claims vis-à-vis future claims. This is depicted in Figure 3-8. The lending curve represents an aggregation of the amounts of desired lending for all economic units at various interest rates. In other words, any point on the curve represents the horizontal sum of different individuals' desired lending at the particular interest rate involved. In terms of our example in the lower panel of Figure 3-7, the desired loans of the individual at the two different rates were $X_0^* - C_0^*$ and $X_0^{**} - C_0^{**}$. Similarly, the borrowing curve represents an aggregation of the amounts of desired borrowing for all economic units at various interest rates. (In the example in the upper panel of Figure 3-7, desired borrowings are $C_0^* - X_0^*$ and $C_0^{**} - X_0^{**}$ for the two interest rates.)

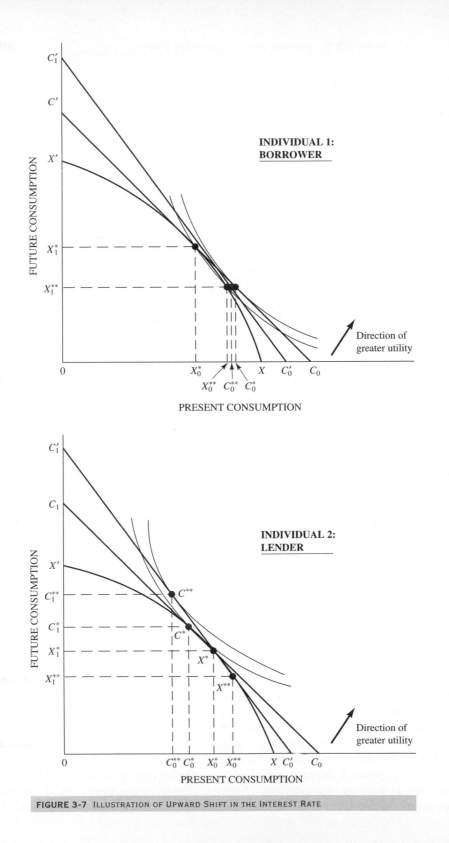

FIGURE 3-7 Illustration of Upward Shift in the Interest Rate

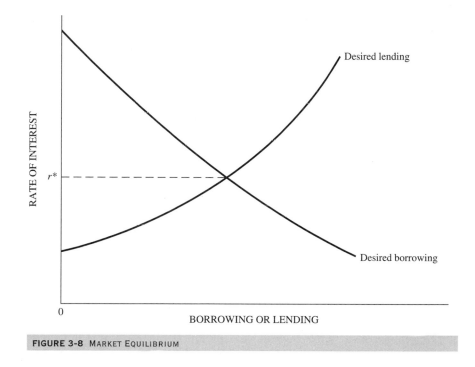

FIGURE 3-8 MARKET EQUILIBRIUM

The lending and borrowing curves in Figure 3-8 intersect at the equilibrium rate of interest, r^*. At this rate, desired lending equals desired borrowing and the market is in equilibrium. Recall that the rate of interest is a measure of the price of current consumption claims in relation to future consumption claims. The curves in Figure 3-8 represent an aggregation of production-consumption optimums for all individuals under varying interest rates, as illustrated in Figure 3-7 and earlier figures. Thus, the equilibrium market rate of interest embodies the desired lending and borrowing behavior of all economic units according to their productive opportunity sets and their utility preferences. Shifts in these factors will cause shifts in desired lending or borrowing and in the equilibrium rate of interest.

What we have described is a **neoclassical loanable funds theory** of market equilibrium. Savings, or forgoing immediate consumption, are the source of loanable funds, and investments are the use of funds. The market rate of interest changes in order to bring about equilibrium when aggregate desired lending and/or borrowing in Figure 3-8 change. In a sense, the loanable funds theory allows for a full equilibrium analysis of an economy and of its financial market. When all forces are in equilibrium, the interest rate is determined automatically.

At the beginning of this section, we invoked the assumption of certainty with respect to the future. As a result, our problem was reduced to showing the determination of the riskless rate of interest. Assuming no transaction costs or other market impediments, this became the rate at which all individual economic units could either borrow or lend. When we leave the world of certainty, however, we must consider risk. In the remainder of this chapter, we present an overall framework for determining interest rates under conditions of risk and uncertainty. In subsequent chapters, we extend this analysis to consider the factors that give rise to risk and their impact on market rates of interest. In other words, we proceed from the general to the specific.

INTEREST RATES IN A WORLD WITH RISK

When we leave the riskless world assumed in the previous section, the determination of interest rates is altered. With risk, for example, we can and do have multiple financial instruments. This contrasts with the previous section, where there was but one financial instrument—a riskless contract between the borrower and lender. This contract bore an interest rate that was the same for all such contracts in the market. Stated another way, only one rate of interest prevailed: the risk-free rate. In a world characterized by risk, different interest rates occur. This is the topic we wish to study.

BEHAVIOR OF INDIVIDUAL ECONOMIC UNITS

Interest rates in risky financial markets cannot be analyzed in isolation. They depend not only on interest rates in other financial markets but also on the real sector of the economy and on consumption. All these factors interact to determine an equilibrium structure of interest rates. In this section we study the behavior of individual economic units in choosing assets and issuing financial liabilities. An understanding of this behavior allows us later to examine how economic units interact to determine interest rates in the economy.

As discussed in chapter 2, the balance sheet for an economic unit at any moment is as follows.

Assets	*Liabilities and Net Worth*
Money	Financial liabilities
	1
Other financial assets	2
1	.
2	.
.	.
.	n
.	
n	
Real assets	
1	
2	
.	
.	Net worth
.	
n	

The assumption is that the economic unit adjusts its balance sheet toward a desired, or preferred, mix of assets and liabilities in keeping with changes in interest rates, investment opportunities, wealth, and other factors. It may increase its total asset holdings only if its net worth increases, it issues additional financial liabilities, or both. In turn, a change in net worth can be the result of two occurrences: (1) current expenditures less than or more than current income, and (2) capital gains or losses on financial assets and liabilities and on real assets over the period.

Consumption clearly represents an alternative to holding assets or issuing financial liabilities and, accordingly, influences the desired totals in the balance sheet for the economic unit. A household, for example, has several choices to make in the allocation of its wealth and income. To purchase a house, it may have to save, by consuming less than its income, until it has accumulated sufficient funds for a down payment. The alternative to purchasing a house in this case would be increased consumption. If the household were already consuming less than its current income, the alternative might be increasing its financial assets. A household must decide not only on the proportion of income to save but also on where these savings are to be employed—that is, what type of asset is to be increased (money, other financial assets, or real assets) or what type of financial liability is to be paid off. A business corporation, on the other hand, may purchase a piece of capital equipment by retaining its earnings, by reducing its financial assets, or by increasing its financial liabilities.

These examples are sufficient to illustrate the complexities that face the individual economic unit in determining the total amount and composition of financial assets it holds and the amount and composition of financial liabilities it issues. How does the individual economic unit adjust its holdings of assets, its financial liabilities, and its consumption to achieve a preferred position? It does so on the basis of maximizing total utility. At a moment in time, the economic unit increases its financial liabilities to finance its holding of money, other financial assets, and real assets as long as it can increase its total utility by doing so. Over time the economic unit can increase or decrease its marginal propensity to consume. Changes in net worth affect and are affected by consumption, the holdings of various assets, and the financial liabilities issued. Thus, all these factors are interdependent with respect to the utility preferences of an economic unit and its behavior.

UTILITY FOR FINANCIAL ASSETS

Assuming that economic units attempt to maximize their total utility, we must consider now the utility derived from holding various assets and from issuing financial liabilities. This consideration is fundamental to understanding how economic units in an economy interact to determine interest rates. For **financial assets** other than money, we assume that the preferences of economic units are based on a two-parameter utility function; these parameters are (1) the expected return from the instrument and (2) the risk involved in holding it.[2] If the future were known, no risk would be involved in holding a financial asset. The income stream would be certain. Because utility is associated positively with return, all economic units would try to maximize their total return from the holding of financial assets by investing in the financial asset that promised the greatest return. With certainty about the future and perfect capital markets, however, arbitrage

---

[2] For a justification of this approach, see James Tobin, "Liquidity Preference as Behavior Towards Risk," *Review of Economic Studies* 25 (February 1958): 65–86.

would assure that every financial asset yielded no more than the risk-free rate, as determined in the previous section.

When the future is *not* known, the utility function of an economic unit is more complex. The economic unit must consider the range of possible returns. To reduce the problem to manageable proportions, we assume that individuals are able to summarize their beliefs about the probability distribution of possible returns from a financial asset or portfolio of financial assets in terms of the **expected return** and the **standard deviation** of the distribution. By diversifying one's holdings of financial assets, the risk-averse economic unit is able to reduce the dispersion of the probability distribution of possible returns relative to the expected value of return for that distribution.[3] Put another way, the risk to the investor will be less compared to the expected return.

The individual economic unit is assumed to have a preference function with respect to the expected return and risk from holding a portfolio of financial assets. In other words, it is assumed to make optimal portfolio decisions on the basis of these two parameters. For a risk-averse investor, utility increases at a decreasing rate with successive increments in wealth. Therefore, the greater the standard deviation of the probability distribution of possible returns for an investment is, the less the expected utility of that investment is and the less desirable it becomes.

Determination of the optimal portfolio of financial assets can be facilitated by several equilibration models. These include the capital asset pricing model, multivariable and multifactor models, and the arbitrage pricing theory. As these are explained in a companion text, we do not do so here.[4] Whatever the model used, all economic units are assumed to select portfolios of financial assets in such a way as to maximize their expected utility. In turn, utility preferences are assumed to be formulated on the basis of the expected return and the standard deviation of the probability distribution of possible returns.

UTILITY FOR FINANCIAL LIABILITIES

We assume also that the issuance of **financial liabilities** can be analyzed on the basis of a two-parameter utility function. Because an economic unit must pay the return on a financial liability, it would have a negative utility for doing so, all other things remaining the same. Consequently, $\partial U/\partial e < 0$, where e is the expected return on the financial liability. If an economic unit is a risk averter, it would prefer less variance to more variance, holding constant the expected return, so $\partial U/\partial v < 0$, where v is the standard deviation for the financial liability. For the risk seeker, $\partial U/\partial v > 0$. For a financial liability, variance pertains to the dispersion of the probability distribution of possible future market prices. For fixed-income financial liabilities, the issuer knows with certainty its contractual obligation to meet interest and principal payments. After issuance, however, the instrument fluctuates in market price because of changes in the overall level of interest rates and because of changes in perceived risk by investors.

---

[3] All the work along this line is an outgrowth of the classic work of Harry M. Markowitz, *Portfolio Selection: Efficient Diversification of Investments* (New York: John Wiley & Sons, 1959).

[4] James C. Van Horne, *Financial Management and Policy,* 11th ed. (Upper Saddle River, NJ: Prentice Hall, 1998), chapters 3–4.

UTILITY FOR OTHER ASSETS

In the previous discussion, we considered the effect of holding financial assets and issuing financial liabilities on the utility of an economic unit. We now must consider the utility arising from the holding of other assets. Because our primary interest is in financial instruments, however, our examination necessarily is brief. Afterward, the maximization of utility for an economic unit in its holdings of assets, in its issuance of financial liabilities, and in its consumption is considered. Having established these building blocks, we deal in the remainder of the chapter with how economic units interact to determine interest rates in an economy.

Because **money** is a medium of exchange and other financial assets are not, it was not included in our previous discussion. If it were not for money, of course, trading would have to be done on the basis of exchanging one good for another. Because of obvious inefficiencies of a barter system, money has come to serve as the accepted medium of exchange in acquiring goods and services. In addition, it serves as the unit of account in the pricing of such. The expected value of return for holding money is zero, but no risk is involved other than the erosion of purchasing power with inflation.

Unlike financial assets, **real assets** are held for the physical services they provide the owner. These assets may be productive, such as a machine tool, or may be designed to satisfy the wants of economic units, such as a house or a consumer durable. Real assets are tangible; they cannot be produced instantaneously but only over time. The marginal utility arising from owning a real asset must be related to the services it provides. In the case of a productive asset, it usually is related to the marginal profitability of another unit of input. In analyzing profitability one must take account of the interdependence of inputs in the production function. It is the partial derivative of profitability with respect to the asset that is important. The marginal utility of consumer durables and dwellings is much more difficult to measure. Here, marginal utility must be related to the want satisfaction the asset provides the owner.

The holding of certain real assets can be explained in terms of the overall portfolio of the owner. Business firms, on the one hand, hold capital assets for the return they are expected to provide. Households, on the other hand, do not appear to acquire consumer durables on the basis of portfolio considerations. However, the acquisition of a home has portfolio implications, for generally it is the largest asset holding of the household. Although the model developed in this chapter implies an independence of the utility function for real assets from that for financial assets, the holding of certain real assets can be explained in terms of an expected return-risk trade-off for the economic unit as a whole. In these cases, the interdependence of real and financial assets must be recognized in the final determination of an optimal portfolio.

MARKET EQUILIBRIUM

The amount of money, financial assets, and real assets held; the amount of financial liabilities issued; and consumption are determined by an economic unit on the basis of maximizing its total utility, subject to net worth and income constraints. In equilibrium, the marginal utility derived from holding each asset is the same. **Marginal utility** is defined as the change in total utility that accompanies an increase of \$1 in a particular asset. Thus, the marginal utility derived from the last dollar increase in financial asset 1 must equal the marginal utility derived from the last dollar increase in money; in financial assets 2, 3, and n; and in real assets 1, 2, . . . , n. In equilibrium, the following equation holds.

$$
\frac{\text{MU money}}{P \text{ money}} = \frac{\text{MU FA}_1}{\text{PFA}_1} = \frac{\text{MU FA}_2}{\text{PFA}_2} = \frac{\text{MU FA}_n}{\text{PFA}_n}
$$
$$
= \frac{\text{MU RA}_1}{\text{PRA}_1} = \frac{\text{MU RA}_2}{\text{PRA}_2} = \frac{\text{MU RA}_n}{\text{PRA}_n}
$$

        (3-2)

Here MU stands for marginal utility, P for price per unit, FA_n for financial asset n, and RA_n for real asset n. In other words, maximum satisfaction occurs at the point at which the marginal utility of a dollar's worth of money equals the marginal utility of a dollar's worth of financial asset n and the marginal utility of a dollar's worth of the other assets held. If this equation is not satisfied, an economic unit can increase its total utility by shifting from an asset with a lower ratio of marginal utility to price to one with a higher ratio. By such shifting, equilibrium will eventually be achieved, where the ratios of marginal utility to price are all equal to some constant λ. If the price of money is 1, $\lambda = \text{MU}$ money/1, or the marginal utility of money.

    For simplicity in analysis, we hold constant the effect of consumption by considering the balance sheet of an economic unit at only a moment in time. Over time, of course, an economic unit can have current expenditures. Then, in equilibrium, the marginal utility derived from a dollar's worth of current expenditures must equal that derived from a dollar's worth of each asset held. In other words, consumption competes with the holding of assets in the maximization of total utility. This implies that the marginal utility of savings (current income less current expenditures) must be evaluated in relation to the satisfaction derived from the assets into which savings are put. To facilitate later analysis, however, we hold constant the effect of savings and consumption and assume that an economic unit will not sell assets, use money, or issue financial liabilities for consumption.

    Financial liabilities represent a negative marginal utility to the issuer. An economic unit does not issue a financial liability for its own sake, but rather to acquire assets. As long as the positive marginal utility from an additional dollar's worth of assets exceeds in absolute magnitude the negative marginal utility from the issuance of an additional dollar of financial liabilities, the economic unit will issue financial liabilities. In equilibrium, the negative marginal utility per dollar's worth of each financial liability should be the same. Moreover, the ratio of marginal utility to price for each financial liability should equal the ratio of marginal utility to price for each asset (if we ignore the sign of the ratio). For the risk averter, we would expect the negative ratio of marginal utility to price to increase at an increasing rate as a financial liability is increased beyond some point.

MAXIMIZING UTILITY FOR THE ECONOMIC UNIT

At any moment in time, the holding of financial assets and the issuance of financial liabilities are constrained by the net worth of the individual economic unit

$$
M + \text{FA}_1 P_{\text{FA}_1} + \text{FA}_2 P_{\text{FA}_2} + \cdots + \text{FA}_n P_{\text{FA}_n} + \text{RA}_1 P_{\text{RA}_1} + \text{RA}_2 P_{\text{RA}_2}
$$
$$
+ \cdots + \text{RA}_n P_{\text{RA}_n} - \text{FL}_1 P_{\text{FL}_1} - \text{FL}_2 P_{\text{FL}_2} - \cdots - \text{FL}_n P_{\text{FL}_n} = \text{NW}
$$

        (3-3)

where FA_n is the quantity of financial asset n, P_{FA_n} is the price per unit of that asset, FL_n is the quantity of liability n, and P_{FL_n} is the price per unit of that financial liability. The individual economic unit will try to maximize its total utility by changing its asset holdings and liabilities issued, subject to its net worth constraint. Its objective function is

$$\max X = U(M, X, R, Y) \tag{3-4}$$

subject to

$$M + \sum_i P_i x_i + \sum_k P_k r_k - \sum_j P_j y_j = NW \tag{3-5}$$

where

$X =$ a column vector of x_i, where x_i is the quantity of the ith financial asset
$P_i =$ price per unit of the ith financial asset
$R =$ a column vector of r_k, where r_k is the quantity of the kth real asset
$P_k =$ price per unit of the kth real asset
$Y =$ a column vector of y_j, where y_j is the quantity of the jth financial liability
$P_j =$ price per unit of the jth financial liability

Recall that the utility to an economic unit of holding financial assets and issuing financial liabilities was assumed to be based on the expected value and standard deviation of the probability distributions of possible returns. Each economic unit forms expectations about possible returns from all feasible portfolios of financial assets and all feasible combinations of financial liabilities. We recognize, however, that an economic unit is limited in the number of financial assets it can consider at one time. It simply is unable to form expectations about the universe of financial assets available to it for investment; consequently, the number of feasible portfolios is restricted. Once the optimal portfolio of financial assets and the optimal combination of financial liabilities are determined by an economic unit, it then increases or decreases them to maximize its total utility, in keeping with Equations (3-4) and (3-5).

In summary, the individual economic unit maximizes its utility according to Equation (3-4) by varying M, X, R, and Y, subject to the net worth constraint. **In equilibrium, the marginal utility per dollar of money equals the marginal utility per dollar of the optimal financial asset portfolio, which, in turn, equals the marginal utility per dollar of real assets held.** In addition, the negative marginal utility per dollar of the optimal combination of financial liabilities must equal the ratio for the assets (if we ignore the sign). If it were less, an economic unit could increase its total utility by increasing its financial liabilities and increasing its holdings of assets.

THE ACTION OF ALL ECONOMIC UNITS

The action of all economic units in an economy maximizing their utility according to Equation (3-4) determines market prices for real and financial assets in that economy. Whereas prices in Equation (3-5) are assumed to be given for the individual economic unit, they are not given for economic units collectively. These economic units act to maximize their individual utilities, and in doing so, they determine market prices and interest rates in the economy. For the economy as a whole, financial assets equal financial liabilities. Accordingly, market prices must adjust so that in equilibrium, no excess demand or excess supply exists.

The equilibrium structure of financial asset prices and interest rates is the result of a complex blending of the expectations, net worths, incomes, and utility functions of all economic units in an economy. This structure is affected by the utility preferences of economic units regarding money, real assets, financial assets, and financial liabilities. For example, an increase in the marginal utility of all economic units toward holding real assets would lead, *ceteris paribus,* to a greater aggregate demand for real assets, higher prices for these assets, a lower aggregate demand for financial assets, and a greater aggregate supply of financial liabilities. For equilibrium to be achieved, prices of financial instruments would have to decline and interest rates rise.

Equilibrium in financial markets requires that the total quantity of a financial instrument demanded equals the total quantity an economic unit desires to issue. The relative influence of an economic unit on market price depends on its net worth, its utility preferences, its expectations, and its existing holdings of assets and liabilities. On the supply side of the market, the quantity of a particular financial liability that an economic unit desires to issue also depends on these factors. In a modern economy, most economic units exert at least some influence on interest rates. Differing expectations, net worths, and utility functions of economic units, however, make determination of equilibrium prices of financial instruments in an economy an extremely complex process involving the interaction of all economic units in the economy. Perhaps the key element in this process is expectations. On the basis of expectations as to return, variance, and covariance, different financial instruments are perceived differently by different economic units. Economic units in need of funds must compete for them on the basis of the expected return paid. (Actually, the need for funds and the expected return paid are determined simultaneously.) Through the interaction of the various economic units, interest rates are determined and savings are allocated in the economy.

❖ SUMMARY

In a riskless world, individuals maximize their utility by first seeking a productive optimum between *current* consumption claims and *future* consumption claims. This optimum occurs at the point of tangency between their production opportunity curve and the market exchange line. Individuals then move up (lend) or down (borrow) the line until a point of tangency is reached with the highest indifference curve. At this point, present and future want satisfaction are maximized. When all economic units behave in this manner, the slope of the market exchange line, which represents the interest rate, shifts until the amount of desired lending equals the amount of desired borrowing at the particular interest rate involved. Thus, the equilibrium rate of interest embraces the productive opportunity sets and utility preferences of all economic units.

A risky world has not one but many interest rates. A general equilibrium framework is necessary to understand their determination. The individual economic unit continually adjusts its asset holdings and liabilities toward a preferred mix of assets, liabilities, and consumption. At the preferred mix, the wealth and income of the unit are allocated optimally. The economic unit adjusts its mix to maximize its total utility. In equilibrium, the marginal utilities of each dollar of money, each dollar of each financial asset, and each dollar of each real asset are the same. These ratios are also equal to the negative marginal utility of each dollar of each financial liability (if we ignore the sign).

The utility preferences for holding financial assets and issuing financial liabilities are assumed to be based on the expected value and the dispersion of the probability distribution of possible returns. In either case, it is the portfolio of assets or liabilities that is important, for an economic unit can reduce dispersion of its portfolio through diversification. Individual economic units maximize their total utility arising from holding money, financial assets, and real assets; from issuing financial liabilities; and from consuming, subject to wealth and income constraints. The behavior of all economic units in a closed economy maximizing their total utility in this manner determines interest rates on financial instruments in that economy. In equilibrium, the total amount of financial assets demanded must equal the total amount supplied; no excess demand or excess supply can exist in financial markets. Interest rates adjust to clear these markets and are the result of a complex interaction of all economic units in the economy.

❖ SELECTED REFERENCES

Bierwag, G. O., and M. A. Grove, "On Capital Asset Prices: Comment," *Journal of Finance* 20 (March 1965): 89–93.

Cochrane, John H., "New Facts in Finance," working paper, *National Bureau of Economic Research* (June 1999).

Elton, Edwin J., Martin J. Gruber, and Christopher R. Blake, "Fundamental Economic Variables, Expected Returns, and Bond Fund Performance," *Journal of Finance* 50 (September 1995): 1229–56.

Fisher, Irving, *The Theory of Interest.* New York: The Macmillan Co., 1930.

Markowitz, Harry M., *Portfolio Selection: Efficient Diversification of Investments.* New York: John Wiley & Sons, 1959.

Sharpe, William F., Gordon J. Alexander, and Jeffery V. Bailey, *Investments,* 6 ed. Upper Saddle River, NJ: Prentice Hall, 1999.

Van Horne, James C., *Financial Management and Policy,* 11th ed., chapters 2–4. Upper Saddle River, NJ: Prentice Hall, 1998.

CHAPTER 4

PRICES AND YIELDS FOR BONDS AND MONEY MARKET INSTRUMENTS

Fixed-income securities involve investing funds today with the promise of cash returns in the future. As a result, the time value of money is involved. Indeed, it underlies the valuation of all instruments investigated in this book. The time value of money merely means that a dollar today is worth more than a dollar to be received in the future.

REVIEW OF PRESENT VALUES

We want to know the amount of money that an instrument is worth today if it pays so many dollars in the future. This value depends on the rate of interest, r, which prevails and the length of time to the future payment. Suppose A is an amount of funds we are to receive one year from now. The present value (PV) of this amount is

$$PV = \frac{A}{(1 + r)} \tag{4-1}$$

If the amount is $100 and the interest rate is 7.5 percent, the present value is

$$PV = \frac{\$100}{(1.075)} = \$93.02$$

If the interest rate to us is 7.5 percent, we should be willing to pay $93.02 for the opportunity to receive $100 one year hence. In present-value language, r is known as the **discount rate.**
    The present value of a sum to be received 2 years from now is

$$PV = \frac{A}{(1 + r)^2} \tag{4-2}$$

where 2 is the exponent of $1 + r$. For our example,

$$PV = \frac{\$100}{(1.075)^2} = \$86.53$$

48

We see that a sum to be received two years from now is worth less than a sum to be received one year from now. Indeed, that is what present value is all about.

ANNUITIES

Rather than receive a single sum in the future, many financial contracts call for equal periodic payments. Such a stream of payments is known as an **annuity.** Suppose that a contract calls for equal payments at the end of each of the next three years, and that these payments are designated A_1, A_2, and A_3. The present value of this stream is

$$PV = \frac{A_1}{(1 + r)} + \frac{A_2}{(1 + r)^2} + \frac{A_3}{(1 + r)^3}$$

If the payment stream were $10 per year and the interest rate again were 7.5 percent, we would have

$$PV = \frac{\$10}{(1.075)} + \frac{\$10}{(1.075)^2} + \frac{\$10}{(1.075)^3} = \$26.01$$

We can express mathematically the present value of amounts to be received in the future as

$$PV = \sum_{t=1}^{n} \frac{A_t}{(1 + r)^t} \tag{4-3}$$

where t is the number of periods until the payment is to be received, n is the last year in which payment is to be received, and the Greek Sigma sign represents the sum of payments going from period 1 through period n.

PRESENT VALUE WHEN INTEREST IS COMPOUNDED MORE THAN ONCE A YEAR

When interest is compounded more than once a year, the formula for calculating present values must be revised. Instead of dividing by $(1 + r)$ to the appropriate power, as we do with annual compounding, the present value is determined by

$$PV = \sum_{t-1}^{n} \frac{A_t}{\left(1 + \dfrac{r}{m}\right)^{mt}} \tag{4-4}$$

where m is the number of times a year interest is compounded and, again, r is the discount rate. The present value of $100 to be received at the end of year 3, with a discount rate of 10 percent compounded semiannually, is

$$PV = \frac{\$100}{\left(1 + \dfrac{0.10}{2}\right)^{(2)(3)}} = \$74.62$$

For other compounding intervals, we change m in the formula from 2 to whatever number is appropriate.

CONTINUOUS COMPOUNDING

When interest is compounded continuously, the present value of a cash flow at the end of the year n is

$$PV = \frac{A_n}{e^{rn}} \qquad (4\text{-}5)$$

where e is approximately 2.71828. The present value of $100 to be received at the end of 3 years with a discount rate of 10 percent compounded continuously is

$$PV = \frac{\$100}{2.71828^{(0.10)(3)}} = \$74.08$$

On the other hand, if the discount rate is compounded only annually, we have

$$PV = \frac{\$100}{(1.10)^3} = \$75.13$$

Thus, the fewer times a year the discount rate is compounded, the greater the present value is. This relationship is just the opposite of that for terminal values. To illustrate the relationship between present value and the number of times a year the discount rate is compounded, consider again our example involving $100 to be received at the end of 3 years with a discount rate of 10 percent. The following present values result from various compounding intervals.

Compounding	Present Value
Annually	$75.13
Semiannually	74.62
Quarterly	74.36
Monthly	74.17
Continuously	74.08

We see that present value decreases, but at a decreasing rate as the compounding interval shortens, the limit being continuous compounding. With these time-value-of-money concepts in place, we turn now to bond valuation.

THE PRICE OF A BOND

The market price of a fixed-income security is the present value of the promised cash flows, discounted at the appropriate rate of interest. This rate is known as the **yield-to-maturity** (YTM).

COUPONS AND PRINCIPAL PAYMENTS

The return on bonds has two components: coupons and the final principal payment. The **face value** of virtually all bonds is $1,000, and this is the final principal payment due at maturity. However, the pricing convention is to treat the face value as $100. The coupon is expressed in terms of a percent of face value. If a bond has a coupon rate of 6.5 percent, the annual coupon payment is $0.065 \times \$100 = \$6.50$.

Most bonds call for coupon payments to be made semiannually. Hence, we will *assume semiannual coupon payments* in all that follows. These semiannual payments are an annuity mathematically, whereas the final principal payment of $100 at maturity is a single payment at that time. The price, P, of a bond is simply the present value of the following.

$$P = \sum_{t=1}^{2n} \frac{C/2}{\left(1 + \dfrac{r}{2}\right)^t} + \frac{\$100}{\left(1 + \dfrac{r}{2}\right)^{2n}} \tag{4-6}$$

where, as before, n is the number of years to maturity, C is the annual coupon payment, r is the annualized yield to maturity, and t is now the number of six-month periods to the payment, be it coupon or principal.

To illustrate, suppose that the 8 percent bonds of Zelta Rao Corporation have 12 years to maturity and that the interest rate, or yield to maturity, is 7.60 percent. As a result, the market price of a bond is

$$P = \frac{\$4}{(1.038)} + \frac{\$4}{(1.038)^2} + \frac{\$4}{(1.038)^3} + \cdots + \frac{\$104}{(1.038)^{24}} = \$103.11$$

The final combined coupon and principal payment of $104 is 24 six-month periods in the future, which, of course, is two times the number of years to maturity. Because the coupon rate, 8 percent, is more than the required interest rate, 7.60 percent, the present-value price is more than the bond's face value. The bond is said to trade at a premium. This premium is amortized over the life of the instrument, and that is the reason the investor receives less return than the bond's coupon rate.

What would happen if the yield-to-maturity were 8.50 percent? When we solve for P in the above equation, we find it to be $96.28. Under these circumstances, the bond is said to trade at a discount. On the basis of these calculations, several observations are in order.

1. When the yield-to-maturity of a bond is less than its coupon rate, the bond sells at a **premium** above its face value of $100.
2. When a bond's yield-to-maturity is more than its coupon rate, the bond sells at a **discount.** That is, its price is below $100.
3. When yield-to-maturity equals the coupon rate, the price of the bond equals its face value of $100.

The relationship between the price of a bond and its yield-to-maturity is shown in Figure 4-1. We see that mathematically as yield rises, price decreases, but at a decreasing rate. The nature of this convex relationship is examined in chapter 7.

PRICE WHEN NEXT COUPON PAYMENT IS LESS THAN SIX MONTHS AWAY

In the computations above, we assume the next coupon payment to be exactly six months in the future. While this is true at the date of issue, it is not the case for a seasoned bond except for two days a year. When the next coupon payment is less than six months away, we must take account of **accrued interest** in calculating the market price of the bond.

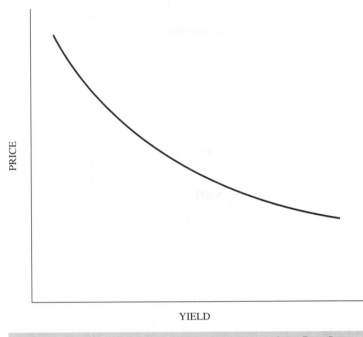

PRICE

YIELD

FIGURE 4-1 RELATIONSHIP BETWEEN PRICE AND YIELD FOR A LONG-TERM BOND

For Treasury notes and bonds, interest between coupon payment dates is accrued in a linear manner on the basis of a 365-day year. Most corporate bonds use linear accrual, but it is on the basis of a 360-day year in which each month is assumed to have 30 days.

Consider a hypothetical 8½ percent coupon Treasury bond that matures 11 years from the next coupon payment date of February 15 and that has a yield-to-maturity of 6.2 percent. Suppose on January 12 we wish to value this bond. There are 34 days to the next coupon payment on February 15, and 184 days between the last payment on August 15 of the prior year and February 15. The settlement price, SP, which is really the present value of the bond, is

$$SP = \frac{\$4.25}{(1.031)^{\frac{34}{184}}} + \frac{\$4.25}{(1.031)^{\frac{34}{184}}(1.031)} + \frac{\$4.25}{(1.031)^{\frac{34}{184}}(1.031)^2}$$

$$+ \cdots + \frac{\$104.25}{(1.031)^{\frac{34}{184}}(1.031)^{22}} = \$121.70$$

The buyer of the bond on January 12 receives the full $4.25 coupon payment on February 15. However, he or she must give up part of it to the seller who has held the bond for $184 - 34 = 150$ days. Therefore, the seller is entitled to

$$(150/184)(\$4.25) = \$3.46$$

This amount is reflected in the settlement price.

The market price of the bond is the settlement price minus the accrued interest.

$$P = \$121.70 - \$3.46 = \$118.24$$

This is the market price reported for a bond with the yield, coupon rate, and maturity used in our illustration. Programs embedded in calculators compute the accrued interest and deduct it from the present value (settlement price) to show the correct market price. For ease of understanding, we will not make any further accrued interest calculations, but simply assume the next coupon payment is six months away.

ZERO-COUPON BONDS

As the name implies, a zero-coupon bond pays no interim coupon. Rather, the issuer promises to make a single payment at a specified future date. This payment is the face value of the bond, $100. The present-value price of a zero-coupon bond is

$$P = \frac{\$100}{\left(1 + \dfrac{r}{2}\right)^{2n}} \tag{4-7}$$

where P is the present market price of the bond, $100 is its face value, r is the yield-to-maturity, and n is the maturity. The yield is simply the internal rate of return discussed earlier. The normal pricing convention is to use semiannual compounding as shown, as opposed to annual compounding.

Suppose Betatron Corporation issued a zero-coupon bond with a face value of $100 and a maturity of 10 years and that the yield-to-maturity is 12 percent. This implies a market price of

$$P = \frac{\$100}{(1.06)^{20}} = \$31.18$$

The investor puts up $31.18 today for the promise to receive $100 in 10 years. The return of 12 percent compounded semiannually is embraced in the discount from face value—$31.18 versus $100 in 10 years.

YIELD CALCULATIONS FOR BONDS

As we have implied but now state formally, the **yield-to-maturity** (YTM) on a bond is the rate of discount that equates the present value of all future coupon payments and face value at maturity with the market price of the bond. With semiannual coupon payments, we solve the following equation for r, the yield-to-maturity[1]

$$P = \frac{C/2}{\left(1 + \dfrac{r}{2}\right)} + \frac{C/2}{\left(1 + \dfrac{r}{2}\right)^2} + \cdots + \frac{C/2}{\left(1 + \dfrac{r}{2}\right)^{2n}} + \frac{\$100}{\left(1 + \dfrac{r}{2}\right)^{2n}} \tag{4-8}$$

---

[1] For a portfolio of bonds, yield-to-maturity is not a weighted average of the yields-to-maturity of the individual bonds. Rather, calculating a portfolio's yield-to-maturity involves the following steps: (1) Sum the market prices for all bonds in the portfolio. (2) For each future period, sum the coupon and principal payments for all bonds in the portfolio. (3) Solve for the rate of discount that equates the present value of cash flows determined in step 2 with the market value of the portfolio at time 0, step 1.

where P is the present market price of the bond, C is the annual coupon payment, and n is the number of years to maturity. Because of semiannual compounding, the annual coupon rate is divided by 2, and the total number of periods to maturity is found by multiplying the years to maturity by 2.

To illustrate, if an 8 percent coupon bond has 13 years to maturity and the present market price is $96, Equation (4-8) becomes

$$P = \frac{\$4}{\left(1 + \frac{r}{2}\right)} + \frac{\$4}{\left(1 + \frac{r}{2}\right)^2} + \frac{\$4}{\left(1 + \frac{r}{2}\right)^3} + \cdots + \frac{\$104}{\left(1 + \frac{r}{2}\right)^{26}}$$

When we solve for r, we find the yield-to-maturity to be 8.51 percent. When a bond trades at a discount, $96 versus the face value of $100, its yield-to-maturity is greater than the bond's coupon rate. Were the market price $105, so that the bond traded at a premium instead of at a discount, the yield-to-maturity—substituting $105 for $96 in the equation—would be 7.39 percent. Because of the premium, the yield-to-maturity is less than the coupon rate.

IMPLICIT REINVESTMENT RATE ASSUMPTION

As with the calculation of bond price, implicit in a yield-to-maturity calculation is that all coupon payments are reinvested at the YTM. If the average reinvestment rate for interim coupon payments turns out to be lower than the YTM, the bond's effective return will be less than its yield-to-maturity calculated at the time of purchase. Contrarily, if the average rate of interest that can be obtained on reinvesting interim coupon payments is greater than the YTM, the effective return will be higher than the bond's yield-to-maturity.

CURRENT YIELD

Sometimes investors are interested in the **current yield** on a bond. This is simply

$$\text{Current yield} = \frac{\text{Annual coupon in dollars}}{\text{Market price}} \qquad \textbf{(4-9)}$$

For our earlier example of an 8 percent bond with a $96 market price, the current yield is $8/$96 = 8.33 percent, different from the 8.51 percent yield-to-maturity. The difference arises because the discount is not amortized in the calculation of the current yield, whereas it is amortized with yield-to-maturity. In other words, the current yield takes account only of coupon payments and not of the other source of return, namely the amortization of any discount or premium. Only when the market price equals $100 will the current yield and the yield-to-maturity be the same.

HOLDING-PERIOD RETURN

The yield-to-maturity usually will differ from the holding-period yield if the security is sold prior to maturity. The *holding-period return,* or *realized return,* is the rate of discount that equates the present value of coupon payments, plus the present value of terminal value at the end of the holding period, with the price paid for the bond.

For example, suppose a bond with an 8 percent coupon with 12 years to maturity were bought for $105. As we can determine, its yield-to-maturity at the time of purchase is 7.37 percent. After purchase, interest rates for this type of borrower increase. Two years later the bond has a market price of $94, at which time it is sold. The holding-period return is

$$\$105 = \frac{\$4}{\left(1 + \dfrac{r}{2}\right)} + \frac{\$4}{\left(1 + \dfrac{r}{2}\right)^2} + \frac{\$4}{\left(1 + \dfrac{r}{2}\right)^3} + \frac{\$4}{\left(1 + \dfrac{r}{2}\right)^4} + \frac{\$94}{\left(1 + \dfrac{r}{2}\right)^4}$$

Here r is found to be 2.48 percent. While the bond originally had a yield-to-maturity of 7.37 percent, the subsequent rise in interest rates resulted in its being sold at a loss. Although the coupon payments more than offset the loss, the holding-period yield is quite low.

YIELD-TO-MATURITY FOR ZERO-COUPON BONDS

To calculate the yield-to-maturity for a *zero-coupon bond,* we solve for r in the following:

$$P = \frac{\$100}{\left(1 + \dfrac{r}{2}\right)^{2n}} \tag{4-10}$$

where, as before, n is the number of years to maturity and P is the market price of the bond. The semiannual compounding convention is invoked. If a zero-coupon bond had $8\frac{1}{2}$ years to maturity and its market price were $48, we would have

$$\$48 = \frac{\$100}{\left(1 + \dfrac{r}{2}\right)^{17}}$$

When we solve for r, we find it to be 8.82 percent.

YIELD FOR PERPETUITIES

With a *perpetuity,* a fixed-coupon payment is expected at equal intervals forever. The British Consol, a bond with no maturity date, carries the obligation of the British government to pay a fixed coupon perpetually. If the investment required an initial cash outflow at time 0 of A_0 and were expected to pay A^* at the end of each year forever, its yield is the discount rate, r, that equates the present value of all future cash inflows with the present value of the initial cash outflow.

$$A_0 = \frac{A^*}{(1 + r)} + \frac{A^*}{(1 + r)^2} + \cdots + \frac{A^*}{(1 + r)^n} \tag{4-11}$$

In the case of a bond, A_0 is the market price of the bond, and A^* is the fixed annual interest payment. When we multiply both sides of Equation (4-11) by $(1 + r)$, we obtain

$$A_0(1 + r) = A^* + \frac{A^*}{(1 + r)} + \frac{A^*}{(1 + r)^2} + \cdots + \frac{A^*}{(1 + r)^{n-1}} \tag{4-12}$$

Subtracting Equation (4-11) from Equation (4-12), we get

$$A_0(1 + r) - A_0 = A^* - \frac{A^*}{(1 + r)^n} \qquad \text{(4-13)}$$

As n approaches infinity, $A^*/(1 + r)^n$ approaches 0. Thus,

$$A_0 r = A^*$$

and

$$r = \frac{A^*}{A_0} \qquad \text{(4-14)}$$

Here r is the yield on a perpetual investment costing A_0 at time 0 and paying A^* at the end of each year forever. Suppose that for $102 we could buy a perpetual bond that was expected to pay $8 a year forever. The yield of the security would be

$$r = \frac{\$8}{\$102} = 7.84 \text{ percent}$$

Because of the premium, its yield is less than the bond's coupon rate. With a perpetuity, no amortization of the premium or discount occurs, so its yield is the current yield defined earlier.

MONEY MARKET INSTRUMENT RETURNS

Up to now, our calculations of returns have been based on strict application of present-value techniques. These calculations hold for capital market instruments, such as bonds and notes. Sometimes the yield-to-maturity is called the "true" yield, to be distinguished from the yield we are about to calculate.

BANK DISCOUNT RATE

For money market instruments, such as Treasury bills, bankers' acceptances, and commercial paper, yields are calculated in a different way. Before computers and sophisticated calculators, a formula was devised to make the calculations easy to do by hand. This formula employs the **bank discount rate method,** and it continues to this day.

Money market instruments carry no coupon but are sold on a discount basis from a face value of $100. The latter is received at maturity. The yields on these instruments are quoted in terms of the bank discount rate, which is

$$\text{bank discount rate} = \left(\frac{d}{\$100} \times \frac{360}{t} \right) \qquad \text{(4-15)}$$

where d is the dollar amount of the discount and t is the number of days to maturity. For example, if the discount on a Treasury bill were $1.90 and it had 88 days to maturity, its yield on a bank discount rate basis would be

$$\left(\frac{\$1.90}{\$100} \times \frac{360}{88} \right) = 7.77\%$$

Several things are apparent from the formula. First, it is based on the face value of the instrument as opposed to the money actually invested, which in our example is $98.10. Second, it assumes a 360-day year as opposed to a 365-day year.

If the instrument has a maturity of less than six months, one can convert the bank discount rate to what is known as an **equivalent bond yield,** using the following formula:

$$\text{equivalent bond yield} = \frac{365 \times \text{BDY}}{360 - (t \times \text{BDY})} \qquad \textbf{(4-16)}$$

where BDY is the bank discount rate yield in decimal form. For our example, the equivalent bond yield is

$$\frac{365 \times 0.0777}{360 - (88 \times 0.0777)} = 8.03\%$$

The equivalent bond yield is higher than the bank discount rate owing to the discount effect and the 365-day-year effect.

Equation (4-16) does not take account of compound interest—that is, interest being earned on interest. If the compounding interval in our example were every 88 days, the effective return would be

$$\left(1 + \frac{\$1.90}{\$98.10} \right)^{\frac{365}{88}} - 1 = 8.28\%$$

IMPLICATIONS

The discount, 365-day year, and compounding effects cause the bank discount rate to be lower than the "true" yield using present-value techniques. Whereas the bank discount rate in our example was found to be 7.77 percent, the "true" yield was 8.28 percent. The equivalent bond yield goes only part of the way to redressing the difference. The import of this discussion is that you cannot compare money market yields with capital market yields unless you adjust the former. Otherwise you are comparing apples with oranges.

A Treasury bond with less than six months to maturity trades at a discount from the $100 to be paid at maturity. A Treasury bill of identical maturity also trades at a discount from $100. Economically, the two instruments are the same, yet the reported yield for the Treasury bill will be lower than that for the Treasury bond. The biases inherent in calculation of yield for a money market instrument quoted on a bank discount rate basis must be recognized and suitable adjustments made.

❖ SUMMARY

The price of a bond is the present value of the stream of coupon payments, together with the present value of the face value of $100 at maturity. The coupon stream of equal payments is an annuity. When interest is compounded more than once a year, the present value of a future payment is less, the limit being that occurring with continuous compounding.

Virtually all coupon bonds pay interest semiannually, and the formula for solving for price and yield-to-maturity was presented. When the yield-to-maturity is less than the coupon rate, a bond sells at a premium above its face value. When more, the bond sells at a discount. In situations when there is less than six months to the next coupon payment, interest is accrued, which affects the pricing formula. Zero-coupon bonds pay no coupons, the yield being embraced in the discount in market price from the payment of $100 at maturity.

The yield-to-maturity is the discount rate that equates the present value of coupon payments and principal payment with the bond's market price. This measure usually differs from the current yield, which is the annual coupon divided by market price, and from the holding-period return realized on the sale of a bond prior to maturity. The yield of a perpetuity is its current yield.

Money market instruments are quoted on a different basis from that used for capital market instruments, with the result that yields are biased and low in relation to the "true" yield calculated for bonds. The bank discount rate method fails to take account of discount, compounding, and 365-day-year effects. As a result, money market rates cannot be compared directly with capital market rates unless the former are adjusted for these biases.

❖ **Selected References**

Cissell, Robert, Helen Cissell, and David C. Flaspohler, *Mathematics of Finance,* 10th ed. Boston: Houghton Mifflin, 1996.

Fabozzi, Frank J., *Bond Markets, Analysis and Strategies,* 4th ed, chapters 2–3. Upper Saddle River, NJ: Prentice Hall, 2000.

Rusbarsky, Mark, and David B. Vicknair, "Accounting for Bonds with Accrued Interest in Conformity with Brokers' Valuation Formulas," *Issues in Accounting Education* 14 (May 1999): 233–53.

Stigum, Marcia, and Franklin L. Robinson, *Money Market & Bond Calculations.* Chicago: Irwin Professional Publishing, 1996.

Taggart, Robert A., "Using Excel Spreadsheet Functions to Understand and Analyze Fixed Income Security Prices," *Journal of Financial Education* 25 (Spring 1999): 46–63.

Van Horne, James C., *Financial Management and Policy,* 11th ed., chapter 2. Upper Saddle River, NJ: Prentice Hall, 1998.

INFLATION AND RETURNS

The consideration of interest rates in the financial market must be expanded to include the effect of inflation on returns. Because interest and principal payments are expressed in terms of money and because the monetary standard changes over time, the **real rate of return** realized by the holder of a financial asset can differ from its money, or **nominal return.** From the previous chapter, we know that the return from a security is the rate of discount, which equates the present value of the stream of interest and principal payments—including the selling price —with the purchase price. For the nominal return, the cash flows received are in current dollars at the time of receipt. They have not been adjusted for inflation.

With inflation, these dollars will be worth less in purchasing power than were the dollars put out at the time the security was bought. As a result, the *realized rate of return* on the security will be less than the nominal return. To illustrate, suppose the expected nominal return on a security to be held 5 years is 7 percent and that expectations are realized. If the rate of inflation over the period turns out to be 4 percent per annum, the real rate of return is less than the nominal return. In this case, the *realized* real return is approximately 3 percent. The *realized* real return, then, is simply the return realized when dollars received in the future are placed on the same purchasing-power basis as the dollars put out to buy the security.

At the outset, we need to distinguish between the real rate of interest in theory and realized real rates of return. The former is the rate that brings into equilibrium *ex ante* savings and investments, abstracting from inflation. Expressed differently, it is the equilibrium rate at which real wealth produces real income. In this sense, the real rate of interest will always be positive, though it varies with changes in such things as the underlying ability of a nation to produce goods and services and in the real savings rate. In contrast, the realized real rate of return is, as we have defined it, the nominal rate less the inflation rate that actually occurs. If inflation turns out to be much higher than expected, the realized real return can be negative.

THE HISTORICAL RECORD IN BRIEF

The relationship between inflation and interest rates has varied over time. Prior to World War II, the relationship, if any, was obscure. In fact, it was difficult to suggest that inflation expectations had any systematic effect on interest rates from the 1860s to World War II.[1] Since World War II, a relationship of sorts has emerged, in which interest rates are a positive function of inflation. Figure 5-1 depicts long- and short-term interest rates, together with the annual rate of inflation in the post–World War II period. Several things are apparent from the figure. First, there was an upward trend in all three series until 1980, after which inflation, followed by interest rates, declined until 1987.

After this, inflation fluctuated with no particular underlying trend until 1997–1999, when it moved somewhat below 2 percent on average. To a limited extent, the long-term bond rate mirrored this pattern of lower post-late-1980s inflation. In contrast, the Treasury bill rate declined dramatically in the early 1990s rose in the mid-1990s, and then declined some. Most attribute this behavior to monetary policy actions directed at forcing short-term rates down, then up, and then down slightly at the end of the time frame portrayed in the figure.

Figure 5-2 displays the real rate of interest on long-term U.S. Treasury bonds from 1975 to 1999. This is simply the longest-term Treasury bond (30 years) minus the inflation rate as depicted by the consumer price index. In the mid-1970s, the real return tended to be reasonably stable, averaging around 1 percent. As inflation accelerated to around 13 percent in 1979 and 1980, nominal interest rates rose but not as rapidly as inflation. As a result, the real rate turned negative. The nominal interest rate continued to rise in 1981, eventually reaching 15 percent. As inflation abated, this combination caused the real rate to rise in that year. In 1982, inflation fell dramatically, to around 4 percent by early 1983. Nominal interest rates declined but by a much lesser magnitude. As a result, the real rate of interest continued to increase through the mid-1980s. For the remainder of the 1980s, inflation fluctuated around 4 percent, but nominal interest rates declined so as to bring the real rate to about 4 percent. In the 1990s, inflation came down to 3 percent and then to roughly 2 percent. The nominal yield declined on average, and again the real rate averaged about 4 percent. Recognize that reported Consumer Price Index (CPI) inflation rates fluctuate from quarter to quarter. Also, nominal rates are based on expected future inflation, not necessarily the most recent inflation. As a result, fluctuations occur in the line shown in Figure 5-2. Still, generalizations are possible.

In a subsequent section, we summarize the results of a number of empirical studies that bear on the question of the response of interest rates and returns to unexpected changes in inflation. Our purpose here is to present general background information so that we have some historical perspective as we explore certain concepts regarding inflation and returns. We now turn to these concepts.

THE NATURE OF INFLATION PREMIUMS

The difference between the nominal return and the expected real return is known as an **inflation premium.** While the actual inflation premium realized for a holding period is straightforward, the expected inflation premium is more complicated. In a loanable

---

[1] See Lawrence H. Summers, "The Non-Adjustment of Nominal Interest Rates: A Study of the Fisher Effect," *A Symposium in Honor of Arthur Okun,* ed. James Tobin (Washington, DC: Brookings Institution, 1983).

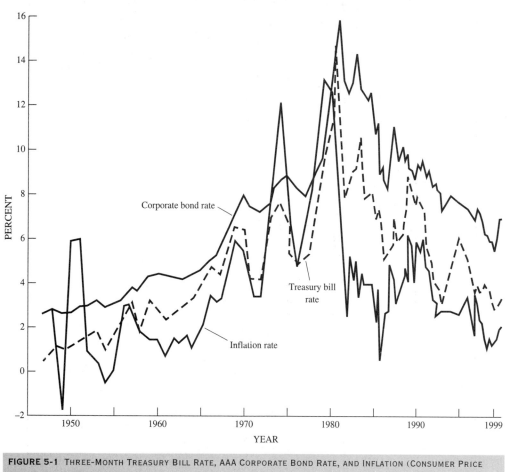

FIGURE 5-1 THREE-MONTH TREASURY BILL RATE, AAA CORPORATE BOND RATE, AND INFLATION (CONSUMER PRICE INDEX), 1947–1999

funds framework, both the supply and the demand functions for funds are affected by inflation expectations. The supply of and demand for loanable funds can be expressed as

$$S = S(r, \alpha, X)$$
$$D = D(r, \alpha, Y) \tag{5-1}$$
$$S = D$$

where S and D are the supply and demand for funds, r is the nominal rate of interest, α is the expected rate of inflation, X is the vector of other factors influencing supply, and Y is the vector of other factors affecting demand. Other factors include such things as the expected returns on other assets, real economic activity variables, and wealth.

When supply and demand are equated in the market equilibrium process described in chapter 3, both the nominal interest rate, r, and the supply of loanable funds are determined. The difference here is that we assume a given level of expected price inflation, designated by α, which was not an explicit variable in chapter 3. Given this level, the market equilibrium is shown in the upper panel of Figure 5-3. The intersection of

FIGURE 5-2 LONG-TERM TREASURY BOND YIELD MINUS INFLATION RATE (CPI) 1975–1999

the curves for supply (lenders) and demand (borrowers) determines the nominal interest rate, r, and the quantity of loanable funds outstanding, Q.

Suppose the rate of inflation unexpectedly increases to a new and higher level, denoted by α'. As shown in the bottom panel of Figure 5-3, the supply curve shifts upward and to the left. Because of the increase in expected inflation, lenders, or suppliers of loanable funds, demand a higher nominal rate of interest. On the other hand, borrowers are willing to pay a higher nominal return, and the demand curve shifts upward and to the right.[2] The intersection of the new supply and demand curves determines the new equilibrium rate of interest, r', and the new quantity of loans outstanding, Q'.

UNANTICIPATED INFLATION

The key then is an **unanticipated change** in expected inflation, which leads to a new equilibrium. Expected inflation already is embraced in market-determined nominal rates of interest. If the present rate of inflation is 3 percent and it shifts upward to 5 percent in a way unanticipated by market participants, the result is a 2 percent unanticipated increase in inflation. Only with an unanticipated change in expected inflation would nominal interest rates change.

In the preceding example, the unanticipated increase in expected inflation, $\alpha' - \alpha$, leads to an increase in the nominal interest rate, $r' - r$, and to a decrease in the quantity of loans outstanding, $Q - Q'$. While an unanticipated increase in inflation would be

---

[2] Throughout, we abstract from the issue of default by assuming all borrowers have the same degree of default risk.

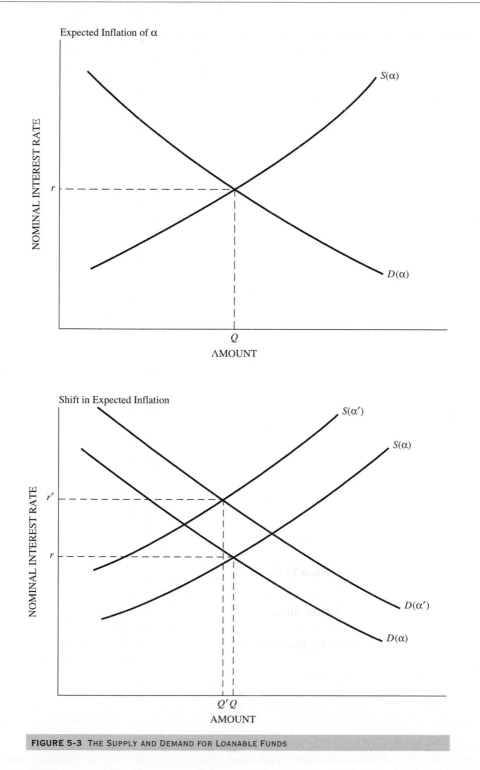

FIGURE 5-3 THE SUPPLY AND DEMAND FOR LOANABLE FUNDS

expected to increase nominal interest rates by some amount, whether the quantity of loans outstanding increases or decreases depends on the reaction of the supply and demand curves in the figure to unexpected changes in inflation, holding constant other factors. Moreover, the shift in nominal interest rate, $r' - r$, may or may not equal the change in inflation, $\alpha' - \alpha$. Let us focus now on the response of interest rates to unexpected changes in inflation, bearing in mind the overall equilibrium process of supply and demand for loanable funds in the face of inflation.

THE FISHER EFFECT

Many years ago, Irving Fisher expressed the nominal rate of interest on a bond as the sum of the real rate of interest and the rate of price change expected to occur over the life of the instrument. More formally, the nominal rate, r, is

$$1 + r = (1 + R)(1 + \alpha)$$
$$r = R + \alpha + R\alpha \tag{5-2}$$

where R is the real rate and α is the rate of inflation per annum expected to prevail over the life of the instrument.[3] Where inflation is only moderate, the cross-product term, $R\alpha$, is small and is usually ignored in the formulation. As a result, we have

$$r = R + \alpha \tag{5-3}$$

Traditionally, this formulation is known as the **Fisher effect.** It states merely that the nominal rate of interest embodies in it an inflation premium sufficient to compensate lenders for the expected loss of purchasing power associated with the receipt of future dollars. Put another way, lenders require a nominal rate of interest sufficiently high for them to earn an expected real rate of interest. In turn, the real rate required is a function of productive returns on real assets in our society plus a risk premium commensurate with risk of the borrower. The Fisher effect implies that if expected inflation rises by 1 percent, the nominal interest rate will rise by 1 percent as well. In other words, the effect is one-to-one. If r and α are the nominal rate and the expected inflation rate now, and r' and α' are those that prevail after a change in expected inflation, the Fisher effect suggests that

$$r' - r = \alpha' - \alpha \tag{5-4}$$

According to this expression, the nominal rate of interest fully adjusts to changes in expected inflation; that is, the relationship of changes in nominal interest rates to changes in expected inflation is one-to-one. Expressed differently, the Fisher hypothesis implies that the real rate of interest and inflation are largely independent of one another. In fairness to Fisher, he did not state that there was likely to be a strong, short-run relationship between expected inflation and nominal interest rates. However, Equation (5-4) has come to be called the Fisher effect even though the author viewed the equation as a long-run equilibrium.

For a given period of time, the realized, or *ex post,* real return is simply the actual nominal rate of interest less the inflation rate that prevailed over the interval examined. However, this *ex post* return is not what is reflected in the Fisher effect. Rather, it is the

[3] Irving Fisher, "Appreciation and Interest," *Publications of the American Economic Association* 11 (August 1896): 1–100.

expected, or *ex ante,* inflation that is subtracted from the nominal rate of interest to give the expected, or *ex ante,* real rate of interest. Fisher implied that this real rate is relatively constant over time because it is the marginal rate of return on the capital stock of a nation.

NOMINAL INTEREST RATES AND INFLATION, THEORETICALLY

The questions of whether the relationship between changes in nominal interest rates and changes in expected inflation is one-to-one, and whether the real rate of interest is constant over time, are subjects of considerable controversy, both theoretically and empirically. On a theoretical level, there are reasons that the nominal interest rate may not conform exactly to changes in inflation. Arguments exist to justify the relationship's being less than one-to-one, as well as more. Robert Mundell, followed by James Tobin, presents a theory in which changes in the expected rate of inflation raise or lower the nominal rate of interest by less than the expected inflation rate change.[4] In the case of an increase in expected inflation, this change is said to be reflected in both an increase in the nominal rate of interest and a decrease in the real rate. (The change in the differential between the two rates equals the increase in the expected rate of inflation.)

The crux of Mundell's contention that the real rate of interest declines under such circumstances is that inflation reduces real money balances. In other words, money assets depreciate in real terms. As a result, real wealth declines, and this stimulates increased savings. In turn, this brings downward pressure on the real rate of interest. Finally, the decline in the real rate of interest stimulates investment and an acceleration in growth, according to this theory.

In the case of a decrease in expected inflation, the opposite occurs. Here the real rate rises and, as a result, the nominal rate falls by less than the change in inflation. Accompanying this is a deceleration of growth. Mundell concludes that fluctuations in the rate of inflation affect real economic activity and not just nominal rates of interest. Thus, the Mundell-Tobin hypothesis is that real rates of interest fluctuate over time in part because of the portfolio adjustments that accompany a change in expected inflation. Because the change in real rate is opposite to that of the change in expected inflation, the response of the nominal rate of interest to the expected inflation change is less than one-to-one. In other words, a negative correlation would prevail between expected inflation and the real rate of interest.

TAX EFFECTS

The principal argument for the response's being more than one-to-one has to do with taxes. This argument has been advanced by Michael R. Darby and by Martin Feldstein.[5]

---

[4]   Robert Mundell, "Inflation and Real Interest," *Journal of Political Economy* 71 (June 1963): 280–83; and James Tobin, "Money and Economic Growth," *Econometrica* 33 (October 1965): 671–84.

[5]   Michael R. Darby, "The Financial and Tax Effects of Monetary Policy on Interest Rates," *Economic Inquiry* 13 (June 1975): 266 76; and Martin Feldstein, "Inflation, Income Taxes and the Rate of Inflation: A Theoretical Analysis," *American Economic Review* 66 (December 1976): 809–20.

With taxes, a rise in expected inflation results in a rise in nominal rates of a greater percentage than the rise in inflation. The after-tax real return to a lender whose loan is specified in nominal dollars is

$$R^* = r - rt - \alpha \tag{5-5}$$

where

r = nominal rate of interest
t = marginal tax rate
α = expected rate of inflation

all of which are expressed in terms of the length of the loan.

Rearranging Equation (5-5), the nominal rate of interest is

$$r = \frac{(R^* + \alpha)}{(1 - t)} \tag{5-6}$$

Suppose now that expected inflation increases from α to α' but that the marginal tax rate remains unchanged, as does the after-tax real return that is required. Equation (5-6) shows that the nominal rate must rise by

$$\Delta r = \frac{\alpha' - \alpha}{(1 - t)} \tag{5-7}$$

If the tax rate were positive, the nominal rate would increase by more than the increase in anticipated inflation. This rise is needed simply to pay the additional taxes. The higher the tax rate is, the greater the nominal rate increase that is required.

To illustrate, suppose the expected rate of inflation is presently 3 percent and that it rises to 5 percent. If the lenders' effective tax rate is 40 percent, the nominal interest rate must rise by

$$\Delta r = \frac{5\% - 3\%}{(1 - 0.4)} = 3\tfrac{1}{3}\%$$

in order for lenders to be as well off in real terms on new loans as they were before the change in expected inflation. The implication is that lenders require compensation not only for inflation but for the additional tax burden, as well. This implication implies a positive correlation between expected inflation and the before-tax real rate of interest.

EXPECTED INFLATION AND INFLATION RISK PREMIUMS

A number of scholars break down the overall inflation premium into two components: one for expected inflation and the other for the risk associated with changing inflation. Thus,

$$r = R + Exp. + IP \tag{5-8}$$

where, as before, r is the nominal interest rate, R is the real rate, but *Exp.* is expected future inflation over the life of the instrument and *IP* is the inflation risk premium. Instead of two components in the nominal yield formulation as in Equation (5-3), there now are three. *IP* might be expected to increase with maturity. Not only is it more difficult to forecast inflation for the more distant future, but the consequences of an incorrect forecast are greater.[6] The latter is merely to say that the mathematical price-yield relationship depicted in chapter 4 is greater when the maturity of the instrument is longer.

EMPIRICAL EVIDENCE ON NOMINAL INTEREST RATES

Theoretically, we see—depending on the strength of the argument—that inflation may affect nominal interest rates in different ways. The Fisher effect postulates a one-to-one change in the nominal rate of interest to a change in expected inflation. Other arguments suggest that it is less than one-to-one (Mundell-Tobin) or more than one-to-one (Darby-Feldstein). The actual effect is an empirical question, and one to which a great deal of inquiry has been directed.

PROBLEMS IN EMPIRICAL TESTING

Several problems arise in empirical testing for the effect of inflation on nominal rates of interest. For one thing, both the real rate and expected inflation are not directly observable. Moreover, the real rate is not necessarily constant over time or independent of inflation.

Several proxies have been derived for the real rate of interest. In the capital market equilibrium approach, one attempts to infer rates of expected inflation from differences in the expected returns on two different types of assets: an asset whose return tends to be expressed in real terms and an asset whose return tends to be expressed in nominal terms. Fisher studied the difference in yield on bonds payable in gold and bonds payable in money. Milton Friedman and Anna J. Schwartz, as well as a number of others, have used the difference in return on stocks and bonds.[7] The idea is that stocks and bonds are close substitutes and that equilibrium in the capital markets is based on expected real returns and not nominal returns.

A second approach to estimating the real rate of return is a loanable funds model. In this approach, the real rate is broken down into two components: (1) *the equilibrium real rate,* which equates *ex ante* savings and investment; and (2) the *deviation of the current real rate from the equilibrium rate.* The equilibrium real bond rate is said to be a function of such variables as the change in real output, the federal deficit, real income, tax rates, real wealth, and risk. The deviation of the current real bond rate from the equilibrium real rate is said to depend on the variables that shift the demand for bonds, such as changes in the monetary aggregates. In yet another approach to estimating the real bond rate, a Keynesian liquidity-preference model may be employed. Here, the principal determinants of the real bond rate are the real stock of liquidity and the level of real income.

All these approaches represent attempts to estimate the real expected rate of return on bonds. As the latter is not directly observable, these indirect estimates vary from study to study depending on the model used and the sample period studied. The

---

[6] See Pu Shen, "How Important Is the Inflation Risk Premium?" *Economic Review of the Federal Reserve Bank of Kansas City* 84 (4th Quarter, 1998): 35–47.

[7] Milton Friedman and Anna J. Schwartz, *A Monetary History of the United States, 1867–1960* (New York: National Bureau of Economic Research, 1963): pp. 583–84.

concern, of course, is with the expected future real rate of interest, not the present or past real rates. Consequently, past levels of, and changes in, various series of data may not be a good proxy for the expected future real rate of interest.

Similarly, estimates of the inflation premium often are based on past levels of, and changes in, some price index. Here, too, the past may not be a good proxy for the future, particularly when inflation is rapidly changing as it was in the 1970s and 1980s. It is not surprising then that when past inflation rates are used, the distributed lag estimates of future inflation vary widely.

Another approach is to use direct inflation estimates by government and business economists as well as by consumers. Short-term inflation forecasts are made by the staff of the Board of Governors of the Federal Reserve System, by the Survey Research Center of the University of Michigan in their survey of consumers, by the Livingston Survey of business economists, and by the Data Resources, Inc. economic consulting firm.[8] However, direct inflation estimates also have a number of sampling and other problems.

TESTING FOR THE EFFECT OF INFLATION

Despite these problems, numerous direct and indirect tests have been made of the effect of inflation on interest rates. There are too many for all to be discussed, but I will give a representative overview.

Little evidence is cited of a relationship between inflation and interest rates prior to the 1960s. Figure 5-4 depicts bond rates and inflation from 1870 to 1999. As shown, little relationship can be seen up to the 1960s; this crude insight is supported by sophisticated statistical studies of the stochastic process of inflation and interest rates.[9] Fisher himself regressed the nominal rate of interest on a geometrically declining weighted average of past inflation rates and found only a weak relationship for the earlier part of the 1900s. In contrast, a strong, positive relationship between inflation and nominal interest rates was evident in the 1960s and 1970s. It is fair to say that from the 1960s on, bond yields have been correlated with inflation, such that permanent movements in actual inflation are associated with underlying movements in bond yields.[10] Moreover, the response of bond yields to changes in inflation has been found to be larger for taxable bonds, like Treasuries, than for tax-exempt, municipal bonds.[11] This is consistent with the Darby-Feldstein argument that the presence of taxes requires a more pronounced change in nominal rates to a change in inflation in order to offset the increased tax bite.

Robert B. Barsky argues that the lack of relationship in the earlier period may be due to a change in the forecastability of inflation around 1960.[12] Before that time, and particularly before 1930, inflation was largely unpredictable, based on past inflation. In other words, it was essentially random. From 1930 to 1959, Barsky finds a modest de-

---

[8] See Robert Darin and Robert L. Hetzel, "An Empirical Measure of the Real Rate of Interest," *Economic Quarterly of the Federal Reserve Bank of Richmond* 81 (Winter 1995): 17–47, for an analysis of their accuracy.

[9] See Lawrence H. Summers, "The Non-Adjustment of Nominal Interest Rates"; and Robert B. Barsky, "The Fisher Hypothesis and the Forecastability and Persistence of Inflation," *Journal of Monetary Economics* 19 (March 1987): 3–24.

[10] Yash P. Mehra, "The Bond Rate and Actual Future Inflation," *Economic Quarterly of the Federal Reserve Bank of Richmond* 84 (Spring 1998): 27–47.

[11] William J. Crowder and Mark E. Wohar, "Are Tax Effects Important in the Long-Run Fisher Relationship? Evidence from the Municipal Bond Market," *Journal of Finance* 54 (February 1999): 307–17.

[12] Ibid.

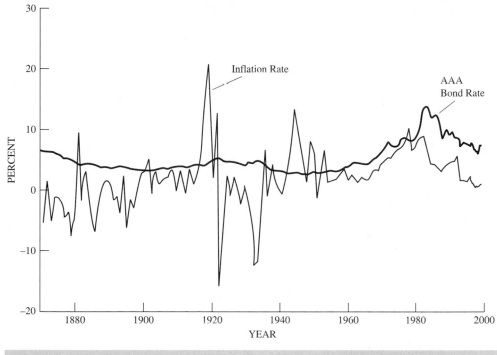

FIGURE 5-4 INFLATION AND INTEREST RATES, 1870–1999

gree of forecastability, followed by the 1960–1979 period when inflation was highly predictable. To the extent that changes in inflation are unpredictable, one would expect little or no relationship between inflation and nominal rates of interest. Barsky contends
that the observed absence of a Fisher effect prior to 1930, and its strong emergence in
1960 to 1979, can be attributed to changes in inflation's predictability as opposed to any
change in the structural relationship between nominal rates and expected inflation. This
and other empirical studies suggest that the relationship between nominal interest rates
and expected inflation is strongest during periods when trends in inflation and interest
rates are detectable, not during trendless periods of time.

As to an inflation risk premium being embraced in nominal interest rates, studies
of British bonds find evidence of a sizable premium—upwards of 1 percent on average.[13] Moreover, the premium has been found to widen with maturity and to vary positively with the differential between nominal and real yields. This differential is likely to
be a proxy for inflation uncertainty.

A SUMMING UP

Although empirical results are mixed, most studies point to a positive relationship
between unanticipated changes in inflation and changes in nominal rates of interest

---

[13] Pu Shen, "How Important Is the Inflation Risk Premium?" *Economic Review of the Federal Reserve
Bank of Kansas City* 83 (4th Quarter, 1998): 35–47; and Martin D. D. Evans, "Real Rates, Expected Inflation, and Inflation Risk Premia," *Journal of Finance* 53 (February 1998): 187–218.

during the last 35 years. Before 1960, little relationship existed. The responsiveness of interest rates to unanticipated changes in inflation is not consistent over time, nor does the real rate of interest appear to be constant. A number of studies suggest a negative correlation of the real rate with expected inflation. A host of factors in addition to inflation affect interest rates. Our ability to explain, let alone predict, nominal rates of interest in terms of inflation leaves a good deal to be desired.

NOMINAL CONTRACTING EFFECTS

With an unanticipated change in inflation, contracts specified in nominal terms are affected. Debtor-creditor claims are one example of redistribution consequences when unexpected inflation occurs. Another example is the tax contract between corporations and the government, on which depreciation tax shields on capital assets are historically based. A third example is the increased tax burden arising from inflation-induced accounting profits on inventories. We consider these as well as other issues in this section.

DEBTOR-CREDITOR CLAIMS

Whenever an unanticipated change in inflation occurs, an existing loan is not repaid in keeping with the real return expected at the time the loan was made. If an unanticipated increase in inflation occurs, the borrower tends to gain. This gain occurs in an opportunity sense in that the loan is repaid with "cheaper" money than originally anticipated. To illustrate, suppose the nominal rate of interest on a 10-year loan is 8 percent, of which 4 percent is the expected real rate and 4 percent represents a premium for expected inflation. However, suppose that over the 10 years, inflation of 6 percent per annum actually occurs. As a result, the borrower's real interest cost is 2 percent instead of 4 percent. The lender loses because the real return is less than anticipated at the time the loan contract was made. With an unanticipated decrease in inflation, the borrower loses, in that the loan has to be repaid in more "expensive" dollars than originally anticipated, whereas the lender gains.

    Unanticipated increases in inflation result in a transfer of real wealth from net creditors to net debtors, whereas the opposite occurs with unanticipated decreases. A *net creditor* is defined as an economic unit whose financial assets exceed its financial liabilities, whereas the opposite holds for the *net debtor*. Whether a given economic unit gains or loses with respect to inflation depends on whether an unanticipated increase or decrease in inflation occurs and whether the economic unit is a net debtor or a net creditor. In the aggregate, nonfinancial corporations have been consistent net debtors. However, individual companies can be net debtors or net creditors, and this can vary over time.

DEPRECIATION

Other nominal contracting effects may be reflected in depreciation and inventories. Depreciation charges, based on the historical costs of assets acquired in the past, do not change with inflation. If inflation results in larger operating cash flows, an increasing portion of these cash flows is subject to taxation. Because the corporation is able to deduct only historical cost depreciation and not replacement cost depreciation, its real rate of return is lower, creating a depressing influence on share value, all other things the same.

INVENTORIES

Under certain circumstances, the same phenomenon applies to inventories. Inventories can be deducted as a corporate expense only when sold or put into a product that is sold. Moreover, they are deductible only at original cost—not at replacement cost. If a company uses the first-in, first-out (FIFO) method of inventory accounting, recorded inventory costs will be lower than replacement costs in an inflationary world. The reason is that the inventory first in was acquired in the past at a lower cost than presently prevails. When this cost is used in the cost of goods sold, accounting profits are overstated, and this overstatement results in higher taxes than would be paid if replacement costs were used. In other words, the real return on capital is lower, owing to the increased tax bite on operating cash flows. The problem can be reduced substantially if the company uses the last-in, first-out (LIFO) method of inventory accounting. With this method, the inventory last in is used in the cost of goods sold, and the cost figure here approximates the replacement cost of the inventory sold. In general, the more capital intensive the firm, the greater the influence of depreciation and inventory (FIFO) considerations, and the greater the difference is between accounting and real profits in an inflationary environment.

CORPORATE VALUE

Another nominal contracting issue has to do with a firm's pension plan and its explicit as well as implicit obligation to existing and future employees. As this aspect is very involved, we do not describe it. The effect of nominal contracts is particularly important when it comes to the valuation of a corporation. Unanticipated changes in inflation should be reflected in common stock prices. Individual stocks may be affected differently, depending on the nature of the nominal contracting.

EMPIRICAL TESTING

Nominal contracting effects have been examined in a number of studies. With respect to debtor-creditor claims, most empirical work supports the notion of a wealth transfer from net creditors to net debtors in times of unanticipated inflation. Other studies have focused on the broad impact of nominal contracting effects on corporate stock values. Some scholars find a relationship between stock returns and unexpected inflation due to debtor-creditor, depreciation tax-shield, and inventory tax-shield effects. Others find little evidence of the redistribution of corporate wealth accompanying an unanticipated change in inflation.

The results of empirical tests of the nominal contracting hypothesis are somewhat mixed. Most of the tests have involved only corporations, with a focus on stock returns as a proxy for wealth. Often, sorting out the effect of nominal contracts from the many other factors that affect these returns is difficult. Still, a number of recent studies support the notion that nominal contracting causes wealth transfers when unanticipated changes in inflation occur.

INFLATION-INDEXED BONDS

Certain countries have issued inflation-linked bonds. Among these are Australia, Canada, Israel, Sweden, the United Kingdom, and most recently, the United States.

THE MECHANICS

The interest payment on a bond typically is linked to a consumer price or retail price index. The bond usually has a stated coupon rate that is low relative to existing nominal interest rates, say 4 percent. Effectively, this coupon rate approximates the real rate of return on the investment. The adjustment for inflation usually occurs in the face value of the bond. By adjusting upward the face value for inflation and paying 4 percent against this ever-increasing value, the investor is largely protected against inflation. However, there usually is a lag between the inflation that occurs and the adjustment in the face value of the instrument and, hence, in the interest payment. For the United Kingdom, the lag is approximately eight months. This means that the investor is not compensated for inflation during the eight months prior to a coupon payment.

The final principal payment is the face value of the instrument, which has been adjusted upward for inflation over the life of the instrument albeit with a lag. The greater the inflation is, the greater the final principal payment is and vice versa. As is apparent, the uncertainty introduced with these procedures revolves around the lag.[14]

BEHAVIOR OF TIPS

In early 1997, the U.S. Treasury introduced Treasury Inflation Protected Securities, known as **TIPS.** Issues of 5-, 10- and 30-year maturities have been offered, and the Treasury has had a program of quarterly issuance. A Dutch-auction procedure is used. Bids are in terms of real yield, and the coupon is set in increments of 1/8 percent on the basis of the clearing yield. To date, coupons have ranged from 3⅜ to 3⅞ percent. The **tax treatment** of TIPS is disadvantageous to taxable investors. The investor is taxed annually on the coupon payment, received in cash, plus the accretion in principal using the constant interest method described in chapter 15. The latter is "phantom" income, which you receive only at maturity or when you sell the security. As a result, TIPS appeal primarily to tax-free institutional investors.

Because of limited supply and segmented demand, TIPS do not enjoy nearly the liquidity that regular Treasury securities command, particularly newly issued securities known as "on-the-run" securities. The daily trading volume is substantially less, and the bid/ask spreads are wider.[15] The correlation of nominal Treasury yields and TIPS yields is variable. Historical yields are shown for 5-, 10-, and 30-year TIPS in the upper panel of Figure 5-5, and for 10-year TIPS and United Kingdom inflation-indexed bonds in the

---

[14]　For studies bearing on British and Israeli inflation-linked bonds, respectively, see Roger H. Brown and Stephen M. Schaefer, "Ten Years of the Real Term Structure: 1984–1994," *Journal of Fixed Income* 5 (March 1996): 6–22; and Shmuel Kandel, Aharon R. Ofer, and Oded Sarig, "Real Interest Rates and Inflation: An Ex-Ante Empirical Analysis," *Journal of Finance* 51 (March 1996): 205–25.

[15]　Robin Grieves and Michael W. Sunner, "Fungible STRIPS for the U.S. Treasury's Inflation-Indexed Securities," *Journal of Fixed Income* 9 (June 1999): 55–62.

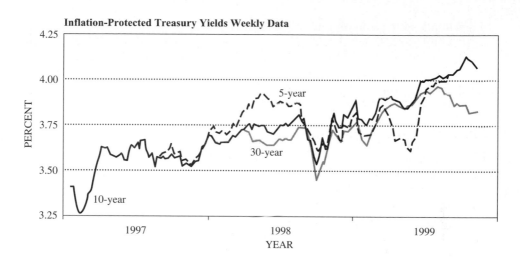

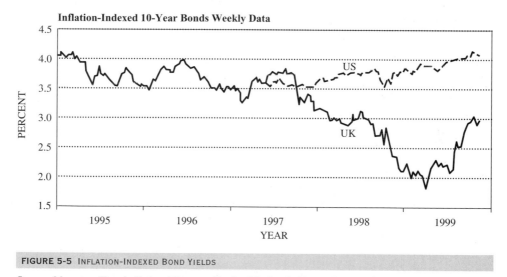

FIGURE 5-5 INFLATION-INDEXED BOND YIELDS

Source: Monetary Trends. Federal Reserve Bank of St. Louis (December 1999).

lower panel. As seen, since 1997 the inflation-indexed yield has been higher in the United States than in the United Kingdom. One reason is the lesser quantity and liquidity of the U.S. bonds. For portfolios of bonds, TIPS provide substantial diversification benefits in lowering volatility in relation to real return. In addition to the Treasury, various agencies of the U.S. government as well as private financial institutions have issued inflation-linked securities.

IMPLIED INFLATION EXPECTATIONS

One can compare the yield for a TIPS bond with that of a regular Treasury security with approximately the same maturity. The differential is known as the **TIPS spread.** This spread is a function of the inflation expectations, as well as of the inflation risk premium. [See Equation (5-8), explained earlier]. For example, on September 24, 1999, the 30-year

TIPS bond, with a coupon rate of 3⅞% and a maturity of April, 2029, yielded 4.06 percent. At the same time the 5¼% Treasury bond of February, 2029, yielded 6.07 percent, giving a TIPS spread of 2.01 percent. This spread varies over time. The spread averaged 1.50 percent in the last half of 1998, with a pronounced increase in spread in 1999. Most attribute this widening to the expectation of rising inflation as opposed to any significant increase in the inflation risk premium.

It is possible, of course, that the inflation risk premium increased some. However, survey data of financial market economists collaborated the upward shift in inflation expectations. In a study of U.K. government-indexed bonds versus regular bonds, Pu Shen found that inflation expectations in 1996–1997 averaged 3.1 percent and that inflation risk premiums for 10-, 15-, 20-, and 25-year bonds were 0.74 percent, 0.89 percent, 0.98 percent, and 1.04 percent, respectively.[16] The U.K. indexed-bond market is a more established and liquid market than the U.S. indexed-bond market, so perhaps more credence can be placed on inflation risk premiums increasing with maturity.

OTHER ASPECTS

Inflation-linked bonds are more actively discussed when inflation is volatile and rising. Their issuance by a government may have signaling implications to financial markets. It may convey an intent of the government to quell inflation. However, this need not be the case. In the 1990s, the inflation that prevailed in advanced industrial countries was neither high nor volatile. As a result, there was not a push to provide such products. In other words, there was not a substantial degree of market incompleteness. Somewhat surprisingly, the United States announced inflation-indexed bonds in 1996 when U.S. interest rates were relatively low and stable.

Rather than being linked to some government inflation index, a bond can be linked to a commodity price index. A limited number of bonds of this sort have been issued. The problem here is that commodity prices are not always a good proxy for overall inflation. To the extent that an investor is concerned with inflation in the overall economy, a commodity-price link may not afford suitable protection against the loss of purchasing power.

❖ SUMMARY

Changing inflation has an important and pervasive influence on interest rates. With inflation, the expected real return on a security is less than its nominal return, and the difference is known as an inflation premium. The Fisher effect suggests that the nominal return on a bond is the sum of the real rate of interest plus the rate of inflation expected over the life of the instrument. Implied is that the real rate is constant over time and that changes in nominal interest rates are highly responsive to unanticipated inflation.

Thus, the Fisher effect implies that the nominal rate of interest changes exactly, or on a one-to-one basis, with changes in expected inflation. In theory, a real money effect argues for a less than one-to-one relationship, whereas a tax effect argues for a more than one-to-one relationship. It is important to distinguish between anticipated inflation, which is embodied in existing interest rates, and unanticipated inflation, which is not. The overall spread between the nominal rate and the real rate, which we have called

---

[16]Shen, *Ibid.*

the inflation premium heretofore, is comprised of expected future inflation and an inflation risk premium that reflects the uncertainty associated with the inflation forecast. Certain empirical evidence was reviewed with regard to the effect of inflation on interest rates, after first exploring problems that plague such testing. Many studies find a positive relationship between changes in nominal interest rates and changes in expected inflation, and evidence of an inflation risk premium can be found in addition to expected inflation being embraced in the nominal rate.

Nominal contracting pertains to such things as debtor-creditor claims, inflation-induced inventory profits, depreciation tax shields, and pension plans. As a result of these contracts, wealth transfer may occur whenever an unanticipated change in inflation occurs. Empirical tests were examined, and much of the evidence on corporate stock prices was found to be consistent with the nominal contracting hypothesis.

Inflation-indexed bonds are issued to buffer investors against changing inflation. Both interest and principal payments are related to the inflation that has occurred, with a lag. The U.S. Treasury product, TIPS, was introduced in 1997; they are issued quarterly. The demand for the product is segmented, as taxable investors are taxed annually on the accretion in principal, which they do not receive in cash. The TIPS spread is the yield differential between a TIPS bond and a regular Treasury bond of like maturity. Implied in this spread is inflation expectations.

❖ SELECTED REFERENCES

Barsky, Robert B., "The Fisher Hypothesis and the Forecastability and Persistence of Inflation," *Journal of Monetary Economics* 19 (March 1987): 3–24.

Bernard, Victor L., "Unanticipated Inflation and the Value of the Firm," *Journal of Financial Economics* 15 (March 1986): 285–321.

Brown, Roger H., and Stephen M. Schaefer, "Ten Years of the Real Term Structure: 1984–1994," *Journal of Fixed Income* 5 (March 1996): 6–22.

Crowder, William J., and Mark E. Wohar, "Are Tax Effects Important in the Long-Run Fisher Relationship? Evidence from the Municipal Bond Market," *Journal of Finance* 54 (February 1999): 307–17.

Darby, Michael R., "The Financial Effects of Monetary Policy on Interest Rates," *Economic Inquiry* 13 (June 1975): 266–76.

Evans, Martin D. D., "Real Rates, Expected Inflation, and Inflation Risk Premia," *Journal of Finance* 53 (February 1998): 187–218.

Evans, Martin D. D., and Karen K. Lewis, "Do Expected Shifts in Inflation Affect Estimates of the Long-Run Fisher Relation?" *Journal of Finance* 50 (March 1995): 225–53.

Evans, Martin, and Paul Wachtel, "Interpreting the Movements in Short-Term Interest Rates," *Journal of Business* 65 (July 1992): 395–429.

Fama, Eugene F., "Short-Term Interest Rates as Predictors of Inflation," *American Economic Review* 65 (June 1975): 269–82.

Fama, Eugene F., and Michael R. Gibbons, "Inflation, Real Returns and Capital Investment," *Journal of Monetary Economics* 9 (May 1982): 297–323.

Feldstein, Martin, "Inflation, Income Taxes and the Rate of Inflation: A Theoretical Analysis," *American Economic Review* 66 (December 1976): 809–20.

Fisher, Irving, "Appreciation and Interest," *Publications of the American Economic Association* 11 (August 1896): 1–100.

Hendershott, Patric H., and James C. Van Horne, "Expected Inflation Implied by Capital Market Rates," *Journal of Finance* 28 (May 1973): 301–14.

Kandel, Shmuel, Aharon R. Ofer, and Oded Sarig, "Real Interest Rates and Inflation: An Ex-Ante Empirical Analysis," *Journal of Finance* 51 (March 1996): 205–25.

Kessel, Reuben A., "Inflation-Caused Wealth Redistribution: A Test of a Hypothesis," *American Economic Review* 46 (March 1956): 43–66.

Lamm, R. McFall, Jr., "Asset Allocation Implications of Inflation Protection Securities," *Journal of Portfolio Management* 24 (Summer 1998): 93–100.

Mehra, Yash P., "The Bond Rate and Actual Future Inflation," *Economic Quarterly of the Federal Reserve Bank of Richmond* 84 (Spring 1998): 27–47.

Mundell, Robert, "Inflation and Real Interest," *Journal of Political Economy* 71 (June 1963): 280–83.

Roll, Richard, "U.S. Treasury Inflation-Indexed Bonds: The Design of a New Security," *Journal of Fixed Income* 6 (December 1996): 9–28.

Shen, Pu, "How Important Is the Inflation Risk Premium?" *Economic Review of the Federal Reserve Bank of Kansas City* 83 (4th Quarter, 1998): 35–47.

Siegel, Jeremy J., "The Equity Premium: Stock and Bond Returns Since 1802," *Financial Analysts Journal* 48 (January–February 1992): 28–38.

THE TERM STRUCTURE OF INTEREST RATES

In chapters 3 and 5, our focus was on the determination of equilibrium rates of interest in the economy with and without the consideration of inflation. We assumed implicitly either a single rate of interest or interest rates in general. In this and subsequent chapters, we are concerned with why rates of interest differ for different financial instruments. We study the relationship among yields on fixed-income securities by examining the term structure of interest rates in this chapter, the effect of coupon rates in the next, default risk in chapter 8, and the effect of option-type features and taxes in later chapters. In each of these chapters, we attempt to hold constant the other factors. Together, these factors should allow us to explain most of the observed differences in yield and expected return for fixed-income securities.

DEFINITION OF TERM STRUCTURE

The relationship between yield and maturity on securities differing only in length of time to maturity is known as the **term structure of interest rates.** All factors other than maturity must be held constant if the relationship studied is to be meaningful. A term structure may be approximated graphically by plotting yield and maturity for like securities at a moment in time. Maturity is plotted on the horizontal axis and yield is plotted on the vertical axis, and their relationship is described by a **yield curve** fitted to the observations.

Examples of yield curves for zero-coupon Treasury securities are shown in Figure 6-1. These securities are known as STRIPS, "Separate Trading of Registered Interest and Principal of Securities." Often, yield curves are upward-sloping, as shown in the figure, though here they are slightly downward-sloping at the far end of the maturity spectrum. (We go into the reasons in chapter 7.) Occasionally, the yield curve is downward-sloping throughout all but the early maturities. While such a shape is not typical, it has occurred in times of uncertainty and/or reduced supply of long-term bonds. In what follows, we concentrate on **pure discount,** or zero-coupon, securities of the highest quality—namely, Treasury securities. These are the instruments to which the theory on the term structure applies. In the next chapter, we relax the assumption of holding constant the coupon rate and allow for instruments with different coupon rates.

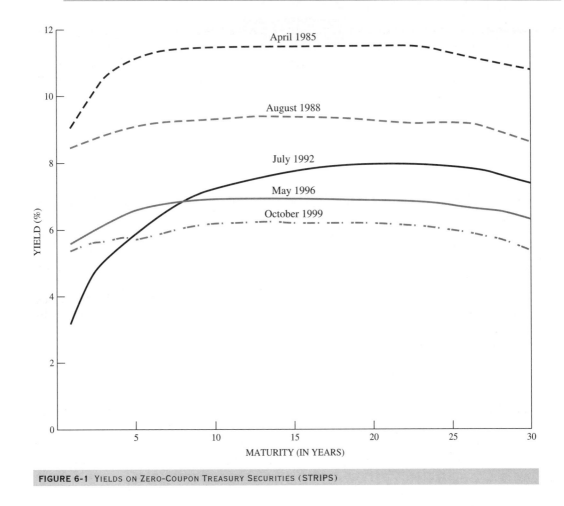

FIGURE 6-1 Yields on Zero-Coupon Treasury Securities (STRIPS)

Notice in Figure 6-1 that there is a dip in yield at the end of the yield curve, namely for the 30-year security. This is due to excess demand for newly issued bonds vis-à-vis securities issued earlier. The most recently issued Treasury bond is known as an **on-the-run** security. After the passage of time, a new 30-year bond will be issued and the older one becomes an **off-the-run** security. On-the-run securities enjoy greater liquidity than off-the-run securities, and tend to trade at lower yields. In addition to 30-year bonds, the Treasury issues new 2-year, 3-year, 5-year, and 10-year notes in its quarterly refundings of the federal debt. These, too, are known as on-the-run securities. The dip in the yield curve is less pronounced for these maturities. For the October 1999 yield curve, a time when liquidity was very much an issue, the dip is evident only for the 5-year security. Recognize that new Treasury issues are coupon issues, but that the coupon yield curve drives the zero-coupon yield curve for reasons we discuss in chapter 7.

In this chapter, we investigate why the term structure of interest rates has different shapes and different overall levels over time. It generally is agreed that expectations of the future course of interest rates are an important influence; controversy arises, however, as to other important influences. We begin by considering the pure expectations theory, where the term structure is explained entirely by interest-rate expectations. Using this theory as a building block, we then consider additional theories for explaining the yield-maturity relationship on securities differing only in the length of time to maturity.

THE PURE EXPECTATIONS THEORY

In broad terms, the expectations theory states that the **expected** one-period rate of return on investment is the same, regardless of the maturity of security in which one invests. That is, if an individual's investment horizon were one year, it would make no difference whether he or she initially invested in a one-year security, invested in a two-year security and sold it at the end of one year, or invested in a five-year security and sold it at the end of one year. The expected holding-period return at the time of initial investment would be the same for all possible maturity strategies. This theory was first expressed by Irving Fisher and was developed further by Friedrich Lutz.[1]

FORWARD RATES OF INTEREST

The rate of interest, or yield, on an actual bond of a particular maturity is known as its **spot rate of interest.** (See chapter 4 for the mathematics of yields.) When considering the expectations theory, it is useful to transform spot rates of interest into **forward rates.** In a formal contract, the forward rate is that rate at which two parties agree to lend and borrow money for a specified period of time in the future. For example, a **forward contract** might be for a two-year loan beginning one year in the future, or for a one-year loan beginning three years hence. Such an arrangement represents an explicit contract.

　　Forward rates also can be implicit. Implied in the term structure at any moment is a set of forward rates.[2]

$$(1 + {}_tR_n)^n = (1 + {}_tR_1)(1 + {}_{t+1}r_{1t})(1 + {}_{t+2}r_{1t}) \cdots (1 + {}_{t+n-1}r_{1t}) \qquad \textbf{(6-1)}$$

where ${}_tR_n$ represents the actual spot rate of interest at time t on an n-period loan, ${}_tR_1$ is the actual rate on a one-period loan at time t, and ${}_{t+1}r_{1t}$, ${}_{t+2}r_{1t}$ and ${}_{t+n-1}r_{1t}$ are forward rates for one-period loans beginning at times $t+1$, $t+2$, and $t+n-1$, implied in the term structure at time t. Thus, a loan for four years is equivalent to a one-year loan plus

---

[1] Irving Fisher, "Appreciation and Interest," *Publications of the American Economic Association* 11 (August 1896): 23–29, 91–92; and F. A. Lutz, "The Structure of Interest Rates," *Quarterly Journal of Economics* 55 (November 1940): 36–63.

[2] For such a derivation, see, for example, J. R. Hicks, *Value and Capital*, 2nd ed. (London: Oxford University Press, 1946), pp. 141–45. If coupon bonds were involved, the formula implicitly assumes that the coupon payments are reinvested, with the lender receiving the principal and reinvesting interest at maturity. The formula contrasts with one in which interest and principal payments are discounted back to present value in accordance with the times when they are to be received.

a series of forward contracts, each renewing the loan for a successive year. The formula for deriving the one-period forward rate beginning at time $t + n$, implied in the term structure at time t, is

$$1 + {}_{t+n}r_{1t} = \frac{(1 + {}_tR_1)(1 + {}_{t+1}r_{1t})\cdots(1 + {}_{t+n-1}r_{1t})(1 + {}_{t+n}r_{1t})}{(1 + {}_tR_{1t})(1 + {}_{t+1}r_{1t})\cdots(1 + {}_{t+n-1}r_{1t})}$$

$$= \frac{(1 + {}_tR_{n+1})^{n+1}}{(1 + {}_tR_n)^n} \tag{6-2}$$

$${}_{t+n}r_{1t} = \frac{(1 + {}_tR_{n+1})^{n+1}}{(1 + {}_tR_n)^n} - 1$$

This formula permits calculation of the implied one-period forward rate for any future period based on actual rates of interest prevailing in the market at a specific time. The forward rate computed need not be a one-period rate, but may span any useful length of time. The calculation of the J-period forward rate beginning at time $t + n$ implied in the term structure at time t is

$${}_{t+n}r_{jt} = \sqrt[j]{\frac{(1 + {}_tR_{n+j})^{n+j}}{(1 + {}_tR_n)^n}} - 1 \tag{6-3}$$

The yield-to-maturity for a pure discount instrument is a geometric average of the forward rates through the maturity date. If the instrument has a maturity of n periods, and our focus is on one-period forward rates, the yield is

$${}_tR_n = [(1 + {}_tR_1)(1 + {}_{t+1}r_{1t})\cdots(1 + {}_{t+n}r_{1t})]^{1/n} - 1 \tag{6-4}$$

where the exponent, $1/n$, is the nth root of the terms contained within the brackets. When forward rates increase (decrease) with maturity, the forward rate for a particular time in the future exceeds (is less than) the yield-to-maturity for a pure discount instrument with that number of periods to maturity. This is merely to say that the end point must be greater (or less) than the average.

The forward rate defined in the manner of Equation (6-2) or Equation (6-3) is merely a mathematical calculation. One version of the pure expectations theory implies that expected future interest rates are equivalent to the computed forward rates. According to this version, ${}_{t+n}\rho_{1t} = {}_{t+n}r_{1t}$, where ρ_1 is the future one-period rate expected at time t to prevail at time $t + n$. To illustrate, suppose the actual rates of interest prevailing in the market were 6 percent for a two-year loan and 6½ percent for a three-year loan. The implied forward rate on a one-year loan two years hence would be

$${}_{t+2}r_{1t} = \frac{(1 + {}_tR_3)^3}{(1 + {}_tR_2)^2} - 1 = \frac{(1.065)^3}{(1.06)^2} - 1 = 7.51\% \tag{6-5}$$

Because forward rates are equivalent to expected future rates, the version of the pure expectations theory discussed implies that the expected one-year rate two years hence is 7.51 percent.

SUBSTITUTABILITY OF MATURITIES

If we ignore transaction costs and assume for a moment that the pure expectations theory is valid, securities with different maturities would be expected substitutes for one another.[3] Prospective investors at any time have three choices: They may invest in an obligation having a maturity corresponding exactly to their anticipated holding period; they may invest in short-term securities, reinvesting in short terms at each maturity over the holding period (known as *rollover*); or they may invest in a security having a maturity longer than the anticipated holding period. In the last case, they would sell the security at the end of the given period, realizing either a capital gain or a loss. According to another version of the pure expectations theory, the investors' expected return for any holding period would be the same, regardless of the alternative or combination of alternatives they chose. This return would be a weighted average of the current short-term interest rate plus future short rates expected to prevail over the holding period; this average is the same for each alternative.[4]

To illustrate, suppose the following yields prevailed in the market for default-free Treasury securities, all of which are pure discount bonds.

Maturity	Percent Yield
1 year	5
2 year	6
3 year	7
4 year	7½

The one-year forward rates, implied in this term structure, may be derived with Equation (6-2) and are found to be

Forward Rate	Percent
$_{t+1}r_{1t}$	7.01
$_{t+2}r_{1t}$	9.03
$_{t+3}r_{1t}$	9.01

If investors have an anticipated holding period of three years, they may invest in the three-year security, from which a yield-to-maturity of 7 percent will be obtained. However, the investor also may invest in a one-year security and reinvest

---

3 For certain technical reasons, they may not be perfect expected substitutes. This concern will be explored later in the chapter.
4 When the holding period is multiperiod, it is better to use a geometric average, as opposed to an arithmetic one, to measure the wealth increment. The geometric average is

$$\overline{R}_j = \left[\prod_{t=1}^{n}(1 + R_{jt})\right]^{\frac{1}{n}} - 1$$

where R_{jt} is the one-period return (in decimal form) for period t, and n is the number of periods in the holding period. The geometric average assumes all one-period returns are reinvested, whereas the arithmetic average implies that each period's return is paid out. While the arithmetic average gives the average return period-by-period, the geometric average gives the average percentage increment in wealth over a particular investment horizon. If a zero-coupon bond goes in price from $50 to $65 to $45.50 over a two-year holding period, the annual returns are +30 percent and −30 percent. The arithmetic average is 0, whereas the geometric average is −4.61 percent. As the investor ends up with less money than he or she started with, the geometric average is the appropriate measure of the average change in wealth.

in one-year securities at maturity over the intended holding period. In this case, the expected return is

$$[(1.05)(1.0701)(1.0903)]^{\frac{1}{3}} - 1 = 7\% \qquad \textbf{(6-6)}$$

or the same as that for investment in the three-year security.

Finally, the investor can invest in a four-year security and sell it at the end of three years as a one-year security. Assuming again a pure discount instrument, its price would have to be $74.88 (per $100 face value) for it to yield 7½ percent over four years. At the end of the third year, its expected market price would need to be $91.73 in order for it to provide a return of 9.01 percent in the last year. (The latter is the one-year forward rate beginning three years hence.) Over the three-year holding period, the expected return to the investor can be found by solving the following equation for r.

$$\$74.88 = \frac{\$91.73}{(1 + r)^3} \qquad \textbf{(6-7)}$$

Solving for r, we find it also to be 7 percent. Thus, the investor could expect to do no better by investing in securities with maturities other than three years. Regardless of the maturity in which an investment is made, the expected return at the time of initial investment is the same. In other words, securities of different maturities are perfect substitutes for one another; one maturity strategy is as good as the next. This would follow if market participants were risk neutral.

TECHNICAL PROBLEMS

In our discussion, we have expressed the pure expectations theory in two ways. First, forward rates of interest embodied in the term structure are unbiased estimates of expected future spot rates of interest. Second, for a specific holding period the expected returns arising from different maturity strategies are the same. With respect to the first expression, forward rates will not be unbiased estimates of expected future spot rates if there is autocorrelation of spot rates and/or if the distributions of possible future spot rates are wide. Rather, they will be biased estimates, and usually upward biased if the autocorrelation is positive. With respect to the second expression, expected returns for a holding period are technically the same only for a specific future holding period, not all possible holding periods. (In a strict sense, this holding period should be the next instantaneous interval of time.)

It also follows from this discussion that the second expression of the pure expectations theory is inconsistent with the first.[5] As these arguments are complex, involving stochastic calculus to resolve, we do not delve into them in this book. The interested reader should refer to the reference cited in footnote 5. For most situations, the biases are not large and, in many cases, can be safely ignored. We assume in this chapter that both expressions of the pure expectations theory hold, and move on to consider the more general implications of the theory. However, one should be mindful of the technical problems involved with different expressions of the pure expectations theory.

[5] The classic paper in this regard is John Cox, Jonathan E. Ingersoll, Jr., and Stephen A. Ross, "A Reexamination of Traditional Hypotheses about the Term Structure of Interest Rates," *Journal of Finance* 36 (September 1981): 769–99.

ARBITRAGE AND MARKET EFFICIENCY

Behaviorally, support for the pure expectations theory comes from the presence of risk-neutral market participants who are willing and able to exploit profit opportunities. Should forward rates differ from expected future rates, a large enough speculative element is said to exist in the market to drive the two sets of rates together. With different rates, various market participants, sensing opportunity for expected gain, would exploit the opportunity until it was eliminated. As a result, forward rates would be unbiased estimates of expected future rates (i.e., the two would be the same). Market participants are said to seek to maximize their return based on their expectations. By buying and selling securities of different maturities, the individual can, in effect, engage in forward transactions. Such a transaction may consist only of shifting from a six-year bond to a seven-year one—a shift that is marginally the same as making a forward contract for a one-year loan six years in the future.

The action of these market participants seeking profit results in the term structure's being determined solely by expectations about future interest rates. According to the pure expectations theory, a horizontal yield curve implies that market participants expect future short rates to be the same as the current short rate. A downward-sloping yield curve signifies that future short rates are expected to fall. Investors are willing to buy long-term securities yielding less than short-term ones because they can expect to do no better by the continual reinvestment in short-term securities. On the other hand, a positively sloped yield curve implies that future short rates are expected to rise. Investors are then unwilling to invest in long-term securities unless the yield is in excess of that on short terms. They would be better off investing in short terms and reinvesting at maturity.

Thus, the pure expectations theory implies that the bond markets are highly efficient. Efficient financial markets are said to exist when security prices reflect all available information that bears on the valuation of the instrument. Implied is that market prices of individual securities adjust rapidly to new information. If excess profits were possible, a sufficient number of market participants with sufficient resources would recognize the opportunity and exploit it. In exploiting it, they would cause security prices to be valued in keeping with all available information. Thus, efficient markets imply an absence of market imperfections that impede the rapid diffusion of information and the rapid reaction to this information by market participants.

UNCERTAINTY AND TERM PREMIUMS

If complete certainty existed in the market, it is clear that forward rates would be exact forecasts of future short-term interest rates. Arbitrage would make all maturities consistent with expectations so that the investor would receive the same return regardless of the maturity in which an investment in a pure discount bond is made. The forward rate would contain no compensation for risk. When we go to an uncertain world, however, the question of risk is raised.

Here, J. R. Hicks and others argue, the pure expectations theory must be modified.[6] The longer the maturity of the security is, the greater is said to be the risk of fluctuation

---

[6]   J. R. Hicks, *Value and Capital,* 2nd ed. (London: Oxford University Press, 1946), pp. 146–47.

in value of principal to the investor. Because of this greater risk, investors are said to prefer to lend short. Borrowers, however, are said to prefer to borrow long in order to reduce the risk of inability to meet principal payments. Because of this "constitutional weakness" on the long side, a risk, or term, premium must be offered to induce investors to purchase long-term securities. This premium is over and above the average of the current short rate and expected future short rates.

Therefore, forward rates would be biased estimates of future interest rates, exceeding them by the amount of term premium. As a result, we would have

$$_{t+n}r_{1t} = {}_{t+n}\rho_{1t} + {}_{1+n}L_{1t} \tag{6-8}$$

where $_{t+n}r_{1t}$, as before, is the forward one-period rate beginning at $t+n$ implied in the term structure at time t, $_{t+n}\rho_{1t}$ is the expected future rate for that period, and $_{t+n}L_{1t}$ is the Hicksian term, or liquidity, premium embodied in the forward rate. If risk increases with the remoteness of the future, term premiums would be an increasing function of this distance.

$$0 < {}_{t+1}L_{1t} < {}_{t+2}L_{1t} < \cdots < {}_{t+n}L_{1t} \tag{6-9}$$

The presence of term premiums implies a bias toward upward-sloping yield curves. Indeed, the yield curve could decrease monotonically only when expected future short rates were lower than the current short rate by amounts exceeding their respective term premiums. To illustrate, suppose market participants expected future short-term interest rates to be the same as the current short rate. On the basis of these expectations alone, the yield curve would be horizontal. However, with term premiums embodied in forward rates, the yield curve would be upward-sloping, as illustrated in Figure 6-2. If a positive bias does exist in forward rates, securities of different maturities would not be perfect expected substitutes for one another. Investment in a long-term security would provide a higher expected return than would investment in a short-term security and reinvestment in short terms at each maturity.

If forward rates do contain term premiums, these premiums are not necessarily constant over time. They may vary with changes in the level of interest rates, in the volatility of interest rates, and in the degree of risk aversion of market participants. To repeat

FIGURE 6-2 COMBINED EXPECTATIONS AND TERM PREMIUMS

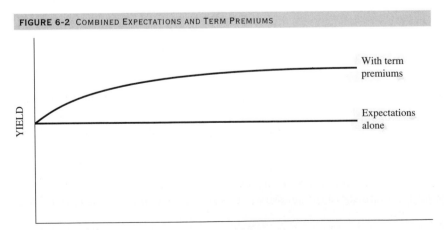

an earlier statement, a key to the liquidity preference theory is that term premiums increase monotonically with the time to maturity.

MARKET SEGMENTATION

A third theory of the term structure suggests that the segmented market behavior of lenders and borrowers basically determines the shape of the yield curve.[7] Because of legal and behavioral restrictions, institutional lenders are said to have preferred maturity ranges in which they operate. For example, commercial banks typically prefer short- to medium-term maturities because of the nature of their deposit liability and a traditional emphasis on liquidity. Insurance companies and other lenders with long-term liabilities prefer longer maturities. On the other hand, borrowers are described as relating the maturity of their debt to their need for funds. Thus, a corporation constructing a plant often takes steps to assure that the maturities of the debt it undertakes in financing the plant correspond to the expected cash flows to be generated from the plant.

In the extreme, a market segmentation theory implies that the rate of interest for a particular maturity is determined solely by demand-and-supply conditions for that maturity, with no reference to conditions for other maturities. In other words, borrowers and lenders have rigid maturity preferences and do not deviate from these preferences no matter how attractive the yields for other maturities are. Thus, the markets for loans would be entirely segmented, or compartmentalized, according to maturity. If there were four segmented markets, for example, there would be four sets of supply and demand curves, as shown in Figure 6-3. Joining together the intersections of these compartmentalized curves would determine the yield curve.

A more moderate version of the segmentation theory is that of Franco Modigliani and Richard Sutch.[8] They suggest that different categories of lenders have *preferred maturity habitats*. While lenders prefer their own habitats, they will leave them if significant yield inducements are available on one side or the other. In the absence of sizable yield inducements, however, lenders will stay in their preferred maturity areas, thereby causing the market for loans to be partially segmented. Therefore, arbitrage across maturities would not entirely eliminate inconsistencies in yield for various maturity areas.

The question we address empirically later in the chapter is whether market segmentation affects the term structure of interest rates over and above the combined influences of expectations and possible systematic risk aversion by lenders. A market segmentation theory on the demand side implies that changes in the relative supplies of various maturities will affect the shape of the term structure of interest rates. For example, if a relatively large quantity of long-term debt is offered, long-term rates presumably would rise relative to short-term rates. The opposite presumably would be true if a relatively large amount of short-term offerings occurred. Thus, the debt

---

[7]   One of the first proponents of this theory was J. M. Culbertson, "The Term Structure of Interest Rates," *Quarterly Journal of Economics* 71 (November 1957): 489–504.

[8]   Franco Modigliani and Richard C. Sutch, "Innovations in Interest Rate Policy," *American Economic Review* 56 (May 1966): 178–197.

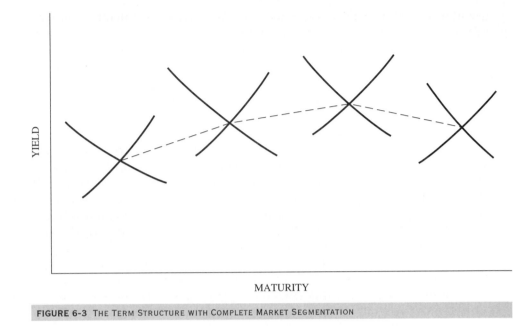

FIGURE 6-3 THE TERM STRUCTURE WITH COMPLETE MARKET SEGMENTATION

management policies of the Treasury, of municipalities, and of corporations would influence the term structure of interest rates if a partial market segmentation theory held.

COX-INGERSOLL-ROSS THEORY

Other theories suggest that the term structure is explained in ways somewhat different from the arguments presented so far. One is the celebrated Cox-Ingersoll-Ross (CIR) model of the term structure.[9] In their approach, CIR specify a general equilibrium model of a continuous-time competitive economy. As the model involves stochastic calculus, which is beyond the scope of this book, we present the main features without going into the details.

GENERAL EQUILIBRIUM NOTIONS

The CIR model is based on individuals maximizing their expected utility from consuming a single good. This good is produced from a finite number of technology states. In maximizing utility, each individual chooses (1) the optimal level of consumption, (2) the optimal proportion of wealth to invest in each production process, and (3) the optimal proportion of wealth to be invested in each of the contingent-claim bonds. The remaining wealth is then invested at the instantaneous riskless rate of interest, or if a shortfall occurs, borrowing to fill the shortfall. According to Cox et al., as in-

---

[9] John C. Cox, Jonathan E. Ingersoll, Jr., and Stephen A. Ross, "A Theory of the Term Structure of Interest Rates," *Econometrica* 53 (March 1985): 385–407.

dividuals make choices and maximize their utilities, the instantaneous interest rate and the expected rates of return on bonds "adjust until all wealth is invested in the physical production processes." The equilibration process is similar to that presented in chapter 3. One feature of the CIR model is that the risk-to-return ratio is the same for all maturity bonds, and arbitrage is the force that brings this about.

TERM STRUCTURE IMPLICATIONS

Focusing on pure discount instruments, CIR endeavor to map the stochastic process underlying bond price behavior. With a single-factor model, CIR assume the state of technology is captured by a single-state variable. They then explore the implications for the term structure.

The authors find that the real price of a bond is a decreasing convex function of the instantaneous interest rate, which merely says that interest rates move together. Moreover, bond prices are a decreasing function of maturity, in keeping with the mathematics of compound interest. A more interesting result is that bond prices are an increasing function of the covariance of the interest rate with wealth. With high covariance, interest rates will tend to be high when wealth is high, and bond prices will be low. When wealth is low, interest rates also will tend to be low and bond prices high. This desirable property has positive marginal utility and, hence, affects the valuation of bonds.

In the CIR formulation, bond prices are also found to be an increasing concave function of interest-rate variance. Cox et al. reason that higher variance reflects more uncertainty about future real production opportunities and, accordingly, more uncertainty about future consumption. As a result, risk-averse investors would value more highly the state-contingent claims of bonds, where certain returns are associated with the various states. On balance, the CIR model suggests that under most circumstances, positive term premiums will be embodied in the term structure of interest rates. With the model, a change in yield anywhere along the term structure is perfectly correlated with changes everywhere else. Moreover, the long-term interest rate converges to a constant or "normal" rate. The long rate, then, can be thought of as the anchor around which the CIR term structure revolves. An important mean-reversion parameter is the adjustment coefficient, which tells us how quickly the long-term rate reverts to its "normal" level.

An example of the CIR model is shown in Figure 6-4, drawn from Peter A. Abken's excellent exposition on the subject.[10] Here the long-term spot rate of interest is assumed to revert to 7 percent. Because risk aversion is assumed (market price of risk = −0.05), a term premium is required. This is reflected by the difference between the forward-rate curve and the expected spot-rate curve. We see that the term premium increases with maturity, which is a feature of the CIR model but not necessarily of other models of this sort.[11]

---

[10] Peter A. Abken, "Innovations in Modeling the Term Structure of Interest Rates," *Federal Reserve Bank of Atlanta Economic Review* 75 (July–August 1990): 222–47.

[11] See Francis A. Longstaff, "A Nonlinear General Equilibrium Model of the Term Structure of Interest Rates," *Journal of Financial Economics* 23 (August 1989): 195–224. In a different approach, Francis A. Longstaff and Eduardo S. Schwartz, "Interest Rate Volatility and the Term Structure: A Two-Factor General Equilibrium Model," *Journal of Finance* 47 (September 1992): 1259–82, develop a two-factor model within the spirit of CIR, the two factors being the short-term interest rate and the volatility of this rate. Finally, George M. Constantinides, "A Theory of the Nominal Term Structure of Interest Rates," *Review of Financial Studies* 5 (Number 4, 1992): 531–52, develops a less restricted one-state-variable extension of the CIR model.

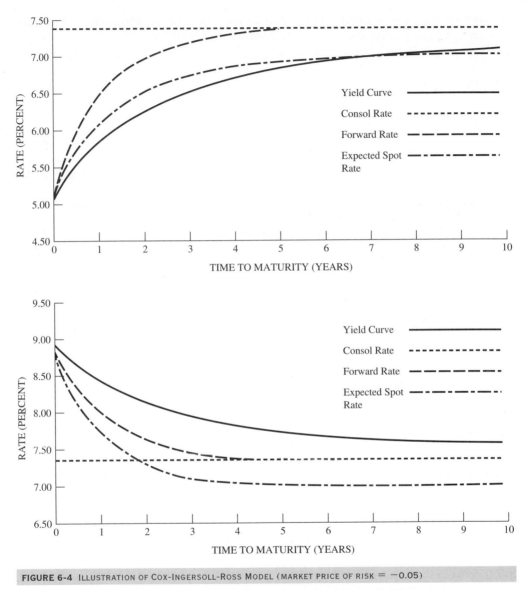

FIGURE 6-4 ILLUSTRATION OF COX-INGERSOLL-ROSS MODEL (MARKET PRICE OF RISK = −0.05)

Source: Peter A. Abken, "Innovations in Modeling the Term Structure of Interest Rates," *Federal Reserve Bank of Atlanta Economic Review* 75 (July–August 1990): 222–47.

The yield curve is that for various maturity pure discount instruments in the spot market. In the upper panel, this curve is below the forward-rate curve, as is the case with upward-sloping yield curves; in the lower panel it is below, as is the case with downward-sloping curves. All this is in keeping with our previous discussion.

Cox, Ingersoll, and Ross extend their model to securities other than bonds—whose payoffs depend on interest rates—such as options and futures contracts on bonds. In addition, they go into multifactor models of the term structure, which permit a wide variety of yield curve shapes.

The advantage of the CIR model of the term structure is that it stems from underlying real economic variables and a general equilibrium in the economy. Therefore, it embraces risk aversion, time consumption preferences, wealth constraints, the factors that give rise to risk premiums, and a variety of investment alternatives. Although this formulation has much virtue, its complexity creates problems in estimating the economic and risk parameters and in making realistic predictions. Researchers working with the CIR model tend to invoke simplifying assumptions. With these, together with the continuous-time mathematics embraced in the model, pricing formulas can be derived for bonds as well as for other instruments.

OTHER MODELS OF THE TERM STRUCTURE

Other models of the term structure exist. Unlike CIR, these are partial equilibrium in nature and try to map the stochastic process governing interest-rate behavior. With a one-factor model, focus is placed on only one point along the term structure. This point usually is either the short-term rate or the long-term rate, with the former employed more often. From changes in this rate, estimates are made of changes in rates for other maturities. These estimates are based on a theoretical model that explains how longer-term rates are connected to the short-term rate, assuming this is the single factor.

MULTIFACTOR MODELS

Multiple-factor models often permit a tighter mapping of interest-rate behavior than does the single-factor model. With multiple factors, rates along the term structure are related to two or more exogenous forces. If these factors were the long-term rate and the short-term rate, changes in all other rates would be functions of changes in these two rates. In other words, their movements are a weighted combination of changes in these two rates. With additional factors, movements in rates along the term structure become a weighted response to changes in three or more factors. Thus, multifactor models attempt to identify the factors that best explain variations in interest rates for all maturities. Two of the better-known models are by Michael J. Brennan and Eduardo S. Schwartz, who fashioned a two-factor model with emphasis on the long-term interest rate and the short-term rate, and by Francis A. Longstaff and Schwartz, where the two factors are the short-term interest rate and the variance of changes in this rate.[12]

Another approach is to map the shape of the term structure. Robert Litterman and José Scheinkman specify the following factors: level, steepness, and curvature of the yield curve.[13] The explanatory power of their model is impressive, although testing was

---

[12] Michael J. Brennan and Eduardo S. Schwartz, "Bond Pricing and Market Efficiency," *Financial Analysts Journal* 38 (September–October 1982): 49–56; Longstaff and Schwartz, "Interest Rate Volatility and the Term Structure: A Two-Factor Equilibrium Model," and Longstaff and Schwartz, "Implementation of the Longstaff-Schwartz Interest Rate Model," *Journal of Fixed Income* 3 (September 1993): 7–14. Another two-factor model of interest is H. Gifford Fong and O. A. Vasicek, "Fixed-Income Volatility Management," *Journal of Portfolio Management* 17 (Summer 1991): 62–65.

[13] Robert Litterman and José Scheinkman, "Common Factors Affecting Bond Returns," *Journal of Fixed Income* 1 (June 1991): 54–61. An application of the modeling to money market rates is found in Peter J. Knez, Robert Litterman, and José Scheinkman, "Explorations into Factors Explaining Money Market Returns," *Journal of Finance* 49 (December 1994): 1861–82.

limited in scope. On average, 97 percent of total variance was explained by the factors for the 13 noncallable Treasury securities tested. As to relative importance, level was by far the most important. It explained 89 percent of the total variance, followed by steepness, which explained 81 percent of the remaining variation in returns.

LATTICE-TYPE MODELS

In another approach to modeling the term structure, researchers have used branching processes to quantify how a bond's price changes from one period to the next. Perhaps the first ones to use this approach were Thomas S. Y. Ho and Sang-bin Lee.[14] They specify a binomial expansion, with bond prices moving either up or down each period. An example of the Ho-Lee model is shown in Figure 6-5.[15] Here we see a zero-coupon bond with five quarters to maturity. At maturity, the bond is worth $1, its face value. Prices and yields (in brackets) are depicted for various states in each of the five quarters. The figure portrays what is known as a **recombining lattice,** where two sets of branches path back to a common middle value at times 3, 2, 1, and 0. With a recombining lattice, the number of nodes after *n* periods is equal to *n*. At the end of time 2, four periods have passed, and we see that there are four nodes. With a **nonrecombining lattice,** there is no constraint and the number of nodes expands geometrically. After four periods there are 16 nodes, which is *n* to the 4th power. Computationally, the recombining lattice can be solved more efficiently, and this becomes important when *n* is large.

At the outset of the example in Figure 6-5, a five-quarter bond is assumed to have a known price of 0.894 and yield of 9 percent. At maturity, of course, it is worth 1.0. The evolution of bond prices between the start and the finish is what is uncertain. The lattice pattern fans out each period, and any individual path is a series of ups and downs. For maturities shorter than five quarters, prices and yields are shown above the data for the five-quarter bond. While the branching processes for them are not illustrated, it is easy to see how they work. Depending on the state path taken, the Ho-Lee model will describe a term structure of interest rates (in the example shown, an upward-sloping one). Because of the complexity, valuation of bonds with any reasonable length of time to maturity requires a computer algorithm.

The Ho-Lee type of lattice model has been extended and refined.[16] Among others, a model by Fischer Black, Emanuel Derman, and William Toy enjoys widespread use within the investment bank of which they were a part.[17] Although this model is similar

14 Thomas S. Y. Ho and Sang-bin Lee, "Term Structure Movements and Pricing Interest Rate Contingent Claims," *Journal of Finance* 41 (December 1986): 1011–29.
15 This example, as well as others involving the Ho-Lee model, is described in Abken, "Innovations in Modeling the Term Structure of Interest Rates."
16 Thomas S. Y. Ho, "Managing Illiquid Bonds and the Linear Path Space," *Journal of Fixed Income* 2 (June 1992): 80–94; David Heath, Robert Jarrow, and Andrew Morton, "Bond Pricing and the Term Structure of Interest Rates: A Discrete Time Approximation," *Journal of Financial and Quantitative Analysis* 25 (December 1990): 419–40; Thomas F. Cooley, Stephen F. LeRoy, and William R. Parke, "Pricing Interest-Sensitive Claims When Interest Rates Have Stationary Components," *Journal of Fixed Income* 1 (March 1992): 64–73; John M. Mulvey and Stavros A. Zenios, "Dynamic Diversification of Fixed Income Portfolios," *Financial Analysts Journal* 50 (January–February 1994): 30–38, and Malcolm C. Easton, "Binary Tree Interest Rate Models with Risk Premiums," *Journal of Fixed Income* 8 (September 1998): 53–59.
17 Fischer Black, Emanual Derman, and William Toy, "A One-Factor Model of Interest Rates and Its Application to Treasury Bond Options," *Financial Analysts Journal* 46 (January–February 1990): 33–39. In their model, interest rates are assumed to be lognormally distributed. For a review of this and other term structure models, see Bruce Tuckman, *Fixed Income Securities* (New York: John Wiley & Sons, 1995), chapters 7 and 8.

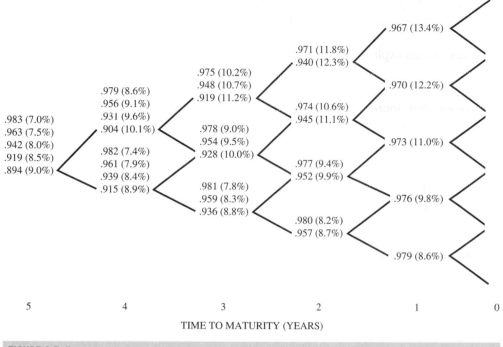

.983 (7.0%)
.963 (7.5%)
.942 (8.0%)
.919 (8.5%)
.894 (9.0%)

.979 (8.6%)
.956 (9.1%)
.931 (9.6%)
.904 (10.1%)

.982 (7.4%)
.961 (7.9%)
.939 (8.4%)
.915 (8.9%)

.975 (10.2%)
.948 (10.7%)
.919 (11.2%)

.978 (9.0%)
.954 (9.5%)
.928 (10.0%)

.981 (7.8%)
.959 (8.3%)
.936 (8.8%)

.971 (11.8%)
.940 (12.3%)

.974 (10.6%)
.945 (11.1%)

.977 (9.4%)
.952 (9.9%)

.980 (8.2%)
.957 (8.7%)

.967 (13.4%)

.970 (12.2%)

.973 (11.0%)

.976 (9.8%)

.979 (8.6%)

| 5 | 4 | 3 | 2 | 1 | 0 |

TIME TO MATURITY (YEARS)

FIGURE 6-5 EVOLUTION OF BOND PRICES IN THE HO-LEE MODEL (YIELDS IN PARENTHESES)

Source: Peter A. Abken, "Innovations in Modeling the Term Structure of Interest Rates," *Federal Reserve Bank of Atlanta Economic Review* 75 (July–August 1990): 228.

to the Ho-Lee model, it allows for volatility changing over time. The impetus for change is a change in the short rate, and this drives all bond price changes. In another variation of the Ho-Lee type of model, David Heath, Robert Jarrow, and Andrew Morton model forward rates as opposed to spot rates.[18] Much work continues on refining and extending lattice-type models to the valuation of derivative securities, both in the academic community and in the investment banking community.

EMPIRICAL EVIDENCE

In recent years, numerous empirical tests have been conducted of the term structure of interest rates. Many of these studies are cited at the end of the chapter. Rather than probe into each of them, I endeavor to give a "thumbnail" synthesis. First, the evidence largely supports the idea that interest-rate expectations affect the shape of the yield curve. Put another way, the term structure appears to contain valuable information as

---

[18] David Heath, Robert Jarrow, and Andrew Morton, "Bond Pricing and the Term Structure of Interest Rates," *Econometrica* 60 (March 1992): 225–62. For an excellent review of various term structure models, see David Backus, Silverio Foresi, and Chris Telmer, "Discrete-Time Models of Bond Pricing," working paper, *National Bureau of Economic Research* (September 1998).

to the expected future course of interest rates. However, scant support can be found for the pure expectations theory. That is to say, forward rates of interest are not unbiased estimates of expected future spot rates of interest. Rather, term premiums appear to be embraced in forward rates and roughly to increase with maturity. Moreover, a number of researchers have found that term premiums vary directly with the volatility of interest rates. Term premium estimates, on average, are sizable. Elton, for example, found them to be around 2¾ percent in the 5-year maturity range when the one-month Treasury bill rate is used for the riskless rate.[19] This contrasts with Dhillon and Laser, who found them to be 0.7 percent when the three-month zero-coupon STRIP is used for the riskless rate.[20] Both offer strong support for term premiums increasing monotonically with maturity.

If the term structure is partially compartmentalized according to maturity, a change in the relative supply or demand in one segment should change the shape of the yield curve. The reason is institutional specialization causing investors and issuers to move from preferred maturity areas only with yield inducements. There has been support for market segmentation having a moderate effect on the term structure. In recent years, the Federal Reserve, the central bank in the United States, seems to be able to affect short-term interest rates in ways that are not entirely transmitted to longer segments of the yield curve. In the long-term area, the reduced supply of 30-year Treasury bonds in 2000 resulted in excess demand and a downward-sloping yield curve beyond 5 years. Thus, market segmentation seems to have an effect.

Limited testing has been done of consumption-based models, such as the Cox-Ingersoll-Ross (CIR) term structure model described earlier. In this regard, certain scholars have found evidence consistent with the term structure containing information about future consumption growth. While some of the properties of the CIR model have been supported empirically, the relationships are not particularly stable over time.

❖ SUMMARY

The term structure of interest rates portrays the yield-maturity relationship on securities that differ only in length of time to maturity and that are pure discount instruments. A number of theories attempt to explain the term structure. The pure expectations theory states that expectations of the future course of interest rates are the sole determinant. One version of the theory implies that securities of different maturity are perfect substitutes in the sense that the expected return is the same, while another version implies that forward rates are unbiased estimates of expected future spot rates of interest. Although this chapter was written as if both versions hold, we pointed out certain technical problems that may not make this so.

A combined theory of expectations and term premiums suggests that market participants prefer to lend short unless offered a premium sufficient to offset the risk of lending long. Thus, the term structure would be affected not only by expectations but

---

[19] Edwin J. Elton, "Expected Return, Realized Return and Asset Pricing Tests," *Journal of Finance* 54 (August 1999): 1199–1220.

[20] Upinder S. Dhillon and Dennis J. Lasser, "Term Premium Estimates from Zero-Coupon Bonds: New Evidence on the Expectations Hypothesis," *Journal of Fixed Income* 8 (June 1998): 52–58.

also by term premiums. If risk increases with the remoteness in the future, these premiums would increase at a decreasing rate with maturity. The presence of term premiums in forward rates of interest implies a bias toward upward-sloping yield curves.

A market segmentation theory implies that maturity preferences of lenders and borrowers are such that they usually will not leave their preferred maturity range to take advantage of yield differentials. As a result, a number of different markets exist, and interest rates are said to be determined by the interaction of supply and demand in each. With partial market segmentation, lenders and borrowers will leave their preferred maturity areas only if yield inducements are offered on either side.

In addition to the theories considered, we also examined the Cox-Ingersoll-Ross theory of the term structure. This model is based on underlying real economic variables and on a general equilibrium in the economy. Various implications result from the model, one of which is that the prices of pure discount instruments are an increasing function of the covariance of the interest rate with wealth. Various additional models of the term structure were presented: multifactor and lattice-type, or branching process, models. These partial equilibrium models attempt to map the stochastic process by which interest rates for different maturity instruments vary over time.

Empirical studies show the important role of expectations in shaping the yield curve. Also, there are indications of forward rates of interest embracing both expectations and term premiums. These term premiums appear to vary with maturity and with the volatility of interest rates. Tests of market segmentation suggest that there may be an effect, particularly in recent years. Finally, we reviewed the limited empirical evidence on consumption and the term structure.

❖ SELECTED REFERENCES

Abken, Peter A., "Innovations in Modeling the Term Structure of Interest Rates," *Federal Reserve Bank of Atlanta Economic Review* 75 (July–August 1990): 222–47.

Backus, David, Silverio Foresi, and Chris Telmer, "Discrete-Time Models of Bond Pricing," working paper, *National Bureau of Economic Research* (September 1998).

Black, Fischer, Emanuel Derman, and William Toy, "A One-Factor Model of Interest Rates and Its Application to Treasury Bond Options," *Financial Analysts Journal* 46 (January–February 1990): 33–39.

Boudoukh, Jacob, Matthew Richardson, Tom Smith, and Robert F. Whitelaw, "Ex Ante Bond Returns and the Liquidity Preference Hypothesis," *Journal of Finance* 54 (June 1999): 1153–67.

Brennan, Michael J., and Eduardo S. Schwartz, "Bond Pricing and Market Efficiency," *Financial Analysts Journal* 38 (September–October 1982): 49–56.

Brown, Roger H., and Stephen M. Schaefer, "The Term Structure of Real Interest Rates and the Cox, Ingersoll, and Ross Model," *Journal of Financial Economics* 35 (February 1994): 3–42.

Brown, Stephen J., and Philip H. Dybvig, "The Empirical Implications of Cox-Ingersoll-Ross Theory of the Term Structure of Interest Rates," *Journal of Finance* 41 (July 1986): 617–30.

Cochrane, John H., "New Facts in Finance," working paper, *National Bureau of Economic Research* (June 1999).

Constantinides, George M., "A Theory of the Nominal Term Structure of Interest Rates," *Review of Financial Studies* 5 (Number 4, 1992): 531–52.

Cox, John C., Jonathan E. Ingersoll, Jr., and Stephen A. Ross, "A Reexamination of Traditional Hypotheses about the Term Structure of Interest Rates," *Journal of Finance* 36 (September 1981): 769–99.

———, "A Theory of the Term Structure of Interest Rates," *Econometrica* 53 (March 1985): 385–407.

Dunn, Kenneth B., and Kenneth J. Singleton, "Modeling the Term Structure of Interest Rates under Non-separable Utility and Durability of Goods," *Journal of Political Economy* 17 (September 1986): 27–56.

Dybvig, Phillip H., Jonathan E. Ingersoll, Jr., and Stephen A. Ross, "Long Forward and Zero-Coupon Rates Can Never Fall," *Journal of Business* (No. 1, 1996): 1–25.

Easton, Malcolm, "Binary Tree Interest Rate Models with Risk Premiums," *Journal of Fixed Income* 8 (September 1998): 53–59.

Elton, Edwin J., "Expected Return, Realized Return and Asset Pricing Tests," *Journal of Finance* 54 (August 1999): 1199–1220.

Ferguson, Robert, and Steven Raymar, "A Comparative Analysis of Several Popular Term Structure Estimation Models," *Journal of Fixed Income* 7 (March 1998): 17–33.

Harvey, Campbell R., "The Real Term Structure and Consumption Growth," *Journal of Financial Economics* 22 (December 1988): 305–33.

Heath, David, Robert Jarrow, and Andrew Morton, "Bond Pricing and the Term Structure of Interest Rates," *Econometrica* 60 (March 1992): 225–62.

Hicks, J. R., *Value and Capital,* 2nd ed. London: Oxford University Press, 1946.

Ho, Thomas S. Y., and Sang-bin Lee, "Term Structure Movements and Pricing Interest Rate Contingent Claims," *Journal of Finance* 41 (December 1986): 1011–29.

Ilmanen, Antti, "Market Rate Expectations and Forward Rates," *Journal of Fixed Income* 6 (September 1996): 8–22.

Ilmanen, Antti, and Ray Iwanowski, "Dynamics of the Shape of the Yield Curve," *Journal of Fixed Income* 7 (September 1997): 47–60.

Litterman, Robert, and José Scheinkman, "Common Factors Affecting Bond Returns," *Journal of Fixed Income* 1 (June 1991): 54–61.

Longstaff, Francis A., and Eduardo S. Schwartz, "Interest Rate Volatility and the Term Structure: A Two-Factor General Equilibrium Model," *Journal of Finance* 47 (September 1992): 1259–82.

Longstaff, Francis A., and Eduardo S. Schwartz, "Implementation of the Longstaff-Schwartz Interest Rate Model," *Journal of Fixed Income* 3 (September 1993): 7–14.

Lutz, Friedrich, A., "The Structure of Interest Rates," *Quarterly Journal of Economics* 55 (November 1940): 36–63.

Meiselman, David, *The Term Structure of Interest Rates.* Upper Saddle River, NJ: Prentice Hall, 1962.

Modigliani, Franco, and Richard C. Sutch, "Innovations in Interest Rate Policy," *American Economic Review* 56 (May 1966): 178–97.

Singleton, Kenneth, "Expectations Models of the Term Structure and Implied Variance Bounds," *Journal of Political Economy* 88 (December 1980): 1159–76.

Tuckman, Bruce, *Fixed Income Securities.* New York: John Wiley & Sons, 1995.

Upinder, Dhillon S., and Dennis J. Lasser, "Term Premium Estimates from Zero-Coupon Bonds: New Evidence on the Expectations Hypothesis," *Journal of Fixed Income* 8 (June 1998): 52–58.

Van Horne, James C., "Interest-Rate Expectations, the Shape of the Yield Curve, and Monetary Policy," *Review of Economics and Statistics* 48 (May 1966): 211–15.

———, "Interest-Rate Risk and the Term Structure of Interest Rates," *Journal of Political Economy* 73 (August 1965): 344–51.

———, "The Term Structure of Interest Rates: A Test of the Segmented Markets Hypothesis," *Southern Economic Journal* 47 (April 1980): 1129–40.

Willner, Ram, "A New Tool for Portfolio Managers: Level, Slope, and Curvature Durations," *Journal of Fixed Income* 6 (June 1996): 48–59.

PRICE VOLATILITY, COUPON RATE, AND MATURITY

Our attention turns now to the relationship between a bond's price and its yield, so we can understand the characteristics of price volatility. In the previous chapter, our focus was on pure discount instruments. By using zero-coupon, default-free Treasury securities, we held constant two important factors that explain differences in expected return and volatility: the coupon rate and default risk. In this chapter, we investigate the effect of different coupon rates on bond valuation. Actually, a coupon bond is no more than a composite of pure discount bonds. Each coupon and principal payment occurs at a specified time in the future and is effectively a zero-coupon instrument. We explore default risk in the next chapter.

We begin this chapter with an analysis of how market-price movements are affected by coupon rates and maturity. We then examine the use of the duration measure, which takes account of the timing of both interest and principal payments, and how volatility is related to it. The yield/price relationship is curvilinear, so it may be appropriate to modify duration using a convexity measure. This is followed by a discussion of how we might immunize the payments stream of a bond investment relative to some desired payments stream. Finally, we explore the implications of the increasing presence of pure discount bonds in the marketplace and the equilibration, through arbitrage, between the market for coupon bonds and the market for zero-coupon bonds.

THE COUPON EFFECT

We know that the longer the maturity of a debt instrument is, the greater is the change in price that accompanies a shift in interest rates. However, price changes also are dependent on the level of coupon. This phenomenon is known as the **coupon effect.** It is important to distinguish the coupon effect that arises from the mathematics of interest rates, to be studied here, from the coupon effect that arises from the call feature, to be examined in chapter 12.

SENSITIVITY OF PRICE TO VARIOUS PROPERTIES

When market yields change, option-free bonds are affected differently depending on their coupon rate and maturity. For a given bond, the lower the coupon is, the greater the price change is for a given shift in interest rates. This relationship is illustrated in Table 7-1 for 10- and 20-year bonds. In the upper part of the table, a yield increase is assumed; in the lower part, a yield decline is assumed. We see that the lower the coupon, the more sensitive market prices are to changes in yields. The reason is that with lower coupons, more of the total return to the investor is reflected in the principal payment at maturity as opposed to nearer-term interest payments.

We see also in Table 7-1 that the 20-year bond column shows more price volatility than the 10-year column, in keeping with our previous discussion. Furthermore, the percentage increase in price when yields decline is greater than the percentage decrease when yields rise. This phenomenon is due to the convex relationship between price and yield, an example of which is shown in Figure 7-1. The point of Table 7-1, however, is to emphasize that one gets different market price movements, depending on the coupon rate. With high coupons, the total income stream (interest and principal payments) is closer to realization than it is with low coupons. The nearer the income stream, the less the present value effect, given a change in yields. Thus, even if high and low coupon bonds have the same maturity, the low coupon bonds tend to be more volatile.

TABLE 7-1   Changes in Price Accompanying a Shift in Yield for Various Coupons

	Yield Increase from 8% to 10%	
Coupon	*Price Decline 10-Year Bond*	*Price Decline 20-Year Bond*
12%	−11.57%	−16.07%
10	−11.96	−16.52
8	−12.46	−17.16
6	−13.11	−18.11
4	−14.02	−19.68
2	−15.33	−22.80
0	−17.42	−31.80

	Yield Decrease from 8% to 6%	
Coupon	*Price Increase 10-Year Bond*	*Price Increase 20-Year Bond*
12%	13.72%	21.31%
10	14.23	22.07
8	14.88	23.11
6	15.73	24.67
4	16.89	27.28
2	18.61	32.37
0	21.32	47.18

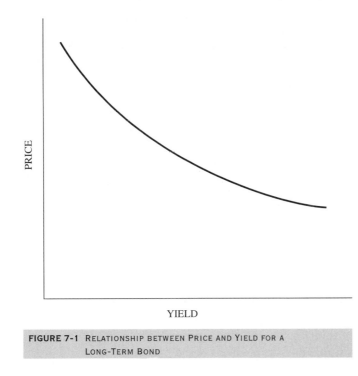

PRICE

YIELD

FIGURE 7-1 RELATIONSHIP BETWEEN PRICE AND YIELD FOR A
LONG-TERM BOND

THE DURATION MEASURE AND ITS
CHANGING BEHAVIOR

The problems associated with different market price movements for different coupon rates have led many to question the usefulness of maturity as a measure of the length of a financial instrument. Instead, they suggest the use of another measure—the duration of a security, which is a weighted average of the times in the future when interest and principal payments are to be received. This measure was first proposed in 1938 by Frederick R. Macaulay in his monumental study of yields.[1] **Macaulay** made it clear that the number of years to maturity is an inadequate measure of the time element of a loan because it tells only the date of final payment and omits essential information about the size and date of payments that occur before the final payment.

To remedy this problem, he proposed the following measure, which he called **duration.**

$$D = \frac{\displaystyle\sum_{t=1}^{n} \frac{C_t(t)}{(1 + R)^t}}{\displaystyle\sum_{t=1}^{n} \frac{C_t}{(1 + R)^t}} \qquad\qquad \text{(7-1)}$$

market value weighted by t (time)

PV of CF = market value

[1] Frederick R. Macaulay, *Some Theoretical Problems Suggested by the Movements of Interest Rates, Bond Yields, and Stock Prices in the United States since 1856* (New York: National Bureau of Economic Research, 1938).

where

C_t = interest and/or principal payment at time t

(t) = length of time to the interest and/or principal payments

n = length of time to final maturity

R = yield-to-maturity

The denominator of the equation is simply the present value of the stream of interest and principal payments—namely, the market price of the bond. The numerator also is a present value, but here the interest and principal payments are weighted by the length of the interval between the present and the time that payment is to be received. Rather than estimate interest rates for each future period and use them to discount the payments to present value, for computational convenience Macaulay used yield-to-maturity as the discount rate throughout. He then employed duration as a measure of the life of a coupon-paying bond.

AN ILLUSTRATION

To illustrate the duration measure shown in Equation (7-1), suppose we own a bond with four years to maturity; it has an 8 percent coupon rate and yields 10 percent to maturity. Assume also that interest payments are received at the end of each of the four years and that the principal payment is received at the end of the fourth year. The duration of the bond is

$$D = \frac{\dfrac{\$80(1)}{(1.10)} + \dfrac{\$80(2)}{(1.10)^2} + \dfrac{\$80(3)}{(1.10)^3} + \dfrac{\$1,080(4)}{(1.10)^4}}{\dfrac{\$80}{(1.10)} + \dfrac{\$80}{(1.10)^2} + \dfrac{\$80}{(1.10)^3} + \dfrac{\$1,080}{(1.10)^4}} = 3.56 \text{ years}$$

If the coupon rate were 4 percent, its duration would be

$$D = \frac{\dfrac{\$40(1)}{(1.10)} + \dfrac{\$40(2)}{(1.10)^2} + \dfrac{\$40(3)}{(1.10)^3} + \dfrac{\$1,040(4)}{(1.10)^4}}{\dfrac{\$40}{(1.10)} + \dfrac{\$40}{(1.10)^2} + \dfrac{\$40}{(1.10)^3} + \dfrac{\$1,040}{(1.10)^4}} = 3.75 \text{ years}$$

If the coupon rate were zero, however, duration would be

$$D = \frac{\dfrac{\$1,000(4)}{(1.10)^4}}{\dfrac{\$1,000}{(1.10)^4}} = 4 \text{ years}$$

Thus, if only a single payment is made, as occurs *with a zero-coupon bond, duration equals maturity.* For coupon bonds, however, duration is always less than maturity.

In summary, duration can be considered a measure of the average life of a debt instrument on a present-value basis. That is, it is a weighted average of the present values of coupon and principal payments. The weights represent portions of the total present value of the bond, which are associated with specific future payments.

RELATIONSHIP BETWEEN DURATION AND MATURITY

For bonds selling at their par value or above, duration increases at a decreasing rate with maturity. For bonds selling at a discount, duration increases at a decreasing rate up to some fairly long maturity, and then declines.[2] The situation is illustrated in Table 7-2 for bonds yielding 6 percent, with semiannual coupon payments. We see that for bonds with a coupon rate of 2 percent, duration declines with maturity after 50 years. For a coupon rate of 4 percent, duration declines in going from 100 years maturity to perpetuity. Thus, for bonds selling at a discount, duration eventually declines with maturity. However, this occurs many years out. For the 6 percent coupon bond selling at par and for the 8 percent coupon bond selling at a premium, duration increases with maturity at a decreasing rate throughout.

The relationships discussed are further illustrated in Figure 7-2.[3] For the zero-coupon bond, a one-to-one relationship exists between duration and maturity, as depicted by the 45 degree line. With coupon bonds, duration is shorter than maturity and the lines are less than 45 degrees. For the discount bond, where yield is greater than the coupon rate, duration increases at a decreasing rate up to a point, after which it declines with further increases in maturity. This point depends on the coupon rate and yield assumed; the greater the divergence, the sooner the point occurs. As maturity increases, duration approaches the duration of a perpetual bond—one that pays a periodic coupon forever. For most discount bonds, the negative relationship between duration and maturity does not occur. It is a factor only with long maturities and deep discounts.

The duration of a perpetual bond is $(1 + R)/R$, or 1 plus the yield over the yield, and it is invariant with respect to maturity. For the par value bond, where yield equals the

TABLE 7-2   Duration for Bonds Yielding 6 Percent with Semiannual Coupons

Years to Maturity	Coupon Rate			
	2%	4%	6%	8%
1	0.995 years	0.990 years	0.985 years	0.981 years
3	2.921	2.852	2.790	2.734
5	4.756	4.558	4.393	4.254
7	6.491	6.111	5.817	5.583
10	8.891	8.169	7.662	7.286
20	14.981	12.980	11.904	11.232
30	18.244	15.485	14.253	13.555
50	19.452	17.129	16.273	15.829
100	17.567	17.232	17.120	17.064
Perpetual	17.167	17.167	17.167	17.167

[2] The first to emphasize these relationships were Lawrence Fisher and Roman L. Weil, "Coping with the Risk of Interest-Rate Fluctuations: Returns to Bondholders from Naïve and Optimal Strategies," *Journal of Business* 44 (October 1971): 408–31.
[3] For additional insight, see G. O. Bierwag, George G. Kaufman, and Alden L. Toevs, "Duration: Its Development and Use in Bond Portfolio Management," *Financial Analysts Journal* 39 (July–August 1983): 16–17, on which this section draws.

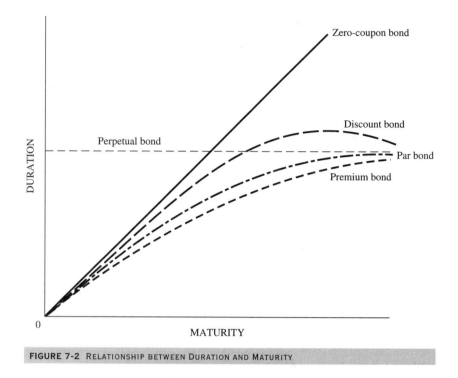

FIGURE 7-2 RELATIONSHIP BETWEEN DURATION AND MATURITY

coupon rate, duration increases with maturity throughout. Finally, for the premium bond, where yield is less than the coupon rate, duration again increases with maturity throughout, but at a lesser rate than with the par value bond.

Thus, the relationship between duration and maturity is different depending on the following factors: (1) whether the bond is zero-coupon or coupon; (2) if the bond is coupon, whether it is perpetual (only the British consols are perpetual); and (3) if the bond is not perpetual, whether it trades at a discount, at par, or at a premium. For non-perpetual coupon bonds, except for the discount bond in the very long maturity area, duration declines with the passage of time.

RELATIONSHIP BETWEEN DURATION AND COUPON PAYMENT

However, this relationship is upset every time a coupon payment is made. As we know, duration is a weighted average of coupon and principal payments, where the weights depend on the nearness of the payment. When a coupon payment occurs, the next coupon becomes six months away, assuming semiannual payments. As a result, duration increases at that moment. With the passage of time, duration declines until the next coupon payment, at which time it again temporarily increases. This phenomenon is illustrated in Figure 7-3 for a par value bond or a premium bond. Although the relationship between duration and maturity is similar to that in Figure 7-2, the line is saw-toothed at the points where coupon payments occur.

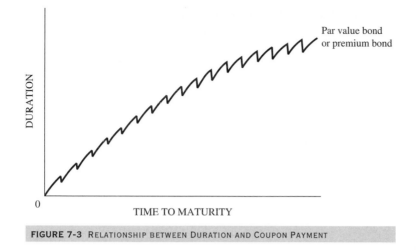

Par value bond
or premium bond

DURATION

0

TIME TO MATURITY

FIGURE 7-3 RELATIONSHIP BETWEEN DURATION AND COUPON PAYMENT

RELATIONSHIP BETWEEN DURATION AND CHANGES IN INTEREST RATES

With the Macaulay duration measures, Equation (7-1), duration depends on the yield-to-maturity. The higher the yield, the shorter the duration, all other things the same. This is illustrated in Figure 7-4 for a specific bond with a given coupon rate and maturity.

As shifts in interest rates occur, the duration of a bond changes. Recall from the previous chapter that a yield curve portrays the relationship between yield and maturity at a moment

FIGURE 7-4 RELATIONSHIP BETWEEN DURATION AND YIELD FOR A SPECIFIC COUPON BOND

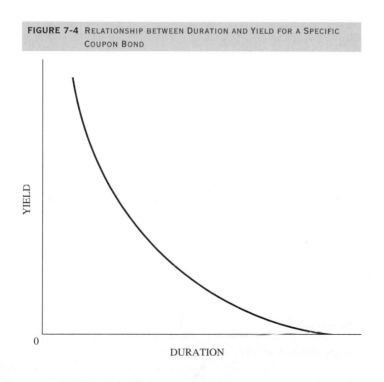

YIELD

0

DURATION

in time. If an instantaneous shift in interest rates occurs, yields change but maturities do not. Consider now a yield curve where duration, instead of maturity, is along the horizontal axis. In Figure 7-5, a base yield-duration curve is shown in the middle. If interest rates shift upward, we see that the new yield-duration curve has shorter durations throughout. Contrarily, if interest rates shift downward, longer durations occur. If volatility is related to duration, this has important implications for a bond's risk. We now turn to this topic.

VOLATILITY AND DURATION

In the duration formula, the denominator is the present value of the payments stream, which is the bond's market price, P_0. We have then

$$D = \frac{\sum_{i=1}^{n} \frac{C_t(t)}{(1 + R)^t}}{P_0} \tag{7-2}$$

Differentiating bond price with respect to the yield-to-maturity,

$$\frac{dP_0}{d(1 + R)} - \frac{P_0}{(1 + R)} D \tag{7-3}$$

which becomes

$$\frac{dP_0}{P_0} = -D \frac{dR}{(1 + R)} \tag{7-4}$$

or

$$\frac{\Delta P_0}{P_0} = -D \frac{\Delta R}{(1 + R)} \tag{7-5}$$

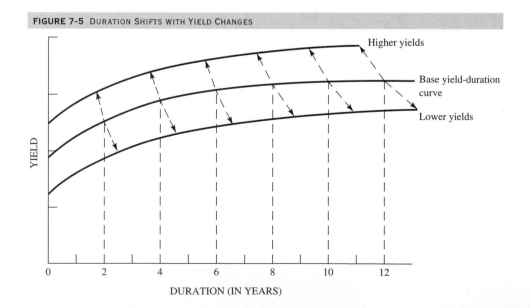

FIGURE 7-5 Duration Shifts with Yield Changes

Thus, the percentage change in bond price due to a percentage change in 1 plus its yield is $-D$.

Suppose the duration of a bond that pays annual interest is eight years, its yield-to-maturity is 10 percent, and interest rates shift up so that the bond's yield goes to 11.1 percent. (This is the equivalent of a 1 percent rise in $1 + R$.) The change in bond price that results is

$$-8\frac{0.011}{(1.10)} = -0.08$$

Thus, the formula suggests that the bond declines in value by 8 percent in response to the increase in 1 plus its yield of 1 percent. This approximation using duration tends to be more accurate the smaller the change in yield.

MODIFIED DURATION FORMULA

Investors use what is known as **modified duration** to estimate the price change that accompanies a change in yield. For a bond that pays interest once a year,

$$MD = \frac{D}{(1 + R)} \tag{7-6}$$

where MD stands for modified duration, D is the Macaulay duration measure determined with Equation (7-1), and R is the yield. For our example, $MD = 8/(1.10) = 7.2727$. With modified duration, the price change that accompanies a change in yield is simply

$$\frac{\Delta P_0}{P_0} = -MD(\Delta R) \tag{7-7}$$

For our example,

$$-7.2727(0.011) = -0.08$$

which is the same as before. The advantage of modified duration is that a change in interest rates can be multiplied directly by it to obtain the expected price change, as opposed to having to express the yield change in terms of 1 plus the yield.

When interest is paid semiannually, Equation (7-6) must be adjusted. **For semi-annual interest, modified duration is**

$$MD = \frac{D}{(1 + \frac{R}{2})} \tag{7-8}$$

where R is simply divided by two. This modified duration measure then is used to estimate the price response to a change in yield for bonds with semiannual coupon payments.

We see that the volatility of a bond is proportional to its duration. Accordingly, two bonds with the same duration should have the same price reaction, percentagewise, in response to a change in interest rates. However, the duration measure is rather restrictive for reasons we are about to discover.

CONVEXITY

While the simple Macaulay duration measure is widely used, it does not take account of certain price/yield characteristics. As we know from Figure 7-1, the relationship between a bond's price and its yield is curvilinear, not linear as implied by the duration measure. In Figure 7-6, we portray the difference. If the yield for a specific bond is R_0 its price will be P_0. We then draw a line tangent to the "true" price/yield relationship at this yield. This tangent line approximates what occurs with the modified duration formula, Equation (7-8):[4] The steeper the tangent line, the longer the duration; the flatter the tangent line, the shorter the duration.

    We see in Figure 7-6 that the larger the change in yield, from R_0, the greater the distance between the tangent line and the true curvilinear relationship between price and yield—thus, the greater the error in the use of the duration measure. In practice, this means that moderate changes in interest rates do not cause substantial errors, but changes of 2 percent or more cause serious problems in estimating the price response to a change in yield.

THE CONVEXITY MEASURE

To better approximate the true relationship between price and yield, we can modify the duration estimate for **convexity.** The measure used is the second derivative of price with

FIGURE 7-6 ILLUSTRATION OF CONVEXITY ERROR FOR PRICE/YIELD RELATIONSHIP

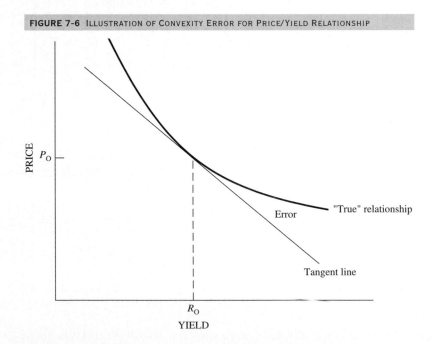

---

[4] If the axes were scaled in logarithms, it would be exact. See G. O. Bierwag, George G. Kaufman, and Cynthia M. Latta, "Duration Models: A Taxonomy," *Journal of Portfolio Management* 14 (Fall 1988): 50–55, for a deeper analysis of the notions probed above.

respect to yield, duration being the first derivative. For the modified duration format, Equation (7-7), convexity is expressed as

$$\text{Convexity} = \frac{d^2P_0}{dR^2}\left(\frac{1}{P_0}\right) \tag{7-9}$$

where d^2P_0/dR^2 is the second derivative of the price-yield function, duration being the first derivative. (The second derivative is the change in the first derivative, namely the slope of the function.) The percentage change in bond price associated with convexity is

$$\frac{\Delta P_0}{P_0} = \frac{1}{2}(\text{Convexity})(\Delta R)^2 \tag{7-10}$$

ILLUSTRATION OF PRICE-CHANGE ESTIMATES USING MODIFIED DURATION AND CONVEXITY

An example best illustrates the calculations. Suppose we have a bond with an 8.4 percent coupon payable semiannually, with six years to final maturity and a yield-to-maturity of 9 percent. As a result, the bond's market price is set at a discount, being $97.26 using the $100 face value convention. We wish to calculate modified duration and convexity, and to estimate the change in price if yield should decline from 9 percent to 7 percent. The example is shown in Table 7-3.

Using the data in Table 7-3, we make the various calculations as follows.

$$\text{Duration} = \$936.54/\$97.26 = 9.629 \text{ half-years} = 4.81 \text{ years}$$

$$\text{Modified Duration} = 4.81/(1.045) = 4.61 \text{ years}$$

$$\text{Convexity} = \$11,246.34/(4 \times 1.045^2 \times \$97.26) = 26.47.$$

TABLE 7-3   Data Used for Modified Duration and Convexity Calculations (8.4% Coupon, 9.0% YTM and 6-Year Maturity)

(1)	(2)	(3)	(4)	(5)
			$[(1) \times (2)]$	
Period	Payment	$(2)/(1.045)^t$	$(1.045)^t$	$(3)(t)(t+1)$
1	$4.20	$4.02	$4.02	$8.04
2	4.20	3.85	7.69	23.08
3	4.20	3.68	11.04	44.17
4	4.20	3.52	14.09	70.44
5	4.20	3.37	16.85	101.11
6	4.20	3.23	19.35	135.46
7	4.20	3.09	21.60	172.83
8	4.20	2.95	23.63	212.64
9	4.20	2.83	25.44	254.36
10	4.20	2.70	27.04	297.49
11	4.20	2.59	28.47	341.62
12	104.20	61.44	737.32	9,585.10
		$97.26	$936.54	$11,246.34

With **semiannual compounding,** unlike annual compounding, you must divide by 4 to determine the bond's convexity.

The estimated price change with a decline in yield from 9 percent to 7 percent using only modified duration is

$$\text{Price change} = -4.61(-0.02) = +9.22\%$$

When we add convexity to modified duration, the estimate is

$$\text{Price change} = -4.61(-0.02) + \frac{1}{2}(26.47)(-0.02)^2 = +9.75\%$$

The addition of convexity recognizes the curvilinear relationship between price and yield, and improves the estimate dramatically when there is a sharp change in yield. The actual price increase mathematically is +9.77 percent, so we see that the estimate is close to the actual increase.

If yield were to increase instead of decrease by 2 percent, the estimated price change using modified duration is −9.22 percent, exactly opposite that shown earlier. With the addition of convexity, we have

$$\text{Price change} = -4.61(+0.02) + \frac{1}{2}(26.47)(+0.02)^2 = -8.69\%$$

Here the addition of convexity blunts the estimate using modified duration alone and in so doing serves as a curvature correction. While modified duration combined with convexity goes most of the way toward the true change in price, greater accuracy is given when you employ higher derivatives in the Taylor expansion (an expression of a mathematical function in calculus).

FURTHER OBSERVATIONS ON CONVEXITY

Several elements produce convexity in a bond. For one, the longer the maturity, usually the greater will be the convexity, all other things the same. The situation is similar with duration, where convexity increases at an increasing rate with duration. Holding yield and duration constant, the higher the coupon rate is, the greater the convexity is. As interest rates decrease, the convexity of a bond increases, and vice versa. These conditions result from the discounting effect in the convexity formula illustrated and are the more important characteristics explaining convexity.

Two bonds with the same duration but different convexities will experience different price changes when a significant change in interest rates occurs. Remember that for moderate changes, the correction for convexity is minimal. As a result, convexity is said to be a desirable property when interest rates are volatile. This is shown in Figure 7-7, where P_0 and R_0 are the present market prices and yields for two bonds with the same duration. We see that Bond 2 has greater convexity than Bond 1. Because there is greater upside price potential when interest rates decline and less downside movement when they increase, the greater convexity of Bond 2 is thought to be desirable.

PORTFOLIO MANAGEMENT

Different investment strategies will produce different results based on convexity. Suppose you wanted your bond portfolio to have a four-year average duration. One way

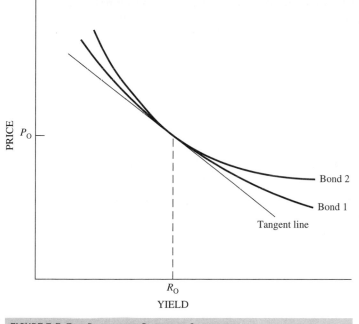

FIGURE 7-7 TWO BONDS WITH DIFFERENT CONVEXITIES

would be with a **bullet** strategy, where all bonds in the portfolio had a duration of exactly four years. Another would be a **barbell** strategy of short- and long-term bonds—say one half with a one-year duration and the other half with a seven-year duration. A third strategy, the **spread,** involves bonds across all durations, but which average four years. In general, the barbell strategy will have the greatest portfolio convexity and the bullet strategy the least. If the yield curve is steeply upward-sloping and is expected to flatten, a barbell strategy will produce better performance than will a bullet strategy. Contrarily, if the yield curve is flat and short-term rates are expected to fall relative to long-term rates, a bullet strategy will produce the best results.

Thus, the convexity of a bond portfolio can be managed depending on the investor's expectations about the volatility of interest rates. Lengthening or shortening the duration of a portfolio represents a "bet" on the direction of interest rates. As we have mentioned before, changing its convexity represents a "bet" on the variance of interest rates. For example, you might wish to increase the convexity of your bond portfolio if you expect interest rates to become more volatile. Contrarily, decreasing portfolio convexity is consistent with an expectation of decreasing volatility. It is important to recognize that we are talking about volatility over the long run. Short-term market volatility is not relevant in the context of managing a bond portfolio for convexity.

However, convexity combined with duration is not necessarily the perfect answer to the question, "What happens to the price of my bond when interest rates change?" As we have stated several times, both measures assume a flat yield curve with parallel shifts. We know that this is not the case, but the question is whether duration and convexity result in a reasonable approximation. If you maximize convexity in the bonds you choose for investment, you also maximize your exposure to twists in the term structure.[5] For example, to increase the convexity of a bond portfolio, you must barbell it. In so doing, you reduce your exposure to the intermediate-term sector of the yield curve. Should this intermediate-term portion decline more sharply in yield than the long-term sector, the barbell strategy may work to your disadvantage. The point of all of this is that convexity does not always help bond performance. Not only does it depend on what you have to pay for convexity in lesser yield to the investor, but also on what happens to the slope and curvature of the yield curve in relation to your duration strategy.

IMMUNIZATION OF BOND PORTFOLIOS

When investors have desired patterns of cash flows to be received at various future times, it is appropriate for them to arrange their bond portfolios in such a way that the desired patterns can be approximated. In other words, they **dedicate** their portfolios to a specific stream of cash payouts and hope to come as close as possible to this stream. To illustrate with a simple example, suppose we were concerned with realizing a single payment five years from today. If a pure discount default-free bond (zero coupon) existed with five years to maturity, it would be an easy matter. We would simply invest in that security. By buying enough of these bonds, we can assure ourselves of the receipt of X dollars five years from now. Because the future value of the position is known with certainty, it is said to be perfectly **immunized,** in that it is insensitive to subsequent fluctuations in interest rates.[6] Put another way, the payoff will precisely equal the amount desired at the end of the horizon.

IMMUNIZATION WITH COUPON ISSUES

Whenever possible, look first to pure discount Treasury securities. A large number of them presently exist. However, because of liquidity or pricing difficulties, you may have to turn to coupon bonds. Here we can also immunize, though usually less than perfectly.

With coupon bonds, two types of risk are germane: *price risk* and *coupon reinvestment risk*. Price risk is the risk that—with changing interest rates—the bond will need to be sold at a different price from what was expected. Of course, price risk could be reduced to zero if bonds whose maturity equaled the intended holding period were selected. However, there would still be coupon reinvestment risk, which is the risk associated with reinvesting the coupons received at yields that are different from the yield of the bond when it was purchased.

Together, these two risks represent the total risk associated with a bond investment for an investor with an intended holding period. Moreover, these risks work in opposite directions. An increase in interest rates reduces the price of a bond but increases the yield possible from reinvestment of coupons. In contrast, a decline in interest rates results in

---

[5] See Jacques A. Schnabel, "Is Benter Better? A Cautionary Note on Maximizing Convexity," *Financial Analysts Journal* 46 (January–February 1990): 78–79; Nelson J. Lacey and Sanjay K. Nawalkha, "Convexity, Risk, and Returns," *Journal of Fixed Income* 3 (December 1993): 72–79; and Wesley Phoa, "Can You Derive Market Volatility Forecasts from the Observed Yield Curve Convexity Bias?" *Journal of Fixed Income* 7 (June 1997): 43–54.

[6] Frederick M. Redington, "Review of the Principle of Life Office Valuations," *Journal of the Institute of Actuaries* 18 (1952): 286–340, was the first to develop the concept and to use the word *immunization.*

a price increase but lowers the yield possible from coupon reinvestment. Thus, the two types of risk are offsetting. To "immunize" a bond investment from subsequent interest-rate changes, these two risks must be balanced so that they are completely offsetting.

AN ILLUSTRATION

To envision this notion, suppose that $1,210 must be realized in two years.[7] At present, the term structure is flat with a 10 percent yield-to-maturity throughout. However, at the end of the first year, a one-time parallel shift in interest rates is possible, either to 12 percent or to 8 percent, as well as the possibility that interest rates will remain unchanged. Available for investment is a two-year bond with a 10 percent annual coupon. For an investment in this bond, the amounts realized at the end of two years under the three possible states of the world are as follows.

	Term Structure Level		
	8%	*10%*	*12%*
Principal payment	$1,000	$1,000	$1,000
Reinvested first-year coupon	108	110	112
Second-year coupon	100	100	100
	$1,208	$1,210	$1,212

Only if interest rates remain at 10 percent can the $1,210 desired at the end of the holding period be realized. If interest rates shift, the bond will not provide perfect immunization. The reason is that the reinvestment rate on the first-year coupon payment changes.

Suppose, however, that a 10 percent coupon bond with 2.1 years to maturity is available. Assume that this bond pays a $10 coupon at maturity (one tenth of a full-year coupon), together with $100 at the end of the first and second years. In this case, the bond will need to be sold before maturity. If interest rates turn out to be 8 percent, the market value of the bond at the end of two years, with one tenth of a year to go, will be approximately $1,002. That is, the $1,000 principal amount and $10 coupon at the end of one tenth of a year will be worth approximately $1,002 at the beginning of the period with an 8 percent discount rate. Contrarily, the market value of the bond at the end of two years will be approximately $998 if the term structure shifts from 10 percent to 12 percent. Therefore, the amounts realized at the end of two years for a 2.1-year bond will be

	Term Structure Level		
	8%	*10%*	*12%*
Market value on sale	$1,002	$1,000	$998
Reinvested first-year coupon	108	110	112
Second-year coupon	100	100	100
	$1,210	$1,210	$1,210

---

[7] This example comes from Jeffrey Skelton, "Recent Results in Term Structure Theory" (Berkeley Program in Finance Seminar, September 13, 1982).

In this case, the bond is perfectly immunized in the sense that the amounts received are exactly the same under all possible states. The changes in principal value at the end of two years exactly offset the changes in reinvestment rate on the first-year coupon.

Using Equation (7-1), the duration of the 2.1-year bond is

$$D = \frac{\dfrac{\$100(1)}{(1.10)} + \dfrac{\$100(2)}{(1.10)^2} + \dfrac{\$1{,}010(2.1)}{(1.10)^{2.1}}}{\dfrac{\$100}{(1.10)} + \dfrac{\$100}{(1.10)^2} + \dfrac{\$1{,}010}{(1.10)^{2.1}}} = 2.0 \text{ years}$$

Thus, the duration is equal to the intended holding period. Whenever the term structure is flat and only parallel shifts in interest rates occur, a bond investment is always immunized when its duration equals the intended holding period.[8] Moreover, one would want to immunize with noncallable bonds. For callable bonds, the actual horizon often is less than maturity due to the bond being called (see chapter 12).

Finally, as interest rates shift, so too does the duration of the portfolio, as illustrated in the previous section. To restore the desired duration, we must reimmunize the portfolio by adding and subtracting bonds. However, there are transactions costs to doing so. Consequently, there are trade-offs between how much slippage in duration is tolerable before reimmunization is necessary. When a sharp change in interest rates occurs, reimmunization will be required where it may not be with only moderate fluctuations. The crucial risk here is the one associated with the reinvestment of coupon cash flows. A number of investment banks and commercial banks provide computer services that endeavor to optimize the reimmunization of a bond portfolio over time.

FISHER-WEIL DURATION

In our illustration, we assumed a flat term structure of interest rates and parallel shifts. Clearly, these assumptions do not hold in practice. As a result, it usually is not possible to achieve perfect immunization simply by finding a coupon bond with a duration equal to the intended holding period. However, the relevant question is, "How effective is the use of Macaulay's duration measure in approximating perfect immunization?" If we could model precisely the stochastic processes governing interest-rate behavior, we could devise an investment strategy that would achieve perfect immunization. To learn whether this is feasible, let us turn to some of the literature.

Fisher and Weil, in their seminal paper on immunization, developed a duration measure that uses weights based on discount rates for each future period.[9] It is

$$D = \frac{\dfrac{C_1 \times 1}{(1 + r_1)}}{P_0} + \frac{\dfrac{C_2 \times 2}{(1 + r_1)(1 + r_2)}}{P_0} + \cdots + \frac{\dfrac{C_n \times n}{(1 + r_1)(1 + r_2)\cdots(1 + r_n)}}{P_0} \qquad \textbf{(7-11)}$$

---

8 For proof of this statement, see G. O. Bierwag and George G. Kaufman, "Coping with the Risk of Interest-Rate Fluctuations: A Note," *Journal of Business* 50 (July 1977): 364–70; and Paul H. Samuelson, "The Effect of Interest-Rate Increases on the Banking System," *American Economic Review,* 35 (March 1945): Appendix B.

9 Fisher and Weil, "Coping with the Risk."

where r_1, r_2, and r_n are estimates of future interest rates and P_0, as before, is the market price of the bond. By not using the yield-to-maturity in the weighting process, the Fisher-Weil duration measure avoids the assumption of a flat yield curve. However, parallel interest-rate shifts are still implied, because unexpected changes in interest rates are assumed to follow an additive stochastic process. To the extent that the shape of the yield curve changes in ways inconsistent with the parallel shift assumption, the Fisher-Weil duration measure will not provide a completely effective immunization technique.

MAPPING THE STOCHASTIC PROCESS

Others have mapped the stochastic process of interest-rate behavior in more sophisticated ways, thereby hoping to obtain better immunization. To the extent that the slope of the yield curve twists or becomes positively or negatively humped, known as a butterfly, more involved immunization strategies than duration may produce better results. A number of such term structure models were analyzed in the last chapter. Moreover, the convexity measure taken up in this chapter can be combined with duration to produce (perhaps) better results as well.

The key is correctly specifying the variance-covariance matrix of bond returns. If this can be done, the model should provide more effective immunization than is possible with a simple Macaulay duration strategy. By allowing for both additive and multiplicative shocks, one may be able to predict better the shape of the yield curve after an unexpected change in interest rates. Figure 7-8 illustrates the situation. The top panel shows the flat yield curve and parallel shifts associated with the simple Macaulay duration measure. The second panel shows the curvilinear yield curves possible with the Fisher-Weil duration measure, but where we still have parallel shifts. Finally, the last two panels illustrate the different shapes possible when multifactor models are employed.

For the latter models to do a better job, the interest-rate stochastic process must be properly specified. In other words, effective immunization can be achieved only if the interest-rate changes which in fact occur are in accord with the process assumed. In turn, this depends on the stability of the stochastic process over time. The proof of the pudding, of course, is in the eating.

TESTING FOR IMMUNIZATION EFFECTIVENESS

A number of tests have been conducted of various immunization strategies based on duration and stochastic models. Fisher and Weil were the first to perform such testing using the duration measures previously described. They concluded that effective immunization was possible. Tests of more sophisticated multifactor models indicate that while some do better than the simple Macaulay duration measure in immunization, it is not by a wide margin.[10] Certain models are proprietary, so we have little information on their usefulness in immunization other than that they are reputed to have promise. An advantage of stochastic models is that they are able to handle bonds having option features.

---

[10] See Robert Litterman and José Scheinkman, "Common Factors Affecting Bond Returns," *Journal of Fixed Income* 1 (June 1991): 54–61, whose results were described in the previous chapter. See also Brian Barrett, Thomas F. Gosnell, Jr., and Andrea J. Heuson, "Yield Curve Shifts and the Selection of Immunization Strategies," *Journal of Fixed Income* 5 (September 1995): 53–64; and Ram Willner, "A New Tool for Portfolio Managers: Level, Slope, and Curvature Durations," *Journal of Fixed Income* 6 (June 1996): 48–59.

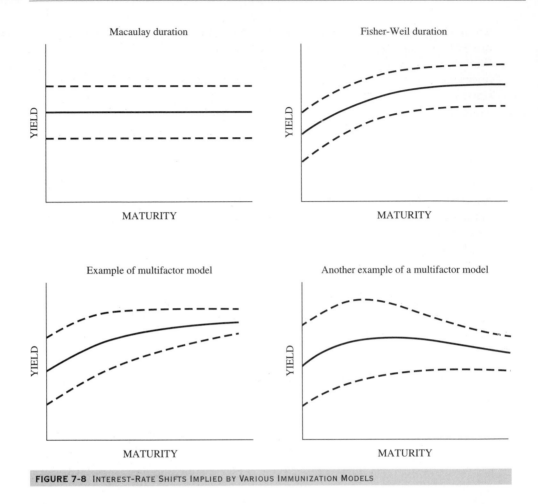

FIGURE 7-8 INTEREST-RATE SHIFTS IMPLIED BY VARIOUS IMMUNIZATION MODELS

However, the Macaulay duration measure continues to be used for immunization purposes. In addition to its simplicity and cost effectiveness, other models have not proven markedly superior over long periods of time. The problem with stochastic models is that the stochastic process governing interest-rate behavior is not stable or consistent over time. This makes past patterns of behavior less useful in predicting the future than is desirable.

ADDITIONAL IMMUNIZATION CONSIDERATIONS

In addition to the immunization procedures described, interest-rate futures markets can be used to obtain similar results. Instead of adjusting the duration of a portfolio by buying and selling bonds, an investor can buy and sell future contracts to achieve approximate immunization. One advantage of using the futures market is that costs of transactions are much less. Financial futures are the subject of chapter 9, and they represent a logical extension of our discussion of immunization.

For the most part, immunization involves a stream of liability outflows over time. Although it is possible to treat each liability outflow as a planning horizon and acquire a bond portfolio to immunize it, other ways are more efficient. A coupon bond generates cash flows that can be applied to more than one liability outflow. Consequently, it is more efficient to immunize in the overall context of the bond portfolio assembled. In this regard, computer routines have been developed for designing portfolios to immunize multiple liability outflows. A number of investment and commercial banks provide such services.

EQUILIBRATION BETWEEN COUPON AND NONCOUPON BOND MARKETS

The presence of zero-coupon bonds in the market began in 1981. At that time, certain corporations began to offer them, as well as bonds with low coupons relative to prevailing rates of interest. Zeros were truly a financial innovation aimed at exploiting what was previously an incomplete market.[11] Institutional investors, particularly pension funds, had an appetite for pure discount bonds for immunization purposes. In addition, other investors also had a desire to eliminate reinvestment risk and/or to make bets on the future course of interest rates using the longest duration bond possible. Whereas the longest duration coupon bond available is only about 14 years, zero-coupon bonds with durations of 30 years are available.

In addition to corporations, agencies of the government, such as the Federal National Mortgage Association (Fannie Mae), and municipalities have been direct issuers of zero-coupon bonds. To the extent the market is incomplete, such issuers tailor their security offerings to the unfulfilled desires of investors and thereby achieve an interest-cost advantage.

COUPON STRIPPING

In addition to original pure discount bonds, a process known as **coupon stripping**—the separation of the coupons from the principal amount of a bond—began in 1982. Once separated, each coupon and each principal payment become separate zero-coupon bonds. For example, if a 6 percent coupon, 5-year bond issue totaling $10 million were stripped, there would be $300,000 in zero-coupon bonds maturing every six months for five years and a $10 million, 5-year, zero-coupon bond. The stripping is indirect.

If an investment bank does the stripping, it first buys a Treasury security and places it in an irrevocable trust. Then participations are sold in the coupon and principal payments. Each participation unit of $1,000 represents partial ownership in a future coupon or a principal payment. When the trust company receives the payment from the Treasury, it pays the participation holders and the units are retired. Thus, each participation unit is a zero-coupon bond and will trade in the market at the appropriate spot rate of interest. Known as *receipt products,* they were created by a number of investment banks.

In 1985, the Treasury introduced its own coupon-strippable product by designating some of its notes and bonds as eligible for stripping. This allows the holder to turn in the

---

[11]   Complete markets exist when every contingency in the world corresponds to a distinct marketable security. Incomplete markets exist when the number and types of securities available do not span these contingencies.

instrument for the zero-coupon parts. However, the unit size is $1,000 for each part. If an investor holds an 11-year, 8 percent bond, semiannual coupon payments of $40 occur for each $1,000 face value bond held. Therefore, one would need $1,000/$40 = 25 bonds for things to work out evenly. Turning the 25 bonds in to the Treasury, the investor obtains 22 zero-coupon instruments entitling him or her to receive $1,000 each six months over the next 11 years and one zero-coupon bond entitling him or her to receive $25,000 as a final principal payment at the end of 11 years. Therefore, the total cash inflow at the end of 11 years is $26,000.

This Treasury product is known as Separate Trading of Registered Interest and Principal of Securities **(STRIPS).** Since their origin in 1985, STRIPS have become the dominant zero-coupon instrument, displacing the receipt-type products issued by investment banks. Registered ownership of STRIPS is by book entry with the Federal Reserve Bank, and each bond created carries a separate CUSIP number for identification. Because callable bonds cannot be easily stripped, the Treasury has focused its borrowings in recent years on noncallable bonds. This accommodates the demand for zero-coupon bonds.

In 1987, the Treasury established procedures for reconstituting the STRIPS. This simply means that one can rebundle the zero-coupon parts and receive the whole bond. In reconstituting, the holder must turn in the previous coupon and principal parts, denoted by *bp* for stripped principal for a bond, by *bn* for stripped principal for a Treasury note, and by *ci* for the stripped coupon. Even though zero-coupon principal and coupon payments have the same maturity and economically are the same, they cannot be used interchangeably in reconstitution. As it is sometimes difficult to acquire principal STRIPS for reconstitution, differential demand causes them to sell at modestly higher prices than coupon STRIPS of identical maturity. Presently, more than 40 percent of all Treasury bonds are held in STRIPS form, whereas around 20 percent of all Treasury notes (original maturity of 2 to 10 years) are held in STRIPS form.

TERM STRUCTURE OF PURE DISCOUNT BONDS

The presence of pure discount instruments and the secondary market for such instruments allow a yield curve based on them to be constructed. This yield curve will differ from a yield curve based on coupon-paying bonds. The former is represented by yield observations for a single payment at the end of year *n*. For coupon-paying bonds, the yield observations pertain to a principal payment at the end of year *n*, together with coupon payments through year *n*. In this case, yield-to-maturity is a weighted average of the pure discount rates applicable to each of the coupon and principal payments. Obviously, the durations of the two bonds are different, and this difference increases with the maturity of the observation, as well as with the coupon rate of the coupon bond. In short, apples and oranges are involved in the construction of the two yield curves.

A hypothetical example of the two yield curves is seen in Figure 7-9. When the yield curve for coupon bonds is upward-sloping, the yield curve for zero-coupon bonds should be above it. This is simply to say that the end point (for zero-coupon bonds) must be greater than the weighted average (for coupon bonds) of all the pure discount rates through the end point. The opposite should occur when the yield curve for coupon bonds is downward-sloping. While the yield curve for coupon bonds should bear a precise relationship with the yield curve for zero-coupon bonds, it will depend on the equilibration between the markets for the two types of bonds.

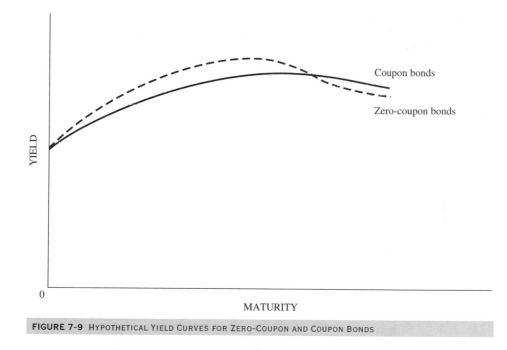

FIGURE 7-9 HYPOTHETICAL YIELD CURVES FOR ZERO-COUPON AND COUPON BONDS

ARBITRAGE EFFICIENCY BETWEEN THE MARKETS

For the two markets to be in equilibrium, arbitrage opportunities must be absent. The equilibration force is the profit motive for being either a coupon stripper or a bond reconstitutor. Market participants will want to be one or the other depending on which way a profit can be made. In equilibrium, there will be an indifference between the two markets.

For a bond to be a candidate for coupon stripping, the sum of its parts must be worth more than the whole bond. We simply take the STRIP market prices for each semi-annual maturity and for the final principal maturity, multiply them times their respective payment amounts, sum them, and then compare this sum with the settlement price of the coupon bond. (See chapter 4 for how to calculate settlement price.) The procedure is illustrated in Table 7-4.

If the sum of the coupon and principal parts, which are present values of single-payment instruments, exceeds the coupon bond's settlement price, the bond would be profitable to coupon strip. If the sum of the parts is less than the whole, an arbitrager would want to be a reconstitutor. By buying the parts in the market, reconstituting them, and selling the whole bond, the arbitrager can earn a profit. If the sum of the parts equals the bond's settlement price, of course, no opportunity exists for arbitrage. In Table 7-4, we see that the sum of the parts, $104.02, almost equals the settlement price of the note, $104.04. With transactions costs, arbitrage possibilities do not exist.

The actions of coupon strippers and bond reconstitutors should bring about an equilibration between coupon and noncoupon bonds. As a result, the zero-coupon yield curve will bear a precise relationship to the coupon yield curve, as illustrated in Figure 7-9. From time to time, however, there appear to be moderate arbitrage profit opportunities from stripping Treasury securities, and minor opportunities from

TABLE 7-4   Arbitrage Efficiency between Coupon and Zero-Coupon Treasuries February 2, 1999

5½% Note of May, 2003 has a market price of $102.52 and a yield to maturity of 4.84 percent. The settlement price is $104.04 based on linear accrual of the next coupon, which is 100 days in the future with 181 days between payments. (See chapter 4.)

For each payment, the following STRIPS prices prevailed on February 2, 1999.

Date	Payment	STRIPS Price	Product
May 1999	$2.75	$98.719	$2.715
Nov. 1999	2.75	96.469	2.653
May 2000	2.75	94.250	2.592
Nov. 2000	2.75	92.063	2.532
May 2001	2.75	89.938	2.473
Nov. 2001	2.75	87.813	2.415
May 2002	2.75	85.750	2.358
Nov. 2002	2.75	84.250	2.317
May 2003	102.75	81.719	83.966
		Sum	$104.021

reconstitution. When they arise, such opportunities may be due to differences in liquidity between the two markets for particular maturity segments.[12]

Demand has been strong for the longest-term, zero-coupon bonds. For one thing, newly issued 30-year Treasury bonds have better liquidity than earlier-issued, 30-year bonds. Known as on-the-run bonds, they enjoy higher demand than somewhat shorter-term off-the-run bonds. This increased demand is reflected also in the zero-coupon market. Additionally, the longest-term STRIPS are sought for immunization purposes, for managing the duration of a bond portfolio, and for speculative purposes. The dip at the long-term end of the yield curve is reflected in Figure 7-9, though it is exaggerated somewhat for purposes of illustration. With arbitrage between the zero-coupon and coupon bond markets, the dip at the end is reflected in both yield curves.

❖ SUMMARY

Volatility in bond prices is due to a number of things. The price/yield relationship, the focus of this chapter, depends on maturity and on the coupon rate: The lower the coupon is, the greater the price change is for a given shift in interest rates. The reason is that more of the total return is realized at maturity when the principal is paid than with in-

---

[12]   Mark Grinblatt and Francis Longstaff, "Financial Innovation and the Role of Derivative Securities: An Empirical Analysis of the Treasury STRIPS Program," working paper, Anderson School at University of California at Los Angeles (January 1996). See also Kok Chew Lim and Miles Livingston, "Stripping of Treasury Securities and Segmentation in the Treasury Securities Market," *Journal of Fixed Income* 4 (March 1995): 88–94.

terim coupon payments. The problems associated with the coupon effect led to the development of the duration measure, which is a time-weighted average of interest and principal payments. Duration represents the average life of an investment on a present-value basis.

For bonds trading at par or above, duration increases at a decreasing rate with maturity, while for discount bonds it eventually declines with maturity. Each time a coupon is paid, the duration of the bond temporarily increases. When interest rates change, so does duration, becoming shorter when interest rates rise and vice versa. Volatility is directly linked to duration, and a formula was presented giving a precise relationship. Instead of duration, many use modified duration when analyzing volatility, which is duration divided by 1 plus the yield.

Duration implies a linear relationship between price and yield. To take account of the curvature of the "true" relationship, a convexity measure was introduced. This measure is the second derivative of price with respect to yield, duration being the first. A convexity correction factor is added to the duration estimate of the price change accompanying a yield change to give, hopefully, a better estimate. However, both measures assume a flat yield curve and parallel shifts.

Immunization consists of arranging a bond portfolio so that its payouts approximate a desired stream of payouts as nearly as possible. A single payout is perfectly immunized if it is insensitive to subsequent fluctuations in interest rates. Whenever feasible, one should immunize with pure discount bonds. With coupon bonds, immunization is more difficult. Both price risk and coupon reinvestment risk are involved, and these risks work in opposite directions. If the term structure were flat and only parallel interest-rate shifts occurred, perfect immunization could be achieved by finding a bond whose duration equaled the intended holding period. As these assumptions do not hold in practice, a number of authors have devised more complicated models to map the stochastic processes governing interest-rate fluctuations.

In recent years, there have been a number of zero-coupon, original-issue bonds, as well as indirect zero-coupon bonds, that result from coupon stripping. The existence of an incomplete market made such instruments valuable in satisfying the needs of certain investors. Equilibration between coupon and noncoupon markets occurs through arbitrage. Market participants will be either coupon strippers or bond reconstitutors, depending on whether the parts are worth more than the whole bond or vice versa.

❖ SELECTED REFERENCES

Barrett, Brian, Thomas F. Gosnell, Jr., and Andrea J. Heuson, "Yield Curve Shifts and the Selection of Immunization Strategies," *Journal of Fixed Income* 5 (September 1995): 53–64.

Bierwag, Gerald O., "The Ho-Lee Binomial Stochastic Process and Duration," *Journal of Fixed Income* 6 (September 1996): 76–87.

Bierwag, G. O., George G. Kaufman, and Alden L. Toevs, "Duration: Its Development and Use in Bond Portfolio Management," *Financial Analysts Journal* 39 (July–August 1983): 15–35.

Bierwag, G. O., George G. Kaufman, and Alden L. Toevs, eds., *Innovations in Bond Portfolio Management.* Greenwich, CT: JAI Press, 1983.

Chance, Don M., and James V. Jordan, "Duration, Convexity, and Time as Components of Bond Returns," *Journal of Fixed Income* 6 (September 1996): 88–96.

Cox, John C., Jonathan E. Ingersoll, Jr., and Stephen A. Ross, "Duration and the Measurement of Basis Risk," *Journal of Business,* 52 (January 1979): 51–61.

Dattatreya, Ravi E., and Frank J. Fabozzi, "The Risk-Point Method for Measuring and Controlling Yield Curve Risk," *Financial Analysts Journal* 51 (July–August 1995): 45–54.

Dolan, Charles P., "Forecasting the Yield Curve Shape: Evidence in Global Markets," *Journal of Fixed Income* 9 (June 1999): 92–99.

Fabozzi, Frank J., *Bond Markets, Analysis and Strategies,* 4th ed., chapter 4. Upper Saddle River, NJ: Prentice Hall, 2000.

Fisher, Lawrence, and Roman L. Weil, "Coping with the Risk of Interest-Rate Fluctuations: Returns of Bondholders from Naive and Optimal Strategies," *Journal of Business* 44 (October 1971): 408–31.

Fong, H. Gifford, and Oldrich A. Vasicek, "A Risk Minimizing Strategy for Portfolio Immunization," *Journal of Finance* 39 (December 1984): 1541–46.

Ho, Thomas S. Y., "Key Rate Durations: Measures of Interest Rate Risks," *Journal of Fixed Income* 2 (September 1992): 29–44.

Hopewell, Michael H., and George G. Kaufman, "Bond Price Volatility and Term to Maturity: A Generalized Respecification," *American Economic Review* 63 (September 1973): 749–53.

Ilmanen, Antti, "How Well Does Duration Measure Interest Rate Risk?" *Journal of Fixed Income* 1 (March 1992): 43–51.

Ilmanen, Antti, and Ray Iwanowski, "Dynamics of the Shape of the Yield Curve," *Journal of Fixed Income* 7 (September 1997): 47–60.

Litterman, Robert, and José Scheinkman, "Common Factors Affecting Bond Returns," *Journal of Fixed Income* 1 (June 1991): 54–61.

Macaulay, Frederick R., *Some Theoretical Problems Suggested by the Movements of Interest Rates, Bond Yields, and Stock Prices in the United States since 1856.* New York: National Bureau of Economic Research, 1938.

Mann, Steven V., "Duration and Convexity Measures When the Yield Curve Changes Shape," *Journal of Financial Engineering* 7 (March 1998): 35–58.

Phoa, Wesley, "Can You Derive Market Volatility Forecasts from the Observed Yield Curve Convexity Bias?" *Journal of Fixed Income* 7 (June 1997): 43–54.

Redington, Frederick M., "Review of the Principle of Life Office Valuations," *Journal of the Institute of Actuaries* 18 (1952): 286–340.

Stanhouse, Bryan, and Duane Stock, "How Changes in Bond Call Features Affect Coupon Rates," *Journal of Applied Corporate Finance,* 12 (Spring 1999): 92–99.

———, "The Impact of Volatility on Duration of Amortizing Debt with Embedded Call Options," *Journal of Fixed Income,* 8 (September 1998), 87–94.

Weil, Roman L., "Macaulay's Duration: An Appreciation." *Journal of Business* 46 (October 1973): 589–92.

Willner, Ram, "A New Tool for Portfolio Managers: Level, Slope, and Curvature Durations," *Journal of Fixed Income* 6 (June 1996): 48–59.

CHAPTER 8

DEFAULT AND LIQUIDITY RISK

In chapters 6 and 7, we examined two reasons for relative differences in market rates of interest—the maturity of a bond and its coupon rate. We also explored the volatility of bond prices as it relates to them. These inquiries gave us some feel for the effect of changing interest rates on risk.

In this chapter, additional risk dimensions are examined—the default risk of a security and its liquidity. The former is the risk that the borrower will default in the contractual payment of principal or interest. The default-risk structure of interest rates depicts the relationship between the yield on securities and their risk of default, holding all other factors constant. The relationship between yield and default risk may be similar to that shown in Figure 8-1. In the figure, yield is plotted along the vertical axis and risk along the horizontal. The intercept on the vertical axis represents the yield on a default-free security; for all practical purposes, it represents the yield on Treasury securities. The figure shows that investors demand a higher yield as perceived risk of default rises.

This chapter deals with default risk on individual fixed-income securities and grades of such securities. In chapter 11, we explore default risk as it pertains to derivative securities like interest-rate swaps. In addition, credit derivatives are examined in that chapter.

RISK PREMIUMS AND PROMISED RATES

A **risk premium** is defined as the differential in yield between a security being studied and a default-free one, with all factors other than default risk being held constant. It is represented in Figure 8-1 by the distance on the vertical axis between the intercept and the yield on the security being studied.

The **promised rate** on a security is the *ex ante* yield at a moment in time. If a corporation issues a bond with an 8 percent coupon rate at a price of $1,000 to the public, the rate promised by the issuer is 8 percent. However, if the bond rises in price so that one month later it yields 7½ percent to maturity, the promised rate at that time would be 7½ percent. Note that the promised rate is not necessarily the rate actually realized if the bond is held to maturity.

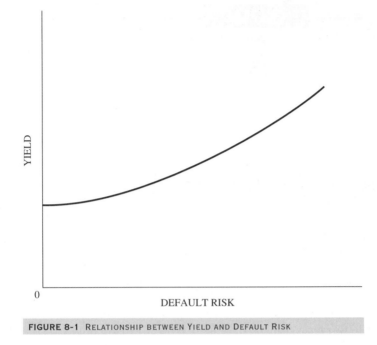

FIGURE 8-1 RELATIONSHIP BETWEEN YIELD AND DEFAULT RISK

The **realized rate** is the rate of discount that equates all payments actually received by investors, including the final principal payment, with the market price of the security at the time the security was purchased. Any difference between the promised rate at the time the security was bought and the realized rate is known as the **loss rate** attributable to default.[1] It is clear that if the issuer does not default in the payment of principal and interest, the promised and the realized rates are the same.

At any moment in time, the risk structure of interest rates is determined by differences between promised rates and **expected rates**—the latter being the rate investors at the margin actually expect to receive. If default is a possibility, the expected yield on a security will be less than the promised one. To carry this reasoning one step further, if financial markets were perfect and investors' risk neutral, the rate expected by investors at the margin would equal the rate on a default-free security. In other words, the difference between the promised rate and the expected rate on a security would correspond to the expected default loss defined earlier.

DISTRIBUTION OF POSSIBLE RETURNS

To better understand this notion, consider the behavior of a prospective investor. At some moment, the investor foresees a number of possible returns associated with owning a risky, fixed-income security. We might picture the investor forming a subjective probability distribution of these returns. This distribution is not symmetrical, but highly

---

[1] This assumes that we have held constant all other factors—in particular, callability. See W. Braddock Hickman, *Corporate Bond Quality and Investor Experience* (New York: National Bureau of Economic Research, 1958), introductory chapter and pp. 64–66.

skewed to the left. For the typical fixed-income security, it is highly probable that the issuer will meet all principal and interest payments. However, no probability exists for the realized yield to exceed the promised yield, assuming the security is held to maturity. The promised rate, then, represents the highest return possible from holding the security to maturity. However, if the issuer defaults in any of the principal or interest payments, the realized rate will be less than this promised rate.

The situation is illustrated in Figure 8-2. The maximum return possible is seen to be the promised yield. Legally, an issuer defaults any time it is unable to make an interest or principal payment. However, degrees of default vary from a simple postponement of an interest payment from one semiannual period to the next, all the way to liquidation involving legal procedures. For each possibility, a probability is attached and the possibilities ordered according to the magnitude of realized return to form the probability distribution shown in the figure. The farther to the left in the figure, the higher is the degree of default. The expected rate for a security is the weighted average of all possible returns. The **expected default loss** is simply the difference between the promised and expected rates.

The expected default loss will correspond to the market risk premium, defined as the differential between the promised yield and the yield on a comparable risk-free security, only if the investor is risk neutral. To the extent that investors at the margin are risk averse and demand a higher return for dispersion and skewness, the risk premium in the marketplace will exceed the default loss expected by these investors.

In summary, investors are assumed to form subjective probability distributions of possible realized returns for each security. Differences in these probability distributions will determine differences in default-risk premiums for the securities and, accordingly, will determine yield differentials between the securities. Figure 8-3 illustrates several of these distributions. The first probability distribution, a, represents the least risky security, while the last, c, is the most risky. On the basis of probability distributions of this sort, risk premiums are assumed to be determined in the market. However, these premiums may or may not conform to the expected default loss.

FIGURE 8-2 DISTRIBUTION OF POSSIBLE RETURNS

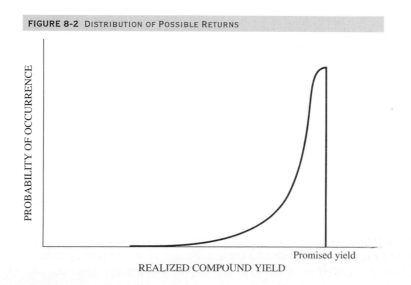

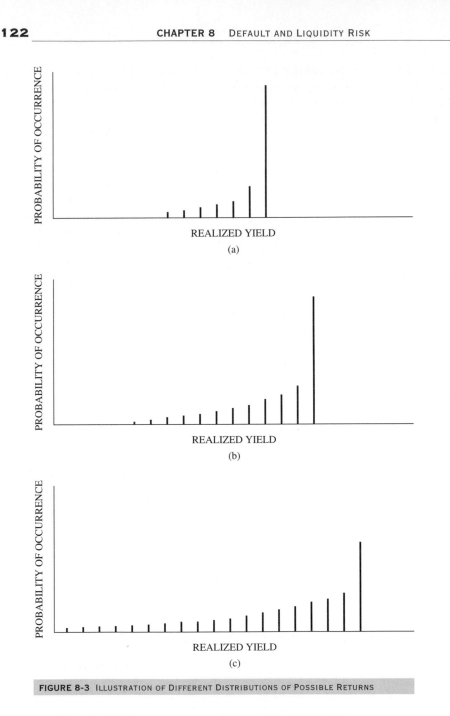

FIGURE 8-3 ILLUSTRATION OF DIFFERENT DISTRIBUTIONS OF POSSIBLE RETURNS

CREDIT RATINGS AND RISK PREMIUMS

For the typical investor, expected returns and risk are judged not by a subjectively for-mulated probability distribution of possible returns but by the credit rating assigned to the bond by investment agencies. The principal rating agencies are Moody's Investors Service and Standard & Poor's. Fitch and Duff & Phelps also rate corporations' credit-worthiness but are not called on to do so nearly as often as are the first two. The issuer of a new corporate or municipal bond contracts with one or more agencies to evaluate and rate the bond as well as to update the rating throughout the bond's life. For this service, the issuer pays a fee that varies with the size and type of security being issued. Moody's and Standard & Poor's rate all U.S. domestic security issues registered with the Securities and Exchange Commission. In some cases, the rating will be unsolicited by the issuer, and this has created a good deal of controversy. While the assignment of a rating for a new issue is current, changes in ratings of existing bond issues tend to lag behind the events that prompt the change. More will be said about this shortly.

Based on their evaluations of a bond issue, the agencies give their opinion in the form of letter grades, which are published for use by investors. In their ratings, the agencies attempt to rank issues according to the probability of default. The highest-grade bonds, whose risk of default is felt to be negligible, are rated triple A. The ratings used by the two agencies, as well as brief descriptions, are shown in Table 8-1. The first four grades in either case are considered to represent **investment-quality** issues, whereas other rated bonds are considered **speculative.** For each rating category, a modifier of 1, 2, or 3 is applied in the case of Moody's (Standard & Poor's uses +, no notation, or − for its modifier). For example, Aa–1 means that a security is in the higher end of the Aa rating category. Baa–3 indicates that it is in the lower end of the Baa category.

Both agencies have a Credit Watch list that alerts investors when the agency is considering a change in rating for a particular borrower. The direction of the change is indicated. Upon studying the situation, the agency may determine that a change in rating is not supported. However, more often than not, a change does occur. In a number of cases, the addition of a company to the Credit Watch list is unexpected, and bond and stock prices react to the announcement.[2] The same occurs for actual rating changes. If the change is unanticipated, a price reaction typically results. If anticipated, market prices already will have adjusted. Because the two agencies work independently, they sometimes attach different ratings to a bond issue; this is known as a split rating. The yield on a split-rated bond tends to be an average of yields for the higher and lower rating categories.[3]

During the last two decades, the number of downgrades of corporate bond ratings has exceeded the number of upgrades. This could be due to cyclical effects or to a general lessening in corporate debt quality. However, it also may be that the rating agencies are getting tougher in the standards they apply. Testing empirically the latter proposition, Blume, Lim, and MacKinlay find support for the notion that agencies have used ever-more-stringent standards in assigning ratings.[4]

A number of scholars have investigated the reasons a rating agency assigns a particular rating. (See references at the end of the chapter.) Using the rating as the dependent variable, they have searched for statistically significant relationships between this variable and measures of past performance. For corporate debt, higher ratings

---

[2] John R. M. Hand, Robert W. Holthausen, and Richard W. Leftwich, "The Effect of Bond Rating Agency Announcements on Bond and Stock Prices," *Journal of Finance* 47 (June 1992): 733–52.

[3] For a review and analysis of credit raters, see Richard Cantor and Frank Packer, "The Credit Rating Industry," *Journal of Fixed Income* 5 (December 1995): 10–34; and Jeff Jewell and Miles Livingston, "Split Ratings, Bond Yields, and Underwriter Spreads," *Journal of Financial Research* 21 (Summer 1998): 185–204.

[4] Marshall E. Blume, Felix Lim, and A. Craig MacKinlay, "The Declining Credit Quality of U.S. Corporate Debt: Myth or Reality?" *Journal of Finance* 53 (August 1998): 1389–1413.

TABLE 8-1	Credit Ratings by Investment Agencies
Moody's	***Explanation***
Aaa	Best quality
Aa	High quality
A	Upper medium grade
Baa	Medium grade
Ba	Possess speculative elements
B	Generally lack characteristics of a desirable investment
Caa	Poor standing; may be in default
Ca	Highly speculative; often in default
C	Lowest grade; extremely poor prospects

Standard & Poor's	***Explanation***
AAA	Highest rating; extremely strong capacity to pay interest and principal
AA	Very strong capacity to pay
A	Strong capacity to pay
BBB	Adequate capacity to pay
BB	Uncertainties that could lead to inadequate capacity to pay
B	Greater vulnerability to default, but currently has the capacity to pay
CCC	Vulnerable to default
CC	For debt subordinated to that with CCC rating
C	For debt subordinated to that with CCC− rating; or bankruptcy petition has been filed
D	In payment default

generally are associated with (1) lower debt ratios, (2) higher return-on-asset ratios, (3) lower relative variation in earnings over time, (4) larger companies, (5) higher-interest coverage ratios, and (6) lack of subordination. The studies varied in explanatory variables employed and in the sample periods tested. Overall, these studies were able to predict correctly anywhere from 60 percent to 90 percent of the ratings assigned by the rating agencies.

LIQUIDITY RISK

As discussed in chapter 1, **liquidity** is the ability to realize value in money. It has several dimensions: the length of time to convert the asset into money; the transaction costs involved; and the certainty of price realized. While default risk and liquidity risk are interelated, in that a greater probability of default is associated with lesser liquidity, the correlation is less than perfect. A bond can have a low probability of default but not be very liquid. All of this discussion pertains to trades in the **secondary market,** after original issuance. Liquidity has several practical aspects.

BID-ASK SPREADS AND PRICE CONCESSIONS

The **bid-ask spread** is one measure of liquidity; the lower the spread the greater the liquidity. Using the $100 face-value convention for corporate bonds, a bid-ask spread of $0.04, or 4 basis points, is consistent with good liquidity. This low spread will occur only for an investment-grade bond with a large amount of bonds outstanding (e.g., MCI-WorldCom). A spread of $0.10, or 10 basis points, for an investment-grade bond indicates lesser liquidity (e.g., Hertz Corporation). For speculative-grade bonds, Ba/BB and lower, spreads of $1.00, 100 basis points, or more are typical. Price spreads can get as high as $5.00, indicating considerable illiquidity and probably a chaotic market. Apart from the spread quoted by a dealer, a price concession may be necessary to sell a specific security. If the trade is large, say 12 percent of the total amount outstanding, or small in dollar amount, say $500,000, the actual bid price may be lower than that quoted. In chaotic markets and "flights to quality," dealers may be unwilling to buy a corporate bond at any price. This happened in October of 1998, triggered by problems in Russia, Asia, and Latin America. In this environment, no bid-ask quotation is provided, and if a sale occurs it must be at substantial price concession from the last traded price.

   Liquidity in the market tends to go in waves. In the early 1990s, liquidity was considerable. As interest rates escalated sharply in 1994, corporate bonds overall became less liquid. Liquidity recovered in 1995 through 1997, but it was not as great as before. Mid-1998 through 1999 was a period of relative illiquidity, particularly for lower-grade bonds. During this time, investment banks reduced rather sharply their **trading inventories** of bonds. Inventories are bonds owned outright, from which dealers sell and buy in order to capture a trading profit. Dealers can quote bid and ask prices without holding inventory in a particular bond, but here they must go into the market as agent for their customer and buy or sell the security. In their reduction of trading inventories in the late 1990s, investment banks caused the corporate bond market to be less liquid.

SIZE AND TIERING

The greater the **size** of a bond issue is, the greater its liquidity is, all other things the same. This means that when more bonds are outstanding, more secondary-market trades will occur and the bond's liquidity will be greater. Size and **tiering** go together in the corporate bond market. Large, well-known corporate issuers enjoy good liquidity for their bonds. The top tier includes telecommunications, media, cable, pharmaceuticals, automotive, and entertainment industries. The bottom tier, at the time of this writing, included gaming, metals, real-estate investment trusts, and textiles. If you hold a lower-grade corporate bond in the bottom tier, it is difficult to sell.

ON-THE-RUN vs. OFF-THE-RUN SECURITIES

Another manifestation of liquidity relates to whether a security has been issued recently. Recently issued securities are said to be on-the-run. They tend to be used for benchmark pricing and to trade more. After aging and/or after a like bond is issued, the security becomes off-the-run. It is traded less often and is less liquid. Admittedly, this statement includes a "self-fulfilling prophecy." The liquidity phenomenon is most evident in the Treasury market, as described in chapter 6. On-the-run 30-year Treasury bonds have traded at yields anywhere from 5 to 30 basis points lower than yields for off-the-run bonds. In late 1999, the yield spread was in the upper part of the range. So even for U.S. Treasury securities, generally considered to be the most liquid bond market in the world, various securities have differences in liquidity. The same phenomenon prevails for corporate and municipal bonds, although it is more difficult to measure.

EMPIRICAL EVIDENCE ON DEFAULT LOSSES

It is useful now to review certain empirical evidence. This evidence pertains only to default risk, there being virtually no studies of liquidity risk. The opportunity to test for default depends on an economic downturn. In a severe economic downturn, a significant number of issues are likely to default. In other words, the probability of default on most securities is small; it takes a sharp downturn to shake out those issuers possessing significant default risk. In this century, the Depression of the 1930s provided the most valid test.

If risk premiums consistently equaled expected default losses by investors at the margin, the average difference between the promised yield at time t and the realized yield at maturity would be expected to equal the average risk premium at time t for a large sample of bonds over a long period of time. The most comprehensive testing of this sort has been by Hickman, who investigated the default experience of fixed-income, single-maturity corporate bonds over the period 1900–1943.[5] The sample consisted of all bonds over $5 million and a 10 percent sample of smaller issues. For the sample, "life span" default rates were computed, depicting the proportion of bonds offered that defaulted between the offering date and extinguishment. In addition, loss rates representing the difference between promised and realized rates were computed.

Hickman's loss rate differed somewhat from the rate used earlier to measure default loss. For one thing, the call feature was not held constant. In addition, certain biases were introduced as a result of the sample period ending January 1, 1944—a time of unusually low interest rates. Harold G. Fraine and Robert H. Mills attempted to correct for these biases by removing the effect of market influences on final liquidating values from the estimates of realized yields and loss rates.[6] The authors derived modified averages for large corporate bonds, using Hickman's data for the period 1900–1943. For bonds that did not default and whose realized yield was in excess of the promised one, they substituted the contractual yield for the realized yield. After these substitutions were made, modified realized yields were computed; these yields are shown in Table 8-2. The results show that when realized yields are modified for gains attributable to changes in interest rates, the realized yield is less than the promised one. Still, the difference between the two yields was somewhat smaller than the typical yield spread between corporate and government securities (the risk premium as defined) from 1900 to 1943. Therefore, the results still appear to be biased.

In a follow-up study, Thomas R. Atkinson extends the analysis of corporate bond quality through 1965.[7] Average annual default rates for the period 1900–1965 were com-

---

[5] Hickman, *Corporate Bond Quality*.

[6] Harold G. Fraine and Robert H. Mills. "Effects of Defaults and Credit Deterioration on Yields of Corporate Bonds," *Journal of Finance* 16 (September 1961): 423–34.

[7] Thomas R. Atkinson, *Trends in Corporate Bond Quality* (New York: National Bureau of Economic Research, 1967).

TABLE 8-2 Promised versus Modified Realized Yields, 1900–1943

Agency Rating	Weighted Mean Annual Rate	
	Promised Yield (%)	*Modified Realized Yield (%)*
I	4.5	4.3
II	4.5	4.3
III	4.9	4.3
IV	5.4	4.5
I-III	4.7	4.3
I-IV	4.8	4.3

Source: Harold G. Fraine and Robert H. Mills, "Effects of Defaults and Credit Deterioration on Yields of Corporate Bonds," *Journal of Finance* 16 (September 1961): 428.

puted. These ratios represent the amount of bonds that went into default during a year divided by the amount of bonds *not* in default at the beginning of the year. The average annual default rates were 2.0 percent in the 1910–1919 decade, 3.2 percent in the Depression of the 1930s, and much lower in other decades. Tying in with the two previous studies, default rates averaged 1.7 percent for the 1900–1943 period and only 0.1 percent for the 1944–1965 period.

Similar in many ways to the Atkinson study, George H. Hempel studied the default experience for municipal securities over the period 1837–1965.[8] The results are reported in terms of number of defaults, as opposed to ratio of default or the relative amount of defaults in dollar terms. As the total number of state and local governments increased dramatically over the period studied, there is a bias toward exaggerating the default experience in the later years relative to the earlier ones. These problems notwithstanding, the numbers are still revealing. They suggest that defaults increase significantly in periods of major depressions. Studying these depressions in more detail, Hempel found the results shown in the following chart.

Depression	*Percent of Debt Outstanding Defaulting*
1837–1843	51.0
1873–1879	24.5
1893–1899	10.0
1929–1937	15.4

Furthermore, he found that most payment problems occurred in the latter stages of a depression. For milder economic reversals, significant debt payment problems did not

---

[8] George H. Hempel, *The Postwar Quality of State and Local Debt* (New York: National Bureau of Economic Research, 1971).

128   CHAPTER 8   DEFAULT AND LIQUIDITY RISK

seem to occur, although some municipalities failed even in good times. As with corporate bonds, then, only a severe economic downturn will cause significant default losses and differences between promised and realized returns for municipal bonds.

MORE RECENT EXPERIENCE

During the last several decades, a distinct relationship has been evident between default rates/losses and credit rating. **Moody's Investors Service** calculates 12-month trailing default rates for the corporate debt that they rate.[9] On the basis of data for 1980–1998, a transition matrix is formed to see what happens to various-grade bonds in going from one year to the next. This matrix is seen in Table 8-3. Take the Ba grade, the top of the noninvestment grades. The chance is 76.5 percent that a bond in this category will remain so for the next year. The chance is 5.2 percent that it will be upgraded to a rating of Baa; 7.4 percent that it will be downgraded to a single B rating; 0.5 percent that it will be downgraded to grade Caa, Ca, or single C; and the chance of default is 1.3 percent. Finally, the chance is 8.5 percent that the bond will be withdrawn from the market. This is a catch-all category for it being called, merged into another company, or something of this sort. Similarly, the transitions for other grades are shown. The greatest probability is that a rating will remain unchanged. This is reflected in the diagonal in bold.

Not surprisingly, the highest incidence of one-year default is for the combined Caa, Ca, and single-C grades, 26.2 percent, followed by the single-B grade, 6.5 percent. Notice also in the table that default for the higher grades is all but nonexistent in going from one year to the next. This does not mean that a double-A or single-A bond never defaults. It can evolve into lower-grade categories and eventually default. However, it does not tend to go directly from an Aa or A grade into default in a single year. Over longer time frames, however, higher-grade bonds can default. In Figure 8-4, cumulative default rates for corporate bonds rated by Moody's are shown for 5-, 10-, 15-, and 20-year time frames. The longer the time frame, the greater the likelihood of default.

TABLE 8-3   Transition Matrix among Moody's Grades from One Year to the Next (Based on 1980–1998 Period, in Percent)

Beginning Rating	Ending Rating								
	Aaa	Aa	A	Baa	Ba	B	Caa–C	Default	Withdrawn
Aaa	**85.4**	9.9	1.0	0.0	0.0	0.0	0.0	0.0	3.6
Aa	1.0	**85.5**	9.2	0.3	0.2	0.1	0.0	0.0	3.6
A	0.1	2.8	**86.6**	5.7	0.7	0.2	0.0	0.0	4.0
Baa	0.0	0.3	6.7	**80.6**	5.7	1.0	0.1	0.2	5.5
Ba	0.0	0.1	0.5	5.2	**76.5**	7.4	0.5	1.3	8.5
B	0.0	0.0	0.2	0.6	6.1	**76.1**	2.5	6.5	8.0
Caa–C	0.0	0.0	0.6	1.0	3.0	6.1	**63.0**	26.2	0.0

Source: Moody's Investors Service.

---

[9] "Historical Default Rates of Corporate Bond Issuers," 1920–1998, Special Comment, *Moody's Investors Service* (January 1999).

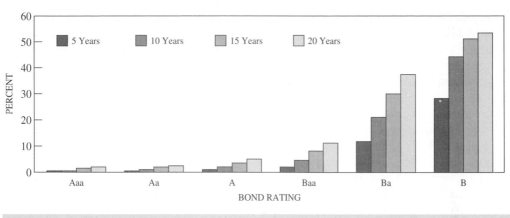

FIGURE 8-4 CUMULATIVE DEFAULT RATES OVER 5, 10, 15, AND 20 YEARS, 1970–1998

Source: Moody's Investors Service.

Even with default, the investor is likely to receive some recovery. While the default rate gives the percentage of corporations in a grade category that default, the **loss rate** is the percentage of estimated loss relative to the bond's face value. It is the combined effect of default occurring and the **severity** of loss to the investor once default occurs. One can think of severity as 1 minus the recovery rate. Moody's estimates recovery rates using the prices of defaulted bonds relative to their face value of $100. For the most recent year at the time of this writing, the average recovery rate was 45 percent, or $45 per $100 of face value, meaning that the severity of loss was 55 percent. Because of the higher incidence of default, the speculative credit grades have much greater loss rates than do investment-grade bonds. According to Moody's, Ba-grade bonds, for example, have more than four times the credit losses that Baa-grade bonds have.

Another major compiler of default rates/losses is Edward I. **Altman,** who focuses only on speculative-grade, high-yield bonds.[10] For 1985 to 1999 (third quarter), the weighted average default rate was approximately 3.2 percent, which is virtually the same as that for the first three quarters of 1999, 3.3 percent. From an average of 2.5 percent in the 1980s, default rates for high-yield bonds peaked at 10.1 percent in 1990 and 10.3 percent in 1991. They then declined to 3.4 percent in 1992 and then averaged about 1.5 percent until picking up to 3.3 percent in 1999. The reasons behind this behavior will be discussed later in the chapter. Because of recovery, we know that the average loss is less than the average default rate. For 1999, Altman finds the average price of the bonds at default to be 31.1 percent. With a loss of principal of 68.9 percent and loss of one half of the coupon, Altman estimates that the loss rate was 2.4 percent for the first three quarters of 1999. This compares with 2.1 percent for the earlier 1978–1998 period.

In addition to Altman, Donaldson Lufkin Jenrette (**DLJ**), an investment bank, studies default for speculative-grade, high-yield bonds. While the methodology is somewhat different from the other two, it is closer to Altman's than to Moody's. For the 1977–1998

---

[10] See Edward I. Altman, "Defaults on High Yield Bonds Remain High in Third Quarter of 1999," working paper, New York University Salomon Center (October 1999). Quarterly, Altman updates data on defaulted high-yield bonds, and they receive widespread attention in the financial and bond academic communities.

period, DLJ estimates the average default rate to be 2.3 percent and the average loss upon default (severity) to be 58.6 percent. For high-yield bonds, DLJ's methodology results in the lowest average default rate, followed by Altman, with Moody's estimates being highest.[11] Unlike the first two, Moody's includes non-U.S. issues (38 percent) in their data bank, and these have a higher incidence of default than U.S. issues do.

For privately placed debt with institutional investors, the loss experience differs somewhat from that for publicly issued debt. Mark Carey found that loss severities were lower for the former than for the latter.[12] With respect to higher-grade debt, there was a higher default rate for private placements than for publicly issued debt. However, the loss severity once default occurred was less. For lower-grade debt, BB or lower, both the default rate and loss severity were less for privately placed debt. Moreover, the lower the credit rating is, the greater the advantage is of private placements over publicly issued debt when it comes to recovery. The author attributes this to the ability of private lenders to write tighter loan contracts and to better monitor the loan.

CYCLICAL BEHAVIOR OF RISK PREMIUMS

An important aspect of yield differentials between various grades of bonds is their cyclical behavior over time. A priori, we might expect risk premiums in the market for bonds to fluctuate in a systematic manner with the business cycle. During periods of economic downturn, the risk premium might be expected to widen, while during periods of economic prosperity, it might be expected to narrow. This pattern of behavior may be attributable to investors' utility preferences for bonds changing with different states of nature. In a recession, their prime concern may be with safety. To invest in more risky bonds, the investor would have to be offered a substantial risk premium. On the other hand, during a period of prosperity, investors may be less concerned with safety and may be willing to bear more risk of default. During such a time, they may tend to seek out the highest-yielding investments. A sufficient number of investors behaving in this manner would narrow risk premiums in periods of prosperity and widen them in times of recession.

A related reason for this behavior relates to liquidity. If liquidity is more valued in a recession than it is in a period of economic expansion, investors may seek out Treasury and other high-grade, marketable securities. In this way, they achieve a high degree of liquidity. This changing preference for liquidity would tend to widen risk premiums in periods of economic contraction and narrow them in periods of economic expansion. Accentuating this phenomenon are occasional "flights to quality," when, in a chaotic and depressed market, investors seek the safest, most liquid investment, namely Treasury securities.

It is important to differentiate these effects from the effect of underlying changes in the default risk of borrowers over the business cycle. In a recession, the default risk for some borrowers increases as their cash-flow ability to service debt deteriorates. The op-

[11] For a comparison of the three default studies (Moody's, Altman, and DLJ), see Sam De Rosa-Farag, Jonathan Blau, Peter Matousek, and Indra Chandra, "Default Rates in the High-Yield Market," *Journal of Fixed Income* 9 (June 1999): 7–31.
[12] Mark Carey, "Credit Risk in Private Debt Portfolios," *Journal of Finance* 53 (August 1998): 1363–87.

posite tends to occur in an economic expansion. While the rating services tend to downgrade issues in the contraction phase of a business cycle and upgrade them in the expansion phase, it is likely that some changes in underlying default risk occur without commensurate adjustments in ratings. In other words, the ratings are "sticky" and do not altogether capture cyclical variations in default risk. The import of all this is that changes in yield differentials between various-grade securities may reflect more than changes in the way investors view risk. They may also reflect underlying changes in default risk.

Recognizing this limitation, let us examine the cyclical behavior of yield differentials. In Figure 8-5, yield differentials between long-term Aaa corporate bonds and Baa corporates are shown for the period 1946–1999. Economic recessions are denoted by the shaded areas. In the figure, we see that the yield differential between these two grades of corporate bonds widened during the recessionary periods. This widening is particularly evident in 1957–1958, 1970, 1974–1975, and 1981–1982. Moreover, during periods of economic expansion, the differential narrowed from the previous peak.

In the 1990s, the yield differential got as low as ½ percent in 1995 and remained relatively low until late 1998. At that time, the "flight to quality" previously described caused quality yield spreads to widen. Recognize that from 1946 to 1982, interest rates rose dramatically, declining thereafter. On a relative basis, the yield differential did not change as much as the figure suggests.

When we examine the yield differential for different grades of municipal bonds, the pattern is less distinct. Figure 8-6 shows the differential between Aaa and Baa municipal bonds during the period 1946–1999. As seen in the figure, the yield differential tends to widen in most of the recessions and declines thereafter. This is particularly evident for the 1981–1982 recession. In the mid-1990s, yield spreads narrowed for both corporate and municipal bonds, as investors reached out on the risk spectrum to obtain yield.

FIGURE 8-5 YIELD DIFFERENTIAL BETWEEN AAA CORPORATE BONDS AND BAA CORPORATE BONDS, 1946–1999

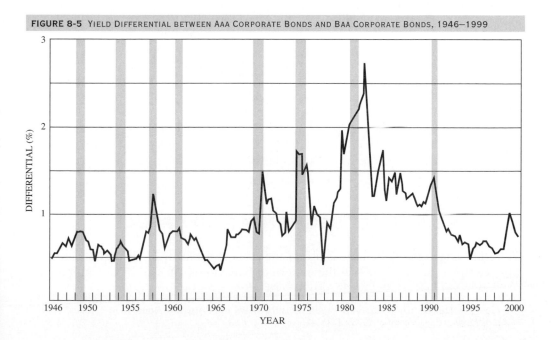

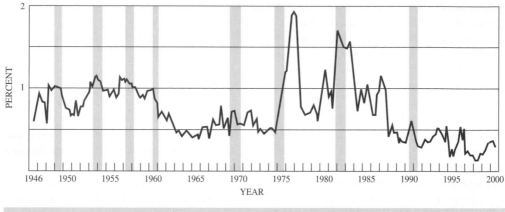

FIGURE 8-6 YIELD DIFFERENTIAL BETWEEN AAA MUNICIPAL BONDS AND BAA MUNICIPAL BONDS, 1946–1999

For municipals, the spread got as low as 0.15 percent in 1997, and increased only moderately in the late-1998 "flight to quality."

Overall, the evidence on municipals gives only moderate support to the notion that risk premiums widen during recessions and narrow during periods of economic expansion. This contrasts with the evidence on corporates, which was stronger. In addition to this evidence, we have results of several regression studies of the cyclical behavior of yield differentials. In most of them, yield spreads are found to vary countercyclically with the business cycle, narrowing during periods of economic expansion and widening during periods of economic downturn. One explanation for this phenomenon is that the utility of investors changes with the changes in the state of the economy. Put another way, investors are said to be more safety conscious in a recession than they are in a period of economic prosperity.

Also affecting risk premiums over time is the changing call risk. This influence on yields is investigated in chapter 12, so we will mention only one aspect here. When interest rates rise, callable bonds are less subject to being called and, hence, are more attractive to investors. When corporate bonds, a number of which are callable, are compared with Treasury bonds, which are not callable, the yield spread between the two may narrow as interest rates rise. In other words, a negative relationship exists between the yield spread and the level of Treasury yields.[13] To correct for this bias, corporate yields often are converted from yield-to-maturity to what is known as **"yield-to-worst."** The yield-to-worst is the yield to the likely call date. This length of time then becomes the relevant maturity for the Treasury yield deducted from the corporate yield.

THE MARKET SEGMENTATION EFFECT

Other investigators say that the cause of the cyclical behavior of yield differentials is more complex. Some argue that the pattern of behavior is affected by institutional re-

---

[13] Gregory R. Duffee, "The Relation Between Treasury Yields and Corporate Bond Yield Spreads," *Journal of Finance* 53 (December 1998): 2225–41.

strictions on investing in and issuing securities. In turn, these restrictions are said to lead to segmented financial markets in the same sense we discussed for the term structure of interest rates. In this case, segmentation refers to the type and grade of security in which one can invest or that one can issue.

Institutional restrictions on the supply side include voter constraints on borrowing by municipalities. In many state and local governments, voter approval is required before a bond issue can be floated. Moreover, some municipalities have a legal ceiling on what they can pay in interest. If interest rates in general move up, these municipalities may be precluded from borrowing unless voter approval to remove the ceiling can be obtained. When inflation occurs, it typically brings with it not only higher interest rates but also increased costs to the municipality and higher property taxes. Because few people like higher taxes, there tends to be a correspondence between inflation and the percentage of bond issues turned down by the electorate. As lower-grade municipalities pay higher interest rates and typically have more funded indebtedness outstanding, it is not unreasonable to expect them to feel restrictions on borrowing to a greater extent than do prime-grade municipalities.

On occasion, corporations also face restrictions on issuing bonds. If a company has outstanding debt that is covered by a loan agreement or bond indenture, frequently the company has restrictions on incurring future debt. This constraint is likely to be more binding for the lower-grade company than it is for the higher-grade company. For both municipalities and corporations, then, it is not unreasonable to expect lower-grade borrowers to feel institutional restrictions to a greater extent than do higher-grade borrowers in times of inflation and economic contraction or stagnation. As a result, the supply of various-grade securities may be affected differently by institutional restrictions over the business cycle.

The demand side has institutional restrictions, as well. For example, a common restriction is the limiting of the types and grades of securities in which certain institutions can invest. In turn, these restrictions on institutions may cause them to select securities different from the ones they would choose if they were free to invest in any security. In other words, institutional restrictions may cause greater relative demand for restricted securities vis-à-vis unrestricted securities, if all other conditions are the same. This notion is illustrated in Figure 8-7, which indicates that restricted investors can invest only in restricted securities, while unrestricted investors can invest in all securities.

The restrictions placed on investment take many forms. Public deposits in commercial banks must be secured by collateral, principally U.S. Treasury or government agency securities. This restriction affects their investment behavior. Life insurance companies and certain other institutions are restricted in their investment by the state in which they operate. They are allowed to invest only in securities on the "legal list." With respect to bonds, this restriction frequently takes the form of investment-grade bonds—those rated Baa/BBB or better. Bonds rated Ba/BB and below would not qualify, and the institution would be precluded from buying them. Similarly, commercial banks tend to be restricted to investment-grade bonds. These are examples of only some of the more important restrictions on the type and grade of security in which an institution may invest.

The combination of restrictions on the supply of and the demand for different types and grades of securities may lead to a market segmentation effect. If significant, this effect would have an influence on the cyclical behavior of yield differentials and

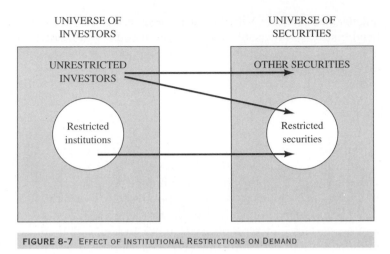

FIGURE 8-7 EFFECT OF INSTITUTIONAL RESTRICTIONS ON DEMAND

risk premiums apart from the influences already discussed. Empirical evidence is mixed with respect to a market segmentation effect on the cyclical behavior of yield differentials. However, there would appear to be some market segmentation premium in going from investment-grade bonds (Baa/BBB or above) to speculative-grade ones (Ba/BB or below).

SPECULATIVE-GRADE, HIGH-YIELD BONDS

The presence of a segmentation premium was one of the reasons for the high-yield bond market. Known also as "junk bonds," a high-yield bond is any bond that has a credit rating of Ba/BB or below.

DEVELOPMENT OF THE MARKET

Prior to the mid-1970s, there were virtually no original issues of such bonds. What bonds there were in this category were the result of rating downgrades. Known as "fallen angels," these bonds were investment grade at the time they were issued. Then in 1976, Drexel Burnham Lambert (DBL), an investment bank, began to court lower-grade companies to issue bonds. At the same time, DBL built an investor market. The principal appeal was the alleged market segmentation premium—considerable reward in higher yield by going from an investment-grade bond to a speculative-grade one, without proportional addition to default risk. With anywhere from a 3 to 5.5 percent yield advantage over Treasury bonds of similar maturity, the return was attractive even after default losses of roughly 1 percent were taken into account. One of the ingredients for a successful financial product is a secondary market, and DBL provided one of sorts.

From its inception, the high-yield bond market expanded rapidly, with growing numbers of issuers and investors. Investors included insurance companies, pension funds, a number of mutual funds that invest solely in high-yield bonds, individuals, and savings and loan associations. While the market was dominated by DBL in the 1970s, other investment banks established high-yield bond departments in the 1980s.

ISSUERS AND USE IN ACQUISITIONS

Initially, issuers of high-yield bonds were corporations that had previously funded their operations through private placements or bank term loans. The development of the high-yield bond market was part of the overall securization of assets described earlier. What occurred was a substitution of public offerings for borrowings in the private market-place, at the expense of depository institutions, insurance companies, and pension funds.

In 1983, high-yield bonds began to play a role in acquisitions, as well as in converting public companies to private through leveraged buyouts. A potential acquirer often was able to obtain a "highly confident" letter indicating the intent of an investment bank to secure financing. Another variation was the bridge loan, in which the investment bank backstopped the acquirer by providing an interim loan pending securing permanent financing for the client. Typically, the ultimate financing included senior debt by banks or finance companies, in which the lender had a lien on virtually all the assets. This debt was followed by junior subordinated debentures, the high-yield bond portion, which usually were equity-linked either through a conversion feature or through options. Finally, a thin layer of common stock constituted the equity base.

RISK VERSUS RETURN

The fact that until the late 1980s, high-yield bonds provided a 3 to 5½ percent yield advantage over Treasuries seemingly gave considerable inducement to the investor. Default rates on a market-based portfolio averaged somewhat more than 2 percent per annum, with actual default losses of only about 1 percent. A market segmentation premium was part of the story, but not the whole story. The underestimation of default risk by investors was a key ingredient. The large growth in high-yield bonds during the 1980s coincided with economic prosperity and declining interest rates. This growth masked underlying default risk, for new high-yield bonds tend not to default for a while. Mortality, or aging, analyses indicated much higher default rates over the life of a bond than the 2+ percent rate cited for a diversified portfolio.[14]

As the 1990–1991 recession developed, the excesses of the 1980s took their toll. A number of highly leveraged transactions ran into difficulty. Default rates on high-yield bonds increased sharply, as we know from our earlier discussion, to more than 10 percent in 1990 and 1991. Highly leveraged companies that avoided default in the 1980s through debt restructurings by DBL and other investment banks no longer were able to do so. Figure 8-8 shows the high-yield bond spread over Treasuries. Maturity is based on the "yield-to-worst" for the high-yield bonds, which takes into account the likelihood of the bond being called. As seen in the figure, the average yield spread over Treasuries went from roughly 500 basis points (5 percent) to more than 1,200 basis points in 1990.

---

[14] See Paul Asquith, David W. Mullins, Jr., and Eric P. Wolff, "Original Issue High Yield Bonds: Aging Analyses of Defaults, Exchanges and Calls," *Journal of Finance* 44 (September 1989): 923–52; Edward I. Altman and Vellore Kishore, "Defaults and Returns on High Yield Bonds," working paper, New York University Stern School of Business (May 1996); and Stuart C. Gilson, "Investing in Distressed Situations: A Market Survey," *Financial Analysts Journal* 51 (November–December 1995): 8–24.

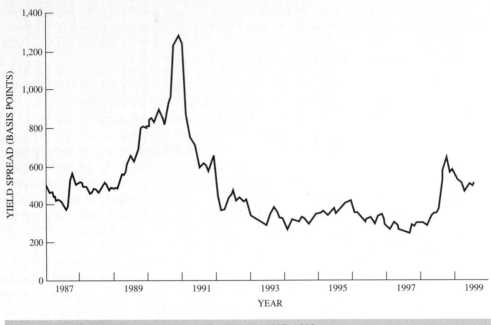

FIGURE 8-8 HIGH-YIELD BOND SPREADS OVER TREASURIES, 1987–1999

In addition to default risk, there was liquidity risk. While a secondary market of sorts existed for high-yield bonds, it was never broad, deep, and resilient—the usual standards for judgment. In a "flight to quality," as occurred in 1990, marketability became nonexistent for all practical purposes. Thus, high-yield bond investors of the mid- to late-1980s underpriced both "true" default and liquidity risks. A major casualty was Drexel Burnham Lambert, the originator of the market, which failed in 1990.

From the shambles of late 1990, the situation improved. Default rates abated, as the poorer credits had already been shaken out. High-yield bonds increased in price, as the yield differential over Treasuries went from more than 1,200 basis points in 1990 to 600 basis points by the end of 1991. (See Figure 8-8.) During 1992 and 1993, there was a revival in high-yield bond financing by corporations, after a hiatus of nearly two years. On the demand side, the market had changed. Mutual funds now were the dominant investor, as thrift institutions, insurance companies, and other institutional investors reduced their presence. From 1992 to 1998, the demand for high-yield bonds was such that the spread fluctuated around 400 basis points. This occurred despite the fact that the net supply of high-yield bonds outstanding doubled. Figure 8-8 shows that in mid-1998, the yield spread widened to more than 600 basis points. This was due to the "flight to quality" described earlier, as well as to the large supply of high-yield bonds coming to market. While the yield spread narrowed somewhat in 1999, it remained wider than during the mid-1990s period. Liquidity problems lingered on in 1999, and the supply of new bonds coming to market during the first half of the year was substantial.

The lower the grade of a bond is, the more it takes on firm-specific characteristics and the less it is related to changes in overall market rates of interest. The yield on a speculative-grade bond has been found to correlate with the corporation's stock return.[15] The lower the grade is in this category, the greater is the correlation. Some institutional investors make assessments of such bonds using stock price movements as a leading indicator.

EVENT RISK

The corporate restructuring movement of the 1980s led to a new risk. It was the risk of a company's involvement in a highly leveraged transaction. When such occurs, the company's existing bonds are downgraded and their prices decline. For example, the RJR Nabisco leveraged buyout in 1989 brought with it a downgrade in bond rating from A to Ba. Investors suffered a market price decline of 11 percent. In short, wealth was transferred, or expropriated, from existing bondholders. This risk has come to be known as **event risk.** Another example was Marriott Corporation's 1992 restructuring of its businesses into two separate companies. The "good" business, which involved services, was largely separated from the "bad" business, which involved asset ownership. Most of the debt remained with the latter, and, not surprisingly, the bonds declined in price.

Event risk is most evident for companies with low to moderate leverage because their bondholders have the most to lose. A more leveraged company cannot increase its leverage as much. With event risk, bondholders should demand a higher yield than would occur without such risk.[16] The hypothetical relationship between risk premium and event risk is shown in Figure 8-9. Here we see that the event risk premium declines with leverage, but that the overall risk premium increases.

The event risk protection that is afforded to bondholders in the indenture varies greatly. Most bond indentures contain little or no protection. One of the stronger covenants is a "super poison put," which enables the bondholder to sell back the bond to the company at face value, or at face value plus a premium, should an increase in leverage or some designated event like a takeover occur. The trigger that activates the poison put clause may be some percentage of voting shares, such as 25 percent, being acquired by a single party. The evidence is mixed as to the protection afforded to bondholders as a result of a super poison put.[17] To the extent the clause serves to entrench management, it may work to the detriment of firm value and ultimately bondholder value.

We should note that not all events are bad; event risk can have an upside. If a lower-graded company merges with a higher-grade one, the debt may be upgraded or even paid off at full face value. This will have a salutary effect on market price.

---

[15] Simon H. Kwan, "Firm-Specific Information and the Correlation between Individual Stocks and Bonds," *Journal of Financial Economics* 40 (January 1996): 63–80.

[16] For amplification of this point, see Steven A. Zimmer, "Event Risk Premia and Bond Market Incentives for Corporate Leverage," *Federal Reserve Bank of New York Quarterly Review* 15 (Spring 1990): 15–30.

[17] See Paul Asquith and Thierry A. Wizman, "Event Risk, Covenants and Bondholder Returns in Leveraged Buyouts," *Journal of Financial Economics* 27 (September 1990): 195–213; Douglas O. Cook and John C. Easterwood, "Poison Put Bonds: An Analysis of Their Economic Role," *Journal of Finance* 49 (December 1994): 1905–20; Leland Crabbe, "Event Risk: An Analysis of Losses to Bondholders and 'Super Poison Put' Bond Covenants," *Journal of Finance* 46 (June 1991): 689–706; and Hugh M. Pratt and Miles B. Livingston, "Effects of Super Poison-Put Clauses on Industrial Debt," *Journal of Fixed Income* 3 (December 1993): 33–45.

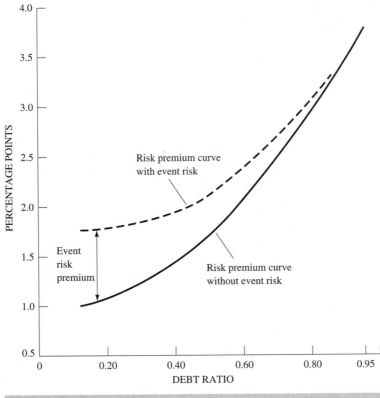

FIGURE 8-9 RISK PREMIUMS WITH AND WITHOUT EVENT RISK

Source: Steven A. Zimmer, "Event Risk Premia and Bond Market Incentives for Corporate Leverage," *Quarterly Review of Federal Reserve Bank of New York* 15 (Spring 1990): 16.

RISK STRUCTURE AND THE TERM STRUCTURE

With differences in both default risk and the length of time to maturity, yield curves may differ for different grades of securities. In other words, the default-risk premium is not necessarily a constant function of the length of time to maturity. If the default-risk premium were 2 percent on a long-term bond, it does not follow that the premium on a short-term security of the same grade also would be 2 percent.

WIDENING YIELD DIFFERENTIALS WITH MATURITY

It may be that the market perceives a higher probability of default the more distant the future is and the lesser the grade of bond is. As the length of time to maturity grows shorter and the issuer does not default, a degree of uncertainty is resolved. With this resolution, investors may require a lesser risk premium. Moreover, as the argument goes, there would be greater relative resolution of uncertainty for lower-grade bonds than for higher-grade ones.[18] As a result, the yield differential between high-grade and low-grade bonds would widen with maturity. Figure 8-10 shows yield curves for AAA and BBB industrial bonds (U.S.) in January 1999. Generally, the yield differential tends to widen with maturity, consistent with the argument above.

CRISIS-AT-MATURITY

If a typical company in a rating category is marginal with respect to servicing debt and meeting the final redemption, the perceived probability of default may increase as maturity grows shorter. Ramon E. Johnson defines this situation as **crisis-at-maturity,** and it implies a narrowing yield differential between high-grade and low-grade bonds as maturity increases.[19] Johnson constructs yield curves based on empirical data for five grades of corporate securities and the comparison of these yield curves with basic yield curves for corporate bonds of the lowest possible default risk. Of particular interest were the yield curves that occurred during the Depression. From 1933 on, the highest-grade issues tended to be upward-sloping, as was the basic yield curve, while lower-grade issues were downward-sloping. Examples of yield curves for 1934 and 1938 are shown in Figure 8-11. The line with the Bs refers to the basic yield curve, while the numbers 1 to 5 refer to different grading categories, from high to low.

Johnson postulated that the downward-sloping yield curves for lower-quality issues, seen particularly during the Depression, were primarily the result of crisis-at-maturity

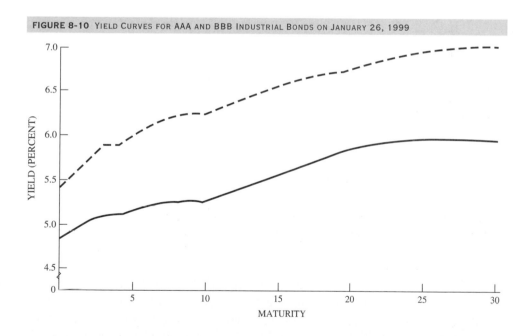

FIGURE 8-10 YIELD CURVES FOR AAA AND BBB INDUSTRIAL BONDS ON JANUARY 26, 1999

18 Robert Litterman and Thomas Iben, "Corporate Bond Valuation and the Term Structure of Credit Spreads," *Journal of Portfolio Management* 17 (Spring, 1991): 52–64; and Jean Helwege and Christopher M. Turner, "The Slope of the Credit Yield Curve for Speculative-Grade Issuers," *Journal of Finance* 34 (October 1999): 1869–84.
19 Ramon E. Johnson, "Term Structures of Corporate Bond Yields as a Function of Risk of Default," *Journal of Finance* 22 (May 1967): 318–21.

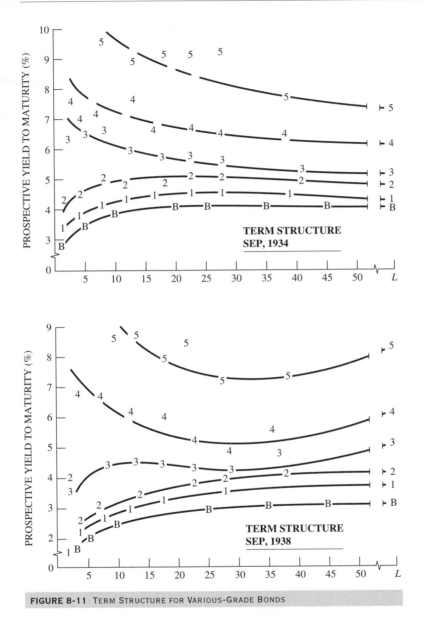

FIGURE 8-11 TERM STRUCTURE FOR VARIOUS-GRADE BONDS

considerations. Upward-sloping yield curves for low-grade bonds occurred only when the prospect for crisis-at-maturity was slight. Moreover, Johnson contended that upward-sloping yield curves for high-grade securities were the result of risk premiums increasing with maturity. On the other hand, U-shaped curves were said to result from a combination of crisis-at-maturity considerations and expectations that default-risk premiums would increase in the future. Similarly, yield curves of other shapes were explained in terms of risk premiums increasing with maturity, crisis-at-maturity, and expectations of changing risk premiums. In addition to Johnson, other scholars have found evidence that crisis-at-maturity is more important during recessions and for lower-grade securities.[20] The decline in yield consistent with crisis-at-maturity occurs mainly for single B and lower rated securities. It has not been observed in recent years for the BBB and AAA comparison, illustrated in Figure 8-10.

The various studies give us insight into the relationship between risk premiums and maturity and how it differs depending on the phase of the economy. It seems clear that risk premiums are not invariant with respect to maturity, though there is little consistent pattern over time. In studying the risk structure of interest rates, we have been concerned with differences in yield for different types and grades of securities, holding maturity constant. However, one must be mindful that the risk structure is different for different maturities and that the relationship between the risk structure and maturity can change over time.

❖ SUMMARY

The relationship between yield and the risk of default is studied through the analysis of risk premiums—the difference between the yield on a security and the yield on a corresponding security that is free of default risk. The promised yield on a security is its *ex ante* yield at a moment in time. The expected yield, on the other hand, is the mean of the probability distribution of possible realized yields. The distribution itself is highly skewed to the left. To the extent that the market is averse to dispersion and skewness to the left of the probability distribution, the risk premium will exceed the default loss expected by investors at the margin.

Most investors rely on credit rating agencies to grade the risk of a corporate or municipal bond. The primary rating agencies are Moody's and Standard & Poor's. Grades for investment-grade securities range from Aaa/AAA to Baa/BBB. For speculative-grade, high-yield bonds, grades range from Ba/BB to single C. The rating methods used by these agencies were explored.

Liquidity is the ability to realize value in money. Liquidity of a bond is judged in terms of the bid-ask spread together with the ability to sell a bond in a short interval of time without significant price concession. Liquidity in the market decreased in the late 1990s. The greater the amount is of a bond issue outstanding, generally the greater its liquidity. Certain industry tiers enjoy greater liquidity in the corporate bond market than do other tiers. Also, on-the-run, newly issued bonds are more liquid than older, off-the-run securities.

Empirical studies of default losses show that default experience is highly correlated with the economic cycle. It is only with a severe economic downturn, such as a depression, that widespread default occurs. However, a number of companies default even in relatively good times, and for speculative-grade, high-yield bonds this percentage rose as high as 10 percent in the 1990s. The transition over time from one grade of bond to another was explored. Because of recovery, the actual default loss rate on a bond is less than the default rate, averaging about 60 percent of the latter.

---

[20] J. B. Silvers, "An Alternative to the Yield Spread as a Measure of Risk," *Journal of Finance* 28 (September, 1973): 933–55; Calvin M. Boardman and Richard W. McNally, "Factors Affecting Seasoned Corporate Bond Prices," *Journal of Financial and Quantitative Analysis* 16 (June 1981): 207–26; Oded Sarig and Arthur Warga, "Some Empirical Estimates of the Risk Structure of Interest Rates," *Journal of Finance* 44 (December 1989): 1351–60; and Jerome S. Fons, "Using Default Rates to Model the Term Structure of Credit Risk," *Financial Analysts Journal* 50 (September–October 1994): 25–32.

An important facet of the default-risk structure of interest rates is the cyclical behavior of risk premiums. Various evidence indicates a tendency for risk premiums to widen during a period of economic contraction and to narrow during a period of expansion. This is consistent with investors' utility preferences changing with the state of the economy—investors being more concerned with safety in an economic downturn than they are in a period of prosperity.

In addition to the cyclical behavior of risk premiums over time, there may be a market segmentation effect. Various institutional restrictions on the demand for and the supply of bonds of various types and grades were discussed. Market segmentation is one of the reasons for the development of the high-yield bond market, which is comprised of speculative-grade issues rated Ba/BB or less. The development of, and problems associated with, this market were evaluated. The focus was on the changing perception (and reality) of default risk and liquidity risk. With the highly leveraged transactions of the 1980s, event risk affected the valuation of corporate bonds. This is the risk that with a sharp increase in leverage, existing bonds will be downgraded and bondholders suffer a loss.

Finally, the default-risk structure and the term structure of interest rates were examined jointly in an effort to explain differing shapes of yield curves for different risk categories of securities. The idea that uncertainty is resolved as maturity grows shorter and that this resolution is greater for lower-grade bonds implies quality yield spreads widening with maturity. "Crisis-at-maturity" implies risk increasing for lower-grade bonds as maturity approaches. This suggests that quality yield spreads narrow with maturity. This phenomenon was observed during the depression of the 1930s and has been observed at other times for single B and lesser grades of corporate bonds.

❖ SELECTED REFERENCES

Alessandrini, Fabio, "Credit Risk, Interest Rate Risk, and the Business Cycle," *Journal of Fixed Income* 9 (September 1999): 42–53.

Altman, Edward I., "Defaults and Returns on High Yield Bonds," working paper, New York University Solomon Center (January 2000).

Asquith, Paul, David W. Mullins, Jr., and Eric P. Wolff, "Original Issue High Yield Bonds: Aging Analyses of Defaults, Exchanges and Calls," *Journal of Finance,* 44 (September 1989): 923–52.

Asquith, Paul, and Thierry A. Wizman, "Event Risk, Covenants, and Bondholder Returns in Leveraged Buyouts," *Journal of Financial Economics* 27 (September 1990): 195–213.

Atkinson, Thomas R., *Trends in Corporate Bond Quality.* New York: National Bureau of Economic Research, 1967.

Bennett, Thomas L., Stephen F. Esser, and Christian G. Roth, "Corporate Credit Risk and Reward," *Journal of Portfolio Management* 20 (Spring 1994): 39–47.

Blume, Marshall E., Felix Lim, and A. Craig MacKinlay, "The Declining Credit Quality of U.S. Corporate Debt: Myth or Reality?" *Journal of Finance* 53 (August 1998): 1389–1413.

Cantor, Richard, and Frank Packer, "The Credit Rating Industry," *Journal of Fixed Income* 5 (December 1995): 10–34.

Carey, Mark, "Credit Risk in Private Debt Portfolios," *Journal of Finance* 53 (August 1998): 1363–87.

Carty, Lea V., and Jerome S. Fons, "Measuring Changes in Corporate Credit Quality," *Journal of Fixed Income* 4 (June 1994): 27–41.

Cathcart, Lara, and Lina El-Jahel, "Valuation of Defaultable Bonds," *Journal of Fixed Income* 8 (June 1998): 65–78.

Cook, Douglas O., and John C. Easterwood, "Poison Put Bonds: An Analysis of their Economic Role," *Journal of Finance* 49 (December 1994): 1905–20.

DeRosa-Farag, Sam, Jonathan Blau, Peter Matousek, and Indra Chandra, "Default Rates in the High-Yield Market," *Journal of Fixed Income* 9 (June 1999): 7–31.

Duffee, Gregory R., "The Relation between Treasury Yields and Corporate Bond Yield Spreads," *Journal of Finance* 53 (December 1998): 2225–41.

Duffie, Darrell, and Kenneth J. Singleton, "Modeling Term Structures of Defaultable Bonds," *Review of Financial Studies* 12 (No. 4, 1999): 687–720.

Fabozzi, Frank J., ed. *Handbook of Corporate Debt Instruments.* New Hope, PA: Frank J. Fabozzi Associates, 1998.

Fisher, Lawrence, "Determinants of Risk Premiums on Corporate Bonds," *Journal of Political Economy* 67 (June 1959): 217–37.

Fons, Jerome S., "Using Default Rates to Model the Term Structure of Credit Risk," *Financial Analysts Journal* 50 (September–October 1994): 25–31.

Foss, Gregory W., "Quantifying Risk in the Corporate Bond Markets," *Financial Analysts Journal* 51 (March–April 1995): 29–34.

Fridson, Martin S., and M. Christopher Garman, "Valuing Like-Rated Senior and Subordinated Debt," *Journal of Fixed Income* 7 (December 1997): 83–93.

Hand, John R. M., Robert W. Holthausen, and Richard W. Leftwich, "The Effect of Bond Rating Agency Announcements on Bond and Stock Prices," *Journal of Finance* 47 (June 1992): 733–52.

Helwege, Jean, and Christopher M. Turner, "The Slope of the Credit Yield Curve for Speculative-Grade Issuers," *Journal of Finance* 54 (October 1999): 1869–84.

Hempel, George H., *The Postwar Quality of State and Local Debt.* New York: National Bureau of Economic Research, 1971.

Hickman, W. Braddock, *Corporate Bond Quality and Investor Experience.* New York: National Bureau of Economic Research, 1958.

Johnson, Ramon E., "Term Structures of Corporate Bond Yields as a Function of Risk of Default," *Journal of Finance* 22 (May 1967): 313–45.

Leland, Hayne E., and Klaus Bjerre Toft, "Optimal Capital Structure, Endogenous Bankruptcy, and the Term Structure of Credit Spreads," *Journal of Finance* 51 (July 1996): 987–1019.

Litterman, Robert, and Thomas Iben, "Corporate Bond Valuation and the Term Structure of Credit Spreads," *Journal of Portfolio Management* 17 (Spring 1991): 52–64.

Longstaff, Francis A., and Eduardo S. Schwartz, "A Simple Approach to Valuing Risky Fixed and Floating Rate Debt," *Journal of Finance* 50 (July 1995): 789–819.

Pedrosa, Monica, and Richard Roll, "Systematic Risk in Corporate Bond Credit Spreads," *Journal of Fixed Income* 8 (December 1998): 7–26.

Sarig, Oded, and Arthur Warga, "Some Empirical Estimates of the Risk Structure of Interest Rates," *Journal of Finance* 44 (December 1989): 1352–60.

Silvers, J. B., "An Alternative to the Yield Spread as a Measure of Risk," *Journal of Finance* 28 (September 1973): 933–55.

Van Horne, James C., "Behavior of Default-Risk Premiums for Corporate Bonds and Commercial Paper," *Journal of Business Research* 7 (December 1979): 301–13.

———, "Optimal Initiation of Bankruptcy Proceedings by Debt Holders," *Journal of Finance* 31 (June 1976): 897–910.

Zimmer, Steven A., "Event Risk Premia and Bond Market Incentives for Corporate Leverage," *Federal Reserve Bank of New York Quarterly Review* 15 (Spring 1990): 15–30.

DERIVATIVE SECURITIES: INTEREST-RATE FUTURES AND FORWARD CONTRACTS

Up to now we have considered only *primary* financial instruments, which evidence direct claims against some other party. These instruments are traded in the *spot market* with prices set by the usual forces of supply and demand. In contrast, a **derivative security** derives its value from an underlying, primary instrument. In this chapter and the next four, we consider such derivative instruments as interest-rate futures, forward contracts, swaps, debt options, and instruments derived from mortgages. Our purpose in this chapter is to explore interest-rate futures and forward contracts. In many ways, the two contracts are similar, but certain important differences exist. As forward contracts were introduced in chapter 6, our treatment of them here will brief.

INTRODUCTION TO FUTURES CONTRACT

A **futures contract** is a standardized agreement that calls for the delivery of a commodity at some specified future date. In the case of financial futures, the commodity is a security. Transactions occur either on an **exchange** or through an investment bank in what is known as the **over-the-counter market.** With an exchange transaction, the clearinghouse of the exchange interposes itself between the buyer and the seller. Its creditworthiness is substituted for that of the broker on the other side of the transaction, and each exchange has a number of rules governing transactions. While the clearinghouse affords the market participant a degree of safety, if the broker should default, the participant may be hurt.[1]

As in commodities, few financial futures contracts involve actual delivery at maturity. Rather, buyers and sellers of a contract independently take off-setting positions to close out the contract. The seller cancels a contract by buying another contract; the buyer cancels by selling another contract. As a result, only a small percentage of con-

---

[1] For an analysis of this problem, see James V. Jordan and George Emir Morgan, "Default Risk in Futures Markets: The Customer-Broker Relationship," *Journal of Finance* 45 (July 1990): 909–33.

tracts come to actual delivery. The *open interest* is the number of futures contracts outstanding that have not been closed.

While futures markets for commodities have been around for some time, the first financial futures market began in 1975. The number of markets has grown, and their development and use represent an important financial innovation. Table 9-1 lists the more active markets for interest-rate futures contracts. In addition to these markets, futures markets exist for a number of other instruments and currencies. We should point out that there are options on futures contracts, which will be discussed in chapter 10.

Futures markets have not only grown in importance over time, but they have changed. Their growth can be attributable to the increased desire by many market participants to shift risk in the face of interest-rate volatility. Another factor is that transactions costs are lower in futures than they are in the spot market. The globalization of finance is yet another factor. At one time, the U.S. Treasury bill futures market was the dominant market for short-term instruments. As more and more loan arrangements were geared to the London InterBank Offer Rate (LIBOR), the Eurodollar market came to prevail. The Treasury bill futures market slipped in volume and eventually withered to where now it is inconsequential. A number of other futures markets have been tried, including a market for Government National Mortgage Association (GNMA),

TABLE 9-1   More Active Interest-Rate Financial Futures Markets

Market	Eurodollars	Eurobor	Euroyen
Contract size:	$1 million	€ 1 million	¥ 100,000,000
Security delivered:	Cash settlement at LIBOR rate for 3-month CDs	Cash settlement at 3-month rate for prime-grade Euro currency borrowings	Cash settlement at rate for 3-month Yen CDs
Exchanges:	CME, LIFFE	LIFFE, MATIF	CME, SIMEX

Market	Treasury Notes	Treasury Bonds
Contract Size:	$100,000	$100,000
Security delivered:	For 5-year note market, a Treasury note with 4.25 to 5.25 years to maturity. For 10-year note market, 6.5 to 10 years, both based on 8% coupon	15-year or more maturity Treasury bond based on 8% coupon
Exchanges:	CBT	CBT

Note: LIBOR = London InterBank Offer Rate
CME = Chicago Mercantile Exchange
LIFFE = London International Financial Futures Exchange
MATIF = Marche a Terme International de France
SIMEX = Singapore International Monetary Exchange
CBT = Chicago Board of Trade

pass-through mortgages, commercial paper, bank certificates of deposit (CDs), and corporate bonds. However, for one reason or another, they have faded from the scene. Unless trading volume reaches and stays above a necessary threshold, a market does not have sufficient liquidity to be viable.

FEATURES OF FUTURES MARKETS

MONEY MARKET INSTRUMENTS

To illustrate a transaction, consider first the market for Eurodollars. Each contract is for $1 million face value of Eurodollar deposits, with delivery each month for several months in the future, after which delivery can occur only in March, June, September, and December. At present, the market extends out nearly ten years—by far the longest of any of the exchange markets. In the case of Eurodollars, no physical settlement is made on the delivery day. Rather, it is a cash settlement procedure against the average LIBOR deposit rate that prevails on the settlement day. In contrast, the Treasury bill futures market calls for the actual delivery of a 90- to 92-day bill. Cash settlements involve fewer complications concerning delivery, but the derivation of an index, such as obtaining and averaging Eurodollar quotations, also has its problems.

MARGIN REQUIREMENTS

When transacting in a futures contract, an investor must put up **margin** as a security deposit. The exchange sets the minimum margin requirement, but a brokerage firm may ask for more. Only competition limits the amount of margin a firm requires. At the time of this writing, the margin requirement on Eurodollar futures was around $2,000 per $1 million contract, whereas that on Treasury bond futures also was $2,000, but for a $100,000 contract. In general, the more volatile the futures market for a particular instrument, the higher the margin required. In putting up margin, one can use cash or an interest-bearing security such as Treasury bills. In either case, the initial margin put up earns a market rate of interest. Margin is *not* the investment. One must have deeper pockets to withstand adverse price movements. Otherwise, chances of being wiped out are high.

Both **initial** and **maintenance** margin requirements are established. Typically, the maintenance requirement is 75 to 80 percent of the initial margin requirement. It works as follows. Suppose the initial and maintenance margin requirements on Treasury bond futures are $2,000 and $1,500, respectively. Initially, both the buyer and the seller (writer) of the contract put up $2,000. If interest rates rise, the value of the buyer's position declines. As long as the decline is less than $500 per $100,000 contract, the buyer is not obligated to put up additional margin. However, if the cumulative decline in value comes to $501, the buyer's margin account would stand at $1,499. He or she would get a margin call from the brokerage firm and be obligated to restore the account to the initial level, in this case to $2,000.

The control limit use of two margin levels reduces the number of margin calls, though they do occur with sharp price movements. If the buyer is unable to restore his or her margin account, the brokerage firm will sell out that position and remit whatever is left over to the buyer. If the futures contract rises in value, the buyer may draw off the excess margin.

MARKING-TO-MARKET AND PRICE MOVEMENTS

Each day, the futures contract is **marked-to-market** in the sense that it is valued at the closing price. Price movements affect the margin positions of buyers and sellers in opposite ways. Every day there is a winner and a loser, depending on the direction of price movement, for it is a zero-sum game. Margin settlements must be made in keeping with the procedures just outlined. Unlike spot market instruments, settlements occur not at the end of the contract but daily. This is a distinguishing feature of the futures markets.

LONGER-TERM INSTRUMENTS

The features of longer-term contracts, such as Treasury bond futures, are somewhat different from those for Eurodollars and Treasury bills. As mentioned, the trading unit for a single contract is $100,000, in contrast to $1 million for Eurodollars. Delivery months are March, June, September, and December, and contracts go out about 1¼ years. Price quotations are given as a percentage of the face value ($100) of an 8 percent coupon with 20 years to maturity. A quotation of 112⁴⁄₃₂ means 112.125 percent of $100 in face value, or $112.125.

For delivery, any Treasury bond with at least 15 years to the earliest call date or to maturity may be used. Because most bonds have a coupon rate other than 8 percent, the invoice is the settlement price multiplied by a **conversion factor.** Recall that the futures contract settlement price is based on a coupon rate of 8 percent. Therefore, the conversion factor is greater than 1.00 for coupon rates greater than 8 percent, 1.00 for an 8 percent coupon bond, and less than 1.00 for coupon rates less than 8 percent. The greater the deviation is in coupon rate from 8 percent, the greater the deviation is in the conversion factor from 1.00.

Conversion factors are established for each coupon rate and time to maturity. While a formula is used to establish them, conversion factors are readily available to market participants through tables and computer programs. Conversion factors for a 7¼ percent bond and a 9½ percent bond with various times to maturity are shown in Table 9-2. Suppose a 7¼ percent bond with 22 years to maturity were delivered and the Treasury bond futures price at the time were $111⁸⁄₃₂. The settlement price on a $100,000 contract would be

$$\text{settlement price} = \$100,000 \times 1.1125 \times 0.9229 = \$102,672.63$$

This is what the party who is short receives in settlement for delivering the bonds. With conversion factors, the idea is to adjust the settlement price for the value of the bonds to be delivered.

QUALITY DELIVERY OPTIONS

Treasury bond futures have several delivery options. Known as quality options, these include (1) the specific security to deliver; (2) the delivery day within the delivery month; and (3) the timing in the afternoon of the delivery day, known as the "wild card" option.

TABLE 9-2 Some Conversion Factors for Treasury Bond Futures

Time to Maturity (years)	7¼% Coupon	9½% Coupon
15	0.9352	1.1297
16	0.9330	1.1341
17	0.9310	1.1381
18	0.9291	1.1418
19	0.9274	1.1453
20	0.9258	1.1484
21	0.9243	1.1514
22	0.9229	1.1541
23	0.9217	1.1566
24	0.9205	1.1590
25	0.9194	1.1611
26	0.9184	1.1631
27	0.9175	1.1649
28	0.9167	1.1666
29	0.9159	1.1682
30	0.9152	1.1697

Concerning the first, more than 20 meet the criterion of 15 or more years to maturity or to the first call date. Naturally, the party obligated to deliver will want to do so with the "cheapest" bond of those that qualify. This bond is the one with the *smallest:*

$$\text{spot market price} - \left(\begin{array}{c}\text{futures price} \\ \text{at settlement}\end{array}\right)\left(\begin{array}{c}\text{conversion} \\ \text{factor}\end{array}\right) \qquad \textbf{(9-1)}$$

As the party delivering will be short the bond, he or she is interested in minimizing the cost to deliver in Equation (9-1). The bond that is **cheapest to deliver** is well known in the market, and equilibrium occurs in relation to it. Because the conversion factor adjustment is imperfect, different bonds will be cheapest to deliver at different times owing to differences in maturity, callability, and coupon rate. The relationship is complicated by changes in interest rates, and no easy generalizations are possible.[2] For the cheapest-to-deliver bond, its price now and the futures price can be used to calculate a return, which is the *implied repo rate.* By definition, the cheapest-to-deliver bond will be the one with the highest implied repo rate among the Treasury bonds with 15 years or more to maturity.

The second option has to do with when to deliver during the delivery month. For maturing contracts, trading is closed the last seven business days of the month. This means that all contracts must be settled pricewise by the 20th to the 22nd of the delivery month. However, the actual delivery of a security can occur up to the last business

---

[2] For an analysis of bonds as to their delivery option value, see Miles Livingston, "The Effect of Coupon Level on Treasury Bond Futures Delivery," *Journal of Futures Markets* 7 (no. 3, 1987): 303–9; Michael L. Hemler, "The Quality Delivery Option in Treasury Bond Futures Contracts," *Journal of Finance* 45 (December 1990): 1565–86; and Mark Koenigsberg, "A Delivery Option Model for Treasury Bond Futures," *Journal of Fixed Income* 1 (June 1991): 75–88.

day of the month. This means that the party obligated to deliver may choose a different bond from what he or she would have chosen on the final settlement day (seven business days before the end of the month). Thus, the bond that is cheapest to deliver has a time dimension.[3]

The wild card option pertains to the fact that while trading closes at 4 P.M. Chicago time, the futures settlement price for delivery purposes is 2 P.M. Moreover, the party has until 8 P.M. to notify the clearinghouse of its intention to deliver. Hence, a two-hour window occurs in which one can buy late in the day and settle at the 2 P.M. price. In the dealer market, trading can occur over the entire six-hour time span. These possibilities exist for each eligible day in the delivery month.[4]

These delivery options work to the advantage of the party making delivery (i.e., the one with a short position). Simply put, the party has potential choices that may prove to be of value. The greater the value of the options is, of course, the lower the price of the futures contract should be. Various people have tested for this downward bias. While it is confirmed, there appear to be opportunities for arbitrage. For various sample periods, futures prices have been found to be too high or too low relative to the value of the delivery options, indicating that such options are undervalued or overvalued.

The greater the number of delivery options is and the greater the ambiguity with which they are defined, the less likely a futures market is to prosper. The party that is short will always want to deliver the lowest-quality instrument. When there is considerable latitude, things become unsettled in the market. Ultimately, market participants lose faith, particularly after a rapid change in interest rates and/or twist in the term structure. The viability of a market is jeopardized when the contract is flawed at the time of origin. It is essential that the value of any delivery option be tightly constrained. History tells us the market will not otherwise survive.[5]

HEDGING AND SPECULATION

Hedging is taking a future contract position opposite a position taken in the spot market. The purpose is to reduce risk exposure by protecting yourself from unexpected price changes. In contrast, a **speculator** takes positions in futures markets in the pursuit of profits and assumes price risk in this endeavor. In other words, a long or short position is undertaken without an offsetting position in the spot market. The speculator buys or sells futures contracts based on his or her interest-rate expectations. Why not use the spot market? Because it often is more expensive with respect to transactions costs and slower in execution than is the futures market.

---

[3] For an evaluation of the worth of the end-of-the-month option, see Marcelle Arak and Laurie S. Goodman, "Treasury Bond Futures: Valuing the Delivery Options," *Journal of Futures Markets* 7 (no. 3, 1987): 269–86.

[4] See Alex Kane and Alan J. Marcus, "Valuation and Optimal Exercise of the Wild Card Option in the Treasury Bond Futures Market," *Journal of Finance* 31 (March 1986): 195–207, for one type of modeling of this option.

[5] For an excellent analysis of what happens when a contract is flawed, see Elizabeth Tashjian Johnston and John J. McConnell, "Requiem for a Market: An Analysis of the Rise and Fall of a Financial Futures Contract," *Review of Financial Studies* 2 (no. 1, 1989): 1–23.

SOME HEDGING FUNDAMENTALS

The principles of hedging are the same regardless of the type of hedge undertaken. Suppose you wish to hedge an asset you own with an offsetting instrument. You hope that downward price movements in the value of your asset will be offset by upward movements in the value of the instrument with which you hedge. Suppose the asset you own is X and the instrument with which you hedge is Y. The expected change in value of these two instruments can be reflected as

$$\text{Value of } \overline{X} = a + \delta \, (\text{Value of } \overline{Y}) \qquad (9\text{-}2)$$

↗ elasticity

where both changes in value are expected, a is a constant, and delta (δ) reflects the sensitivity of expected changes in X to changes in the value of Y. If this delta were 0.6, it would suggest that on average X goes up or down in value by 0.6 percent with a 1 percent change in the value of Y.

The delta tells us the number of units of Y that should be used to hedge our position in X. The delta is known as the **hedge ratio.** If the delta were 0.6 as assumed above, we would make an offsetting commitment of $0.60 in Y for every $1.00 of investment in X. This delta hedge would be expected to offset the risk of holding X. However, the offset usually is not perfect, for reasons we will illustrate shortly.

Because the values of the two instruments change over time, so does the relationship between them. The delta in Equation (9-2) is not constant over time and must be adjusted if risk is to be minimized. This adjustment is known as **dynamic hedging,** and it must be done with an eye to transactions costs. With this general discussion of hedging in mind, we turn now to the futures market, first describing the relationship between futures and spot prices.

FUTURES AND SPOT PRICES

Futures prices presumably convey expectations about spot, or actual, prices to prevail in the future. Similar to our examination of the term structure of interest rates in chapter 6, the question is whether they are biased estimates of future spot prices. The **expectations hypothesis** holds that they are not. This hypothesis suggests that the present price of a futures contract represents the market's consensus expectation of the future spot price. It is an unbiased estimate, and there is no risk premium.

The **theory of normal backwardation,** by John Maynard Keynes, implies that in the overall market, hedgers want to transfer risk to speculators. A price concession must be offered to entice speculators into the market. That is, the futures price must be less than the expected future spot price. This price inducement is said to diminish as the delivery date approaches, so that futures prices rise during their lives. This theory implies that hedgers are short on a net basis in their futures position. That is, they are net sellers of futures contracts, hedging against a rise in interest rates.

A **normal contango theory** works in the opposite direction. It is based on the notion that hedgers are long on a net basis in the futures market. That is, they are net buyers of futures contracts. In order to entice speculators into taking short positions on a net basis, they must be rewarded with a futures price in excess of the expected spot price. Again, as the delivery date approaches, the premium diminishes in size.

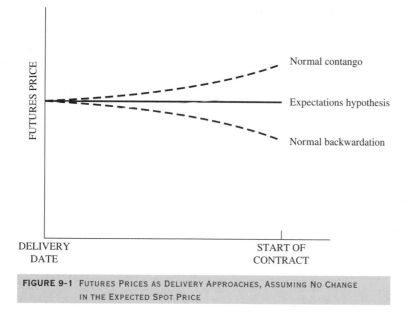

FIGURE 9-1 FUTURES PRICES AS DELIVERY APPROACHES, ASSUMING NO CHANGE
IN THE EXPECTED SPOT PRICE

The three theories are illustrated in Figure 9-1, under the assumption that the expected spot price does not change over the life of the contract. As the concepts involved are familiar from our discussion in chapter 6, we will not dwell on them further.

LONG HEDGES

A **long hedge** involves buying (going long in) a futures contract. It is generally employed to lock in an interest rate that is believed to be high. Suppose an investor will have $1 million to invest in Treasury bonds two months hence—on November 1, for example. The investor believes interest rates have peaked at present and wishes to lock in the current rates (on September 1), even though the funds will not be available for investment for two months.

Suppose the conditions shown in Table 9-3 held for September 1 and November 1, respectively. In the example, we ignore transaction costs and margin deposits. We also assume the use of 8 percent coupon bonds in the spot market, so we do not need a conversion factor. The investor buys 10 futures contracts on September 1, and prices rise

TABLE 9-3   Illustration of a Long Hedge

Cash Market	Futures Market
September 1:	September 1
8% Treasury bond sells at $106^{15}/_{32}$. Investor wants to lock in yield.	Buys 10 December Treasury bond futures contracts at $107^{9}/_{32}$.
November 1:	November 1:
Buys $1 million of 8% Treasury bonds at $113^{6}/_{32}$.	Sells 10 December bond futures contracts at $113^{17}/_{32}$.
Loss: $67,187.50	Gain: $62,500

and yields fall as expected. By selling the contracts on November 1, the investor realizes a gain of $62,500. On the same day, the investor purchases $1 million in Treasury bonds at a higher price and lower yield than prevailed on September 1. The opportunity loss is $67,187.50. Thus, the opportunity loss is offset, but not entirely so, by the gain on the futures contracts. The hedge was less than perfect, but it was largely successful in insulating the investor from price changes.

Notice that the use of the futures market provides a **two-sided hedge.** If interest rates rise in our example, you gain in an opportunity sense on your cash-market purchase November 1, but lose on your futures-market position. If interest rates fall, as they do in the example, the opposite occurs. The hedge is two-sided with respect to price risk; you merely lock in a position (except for residual risk, to be discussed shortly). This contrasts with *one-sided hedges,* such as options, which are taken up in chapter 10. The transactions cost of taking a futures position, either for hedging or for speculative purposes, is relatively low. A $100,000 contract is likely to cost less than $50 to establish and settle.

HEDGE RATIOS

When the coupon rate of the spot market instrument differs from 8 percent, we will want a different face-value position in the futures market. For example, if the bond we contemplate investing in has a 10 percent coupon and 13 years to maturity, we know that its price will fluctuate less than the futures price. The reason is that it has a higher coupon and shorter maturity than the 8 percent coupon, 20-year bond underlying the futures contract. As a result, we probably can hedge with fewer futures contracts. The hedge ratio, defined earlier, reflects this relationship; it is the face value of the futures position divided by the face value of the spot position.

To the extent price volatility is proportional to duration, differences in duration can be used to derive a hedge ratio. Recall from chapter 7 that if interest rates follow the assumptions of Macaulay's duration measure, the percentage change in bond price is $-D[\Delta R/(1 + R)]$, where D is the duration, and the term in brackets is the change in 1 plus the yield. The idea is that the value of the futures position should offset the value of the spot position. Thus,

$$D_f[\Delta R/(1 + R)]_f \times F = D_s[\Delta R/(1 + R)]_s \times S \qquad \textbf{(9-3)}$$

where the f and s subscripts refer to the respective bonds underlying the futures and the spot positions, and F and S refer to the values of these positions. Rearranging Equation (9-3), the hedge ratio becomes

$$\frac{F}{S} = \frac{D_s}{D_f} \times \frac{[\Delta R/(1 + R)]_s}{[\Delta R/(1 + R)]_f} \qquad \textbf{(9-4)}$$

which suggests that the hedge ratio is proportional to the duration ratio times the change in 1 plus the yield ratio.

In our hypothetical example, the duration of the spot position is less than that of the bond underlying the future position. As shorter-term interest rates tend to fluctuate more than longer-term rates, the change in 1 plus the yield for the spot position will be greater than that for the futures position. To illustrate, suppose the duration of the bond underlying the futures position is eight years while that for the spot position is six years.

This gives a duration ratio of $\frac{6}{8} = 0.75$. If the change in 1 plus the yield ratio were 1.12, the hedge ratio would be

$$-\frac{F}{S} = 0.75 \times 1.12 = 0.84$$

If the market value of the spot position (a short position in our example) were $10 million, a futures position of $8.4 million would be necessary to offset it. At $100,000 a contract, this translates into 84 contracts.

The use of this method to derive a hedge ratio gives only an approximation. All the caveats concerning interest-rate behavior and the use of the duration measure discussed in chapter 7 are relevant here. However, the illustration does show that the more volatile the futures position is relative to the spot position, the lower the hedge ratio is.

SHORT HEDGES

A **short hedge** involves the opposite sort of transactions from a long hedge. Here the idea is to sell a futures contract now because of a belief that interest rates will rise. The sale of a futures contract is used as a substitute for the sale of an actual security held. Another example of a short hedge is a corporation that needs to borrow in the future and sells a futures contract now to protect itself against an expected rise in interest rates. Suppose on February 1, a corporation knows it will need to borrow $1 million in the long-term market three months hence. The company believes interest rates will rise and wishes to hedge against this possibility.

Unfortunately, no futures market exists for long-term corporate bonds. Therefore, the company must look to a related market and settles on the Treasury bond futures market. While interest rates in these two markets do not move entirely in concert, a close relationship exists, so a **cross hedge** across markets makes sense. This type of hedge is shown in Table 9-4. Again, we ignore transaction costs and margin deposits. Instead of selling 10 Treasury bond futures contracts, the company sells 12 to bring its total commitment to a little more than $1 million in the futures market. The hedge ratio, which is greater than 1.0, is established in keeping with the considerations in the previous section. Because the cross markets do not have exactly the same price movements, a perfect hedge is not achieved. In this case, the gain in the futures market more than offsets the opportunity loss in the spot market. These examples are sufficient to illustrate the principles of hedging and some of the terms. We turn now to a more in-depth analysis.

TABLE 9-4   Illustration of a Short Cross Hedge

Cash Market	Futures Market

February 1:
    7½% high-grade, 20-year corporate bond sells at 99⅝. Issuer wants to protect against rise in interest rates.
	February 1:
	    Sells 12 June 8% Treasury bond futures contracts at 110²⁄₃₂.

May 1:
    Issues 7½% corporate bond at 91⅞.
	May 1:
	    Buys 12 June 8% Treasury bond futures contracts at 103¹⁴⁄₃₂.

Loss: $75,000	Gain: $79,500

BASIS RISK

The examples show that hedging is not perfect in eliminating all the risk of a position. In hedging, market participants are concerned with fluctuations in the **basis,** which portrays the risk to the hedger. The basis is simply

$$\text{basis} = \frac{\text{spot market}}{\text{price}} - \frac{\text{futures price (adjusted by}}{\text{appropriate conversion factor})} \qquad \textbf{(9-5)}$$

Theoretically, the spot price less the futures price should equal the *cost of carry.* The cost of carry is the cash return, or yield earned, on the asset less the net financing cost. A *positive carry* occurs when the former exceeds the latter; a *negative carry* occurs when the opposite prevails. With a positive carry, the spot price should exceed the futures price; with a negative carry, it should be less than the futures price.

While this is how things should work, hedgers face uncertainty as to what basis will prevail when they close out their futures contracts. This is known as **basis risk.** For example, if the hedger holds 8 percent Treasury bonds long and sells futures contracts in an equivalent amount, both the spot price and the futures price are uncertain at the closeout. At this close, the hedger will receive $\tilde{S}_c$ in the spot market for each bond held long. The futures price at that time is depicted by $\tilde{F}_c$, whereas the futures price at the time the contract is sold is F_0. The latter is known with certainty.

At the closeout, the net funds received are the funds realized from the sale of the bonds held long, together with the gain or loss on the futures position. This can be expressed as

$$\text{net funds received} = Q\tilde{S}_c - Q(\tilde{F}_c - F_0) \qquad \textbf{(9-6)}$$

where Q is the number of bonds involved in both the long position and the short position in the futures market. Rearranging the equation, we have

$$\text{net funds received} = QF_0 + Q(\tilde{S}_c - \tilde{F}_c)$$

Thus, the net funds received depend on the futures price at the time of the hedge, which is known, and the difference between the price received on the sale of bonds in the spot market and the futures price at the close, both of which are uncertain. As both terms of the basis are uncertain at the closeout, the overall hedge is not free of risk. To be sure, risk has been reduced considerably from what would occur with only a long position or only a futures position, because spot and futures markets tend to move in similar ways. However, risk is not totally eliminated and the residual risk is represented by the fluctuations in the basis, or in basis risk, as it is known.

MORE ON BASIS RISK

To illustrate basis risk in a different way, suppose you hold a portfolio of corporate bonds and wish to hedge it. If interest rates rise, the value of your portfolio declines, and vice versa. This is illustrated in the top panel of Figure 9-2. The mathematical relationship between value and interest-rate changes is given by the curvilinear line. Because the corporate bond market is subject to imperfections, there may be deviations about the line, as depicted by the scatter of dots.

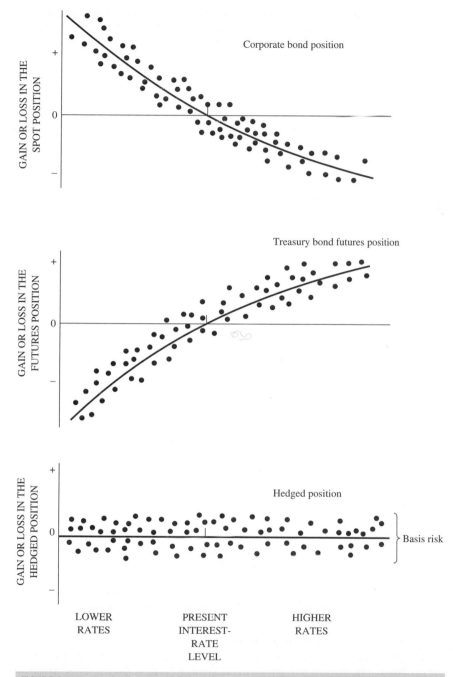

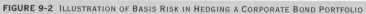

FIGURE 9-2 ILLUSTRATION OF BASIS RISK IN HEDGING A CORPORATE BOND PORTFOLIO

To hedge a portfolio, one would want to write Treasury bond futures contracts. As no viable corporate bond futures market exists, one must resort to a cross hedge. By writing futures contracts, he or she offsets the long position in the spot market with a short position in the futures market. As interest rates rise, the value of the futures contract will increase, and vice versa. The relationship is illustrated by the middle panel of Figure 9-2. Here, too, a random component is depicted by the scatter of dots.

On average, the long and the short positions are offsetting. As shown in the bottom panel of Figure 9-2, the overall position (spot and futures) is insensitive to changes in interest rates. However, there is risk left over, again depicted by the dispersion of dots about the line. This basis risk arises because of somewhat **divergent movements in the spot and futures markets.**

SOURCES OF BASIS RISK

Basis risk has a number of sources. One is the use of a cross hedge as opposed to a direct one; the yield differential between the two markets is uncertain. Another source is a mismatch in maturity. The maturity involved in the futures market may not correspond to the maturity of the instrument(s) one wishes to hedge. The futures markets are confined to 3 months for Eurodollars, 2 to 10 years for Treasury notes, and 15 years or more for Treasury bonds; there are maturity gaps. Also, the bond or note that is cheapest to deliver will change over time. This creates additional uncertainty, as we saw when exploring delivery quality options. The settlement system (marked-to-market) is different from that used in the spot market, which can be a contributing factor to basis risk, as well. Getting the hedge ratio desired may not be possible because the size of the position one wishes to hedge is too small relative to the contract integers of $100,000 or $1 million. Finally, random fluctuations occur in the two markets that either are not removed immediately by arbitrage or are within the transaction-cost boundaries of arbitrage.

For these reasons, a perfect hedge seldom exists. At times, basis risk can be significant. When a number of large market participants, such as investment banks, hedge their positions in the same direction, reversing them can be difficult if they all try to reverse at the same time. The liquidity risk in a chaotic bond market can be substantial.

FORWARD CONTRACTS

The forward contract serves the same economic function as a futures contract, but is different in the detail. The contract itself is arranged in the **over-the-counter market** with an investment bank under a formal agreement. No exchange exists for such contracts; they are arranged privately. The **forward rate** is that rate at which two parties agree to lend and borrow money for a specified period of time in the future. For example, a forward contract might be for a 6-month loan beginning 2 years hence. The forward price is established in keeping with the term-structure notions taken up in chapter 6. The settlement, or delivery, date is explicit in the agreement. In our example, it would be 2 years from now. Also explicit is the source for determining the interest rate that prevails on the settlement date. It might be LIBOR, the Merrill Lynch index on a current coupon maturity Treasury bond, the Bond Buyer's municipal bond index, or some other index.

The buyer of the forward contract agrees to pay the contract rate in the future; the seller agrees to sell funds at that rate. The **notional amount** is the principal involved in the contract upon settlement. Cash settlements are required. If interest rates rise and the settlement rate exceeds the contract rate, the forward-rate buyer benefits in being able to borrow at a lower-than-prevailing interest rate and the seller loses in having to provide funds at a below-market rate. If the settlement rate is less than the contract rate, the opposite occurs. While this is the concept, what actually occurs at settlement is the payment, or receipt, of the present value of the interest differential on the notional amount of the contract. Suppose our forward contract beginning 2 years hence was for 6-month LIBOR at 5.60 percent. At the settlement date in 2 years, interest rates are lower and 6-month LIBOR is 5.20 percent. If the notional amount of the contract is $2.8 million, the interest differential is

$$\text{\$2.8 million} \times (0.056 - 0.052) \times (182/360) = \$5,662.22$$

The seller of the contract owes the buyer this amount on the settlement date. If a contract is reversed prior to the settlement date, the interest differential is figured in the same way, but it must be discounted at the appropriate-maturity interest rate.

For LIBOR and Treasury interest-rate settlement dates going out several years, the forward market is reasonably liquid. Competition among investment banks in the over-the-counter market assures such. With settlement dates beyond several years, the market becomes more "customized," and quotations among investment banks vary.

IMPLICIT FORWARD ARRANGEMENTS

Rather than arrange an explicit forward contract, we know from chapter 6 that you can create one for yourself. Suppose you wanted to lock in a forward rate on Treasury securities—say a 1-year return starting 2 years from now. You could manufacture your own forward contract by buying a 3-year Treasury security and selling short a 2-year security. (With a short sale, you borrow a security and sell it in the market, both of which are through an investment bank. You have the obligation to return the security to the party from whom it was borrowed. If the security declines in value, you will be able to buy it back at a price lower than that at which it was sold. If it is higher in price, the opposite occurs.) By buying the 3-year security and selling short the 2-year security, you have created a forward contract, which upon delivery 2 years hence provides you with a 1-year security. Embedded in the difference in prices is an implied forward rate of interest, which can be determined using Equation (6-3) in chapter 6. Thus, spot market prices for the term structure of interest rates imply forward rates.

FUTURES AND FORWARD CONTRACT DIFFERENCES

Futures and forward contracts have several important institutional differences. The former is traded on an exchange with settlements through a clearinghouse, whereas forward contracts are arranged over the counter with little in the way of a secondary market. Because of the clearinghouse guarantee, the futures contract tends to be safer than a forward contract arranged with an investment bank. The parties to a forward contract are exposed to **counterparty risk,** which is the risk that the other side will not perform according to all of the conditions of the underlying contract. Counterparty risk must be carefully monitored, and this usually is done by restricting transactions to parties with some minimum credit rating, such as single A or better. The futures and forward contracts differ also in that there are daily settlements of a futures position, while settlement of the forward contract comes only at maturity. As discussed previously, the futures position is marked-to-market with daily settlements throughout the life of the contract. However, the forward contract is not constrained as to contract size, such as multiples of $1 million. Rather, it can be customized to most any amount. Also, the forward contract can be made for any maturity and is not contained to the middle of March, June, September, and December as is true for many futures contracts.

MARKET EFFICIENCY BETWEEN FUTURES AND FORWARD RATES

If a futures rate is out of line with the forward rate for the same interval in the future, arbitrage may be possible. A futures contract on Treasury bills, for example, specifies a given return on 91-day bills so many days in the future, numbering m. If there were an m-day Treasury bill and an $(m + 91)$-day Treasury bill in the spot market, a forward rate could be derived using the formula given in chapter 6. If rates of interest on future contracts differ significantly from forward rates, the markets are said to be inefficient. On the other hand, if arbitrage brings the returns into parity, no further opportunities for arbitrage would exist and the markets would be said to be efficient.

Should the futures rate exceed the forward rate, an arbitrager could buy a futures contract for 91-day Treasury bills delivered m days hence and essentially short a forward contract in the spot market for the same period—namely, m to $m + 91$ days in the future. He or she might accomplish this by establishing a short position in Treasury bills maturing in $m + 91$ days and using the exact proceeds of the short sale to buy Treasury bills maturing in m days. Ignoring transaction costs and margin requirements, the cash inflows from the proceeds of the bills maturing on the mth day will exceed the cash outflow needed to take delivery on the futures contract on the mth day. On the $(m + 91)$st day, the proceeds realized on the maturing bills will equal the outflow associated with maturation of the originally shorted $(m + 91)$-day bills.

If the forward rate exceeds the futures rate, the arbitrager will wish to sell a futures contract for 91-day bills to be delivered m days hence and buy a forward contract for the same time frame. In this case, the latter might be accomplished by establishing a short position in m-day Treasury bills and using the exact proceeds to buy $(m + 91)$-day bills. On the mth day, the Treasury bills held long are used to make delivery on the futures contract. The cash inflows realized from delivery of the bills on this contract will exceed the cash outflow associated with maturation of the originally shorted m-day bills if we again ignore the transaction costs and margin requirements. In both these situations, the arbitrager has no risk. In efficient markets then, arbitrage could be expected to bring forward rates and future rates into parity.

POSSIBLE REASONS FOR DEVIATION OF FORWARD AND FUTURES RATES

However, the futures rate may not equal the forward rate for various reasons. For one thing, arbitrage has transaction costs. These consist of (1) costs involved in opening and closing a futures position, including margin requirements, (2) costs of buying and selling securities long in the spot market, and (3) cost of establishing a short position in the spot market. With respect to a short position, the arbitrager must post collateral equal in value to the securities borrowed, as well as pay a percentage premium for such securities. This premium, around half a percent on an annualized basis, means that the dollar cost of the premium increases with the time to maturity. The effect here is a tendency for forward rates to exceed futures rates for more distant maturities, all other things the same. For both margin deposits on futures contracts and collateral deposits on short positions, securities can be deposited. As a result, the arbitrager does not suffer an opportunity loss on the funds. The costs of opening and closing a futures position and of buying and selling securities long in the spot market are relatively small in magnitude. Moreover, they are nondirectional; they simply establish a band within which arbitrage is not profitable. Only the cost of short selling for longer maturities is directional, and it argues for forward rates exceeding futures rates.

As we know from previous discussion, futures positions are settled daily, while settlement of the forward contract comes only at maturity. Each day the losing party in a futures contract, either the buyer or the seller, must pay the full amount of the futures price change that day. If the daily interest rate at which such funds can be invested is stochastic, the arbitrage hedge described earlier would not be entirely free of risk. Technically, the day-to-day debits and credits must be taken into account. John C. Cox, Jonathan E. Ingersoll, Jr., and Stephen A. Ross argue that the differences in timing of cash flows may create a price discrepancy between forward and futures contracts.[6] They developed a model for valuing the two contracts that incorporates differences in settling-up procedures. The instantaneous interest rate is assumed to follow a mean reverting diffusion process. Under this assumption, they find that if futures and spot prices are positively correlated, the futures contract price will be less than the forward contract price, because more risk is involved with the former. If they are negatively correlated, the futures contract price will exceed the forward contract price. Unless interest rates get very volatile, differences in settling-up procedures on futures and forward contracts result in relatively small differences in prices of the two contracts using the Cox-Ingersoll-Ross (CIR) model.

A third factor perhaps responsible for differences in futures and forward rates is differences in default risk and liquidity on the two types of contracts. The futures contract generally is safer and more liquid than the forward contract, for reasons previously discussed. As a result, the rate of return on a forward contract might be expected to be slightly higher than the futures rate.

Although a number of empirical tests have been conducted to compare returns on futures contracts and derived forward contracts, the evidence is mixed as to market efficiency. These tests look for an absence of arbitrage opportunities as confirmation of market efficiency. Virtually all studies find evidence that futures rates are out of line with forward rates part of the time. For shorter-term contracts, there is largely an absence of arbitrage opportunities once we allow for transactions costs. For longer-term contracts, small arbitrage opportunities seem to emerge from time to time. However,

---

[6] John C. Cox, Jonathan E. Ingersoll, Jr., and Stephen A. Ross, "The Relation between Forward Prices and Futures Prices," *Journal of Financial Economics* 9 (December 1981): 321–46. For empirical support of the Cox-Ingersoll-Ross proposition using Eurodollar data, see Lisa Meulbroek, "A Comparison of Forward and Futures Prices of an Interest-Rate Sensitive Financial Asset," *Journal of Finance* 47 (March 1992): 381–96.

the mispricing found between futures and forward markets decreased sharply from the 1980s to the 1990s. Overall, the markets are largely efficient today.

❖ SUMMARY

The value of a derivative security derives from a primary financial instrument. A futures contract is standardized and traded on an exchange; it calls for delivery of a specific financial instrument or one of a basket of approved instruments at a specified future date. Some markets do not require a delivery instrument, but rather involve a cash settlement based on an interest-rate index. Both the buyer and the seller of a contract must maintain margin as a security deposit. Each day, the value of the contract is marked-to-market, with the losing party required to put up additional margin if the account falls below the maintenance requirement. With longer-term contracts, an adjustment factor converts the futures price, which is based on an 8 percent coupon rate, to an appropriate settlement price for the bond actually delivered. Several quality delivery options are available to the seller of a contract; these options have to do with the specific security delivered and the timing of delivery.

Futures prices may or may not be good estimates of expected future spot prices. The expectations hypothesis says they are unbiased estimates, whereas the theories of normal backwardation and normal contango suggest they are biased estimates, though in opposite directions. Hedging involves taking a futures position opposite to that taken in the spot market in order to reduce exposure to risk substantially. There are long hedges, short hedges, and cross hedges (across different financial instruments). The hedge ratio reflects the number of futures contracts necessary to offset price movements in a spot position. A speculator takes positions in the futures market in anticipation of profiting from interest-rate movements. Hedging usually does not eliminate all risk; basis risk remains. The basis is the spot price minus the futures price, and fluctuations in this basis represent risk to the hedger.

A forward contract is like a futures contract as to its economic purpose, but differs as to institutional detail. Forward contracts are arranged privately through an investment bank in the over-the-counter market and are nonstandardized. The forward rate is the rate at which the two parties agree to lend and borrow money for a specified period of time in the future. Rather than a formal contract, one can manufacture one's own forward contract by buying long one security and selling short a like security with a lesser time to maturity. This is an implicit forward contract. Futures and forward contracts differ in settlement, maturities and sizes possible, and credit risk.

Market efficiency concerns whether arbitrage opportunities exist between the futures and the spot markets. Such opportunities usually are judged by comparing the futures rate with the forward rate embodied in the spot market for the same future period. Several possible reasons for deviations were explored. The empirical evidence on market efficiency was reviewed, and it was sufficiently mixed to make generalizations difficult.

❖ SELECTED REFERENCES

Arditti, Fred D., *Derivatives.* Boston: Harvard Business School Press, 1996.

Cox, John C., Jonathan E. Ingersoll, Jr., and Stephen A. Ross, "The Relation between Forward Prices and Futures Prices," *Journal of Financial Economics* 9 (December 1981): 321–46.

Duffle, Darrell, *Futures Markets.* Upper Saddle River, NJ: Prentice Hall, 1989.

Fabozzi, Frank J., *Bond Markets, Analysis and Strategies,* 4th ed., chapter 21. Upper Saddle River, NJ: Prentice Hall, 2000.

Grinblatt, Mark, and Narasimhan Jegadeesh, "The Relative Pricing of Eurodollar Futures and Forward Contracts," *Journal of Finance* 51 (September 1996): 1499–1522.

Hemler, Michael L., "The Quality Delivery Option in Treasury Bond Futures Contracts." *Journal of Finance* 45 (December 1990): 1565–86.

Hong, Harrison, "A Model of Returns and Trading in Futures Markets," *Journal of Finance,* 55 (April 2000).

Hull, John, *Options, Futures and Other Derivative Securities,* 2nd ed. Upper Saddle River, NJ: Prentice Hall, 1993.

Jarrow, Robert A., and Stuart Turnbull, *Derivative Securities,* 2nd ed. Cincinnati: South-Western, 2000.

Johnston, Elizabeth Tashjian, and John J. McConnell, "Requiem for a Market: An Analysis of the Rise and Fall of a Financial Futures Contract," *Review of Financial Studies* 2 (no. 1, 1989): 1–23.

Lekkos, Ilias, "Distributional Properties of Spot and Forward Interest Rates," *Journal of Fixed Income* 8 (March 1999): 35–54.

Rendleman, Richard J., Jr., "Duration-Based Hedging with Treasury Bond Futures," *Journal of Fixed Income* 9 (June 1999): 84–91.

Rubinstein, Mark, "Derivative Assets Analysis," *Economic Perspectives* 1 (Fall 1987): 73–93.

Smith, Clifford W., Jr., Charles W. Smithson, and D. Sykes Wilford, *Managing Financial Risk,* chapters 6–12. New York: Harper & Row, 1990.

Stoll, Hans R., and Robert E. Whaley, *Futures and Options.* Cincinnati: South-Western, 1993.

Tuckman, Bruce, *Fixed Income Securities,* chapter 14. New York: John Wiley & Sons, 1995.

CHAPTER 10

DERIVATIVE SECURITIES: OPTIONS

Another security that derives from an underlying instrument is the option. The option may have to do with equity, whereby the option holder is able to acquire stock. It may be that the option is to acquire a debt instrument or a futures position, which is like a double derivative security. Option valuation is fundamental not only to understanding certain financial instruments but also to understanding specific features, such as callability, the ability to prepay a mortgage, and sinking funds. In this chapter, our attention is on option-type securities, while in chapters 12 and 13 we focus on option features embedded in various instruments. Fundamental to both is option valuation, which we take up next.

OPTION VALUATION

An **option** is simply a contract that gives the holder the right, but not the obligation, to buy or sell an asset at some specified price. In this chapter, the asset is either common stock, a debt instrument, or an interest-rate futures contract. A **call** option gives the holder the right to buy the asset. A **put** option gives the right to sell the asset. More complex options involve combinations of calls and puts. The price at which the transaction takes place is known as the **exercise** or **strike** price. We might have a call option to buy one share of ABC Corporation's common stock at $31.50 or an option to buy a Treasury bond at $97.125. Another feature is the **expiration** date. In the case of a *European-type* option, it is the only date at which the option may be exercised. In contrast, an *American-type* option may be exercised at any time up to and including the expiration date.

The party providing the option is known as the **writer.** In the case of a call option being exercised, the writer must deliver the asset to the option holder. The writer, of course, receives the exercise price. In the case of a put option being exercised, the writer must buy the asset at the exercise price. Many options are traded on exchanges, such as the Chicago Board of Trade and the Chicago Mercantile Exchange. In other cases, investment banks make markets and these options are traded **over the counter.**

EXPIRATION DATE VALUE OF AN OPTION

Consider first a European type of option, exercisable only on the expiration date. The value of a call option at this date is simply

$$V_0 = \max.(V_a - E, 0) \tag{10-1}$$

where V_a is the market price of the associated asset, E is the exercise price of the option, and max. means the maximum value of $V_a - E$, or zero. If the value of the asset less the exercise price were negative, the option holder would not exercise the option. Therefore, its value is bounded at zero on the downside. To illustrate the formula, suppose a Treasury bond had a value of $98.00 at expiration and the exercise price of a call option is $95.25. The value of the option would be $98.00 - $95.25 = $2.75. If the bond's value were $94, the option value would be zero. The same example can be formulated for a share of common stock.

In Figure 10-1, the value of the asset is on the horizontal axis, and the expiration date value of the option is on the vertical axis. When the value of the asset exceeds the exercise price, the option has a positive value and increases in a linear one-to-one manner with increases in the value of the asset. When the value of the asset equals or is less than the exercise price, the call option has a value of zero.

To determine whether an investor holding an option gains or loses, we must take account of the price, or premium, paid for the option. If we disregard, for the moment, the time value of money and transactions costs, the investor's gain or loss is simply the value of the option at the expiration date less the price paid for it. To break even, the value of the asset must exceed the exercise price by an amount equal to the premium paid for the option. This is illustrated in the top panel in Figure 10-2. Here we see that the investor suffers a loss until the asset rises in price to the point that it equals the exercise price of the option plus the premium. After that, as the asset rises in price, the holder of the option gains.

For the writer, or seller, of the call option, the opposite picture emerges. As shown in the lower panel of Figure 10-2, the writer receives the premium and realizes a gain as long as the value of the asset at the expiration date is less than the exercise price plus the premium. If it is more, the seller loses, and losses deepen with increases in the value

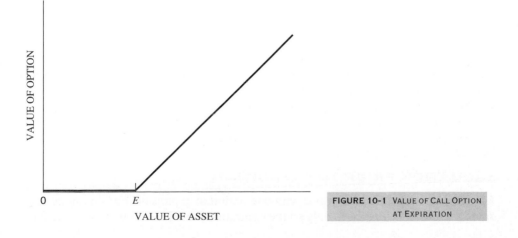

VALUE OF OPTION

0   E

VALUE OF ASSET

FIGURE 10-1 Value of Call Option at Expiration

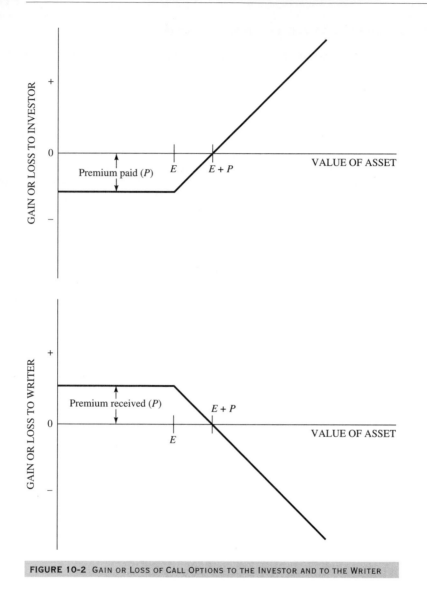

FIGURE 10-2 GAIN OR LOSS OF CALL OPTIONS TO THE INVESTOR AND TO THE WRITER

of the asset. In options, then, the expiration date gain or loss to the investor and to the writer of the option are mirror images of each other. It is a "zero-sum" game in which one can gain only at the expense of the other.

For the put option, the same mirror image occurs, but the directions are opposite those shown in Figure 10-2. In Figure 10-3, the situation is illustrated. In this case, the investor gains and the writer loses if the asset declines in value below the exercise price.

VALUATION PRIOR TO EXPIRATION

Consider now a call option's value with one period to expiration. For simplicity, let us assume that it can be exercised only on the expiration date. The value of the asset at the ex-

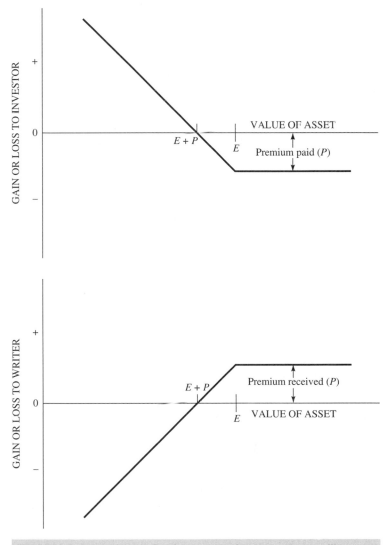

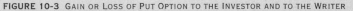

FIGURE 10-3 GAIN OR LOSS OF PUT OPTION TO THE INVESTOR AND TO THE WRITER

piration date is not known but is subject instead to probabilistic beliefs. As long as some time remains until expiration, it is possible for the market value of the option to be greater than its theoretical value. The reason is that the option *may* have value in the future. The actual value of the option might be described by the dashed line in Figure 10-4. If the current asset price is less than the exercise price in the figure, the option is said to be trading **"out of the money."** The further to the left an option is on the dashed line, the deeper the option is "out of the money," and the less the likelihood that it will have value at the expiration date. If the asset price exceeds the exercise price, the option is said to be trading **"in the money,"** whereas if it equals the exercise price, the option is trading **"at the money."**

In general, the longer the period of time until expiration, the greater the value of the option is relative to its theoretical value. This makes sense in that there is more time

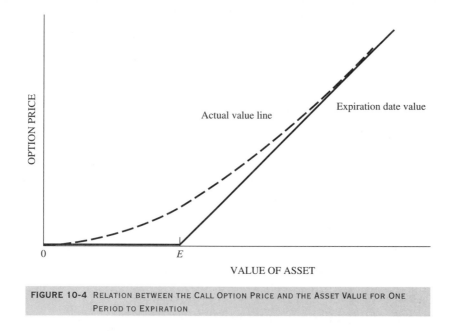

VALUE OF ASSET

FIGURE 10-4 RELATION BETWEEN THE CALL OPTION PRICE AND THE ASSET VALUE FOR ONE
PERIOD TO EXPIRATION

in which the option may have value. Moreover, the further in the future one pays the exercise price, the lower its present value is, and this, too, enhances the option's value. As the expiration date of an option approaches, the relationship between the option value and the asset value becomes more convex, as shown in Figure 10-5. Line 1 represents an option with a shorter time to expiration than that for line 2, and line 2 represents an option with a shorter time to expiration than that for line 3.

Usually, the most important factor in the valuation of options is the price volatility of the associated asset. More specifically, the greater the possibility is of extreme outcomes, the greater the value of the option is to the holder, all other things the same. We may, at the beginning of a period, be considering options on two common stocks that have the following probability distributions of possible values at the expiration of the option.

Probability of Occurrence	Price of Stock A	Price of Stock B
0.10	$30	$20
0.25	36	30
0.30	40	40
0.25	44	50
0.10	50	60

The expected stock price at the end of the period is the same for both stocks: $40. Stock B, however, has a much larger dispersion of possible outcomes. Suppose the exercise prices of options to purchase stock A and stock B at the end of the period are the same—for example, $38. Thus, the two stocks have the same expected values at the end

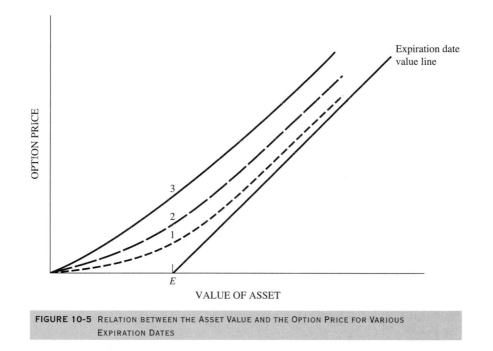

FIGURE 10-5 RELATION BETWEEN THE ASSET VALUE AND THE OPTION PRICE FOR VARIOUS EXPIRATION DATES

of the period, and the options have the same exercise price. The expected value of the option for stock A at the end of the period, however, is

$$\text{Option A} = 0(0.10) + 0(0.25) + (\$40 - \$38)(0.30)$$
$$+ (\$44 - \$38)(0.25) + (\$50 - \$38)(0.10) = \$3.30$$

whereas that for stock B is

$$\text{Option B} = 0(0.10) + 0(0.25) + (\$40 - \$38)(0.30)$$
$$+ (\$50 - \$38)(0.25) + (\$60 - \$38)(0.10) = \$5.80$$

Thus, the greater dispersion of possible outcomes for stock B leads to a greater expected value of option price on the expiration date. The reason is that values for the option cannot be negative. As a result, the greater the dispersion is, the greater the magnitude of favorable outcomes is, as measured by the stock price minus the exercise price. Increases in the volatility of the stock therefore increase the magnitude of favorable outcomes for the option buyer and, hence, increase the value of the option.

HEDGING WITH OPTIONS

Having two related financial assets—an asset and an option on that asset—we can set up a risk-free hedged position. Price movements in one will be offset by opposite price movements in the other. A hedged position can be established by buying the asset (holding it long) and by writing options. If the asset goes up in price, we gain in our long position—that is, in the asset we hold. We lose in the options we have written, because the price we must pay for the asset in order to deliver to the person exercising the option is higher than it was when the option was written. If the asset goes down in price, the opposite occurs. We lose on our long position but gain on the options we have written.

Thus, when one holds a combination of assets and options written, movements upward or downward in the price of the asset are offset by opposite movements in the value of the option position written. If one does this properly, the overall position (long in asset, options written) can be made approximately risk free. The appropriate hedge ratio of stock to options is known as the *option delta;* the fundamentals of hedging were discussed in chapter 9 in the context of interest-rate futures markets. In market equilibrium, one would expect to earn only the risk-free rate on a perfectly hedged position. To the extent that excess returns are available on a fully hedged position, people will have an incentive to take such positions. The impact of their transactions on relative prices will drive out any excess returns that might be earned. As a result, prices will adjust until the return on the hedged position is the risk-free rate and the option is neither overpriced nor underpriced. In Appendix A to this chapter, we show market equilibration across call options, shares of stock, and put options, employing what is known as the **put-call parity theorem.** This explanation should give the interested reader a better understanding of how arbitrage works to bring about market equilibrium.

BLACK-SCHOLES OPTION MODEL

In a seminal paper, Fischer Black and Myron Scholes developed a precise model for determining the equilibrium value of an option.[1] This model is based on the hedging notion discussed earlier. Black and Scholes assume the following: an option that can be exercised only at expiration, with no transaction costs or market imperfections; an asset with no interest, principal, or dividend payments through the expiration date of the option; a known short-term interest rate at which market participants can both borrow and lend; and, finally, asset price movements that follow a random pattern where the probability distribution of returns is normal and variance is constant over time.

Given these assumptions, we can determine the equilibrium value of an option. Should the actual price of the option differ from that given by the model, we could establish a riskless hedged position and earn a return in excess of the short-term interest rate. As arbitragers enter the scene, the excess return will eventually be driven out and the price of the option will equal that value given by the model. To illustrate, suppose the current market price of a share of stock is $20 and the price of a call option is $7. At $20 a share along the horizontal axis in Figure 10-4, suppose the slope of the actual value line is one-half. Therefore, a hedged position can be established by buying a share of stock for $20 and writing two options at $7 each. The *net money* invested in this position is $20 − 2($7) = $6.

This combination of holding one share of stock long and two options short leaves us essentially hedged with respect to risk. If the stock drops slightly in value, the value of the short position goes up by approximately an equal amount. We say *approximately* because with changes in the price of the common and with changes in time, the ideal hedge ratio changes. With a stock price increase, for example, the slope of the line in Figure 10-4 increases. Therefore, fewer options need to be written. If the stock price declines, the slope decreases and more options need to be written to maintain a hedge. As a general rule, the higher the stock price is relative to the exercise price, the less risky the option is and the fewer the options that must be used to hedge. In addition to stock price changes, the actual value line will shift downward as time goes on and the expira-

---

[1] Fischer Black and Myron Scholes, "The Pricing of Options and Corporate Liabilities," *Journal of Political Economy* 81 (May–June 1973): 637–54.

tion date approaches. This was illustrated in Figure 10-5. Thus, one's short position in options must be adjusted from time to time for changes in the stock price and for the passage of time if a riskless hedged position is to be maintained. Arbitrage will assure that the return on this position is approximately the short-term, risk-free rate.

In this context, the equilibrium value of an option that entitles the holder to buy one share of stock is shown by Black and Scholes to be

$$V_0 = V_s N(d_1) - \left(\frac{E}{e^n}\right) N(d_2) \tag{10-2}$$

where

V_s = the current price of the stock
E = the exercise price of the option
e = 2.71828
n = the number of periods to expiration of the option
r = the short-term interest rate continuously compounded
$N(d)$ = the value of the cumulative normal density function

$$d_1 = \frac{\ln(V_s/E) + (r + 1/2\sigma^2)t}{\sigma\sqrt{t}}$$

$$d_2 = \frac{\ln(V_s/E) + (r - 1/2\sigma^2)t}{\sigma\sqrt{t}}$$

$\ln$ = the natural logarithm
σ = the standard deviation of the annual rate of return on the stock continuously compounded
t = the length of time in years to the expiration of the option

The important implication of this formula is that the value of the option is a function of the short-term interest rate, of the time to expiration, and of the variance rate of return on the stock, but it is not a function of the expected return on the stock. The value of the option in Equation (10-2) increases with the increase of the time to expiration, the standard deviation, and the short-term interest rate.

The reason for the first two relationships with option values is obvious from our earlier discussion. The last is not so obvious. Recall that a person is able to take a position in options that will provide the same dollar movements as the associated stock but with a lower net investment. The difference in net money in the option relative to the stock may be invested in short-term market instruments. The greater the return on these investments is, the greater the attraction of the option is relative to the stock, and the greater its value. Another way to look at the matter is that the greater the interest rate is, the lower the present value of the exercise price is that will need to be paid in the future if the option is exercised, and the greater the value of the option. Of the three factors affecting the value of the option, however, the short-term interest rate has the least impact.

In solving the formula, we know the current stock price, the time to expiration, the exercise price, and the short-term interest rate. The key unknown, then, is the standard deviation. This must be estimated. The usual approach is to use the past volatility of the stock's return as a proxy for the future. Black and Scholes, as well as others, have tested the model using standard deviations estimated from past data with good results. Given the valuation equation for options, Black and Scholes derive the ratio of shares of stock to options necessary to maintain a fully hedged position. It is shown to be $N(d_1)$, which was defined earlier. Thus, the Black-Scholes model permits the quantification of the various factors that affect the value of an option.

In Table 10-1, Black-Scholes option values are shown for various assumptions as to standard deviation, exercise price, short-term interest rate, r, and the time to expiration of the option, t. A number of computer programs exist for solving the Black-Scholes pricing formula. It also may be solved by hand with the help of a calculator having a natural logarithm function and with the aid of a normal probability distribution table.

TABLE 10-1   Option Prices from Black-Scholes Equation for Various Parameter Values (Price of Underlying Stock = $40)

r = 5%

Standard Deviation	Exercise Price	t = 1 Month	t = 4 Months	t = 7 Months
0.20	35	5.15	5.77	6.42
0.20	40	1.00	2.18	3.02
0.20	45	0.02	0.51	1.11
0.30	35	5.22	6.26	7.19
0.30	40	1.46	3.08	4.20
0.30	45	0.16	1.26	2.24
0.40	35	5.39	6.90	8.11
0.40	40	1.92	3.99	5.38
0.40	45	0.42	2.11	3.44

r = 10%

Standard Deviation	Exercise Price	t = 1 Month	t = 4 Months	t = 7 Months
0.20	35	5.30	6.29	7.26
0.20	40	1.09	2.54	3.67
0.20	45	0.03	0.65	1.47
0.30	35	5.36	6.72	7.92
0.30	40	1.55	3.42	4.79
0.30	45	0.18	1.45	2.66
0.40	35	5.52	7.31	8.76
0.40	40	2.00	4.31	5.94
0.40	45	0.45	2.33	3.87

r = 15%

Standard Deviation	Exercise Price	t = 1 Month	t = 4 Months	t = 7 Months
0.20	35	5.44	6.81	8.11
0.20	40	1.19	2.94	4.38
0.20	45	0.03	0.82	1.91
0.30	35	5.50	7.18	8.66
0.30	40	1.64	3.78	5.42
0.30	45	0.20	1.67	3.12
0.40	35	5.65	7.73	9.42
0.40	40	2.09	4.65	6.52
0.40	45	0.48	2.57	4.34

With these notions as to option valuation in mind, we are ready to explore various financial instruments having option characteristics.

DEBT OPTIONS

The first is options on debt instruments. Exchange markets for such options began in 1982 with options on individual Treasury securities and options on interest-rate futures contracts. The former have withered, but an over-the-counter market exists for such options. Institutional investors are the primary users of **direct options** on securities, using them to hedge their risk exposure to the specific instrument.

Futures options give the buyer the right, but not the obligation, to buy from, or sell to, a writer a futures contract at a specified price any time during the option period. With a call option, the buyer has the right to purchase the futures contract at the exercise price. With a put, the buyer has the right to sell the futures contract at the exercise price. There are futures options for a number of instruments: Treasury notes, Treasury bonds, Eurodollars, long British Gilts, German government bonds, and others.

One reason futures options have thrived and spot instrument options have not is that there are problems in accounting for and valuing coupon payments when it comes to options on spot instruments. With a futures option, for example, accrued interest does not enter into the settlement. This makes things easier. Also, delivery is not a problem because the deliverable supply of futures contracts is quite large.

FEATURES OF FUTURES OPTIONS

To illustrate certain features, let us explore Treasury bond futures options. Suppose the quotations for such options were those shown in Table 10-2. The September and December dates relate to the delivery dates for the futures contract. (See chapter 9.) However, the option's expiration date is five business days before the beginning of September or December. This lead time is necessary because delivery on the futures contract can occur as early as the first business day of the month.

The strike price is the price per $100 of face value that must be assumed if the option is exercised. Taking the first strike price, the holder of a call option has the right to assume a long position in a Treasury bond futures contract at a price of $108 any time prior to the expiration of the option. Upon exercise, the call writer assumes a short position in the futures

TABLE 10-2   Values of Call and Put Options on Treasury Bond Futures

Strike Price	Calls		Puts	
	September	*December*	*September*	*December*
108	4–55	5–52	0–40	1–43
109	3–21	3–35	1–02	2–18
110	2–02	2–30	1–46	3–08
111	1–06	1–40	2–47	4–12
112	0–35	1–02	4–09	5–44
113	0–18	0–41	5–51	7–08

contract. Remember from chapter 9 that a Treasury bond futures contract assumes an 8 percent coupon rate. The holder of a put option has the right to assume a short position in the contract, again at an exercise price of $108. Upon exercise, the put writer assumes a long position. For both options, a cash settlement does not occur when the option is exercised. Rather, the option holder acquires a long or short position in the futures market with the same margin and marked-to-market requirements as described in chapter 9.

The price of the call option (strike price of 108) in Table 10-2 is 4^{55}⁄₆₄ for the September contract and 5^{52}⁄₆₄ for the December contract. For a $100,000 contract (the minimum size), these quotations translate into $4,859.38 and $5,812.50, respectively. The September put option has a price of ^{40}⁄₆₄ and the December contract 1^{43}⁄₆₄. The higher the strike price, the less valuable the call option and the more valuable the put option. The different prices for September and December reflect the option value associated with a longer time to expiration and, perhaps, different interest-rate expectations.

USE OF DEBT OPTIONS

With a futures contract, an investor's gain or loss depends on interest-rate movements. If one wished to hedge a long position in a fixed-income security, he or she would take a short position in a futures contract; that is, a hedger would write a contract. By such action a hedger largely neutralizes risk; the remaining basis risk was described in chapter 9. Such a hedge is illustrated in the top panel of Figure 10-6.

With an option, the potential loss is limited to the premium paid. This contrasts with a futures position where the loss is not so bounded. If an individual wished to hedge a long position in a fixed-income security, he or she would buy a put option. The situation is illustrated in the bottom panel of Figure 10-6.

Options are particularly suited to hedging risk in one direction. Consider a fixed-rate loan commitment by a financial institution. If interest rates rise, a high proportion of the commitments will be taken down, necessitating the financial institution to make loans at below-market rates of interest. By purchasing a put option, however, the financial institution offsets the value loss that occurs with higher interest rates. If interest rates decline, customers will renegotiate their loans at lower rates and let their commitments expire. Thus, the risk to the financial institution is one-sided—rising interest rates. Effectively, the financial institution has written a put option to its customers. To hedge, it may purchase a put option in the market.

So far we have discussed only put options. However, one can buy call options or write either type of option. The various configurations of price movements are shown in Figure 10-7. The dark lines represent expiration date values of the options as interest rates change. Note that with interest rates on the horizontal axis, the lines are opposite what they would be if prices were used. Also, the lines are curvilinear, reflecting the relationship between value changes and interest rates. Thus, debt options can be used in a number of ways to hedge risk or to place bets on the direction and/or volatility of interest rates.

CAPS, FLOORS, COLLARS, AND CORRIDORS

On occasion, borrowers want to **cap** their short-term, floating-rate borrowing costs. If interest rates should rise beyond some specified ceiling, the borrower pays no more. One vehicle for "manufacturing" your own cap is to purchase a put option. Should interest rates rise, you pay more on your borrowings but gain on your put position. Caps also can

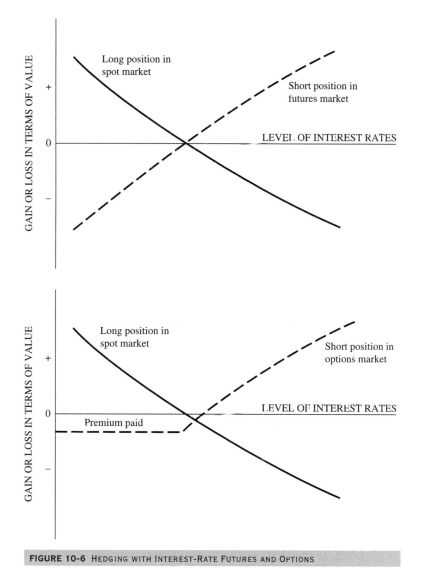

FIGURE 10-6 HEDGING WITH INTEREST-RATE FUTURES AND OPTIONS

be arranged directly with a lender or an investment bank, for a price. Usually the price takes the form of a fee. The presence of a cap protects the borrower, as shown in the top panel of Figure 10-8, relative to what occurs under a straight floating-rate arrangement. The index frequently used in the cap market is the three-month LIBOR rate.

The buyer of cap protection pays an up-front fee, which is like the premium paid on an interest-rate put option. The higher the cap is in relation to existing interest rates and the less their volatility, the lower the fee. For the buyer, the cap pays off if interest rates rise above the cap rate. Otherwise, he or she is out the up-front fee paid. The overall cap contract can be broken down into separate periods. In this sense, we have a series of options with different expiration dates, but all with the same strike price—namely, the cap rate of interest. These options are known as **caplets.** Caplets can be priced off the

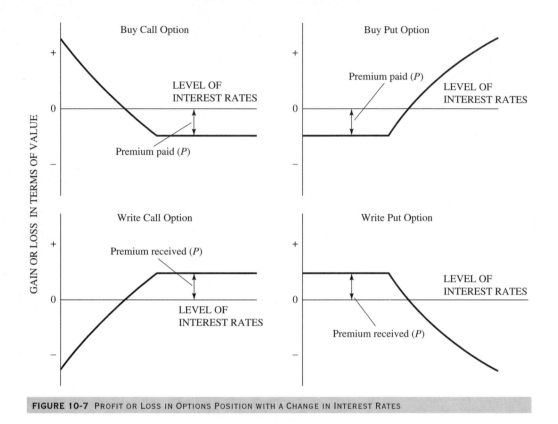

FIGURE 10-7 PROFIT OR LOSS IN OPTIONS POSITION WITH A CHANGE IN INTEREST RATES

forward-rate yield curve. (See chapters 6 and 9.) The value, or up-front fee, for the overall cap is the summation of the individual caplet values. Thus, pricing an overall cap depends upon the yield curve. The steeper its slope is, the more valuable the more distant caplets are. All other things the same, the overall value of the cap increases.

If a borrower is willing to accept a **floor,** in addition to receiving a cap, a **collar** is created. This arrangement is shown in the lower panel of Figure 10-8. If interest rates fall below the floor, the borrower pays the floor rate. If they rise above the ceiling, the borrower pays the cap rate. Only in the intermediate range do borrowing costs vary with underlying short-term interest rates. Like the cap, a floor can be broken down into a series of options, or **floorlets,** that pay off if the interest-rate index, say LIBOR, goes below the floor interest rate. Floorlets also are priced off the forward-rate yield curve, and the value of the overall floor is the summation of the individual floorlet values.

The advantage of the collar is that the cost to the buyer is much less than what an interest-rate cap costs. By accepting a floor, the collar buyer offsets the cost of the cap, usually to a great extent. The pricing of the collar depends on the level of existing interest rates relative to the cap and floor rates, the volatility of interest rates, and the shape of the yield curve. For upward-sloping yield curves, the cap usually costs more than the value of the floor. (This statement is conditioned on the level of interest rates being roughly in the middle of the cap-floor range.) As a result, an up-front fee is charged for the collar. When the yield curve is flat, the floor becomes more valuable relative to the cap. If the yield curve is downward sloping, it is even possible for the buyer of a collar to receive an up-front fee from the seller.

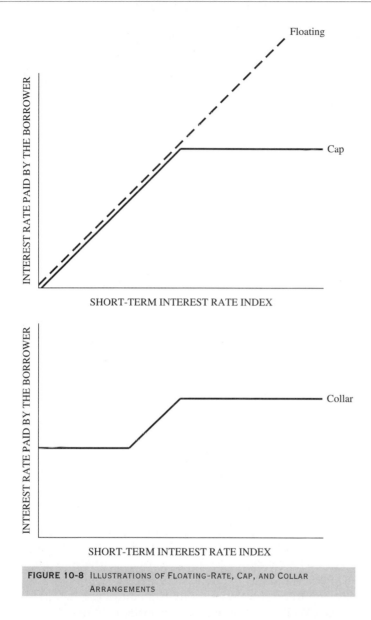

FIGURE 10-8 ILLUSTRATIONS OF FLOATING-RATE, CAP, AND COLLAR
ARRANGEMENTS

Yet another risk-shifting device is the interest-rate **corridor,** illustrated in Figure 10-9. As seen in the figure, the rate paid is constrained only in the middle, the mirror image of the collar. In other words, the buyer of an interest-rate corridor is only partially protected. The corridor is a combination of two caps. A cap is bought at the lower interest-rate strike level, and a second cap is sold at the higher interest-rate strike level. Within the corridor, the cap bought protects the buyer while the cap sold does not work against him or her. Outside the corridor, no protection is provided and the interest rate paid by the borrower floats with the index. When interest rates decline below the lower band, he or she benefits; when they rise above the upper strike level, the effect is adverse.

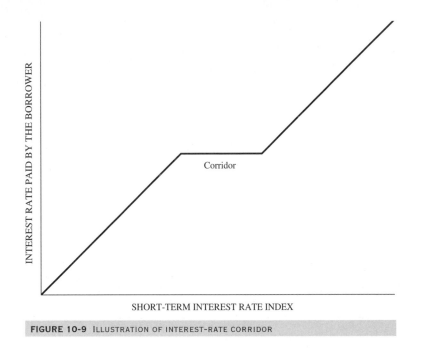

FIGURE 10-9 Illustration of Interest-Rate Corridor

However, this adverse effect is mitigated by the difference between the two strike levels. Expressed differently, the interest cost is what a straight floating-rate loan would cost less the difference between the two strike interest rates.

Other forms of interest-rate protection can be crafted, but these are the major products. The cap, collar, and corridor markets have developed as customized derivative products, and they are available through commercial and investment banks.[2] In turn, these institutions use debt options to insulate their interest-rate risk exposure.

VALUATION OF DEBT OPTIONS

Option pricing models in the spirit of Black-Scholes may be used to value debt options (substituting futures prices and variances for stock prices and variances in the formula). As with any option, the key is the volatility of returns for the associated asset. In this case, volatility has to do with the variability of interest rates. Unlike stock options, where the return variance is assumed to be constant over time, a bond's return variance declines as maturity approaches. While the assumption of constant variance may be reasonable over a short time span, it obviously does not hold over the long run. Variance changes over time. Another problem is the assumption of a constant short-term interest rate, implying a term structure anchored at the short end.

Because prices of fixed-income securities are bounded on the upside by their face value at maturity, a problem occurs in applying standard option pricing formulas. Such formulas assume no limits for the volatility parameter, frequently expressed in terms of

---

2 For a methodology for pricing caps and collars, see Eric Briys, Michel Crouhy, and Rainer Schobel, "The Pricing of Default-Free Interest Rate Cap, Floor, and Collar Agreements," *Journal of Finance* 46 (December 1991): 1879–92.

the lognormal price distribution. Instead of price, many scholars use yield and assume that it conforms to some type of distribution, usually lognormal, at the expiration of the option. Finally, most option models, such as Black-Scholes, are for European options, whereas debt options may be exercised up to and including the expiration date. However, adjustments can be made to come to grips with the problem of early exercise.[3]

Another approach, and one that is commonly used, is the binomial, lattice-type model described in chapter 6. This type of model is grounded in an arbitrage-free equilibrium theory of the term structure of interest rates and attempts to map the stochastic process governing interest-rate movements.[4] The approach is illustrated in chapter 12, so we do not do so here. How accurately one maps volatility is the key to whether or not the model will be successful. Various scholars have studied debt options and have obtained reasonable explanations of their pricing. While the models are not perfect, the average pricing error generally is small.

YIELD CURVE OPTIONS

Just as there are options on interest rates, there are options on yield spreads. The spread is simply a long-term Treasury interest rate minus a shorter-term rate. For the SYCURVE (slope of the yield curve) options of Goldman Sachs, for example, the more popular options are the 2-year to 10-year spread, the 2-year to 30-year spread, and the 10-year to 30-year spread. No deliverable instrument is involved; all settlements are on a cash basis, relative to the spread that prevails on exercise of the option.

The exercise "price" is expressed in terms of basis points. Suppose the exercise, or strike, spread for a 2-year to 30-year call option is 125 basis points, or 1¼ percent. If the actual yield spread turns out to be greater than 125 basis points, the option is "in the money" and can be exercised to advantage. The holder receives 1 cent per $1 of face value for every basis point above the exercise spread. If the actual spread turns out to be 144 basis points and a $1 million call option is involved, the settlement amount is

$$(144 - 125) \times 0.01 \times \$1 \text{ million} = \$190,000$$

Whether the option holder makes money, of course, depends on what was paid for the option. If the premium were $110,000, the net profit would be $80,000 on the contract.

A put option is opposite in direction. If the actual spread is below the exercise spread, the option is "in the money." The gain or loss to option holders of yield curve calls and puts is illustrated in Figure 10-10. The exercise spread is denoted by E in the figure. The principle demonstrated is the same as that for any option (see Figures 10-2 and 10-3). Instead of the value of the asset or interest rates appearing on the horizontal axis,

---

[3] See Robert E. Whaley, "On Valuing American Futures Options," *Financial Analysts Journal* 42 (May–June 1986): 49–59. See also Hans R. Stoll and Robert E. Whaley, *Futures and Options,* chapter 15 (Cincinnati: South-Western, 1993).

[4] See Fischer Black, Emanuel Derman, and William Toy, "A One-Factor Model of Interest Rates and Application to Treasury Bond Options," *Financial Analysts Journal* 46 (January–February 1990): 33–39. Wolfgang Buhler, Marliese Ulrig-Homburg, Ulrich Walter, and Thomas Weber, "An Empirical Comparison of Forward-Rate and Spot-Rate Models for Valuing Interest-Rate Option," *Journal of Finance* 54 (February 1999): 269–305, test various valuation models and find that the best is the one-factor model with proportional volatility.

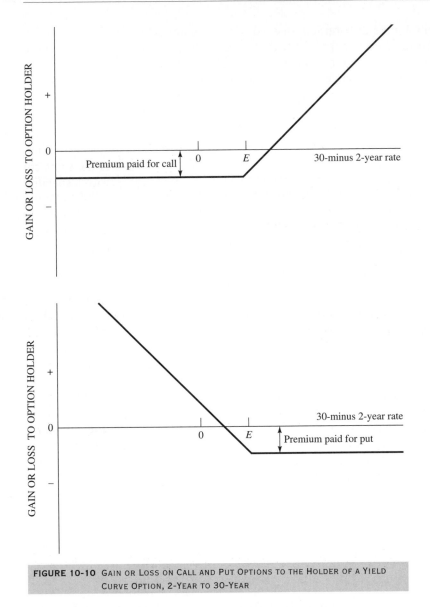

FIGURE 10-10 GAIN OR LOSS ON CALL AND PUT OPTIONS TO THE HOLDER OF A YIELD
CURVE OPTION, 2-YEAR TO 30-YEAR

however, the yield spread appears. As with other options, the yield curve option has an expiration date, at which time it is automatically exercised if it is "in the money."

For the call option holder, the bet being placed is that the term structure of interest rates will widen, whereas with a put option it is predicted to flatten. A number of applications to bond portfolio management are possible. Risk can be more effectively isolated when this financial innovation is used either by itself or in combination with other derivative securities. The greater the volatility of yield spreads is, of course, the more valuable this type of option is and the greater the premium that is charged for its use. However, volatility of a spread is different from the volatility of yield for a specific maturity instrument. As a result, the valuation of these options is more complicated even though some of the same tools are used.[5]

CONVERTIBLE SECURITIES

Convertible securities are forms of options. As such, their valuation depends on the factors described earlier. A convertible security is a bond or a share of preferred stock that can be converted at the option of the holder into common stock of the same corporation. The investor is provided with a fixed return from a bond or with a specified dividend from preferred stock. In addition, the investor has an option on the common stock. As a result, a company is able to sell a convertible security at a lower yield than it would have to pay on a straight bond or preferred stock issue. As the principles are nearly the same, our subsequent discussion will focus only on convertible bonds.

CONVERSION PRICE/RATIO

The ratio of exchange between the convertible security and the common stock can be stated in terms of either a **conversion price** or a **conversion ratio.** Suppose Zapata Corporation's 6 percent convertible subordinated debentures ($1,000 face value) have a conversion price of $43.75. To determine the conversion ratio, we merely divide $1,000 by $43.75 to get 22.86 shares. This is the number of shares of stock a holder will receive upon converting his or her debenture.

The **conversion value** of a convertible security is the conversion ratio of the security times the market price per share of the common stock. If Zapata stock were selling for $48 per share, the conversion value of the debenture would be $22.86 \times \$48 = \$1,097$. At the time of issuance, the convertible security will be priced higher than its conversion value. The differential is known as a **conversion premium.** Zapata's share price at the time of issuance was $38½. Therefore, the conversion premium was $43.75 - \$38.50 = \$5.25$. On a percentage basis, this translates into 13.6 percent. For most issues of convertibles, the conversion premium ranges from 10 to 25 percent. For a growth company, the conversion premium can be in the upper part of this range, or perhaps even higher—like 30 percent, in the case of super growth. For companies with more moderate growth, the conversion premium may be closer to 10 percent. The range itself is established mainly by market tradition.

DEBT PLUS OPTION CHARACTERISTIC

The convertible bond may be viewed as straight debt plus an option to purchase common stock. If the expiration of the option and the maturity of the convertible are the same, then the following roughly holds.

$$\frac{\text{Debt}}{\text{Value}} + \frac{\text{Option}}{\text{Value}} = \frac{\text{Convertible Bond}}{\text{Value}} \qquad \textbf{(10-3)}$$

Both the value of the debt and the value of the option components are affected by the volatility of the company's cash flows. The greater this volatility, the lower the value of

---

[5] See Francis A. Longstaff, "The Valuation of Options on Yields," *Journal of Financial Economics* 26 (July 1990): 97–121.

the debt component but the higher the value of the option component. Thus, risk cuts both ways. As risk increases, it may be that the enhanced value of the option component more than offsets the decline in the debt component. As a result, the interest rate for the convertible may not increase with more firm risk and actually could decrease. Whereas the high-risk company may be unable to sell straight debt, the option characteristic makes the package attractive in the marketplace.

In Appendix B to this chapter, we explore the option characteristics of convertible securities in detail. But now we look at their valuation in more traditional ways.

VALUE OF CONVERTIBLE SECURITIES

As we know, the value of a convertible bond is twofold: its value as a bond and its potential value as common stock. Investors obtain a hedge. If the market price of the stock rises, the value of the convertible is determined largely by its conversion value. If the market for the stock turns down, the investor still holds a bond whose value provides a floor below which the price of the convertible is unlikely to fall.

The bond value of a convertible security is the price at which a straight bond of the same company would sell in the open market. It can be determined by solving Equation (10-4) for B in the case of a bond with semiannual interest payments.

$$ B = \sum_{t=1}^{2n} \frac{C}{\left(1 + \dfrac{r}{2}\right)^t} + \frac{F}{\left(1 + \dfrac{r}{2}\right)^{2n}} \qquad \textbf{(10-4)} $$

where

   B = straight bond value of the convertible
   C = semiannual interest payments determined by the coupon rate
   F = face value of the bond
   n = years to final maturity
   r = market yield to maturity on a straight bond of the same company

In the equation, we assume semiannual interest payments, which are typical with corporate bonds, so the total number of interest payments is two times the years to maturity, n, and the semiannual interest rate on a straight bond is r divided by 2.

Suppose Zapata Corporation's 6 percent convertible debentures have a final maturity of 20 years. If the company is to sell a straight 20-year bond in the current market, the yield will have to be 8.6 percent to be attractive to investors. For a 20-year bond with a 6 percent coupon to yield 8.6 percent to maturity, the bond must sell at a discount. Using the preceding equation and rounding to the nearest dollar, we have

$$ B = \sum_{t=1}^{40} \frac{\$30}{(1.043)^t} + \frac{\$1,000}{(1.043)^{40}} = \$754 $$

Thus, the bond value floor of the company's convertible bonds is $754. This floor suggests that if the price of the common stock were to fall sharply, the price of the convertible would fall only to $754. At that price, the security would sell as a straight bond in keeping with prevailing bond yields for that grade of security.

The bond value floor of a convertible is not constant over time. It varies with (1) interest-rate movements in the capital markets and (2) changes in the financial risk of the company involved. If interest rates in general rise, the bond value of a convertible will decline. If the yield-to-maturity on a straight bond in our example increases from 8.6 percent to 9.0 percent, the bond value of the convertible will drop from $754 to $724. Moreover, the company's credit rating can either improve or deteriorate over time. If it improves and the company is able to sell a straight bond at a lower yield-to-maturity, the bond value of the convertible security will increase, all other things held constant. If the company's credit standing deteriorates and the yield on a straight bond increases, the bond value floor will decline. Unfortunately for investors, when the market price of the stock falls because of poor earnings, the company may have financial difficulty, in which case its credit standing will suffer. As a result, the straight bond value of the convertible may decline along with the decline in its conversion value, giving investors less downside protection than they might have expected originally.

PREMIUMS

Convertible securities frequently sell at premiums over both their bond value and their conversion value. Recall that the conversion value of a convertible is simply the current market price per share of the company's common stock times the number of shares into which the security is convertible. The fact that the convertible bond provides the investor with a degree of downside protection, given the qualifications mentioned previously, often results in its selling at a market price somewhat higher than its conversion value. The difference is known as the **premium-over-conversion value.**

Moreover, a convertible bond typically will sell at a **premium-over-bond value,** primarily because of the conversion feature. Unless the market price of the stock is very low relative to the conversion price, the conversion feature usually will have value, in that investors may eventually find it profitable to convert the securities. To the extent that the conversion feature does have value, the convertible will sell at a premium over its straight bond value.

The trade-off between the two premiums depicts the value of the option to investors and is illustrated in Figure 10-11. The market price of the common is on the horizontal axis; the value of the convertible security is on the vertical. Note that the two axes are on different scales. The diagonal line, which starts at the origin, represents the conversion value of the bond. It is linear, as the conversion ratio is invariant with respect to the market price of the stock. The bond-value line, however, is related to the market price of the common. If a company is doing badly financially, the prices of both its common stock and its bonds are likely to be low. At the extreme, if the total value of the company were zero, both the bonds and the stock would have a value of zero. As the company becomes sounder financially and the common stock increases in price, bond value also increases but at a decreasing rate. After a point, the bond-value line becomes flat, and further increases in common stock price are unrelated to it. At this point, the bond-value floor is determined by what other high-grade bonds sell for in the market. The upper curved line represents the market price of the convertible security. The distance between this line and the bond-value line is the premium-over-bond value, while the distance between the market-value line and the conversion-value line represents the premium-over-conversion value.

We see that at relatively high common-stock price levels, the value of the convertible as a bond is insignificant. Consequently, its premium-over-bond value is high,

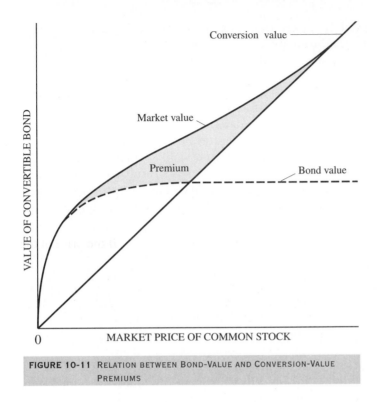

FIGURE 10-11 RELATION BETWEEN BOND-VALUE AND CONVERSION-VALUE PREMIUMS

whereas its premium-over-conversion value is negligible. The security sells mainly for its stock equivalent. Investors are unwilling to pay a significant premium-over-conversion value for the following reasons. First, the greater the premium of market price of the convertible over its bond value is, the less valuable the bond value protection is to the investor. Second, when the conversion value is high, the convertible may be called; if it is, investors will want to convert rather than redeem the bond for the call price. Upon conversion, of course, the bond is worth only its conversion value.

On the other hand, when the market value of the convertible is close to its straight bond value, the conversion feature has little value. At this level, the convertible security is valued primarily as a straight bond. Under these circumstances, the market price of the convertible is likely to exceed its conversion value by a significant premium.

The principal reason for premiums in market price over both conversion value and bond value is the unusual appeal of a convertible as both a bond and an option on common stock. It offers the holder partial protection on the downside, together with participation in upward movements in stock price. Thus, the distribution of possible outcomes is skewed to the right, and this characteristic finds favor with investors. Both the bond-value and the stock-value components of the convertible security can be valued using the option pricing notions discussed earlier. (See Appendix B to this chapter.)

OTHER REASONS FOR PREMIUMS

Although we have concentrated on the main reasons for premiums, other factors appear to have at least a modest influence. Some of their influence stems from the presence of certain impediments to the perfect market assumptions implied earlier in our discussion. For one thing, lower transaction costs on convertible bonds relative to those on common stocks enhance the attractiveness of these bonds. By purchasing convertible bonds and converting them into common stock, investors incur somewhat lower transactions costs than they would by purchasing the stock outright. This attraction should exert upward pressure on the premium-over-conversion value and premium-over-bond value. Yet another influence that may raise premiums is that certain institutional investors, such as life insurance companies, are restricted with respect to investing in common stock. By investing in convertible bonds, they gain the benefits of a common-stock investment without actually investing in common stock.

The length of time to expiration of the convertible option also should affect the premiums. The longer this time frame is, the more valuable the option is. Unlike other options, however, the time to expiration is uncertain. The longest time to expiration is the maturity of the security, but actual expiration typically is shorter. If the price of the common stock increases steadily, the conversion value of the bond eventually will exceed the call price by a comfortable margin. At this point, many companies call the bond issue, causing the investor to convert rather than accept the lower-valued call price. This is known as "forcing conversion," and the timing of such is at the discretion of the issuer.

Another factor is the dividend on the common. The greater the dividend is, the greater the attraction is of common vis-à-vis the convertible security and the lower the premiums, all other things the same. All these influences affect the premiums at which convertible securities sell, but they are less important than the influences discussed in the previous section.

❖ SUMMARY

Many financial instruments have option characteristics. A call option gives the holder the right, but not the obligation, to buy a debt or an equity instrument at a stated exercise price, either on the expiration date, in the case of a European-type option, or up to and including the expiration date, in the case of an American-type option. A put option enables the holder to sell an asset at a stated price. The party who provides either type of option is known as the writer. The key factor in valuing options is the volatility of the associated asset. The more volatile the associated asset's price, the greater the option's value. Value also increases with a longer time to expiration and a higher short-term interest rate. By hedging an underlying asset with options, Black and Scholes developed a precise equilibrium model for option valuation in which the expected return on the hedged position is the risk-free rate. This model and variations of it have widespread use. Arbitrage brings about market equilibrium; the put-call parity theorem is illustrated in Appendix A.

Debt options may be either on a specific spot market instrument or, more commonly, on an interest-rate futures contract. Markets for both calls and puts exist, and the features are similar to other options. However, a futures option gives the holder the right to assume a long or a short position in a futures contract. Debt options are particularly suited to hedging "one-sided" risk: The hedger effectively buys insurance for which a premium is paid. Various scholars have fashioned valuation models that recognize changing variance and other unique aspects associated with debt options.

A variation of option has to do with caps on floating-rate borrowing costs. When a cap is combined with a floor, a collar is created where the interest rate paid varies only within a range. The cap and the collar are priced off the forward yield curve. With a corridor arrangement, the interest rate paid is constant within a range but floats on either side of the corridor. In addition to interest-rate options, there are options on yield spreads between various maturity Treasury securities. The purchaser of a yield spread call option gains if the term structure becomes more steeply upward-sloping, whereas a put option purchaser gains if it flattens. The more volatile the twists in the term structure are, the more valuable these types of options are.

A convertible security can be viewed as straight debt plus an option to buy common stock. The premiums at which a convertible security sells above its conversion value and above its bond value are due to the security's partial downside protection as a bond and its upside potential as stock (the same principle as with any option), the volatility of the common stock, the duration of the convertible option (the issuer calling the bond or its maturing), the dividend on the common, and certain institutional imperfections that affect investors. In Appendix B, we examine convertibles in light of certain option pricing notions.

APPENDIX A
Put-Call Parity

In the equilibration process driven by arbitrage, a relationship exists between put, call, and stock prices. To illustrate, assume European-type put and call options where both have the same exercise price, $30, and the same expiration date. Suppose our strategy is to sell one put option and to buy one call option. If we ignore for now the premiums earned and paid, the expiration date values of the two options are shown in Figure 10A-1. We see that the expiration date value of our put-call strategy is the stock price less the exercise price of $30, described by the diagonal line throughout. Now suppose we buy the stock and borrow the exercise price of the options with a loan maturing at the expiration date. The expiration date value of our position, ignoring interest, is also the stock price minus $30. Thus, the two strategies produce the same result.

In market equilibrium with zero arbitrage opportunity, a precise relationship exists between the market values of the put and the call options and the stock. We have established that the payoff from a strategy of buying a call and selling a put is the same as that from buying the stock and borrowing the exercise price. Taking account of the time value of money, the relationship can be expressed as

$$V_c - V_p = V_s - PV(E) \quad \textbf{(10A-1)}$$

where

V_c = value of call option
V_p = value of put option
V_s = value of share of stock
$PV(E)$ = present value of the exercise price, where the time interval is the time to expiration of the options

Rearranging Equation (10A-1),

$$-V_s + PV(E) + V_c - V_p = 0 \quad \textbf{(10A-2)}$$

which is the put-call parity theorem. This basic expression can be rearranged further to solve for any one of the four values, given the other three. For the value of the call,

$$V_c = V_s + V_p - PV(E) \quad \textbf{(10A-3)}$$

For the value of the put, it would be

$$V_p = -V_s + V_c + PV(E) \quad \textbf{(10A-4)}$$

and for the value of the stock,

$$V_s = V_c - V_p + PV(E) \quad \textbf{(10A-5)}$$

Suppose that a put option had a value of $3, that both options had an exercise price of $30 and six months to expiration, that the interest rate were 4 percent for six months, and that the share

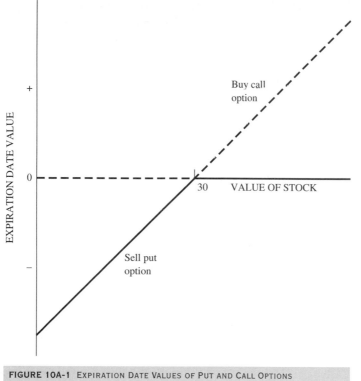

FIGURE 10A-1 EXPIRATION DATE VALUES OF PUT AND CALL OPTIONS

price were $35. If there were no opportunities for arbitrage, the value of the call option would be

$$V_c = \$35 + \$3 - \$28.80 = \$9.20$$

If the call option value were other than this, there would be opportunity for arbitrage.

Thus, the put-call parity theorem may be used to determine whether the stock and the options are priced correctly. Zero arbitrage opportunity means that there is market equilibrium in the prices of all three securities, as was the case in the chapter for the call option and the stock.

APPENDIX B
Application of Option Pricing Concepts to Valuing Convertible Securities

As we know, a convertible security is an option to obtain common stock in a corporation. As with any option, the greater the volatility of the stock and the underlying volatility of firm value are, the greater the value of the option is to the convertible security holder.

In a conceptual sense, the debtholders of a corporation can be viewed as option writers, and equityholders can be viewed as holding an option on the firm's total value. At the maturity of the debt, the equityholders have the option of buying back the firm from the debtholders at a specified price, which is the face value of the debt instrument. In this context, the greater the volatility of the value of the total firm is, the greater the value of the option is to the equityholders. On the other hand, the greater the volatility is, the greater the default risk is in the sense that the firm will be worth less than the debt's face value. If default occurs, equityholders will not exercise their option, bankruptcy by definition will occur, and debt-holders will suffer a loss. In chapter 12, we explore the valuation of the call option on straight debt. Here we find that the greater the volatility of future interest rates is, the greater the value of the call option is to the equityholders and the greater the value loss is to the debtholders. If such interest-rate volatility is anticipated at the time of the loan, lenders will demand a higher interest rate to compensate themselves for the call risk.

All three factors influence the valuation of convertible bonds, and it is useful to explore the interrelationships. What will emerge is not a precise model, if indeed one were possible, but a general overview of the valuation underpinnings. To begin, let us assume that financial markets are perfect, that a firm has no debt other than convertible bonds, and that bondholders and the firm follow optimal strategies. Under these circumstances, optimal strategies consist of (1) bond-holders converting their bonds into stock if the value of the convertible is less than its conversion value; (2) bondholders forcing the firm into bankruptcy and seizing its value if the value of the firm falls below the debt's face value, assuming that the ability to do so is written into the contract; and (3) the firm calling the bonds when their value equals the call price.

Given these actions, the boundaries for the valuation of convertible bonds are shown in Figure 10B-1. If the value of the bonds should exceed the call price, they will be called so their value is bounded on the upside by the call price. On the downside, bondholders will force bankruptcy, should the value of the firm fall below the total face value of the bonds outstanding.[1] Moreover, bond-holders will convert if the value of their bonds falls below the conversion value, so we have another lower boundary. Finally, the total value of the bonds cannot exceed the total value of the firm. As a result of these constraints, the value of the bonds must fall within the shaded area in the figure.

---

[1] This assumes that at the time of the loan, the firm's value exceeds the face value of the bonds.

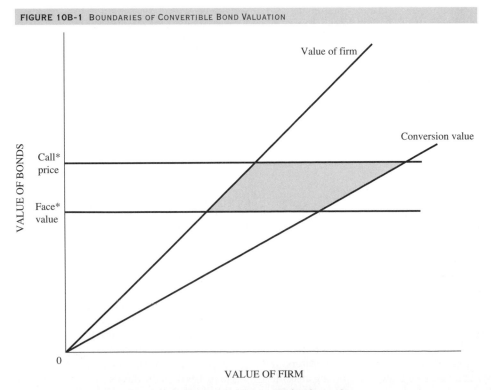

FIGURE 10B-1 BOUNDARIES OF CONVERTIBLE BOND VALUATION

*Represents the total value of all bonds at the call price and at face value.

Within these boundaries, certain relationships are likely to hold. For one, we would expect an inverse relationship between the risk of default and the value of the firm. That is, increases in firm value would be associated with decreases in default risk up to a point. As a result, we might expect the relationship shown in the upper panel of Figure 10B-2. Here we see that the value of the bonds increases at a decreasing rate until the curve eventually turns up, in keeping with the change in conversion value. This phenomenon was discussed in the chapter, and we know that

FIGURE 10B-2 CONVERTIBLE BOND VALUATION WITH DEFAULT RISK

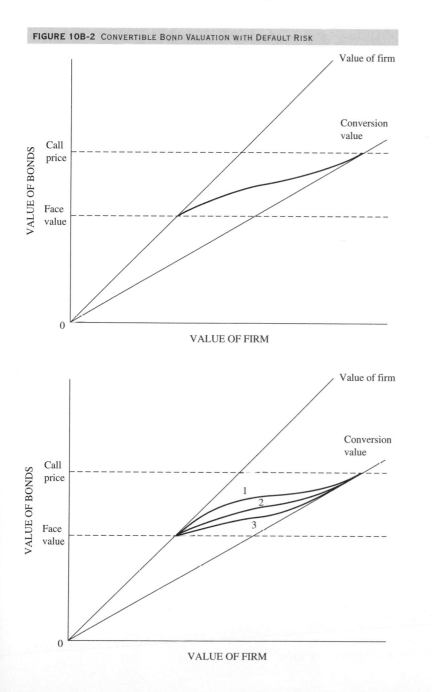

it embraces both default risk and firm value volatility.

For a given firm value, companies can have different business-risk strategies, which result in different default risks. Therefore, the relationship between bond value and firm value will differ, depending on the risk strategy chosen by the firm.

In the bottom panel of Figure 10B-2, risk strategy 1 is safer than strategies 2 and 3, in the sense of less volatility of firm value. Accordingly, the risk of default is less for any level of firm value, and the value of the convertible bonds is higher.

Having considered default risk, we turn now to interest-rate risk. For given levels of firm value

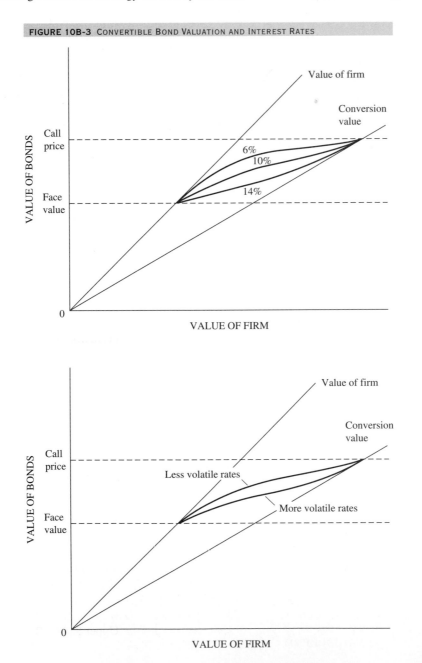

FIGURE 10B-3 CONVERTIBLE BOND VALUATION AND INTEREST RATES

and default risk, the greater the interest rate is, the lower the value of the outstanding convertible bonds is. The relationship is depicted by the upper panel of Figure 10B-3. For a hypothetical interest rate of 6 percent, the bond-value line is higher than it is for interest rates of 10 percent and 14 percent, respectively. This follows, of course, from the valuation of any fixed-income security. Apart from the expected level of interest rates, the greater the volatility of future interest rates is, the greater the value is of the call option to the company, and the lower the value of the convertible security is to the holder. This situation is depicted in the lower panel of Figure 10B-3. Bear in mind that if the bond is called, the holder has the option to convert it into common stock; therefore, the impact of the call is far less than it is in the case of straight debt. Finally, we should point out that in determining whether a convertible security is called, stock-price volatility usually dominates interest-rate volatility.

We have described the more important two-way relationships affecting the valuation of convertible bonds, but other relationships complicate the picture. For one thing, there is likely to be an association among the level of interest rates, default risk, and the value of the firm. High interest rates often are associated with periods of high and uncertain inflation. Consequently, the value of the firm will be less, all other things the same, than it is in times of low inflation, moderate uncertainty, and low interest rates. Similarly, periods of high inflation, great uncertainty, and high interest rates may be characterized by greater default risk. Thus, the volatility of firm value and the volatility of interest rates are not independent, and this makes the valuation of the hybrid convertible security complicated indeed.

Our purpose is not to present a formal model, but to point out the direction of bond-value changes that are likely to accompany parameter changes.[2] This discussion, which draws on concepts of option pricing theory, gives us a richer understanding of the valuation of convertible securities, a topic that will see increasing research in the direction discussed in this appendix.

---

[2] For one approach to modeling the relationships, see Michael J. Brennan and Eduardo S. Schwartz, "Analyzing Convertible Bonds," *Journal of Financial and Quantitative Analysis* 15 (November 1980): 907–29.

❖ SELECTED REFERENCES

Arditti, Fred D., *Derivatives.* Boston: Harvard Business School Press, 1996.

Asquith, Paul, "Convertible Bonds Are Not Called Late," *Journal of Finance* 50 (September 1995): 1275–89.

Bakshi, Gurdip S., and Zhiwu Chen, "An Alternative Valuation Model for Contingent Claims," *Journal of Financial Economics* 44 (April 1997): 123–65.

Black, Fischer, "The Pricing of Commodity Contracts," *Journal of Financial Economics* 3 (March 1976): 161–79.

Black, Fischer, Emanuel Derman, and William Toy, "A One-Factor Model of Interest Rates and Its Application to Treasury Bond Options," *Financial Analysts Journal* 46 (January–February, 1990): 33–39.

Black, Fischer, and Myron Scholes, "The Pricing of Options and Corporate Liabilities," *Journal of Political Economy* 81 (May–June 1973): 637–54.

Brennan, Michael J., and Eduardo S. Schwartz, "Analyzing Convertible Bonds," *Journal of Financial and Quantitative Analysis* 15 (November 1980): 907–29.

Briys, Eric, Michel Crouhy, and Rainer Schobel, "The Pricing of Default-Free Interest Rate Cap, Floor, and Collar Agreements," *Journal of Finance* 46 (December 1991): 1879–92.

Buhler, Wolfgang, Marliese Uhrig-Homburg, Ulrich Walter, and Thomas Weber, "An Empirical Comparison of Forward-Rate and Spot-Rate Models for Valuing Interest-Rate Options," *Journal of Finance* 54 (February 1999): 269–305.

Dietrich-Campbell, Bruce, and Eduardo Schwartz, "Valuing Debt Options: Empirical Evidence," *Journal of Financial Economics* 16 (July 1986): 321–44.

Fabozzi, Frank J., *Bond Markets, Analysis and Strategies,* chapter 22. Upper Saddle River, NJ: Prentice Hall, 2000.

Fabozzi, Frank J., *Measuring and Controlling Interest Rate Risk.* New Hope, PA: Frank J. Fabozzi Associates, 1996.

Heath, D., R. Jarrow, and A. Morton, "Bond Pricing and the Term Structure of Interest Rates: A New Methodology," *Econometrica* 60 (March 1992): 77–105.

Ho, Thomas S. Y., and David M. Pfeffer, "Convertible Bonds: Model, Value Attribution, and Analytics," *Financial Analysts Journal* 52 (September–October 1996): 35–44.

Hull, John, *Options, Futures, and Other Derivative Securities,* 4th ed. Upper Saddle River, NJ: Prentice Hall, 2001.

Jarrow, Robert, and Stuart Turnbull, *Derivative Securities,* 2nd ed. Cincinnati: South-Western, 2000.

Kihn, John, "The Effect of Embedded Options on the Financial Performance of Convertible Bond Funds." *Financial Analysts Journal* 52 (January–February 1996): 15–26.

Longstaff, Francis A., "The Valuation of Options on Yields," *Journal of Financial Economics* 26 (July 1990): 97–121.

Rubinstein, Mark, "Derivative Assets Analysis," *Economic Perspectives* 1 (Fall 1987): 73–93.

Schaefer, Stephen M., and Eduardo S. Schwartz, "Time-Dependent Variance and the Pricing of Bond Options," *Journal of Finance* 42 (December 1987): 1113–28.

Stoll, Hans R., and Robert E. Whaley, *Futures and Options,* chapter 15. Cincinnati: South-Western, 1993.

Tsiveriotis, Kostas, and Chris Fernandez, "Valuing Convertible Bonds with Credit Risk," *Journal of Fixed Income* 8 (September 1998): 95–102.

Whaley, Robert E., "On Valuing American Futures Options," *Financial Analysts Journal* 42 (May–June 1986): 49–59.

DERIVATIVE SECURITIES: INTEREST-RATE AND CREDIT SWAPS

A **swap,** as the name implies, represents an exchange of obligations. The three principal types are currency swaps, interest-rate swaps, and credit swaps. With the first, two
parties exchange interest obligations on debt denominated in different currencies. At
maturity, the principal amounts are exchanged, usually at a rate of exchange agreed to
in advance. With an interest-rate swap, interest payment obligations are exchanged between two parties. Like a series of forward contracts, it is a device for shifting interest-
rate risk. This market is unregulated and began in the early 1980s. With a credit swap,
the idea is to unbundle the credit risk of a fixed-income security and transfer it to someone else. Our focus in this chapter is on interest-rate swaps and credit derivatives; in
chapter 14 we consider currency swaps.

FEATURES OF INTEREST-RATE SWAPS

The most common interest-rate swap is a **floating/fixed** type. For example, a corporation that has borrowed on a fixed-rate basis may swap with a counterparty to make
floating-rate payments. The counterparty, which has borrowed directly on a floating-
rate basis, agrees to make fixed-rate payments in the swap. No transfer of principal occurs; it is **notional** only as to principal amount outstanding. The interest obligation is
what is exchanged, and this usually is done every six months. The exchange itself is on
a net settlement basis; that is, the party who owes more interest than it receives in the
swap pays the difference. Often, the arrangement is blind in that the counterparties do
not know each other. An intermediary—often a commercial or investment bank—
makes the arrangements. Sometimes the intermediary will assume the obligation of one
of the counterparties, but usually this assumption is only temporary until an outside
counterparty can be found.

Typically, floating-rate payments are tied to the London Interbank Offer Rate
(LIBOR) though this does not need to be the case. LIBOR is the rate for top-quality
Eurodollar borrowings by banks. The maturity of LIBOR used as the index can be

one-month, three-months, or six-months with the latter being the most popular. The **frequency of reset** for the floating rate is specified in the swap contract. For standardized swaps, a secondary market exists. This market allows contracts to be reversed or terminated, providing a degree of liquidity to be discussed shortly.

While the floating-rate/fixed-rate swap is the most common, a **basis swap,** or floating-to-floating swap as it sometimes is called, also is used. With this type of arrangement, two floating-rate obligations are exchanged. Typically, the indices used are different for the two instruments. One might be LIBOR while the other is the six-month Treasury bill rate. If a party's assets and liabilities are priced from different indices, a basis swap may put them on the same footing. It is an effort to reduce basis risk (described in chapter 9); hence, the name.

In addition to these standard swaps, there is an array of customized swaps. The swap might involve a timing mismatch of a zero-coupon obligation with a level, periodic payment obligation. It might involve a swap with a reversal feature, or a contingent, option-like component. One of the parties, or both, might have a rate cap or a swap with caps and floors. Often an interest-rate swap is combined with a currency swap. When two or more currencies are brought into the picture, things get complicated rather quickly, as we shall discover in chapter 14.

AN ILLUSTRATION

To illustrate a basic floating-rate/fixed-rate swap, consider the example in Figure 11-1. Company A has an AAA credit rating and is able to borrow directly in the capital markets at a rate of 7 percent for a 10-year loan and at six-month LIBOR plus 0.20 percent for a floating-rate loan. Company B has a BBB credit rating and can borrow directly at 8.20 percent for a 10-year loan and at six-month LIBOR plus 0.75 percent on a floating-rate basis. In our example, Company A borrows directly at a fixed rate of 7 percent and swaps to pay floating rate at LIBOR flat (no premium over LIBOR). It is called the **floating-rate payer.** In contrast, Company B borrows directly in the floating-rate market at six-month LIBOR plus 0.75 percent, and agrees to pay a fixed rate of 7.16 percent in the swap. It is called the **fixed-rate payer.** Finally, the intermediary is interposed between the two parties. It passes the floating-rate payments through directly, but retains 0.04 percent (4 basis points) of the fixed-rate payments as its margin. This rather low margin is typical for "plain vanilla" swaps of the sort illustrated.

At the bottom of the figure is a recap that portrays the "alleged" savings to the two parties. For Company A, its "all-in" cost of floating-rate financing is the LIBOR rate it pays in the swap minus (7.12 percent − 7.00 percent), which represents the excess of what it receives in the swap over its fixed-rate cost of borrowing directly. As a result, it realizes an opportunity savings of 0.32 percent, or 32 basis points, relative to what it would pay to borrow directly on a floating-rate basis. Company B's "all-in" cost of fixed-rate financing is 7.91 percent. This is comprised of the 7.16 percent it pays in the swap plus (LIBOR + 0.75 percent − LIBOR), which represents the excess of its floating-rate cost of direct borrowing over what it receives in the swap. It realizes an opportunity savings of 0.29 percent—29 basis points—relative to the 8.20 percent it would pay to borrow directly on a fixed-rate basis. Thus, both parties as well as the intermediary seem to gain in this floating-rate/fixed-rate swap. From whence do these gains come?

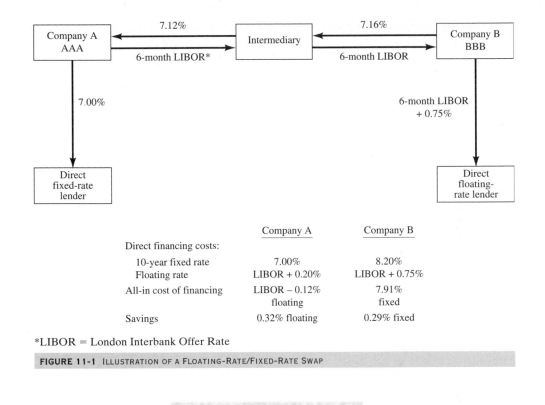

	Company A	Company B
Direct financing costs:		
10-year fixed rate	7.00%	8.20%
Floating rate	LIBOR + 0.20%	LIBOR + 0.75%
All-in cost of financing	LIBOR – 0.12% floating	7.91% fixed
Savings	0.32% floating	0.29% fixed

*LIBOR = London Interbank Offer Rate

FIGURE 11-1 ILLUSTRATION OF A FLOATING-RATE/FIXED-RATE SWAP

VALUATION ISSUES

Is the "value creation" in Figure 11-1 real or imaginary? In efficient and competitive financial markets, we would expect no gains, the process being a zero-sum game between the two parties.[1] To the extent there were intermediation costs, there would be no swaps. Now we know that the swap market has grown dramatically, so there must be other factors at play that explain the situation depicted in Figure 11-1. Let us explore the reasons that have been advanced.

COMPARATIVE ADVANTAGE

One argument is comparative advantage in financing, which rests on the expectation that market segmentation will occur.[2] The claim is that institutional restrictions (regulatory, tax, and tradition) limit the ability of a party to borrow in the way or in the currency desired. Closely allied is an argument that asymmetric information causes the opportunity. Different lenders are said to have access to different information about borrowers. As disclosure requirements in Europe are different from those in the United

---

[1] For proof of this proposition, see Stuart M. Turnbull, "Swaps: A Zero Sum Game?" *Financial Management* 16 (Spring 1987): 15–21.

[2] Leading proponents of this explanation for the existence of the swap market are James Bicksler and Andrew H. Chen, "An Economic Analysis of Interest Rate Swaps," *Journal of Finance* 41 (July 1986): 645–55.

States, for example, a potential corporate borrower may be able to borrow to better advantage in the home market where lenders have an information edge.

As a result of imperfections and disparate information, borrowers are said to have comparative advantage. It may be that United Fruit can borrow more effectively on a term basis in the United States than it can on a floating-rate basis either in the United States or in Europe, while Foreaux Company can place floating-rate debt more effectively in France than it can place term debt either in Europe or in the United States. If United Fruit really wants to borrow on a floating-rate basis and Foreaux really wants to borrow on a term basis, the sensible course is for each to borrow where it has comparative advantage. By swapping interest obligations, both parties can realize cost savings similar to those shown in Figure 11-1, so the argument goes.

The key is whether the arbitrage opportunity persists. One would think that as more and more swaps occur, the rate differences would be reduced and eventually eliminated. In other words, any initial opportunity would be arbitraged out as the swap market seasoned. So while institutional rigidities may persist, arbitrage would eliminate savings possible from comparative advantage. Moreover, informational asymmetry would be reduced as more swaps occur and credit rating services endeavor to fill information gaps. Thus, the comparative advantage argument is suspect.

COMPLETING MARKETS

Swaps are used to manage interest-rate risk, such as a mismatch between the average duration of assets and that of funding sources. Recall from earlier chapters that a complete market is characterized by a set of available securities that spans the desires of investors. It may be that the swap market fills a gap in the overall market to hedge interest-rate risk.[3] The futures, forward, and debt options markets are limited in horizon to about four years. In foreign countries, certain instruments simply are not available. By using the swap market, one can create a synthetic security and may be able to shift risk in ways that otherwise are not available. By exploiting market incompleteness in interest-rate management, the swap may benefit all parties.

CREDIT RISK

Typically the counterparties in a swap are not of equal credit risk. Default risk does not apply to principal; each party is responsible for whatever principal obligation it has incurred in direct borrowings. However, there is default risk with respect to the differential in interest payments. In the beginning, default risk was borne by the two counterparties. However, intermediaries increasingly interposed themselves between the parties in such a way as to assume the default risk. Sometimes an intermediary will take on a swap contract without a counterparty, putting one side of the contract on its own books.

If a counterparty should default on its obligation, the exposed intermediary will need to assume its position. This is known as **replacement risk.** Suppose the fixed-rate payer in the swap defaults. If interest rates decline from the time of the contract, there is a shortfall between the payment required and what could be obtained in the current

---

[3] See Clifford W. Smith, Jr., Charles W. Smithson, and Lee Macdonald Wakeman, "The Evolving Market for Swaps," *Midland Corporate Finance Journal* 3 (Winter 1986): 26–27, for this line of reasoning.

swap market. The exposed intermediary must make up the difference. It can bring in another counterparty to pay the fixed rate, but it will be at a lower rate, and again the intermediary must make up the differential. If interest rates rise, the intermediary will have no difficulty replacing the defaulted counterparty. Thus, fixed-rate default risk depends on two things: (1) the fixed-rate payer's defaulting; and (2) interest rates declining. This combined scenario is more likely in a steep recession than it is at other times.

The condition under which an intermediary is hurt when the floating-rate payer defaults is just the opposite. Should interest rates rise, another counterparty cannot be found to accept the fixed rate contracted for in the swap. Therefore, the intermediary must make up the difference. For floating-rate default to result in a loss, again two things must happen: (1) the floating-rate payer defaults, and (2) interest rates rise. For both fixed-rate payer and floating-rate payer default exposure, the intermediary can liquidate the exposed side of the contract at a loss instead of paying the interest-rate differential for the remainder of the contract.

Smith, Smithson, and Wakeman have identified a number of factors that bear on swap defaults.[4] They maintain that *default risk is lower*

1. the higher the credit ratings of the counterparties and intermediary
2. the less volatile the interest rates
3. the lower the correlation between the contracting firm's value and interest rates
4. the shorter the maturity of the swap
5. the more positively sloped the term structure of interest rates
6. the more the swap is being used to hedge rather than to speculate
7. the better bonded the contract is with performance bonds and other devices.

All but the fifth factor are straightforward. The idea here is that with an upward-sloping term structure, interest rates are expected to rise. As a result, the party paying fixed rate and receiving floating rate is expected to pay larger difference checks in the early part of the contract than in the latter part. Effectively, this shortens the expected duration of the contract from the standpoint of the counterparty.

Differences in default risk may explain some of the apparent cost savings in Figure 11-1. The question is whether default risk is being properly priced in the contract. The fact that there have been negligible defaults has led to aggressive pricing of standard, "plain vanilla" types of swaps. Whether margins are adequate to cover the true risk involved is a subject of debate, and one we will take up shortly.

SKIRTING TAX LAWS AND REGULATIONS

In certain cases, the use of swaps allows a party to get around tax laws and regulations, a topic touched on earlier in the section on comparative advantage. Usually such skirting is possible only when the swap is across two countries. Through swaps, currency and interest-rate risk exposures can be separated, sometimes to tax advantage. In other cases, regulations in one country can be avoided by arranging a cross-border swap.

---

[4]   Clifford W. Smith, Jr., Charles W. Smithson, and Lee Macdonald Wakeman, "The Market for Interest Rate Swaps" (research paper, University of Rochester, 1987).

Known as tax and regulatory arbitrage, the idea is simply to exploit opportunities to reduce tax and regulatory constraints.

SWAP VALUATION: A SUMMING UP

Thus, swaps exist for a number of reasons. Probably the least defensible is that they offer a comparative advantage leading to persistent arbitrage opportunities. Indeed we know that the margin has declined on swaps over the years, indicating the inevitable consequences of arbitrage. Smith, Smithson, and Wakeman contend that part of the net savings shown in Figure 11-1 is an illusion because of prepayment differences. The 10-year loan rate on direct U.S. borrowings often has embraced in it a premium for call risk. In contrast, swaps typically do not have a call option. For this reason alone, the fixed rate in a swap should be lower than the fixed rate on a direct bond issue in the United States. This is simply the yield differential between a callable and a noncallable bond (see chapter 12).

Apart from these considerations, the swap market provides a hedging vehicle not otherwise available in certain maturity areas. It is like a series of forward contracts corresponding to the future settlement dates at which difference checks are paid. (The direction and magnitude of a difference check depend on what happens to the floating rate, the fixed rate being locked in at the inception of the swap.) However, a comparable forward market does not exist. Nor do lengthy futures or options contracts. As a result, the swap market serves to complete the market for risk-shifting devices. Finally, differences in default risk between the parties often are involved. To the extent that credit risk is not properly priced, swaps may give a false impression of economic benefit.

PRICING AN INTEREST-RATE SWAP

Price quotations in the swap market tend to be in terms of the fixed rate paid. A typical quote would be so many basis points over a Treasury security of comparable maturity. This differential is known as the **swap spread.** For example, the swap spread quote for a 5-year swap might be "81 basis points over 5-year Treasuries." The floating-rate quote usually is "flat." That is, the floating rate is set equal to an index, such as 6-month LIBOR, with no premium. In some situations, it will be LIBOR plus so many basis points, with the result that the quote is in terms of both the fixed and the floating rates. However, this is the exception. A term structure of swap rates is reported regularly by the Bloomberg service and by assorted investment banks. Typically, maturities of 2, 3, 4, 5, 7, 10, 15, and 20 years are shown, and the counterparties are assumed to be single A in credit rating or better. Swap spreads tend to widen or narrow as quality yield spreads (default-risk premiums) in general change over time.

A fixed-rate/floating-rate swap can be viewed as a combination of forward contracts extending through the life of the swap agreement. If the forward market is based on, or corresponds to, the same index as the swap, say LIBOR, and if the reset dates on the swap correspond to the settlement dates for the forward contracts, the forward rates can be used to determine the present values of swap cash flows. Assumed in this procedure is that the forward rates are realized and that they equal the LIBOR rates that prevail for various future periods. When a swap is initiated, its present value is approximately zero in the sense that neither counterparty has a gain or loss. This is merely to say that there is equilibrium between what the two counterparties agree to pay. Assuming LIBOR flat (no premium), the **swap rate** for the fixed-rate payer is that interest rate which will equate the present value of the fixed-rate payments with the present value of the floating-rate payments.

AN ILLUSTRATION OF PRESENT-VALUE CALCULATIONS

Suppose we are considering a 5-year swap with a notional amount of $1 million, which is small as swaps go but useful for illustration purposes. The floating-rate payer is assumed to pay 3-month LIBOR flat and the fixed-rate payer 6.50 percent. Both sets of payments are quarterly, as is the reset. For simplicity, we assume that each quarter has the same number of days. (In practice, this will not be the case, and the day count becomes important in the calculations.) This allows us to divide by four. For the fixed-rate cash flow, payments are $0.065 \times \$1$ million $\times 0.25 = \$16,250$ each quarter.

Prevailing forward rates for each future quarter are shown in the second column of Table 11-1. The expected floating-rate cash flows, column 4, are the forward rates for

TABLE 11-1 Calculation of Swap Present Values

(Assumptions: $1 million, 5 years, 6.5% fixed, LIBOR flat floating, quarterly resets)

Future Quarter	Forward Rate	Discount Factor	Floating Cash Flows	PV Floating Cash Flows	Fixed Cash Flows	PV of Fixed Cash Flows
1	0.0551	0.98641	$13,775	$13,588	$16,250	$16,029
2	0.0555	0.97291	13,875	13,499	16,250	15,810
3	0.0559	0.95950	13,975	13,409	16,250	15,592
4	0.0563	0.94619	14,075	13,318	16,250	15,376
5	0.0575	0.93278	14,375	13,409	16,250	15,158
6	0.0594	0.91913	14,850	13,649	16,250	14,936
7	0.0601	0.90552	15,025	13,605	16,250	14,715
8	0.0610	0.89192	15,250	13,602	16,250	14,494
9	0.0619	0.87833	15,475	13,592	16,250	14,273
10	0.0628	0.86475	15,700	13,577	16,250	14,052
11	0.0633	0.85128	15,825	13,472	16,250	13,833
12	0.0637	0.83794	15,925	13,344	16,250	13,616
13	0.0640	0.82474	16,000	13,196	16,250	13,402
14	0.0646	0.81163	16,150	13,108	16,250	13,189
15	0.0650	0.79866	16,250	12,978	16,250	12,978
16	0.0653	0.78583	16,325	12,829	16,250	12,770
17	0.0657	0.77313	16,425	12,699	16,250	12,563
18	0.0662	0.76054	16,550	12,587	16,250	12,359
19	0.0664	0.74812	16,600	12,419	16,250	12,157
20	0.0651	0.73614	16,275	11,981	16,250	11,962
			Total	$263,859		$279,264

the quarter divided by four, times the $1 million notional amount. We also use these forward rates to determine the discount factor for quarter T

$$\text{Discount factor, } T = \prod_{t=1}^{T} \frac{1}{\left(1 + \dfrac{F_t}{4}\right)}$$

where Π is the multiplicative sign and F_t is the forward rate for quarter t. For the first quarter, we have a discount factor of $1/1 + (0.0551/4) = 0.98641$; for the second quarter, $1/\{[1 + (0.0551/4)][1 + (0.555/4)]\} = 0.97291$; and so forth.

EQUILIBRIUM PRICING

When the discount factors are multiplied by the floating-rate and fixed-rate cash flows, we obtain the present values for both. We see in the table that the present value of the fixed-rate cash flows, $279,264, exceeds that of the floating-rate cash flows, $263,859. If pricing is off the forward rates, the 6.5 percent interest rate the fixed-rate payer pays in the swap is simply too high. Equilibrium will not occur at this rate. The fixed rate at which the present values of the two cash flow columns are the same is 6.14 percent (6.1414 percent to be more exact). At this fixed rate, the net present value of the swap is essentially zero (floating-rate cash flow present value minus fixed-rate cash flow present value). With the forward rates in Table 11-1 then, equilibrium pricing would suggest 6.14 percent fixed and LIBOR flat. However, this calculation implies no margin to the financial intermediary that arranges the swap. If the intermediary's profit margin were 4 basis points, the fixed-rate quote would be 6.18 percent.

SECONDARY MARKET VALUES

We use the procedure above to determine the present value of an existing swap. Suppose that when an earlier swap was initiated, the fixed rate was 6.50 percent and interest rates have declined to the point where the forward rates in Table 11-1 now prevail. The present value of the contract for the fixed-rate payer would be $263,859 − $279,264 = ($15,405). It has a negative present value and is "underwater" from the time it was initiated. Expressed differently, the fixed-rate payer is obligated to pay a higher interest rate than what it would need to pay currently. For the floating-rate payer, the contract has a positive present value of $15,405.

For more standardized swaps, a secondary market has developed. More customized swaps sometimes can be exited, but with more difficulty and price concession. In a **swap sale,** you sell your position to another party and there is no further obligation. This differs from a **swap reversal,** in which you arrange a swap opposite to the one held. You now hold offsetting swaps, alike in every way except direction. Although interest-rate risk has been removed, the disadvantage of a swap reversal is that credit risk remains with two counterparties now instead of one.

After a swap is undertaken, interest rates can and do change. As a result, the value of the swap changes as illustrated in our previous pricing example in Table 11-1. Most participants in the swap market are required to *mark-to-market* every day, similar to what occurs in the futures market. Volatility in the swap spread, the difference between the fixed rate in the swap and the rate on a comparable maturity Treasury, is the key. Changes in this spread are due to several underlying causes that have been explored by scholars.[5]

If interest rates should decline, the fixed-rate payer in the swap will suffer a decline in the value of its swap contract. To get someone to take over the position requires that a lower fixed rate be paid. As a result, the contract is worth less. In contrast, the floating-rate payer realizes a gain in value, because the stream of fixed-rate payments it receives is worth more. This is the same as with holding any fixed-income security when interest rates drop. The opposite occurs when interest rates rise. In summary, we have the following:

	Interest Rate Decline	*Interest Rate Increase*
Fixed-rate payer	Loses	Gains
Floating-rate payer	Gains	Loses

An analogy of this profile is found in the futures market. The floating-rate payer in the swap (who receives fixed rate) is like the buyer of an interest-rate futures contract (long position). If interest rates rise, he or she suffers a diminution in value; if they fall, the value of the contract increases. Contrarily, the fixed-rate payer (who receives floating rate) is like the seller of a futures contract (short position). Here an increase in interest rates results in an increase in the value of the futures contract, whereas a decrease results in a decline in value. (See Figure 9-2 in chapter 9 for amplification.)

The interest-rate swap market for standard types of contracts is relatively liquid. Active price quotations can be obtained and there is little difficulty in liquidating a contract. The same liquidity does not prevail with interest-rate forward contracts.

CREDIT RISK, MATURITY, AND SYSTEMIC RISK

Different quality yield spreads prevail for floating-rate and for longer-term, fixed-rate debt. As a result, swaps can be arranged to seemingly improve one's position. This is sometimes known as "credit arbitrage," an unfortunate term in my opinion, but it is useful to explore the concept. While the end result is not materially different from our earlier discussion of default risk in the context of Figure 11-1, the orientation regarding the source of supposed advantage is different.

To illustrate, suppose we have two parties: a AAA-rated bank and a BBB-rated corporation. The bank can borrow at 6-month LIBOR plus 20 basis points in the floating-rate market, whereas the corporation can borrow at 6-month LIBOR plus 70 basis points. The differential is 50 basis points, or ½ percent. Suppose further that for a fixed-rate, 7-year loan, the bank would pay 7 percent, whereas the corporation would pay

5   See Keith C. Brown, W. V. Harlow, and Donald J. Smith, "An Empirical Analysis of Interest Rate Swap Spreads," *Journal of Fixed Income* 3 (March 1994): 61–78.

8.2 percent. Thus, the quality yield spread is 120 basis points, 1.2 percent. Note that the credit spread widens as you go from a 6-month floating rate to a 7-year fixed rate.

Similar to Figure 11-1, we can craft an example in which a swap is seemingly favorable to both parties. This is shown in Table 11-2, where the bank pays floating rate and receives fixed rate in the swap and the corporation pays fixed rate and receives floating rate. In the example, the bank has a net borrowing cost on floating-rate debt of LIBOR minus 10 basis points, whereas the net borrowing cost to the corporation on a 7-year fixed-rate loan is 7.9 percent. Through this synthetic borrowing arrangement, a swap, the bank saves 30 basis points [(LIBOR + 0.2%) − (LIBOR − 0.1%)], and the corporation saves 30 basis points as well: 8.2% − 7.9%. In addition, the intermediary realizes a spread of 10 basis points, reflected in the floating-rate difference in the swap [(LIBOR + 0.5%) − (LIBOR + 0.4%)].

Again, we are back to a situation in which both parties seemingly are able to borrow at lower rates synthetically than they can directly. If the "true" quality yield spread were 50 basis points throughout all maturities, and the direct market was simply mispricing the longer-term, fixed-rate spread, credit arbitrage would be possible. But if the "true" quality yield spread changes with maturity, as we explored in chapter 8, then the supposed advantage is a mirage. Put another way, if the quality yield spreads that were observed in the floating-rate and fixed-rate markets represent "true" differences in default risk between maturities, then synthetic borrowing offers no net advantage. Rather than credit arbitrage, there is a net assumption of credit risk by the intermediary.

DEFAULT PROVISIONS

The credit risk of a swap is lower than that of a loan. As we have discussed, no exchange of principal occurs. As Robert H. Litzenberger points out, there are other reasons.[6] For

TABLE 11-2	Differing Credit Spreads and a Swap Transaction (Received +, Paid −)		
Direct Market:	**Bank AAA**		***Corporation BBB***
Floating rate	−(LIBOR + 0.2%)		−(LIBOR + 0.7%)
Differential		0.5%	
Fixed rate	−7.0%		−8.2%
Differential		1.2%	
Swap Market:			
Floating rate	−(LIBOR + 0.5%)		+(LIBOR + 0.4%)
Fixed rate	+7.6%		−7.6%
Implied Savings:			
Floating rate	−0.3%		−0.3%
Fixed rate	+0.6%		+0.6%
	+0.3%		+0.3%
Net borrowing cost	LIBOR − 0.1%		7.9%
after swap	(Floating)		(Fixed)

Note: LIBOR = London InterBank Offer Rate

6 Robert H. Litzenberger, "Swaps: Plain and Fanciful," *Journal of Finance* 47 (July 1992): 831–50.

one thing, swap positions can be sold, which gives them a degree of liquidity not found in many loans. Also, the treatment of swaps in bankrupt situations is kinder than that of loans. Finally, longer-term swaps often contain triggers to replace counterparties whose investment grade falls below some specified minimum, like single A.

Swap contracts typically are written under an International Swaps and Derivatives Association **(ISDA) master agreement,** which among other things specifies how transactions are netted and closed out in case of default. Downgrade provisions are incorporated in the agreement. While investment-grade counterparties rarely default, the use of downgrade triggers has been shown to reduce significantly the possibility of default.[7] When triggered, the swap contract is terminated, resulting in its liquidation. The key is whether the downgraded counterparty has the wherewithal to make good on the contract so that there is no default loss. If the plunge through a downgrade trigger into distress is rapid, default losses are possible. Still, downgrade triggers seem to reduce the probability and are increasingly being used.

Concern has been expressed about the creditworthiness of the swaps market overall, and this concern has attracted the attention of regulators. Although swap dealers try to balance the risk of individual swaps against other risks, so as to be approximately neutral, hedging credit risk is difficult. Because of the interlocking nature of swaps and lines of credit internationally, a limited number of defaults could trigger a cascade of defaults. This is known as **systemic risk.** In other words, risk is not isolated to a single default and neatly contained; once begun, it may reverberate throughout the financial marketplace. How serious a threat is systemic risk?

VALUE AT RISK

Increasingly, credit discipline is coming into the market for swaps and other derivative products. Many now undertake **value-at-risk** (VAR) analyses. Value at risk is a statistical estimate of how much can be lost on a contract should market prices change by some specified amount corresponding to a probability, like 1 or 5 percent, during a specified interval of time—two days, two weeks, one month, and so on. Typically, simulations based on historical price movements are used to derive the probability distribution of swap values. The system is then "shocked" with other assumptions involving such things as shifts in the term structure of interest rates, changes in the slope of the yield curve, changes in yield volatilities, and different default rates to see how much a portfolio might lose in value.

With respect to credit risk, value at risk is the net cost of replacement of a counterparty times the default ratio assumed either on the basis of historical or projected incidence. For historical, many use the cumulative default risk experience of Moody's.[8] Recognize that principal loss is not involved, as all swap contracts are notional in amount. It is the replacement cost on the differential between fixed rate and floating rate that matters. This is a small percent of the total notional amount of swap contracts outstanding. For a diversified portfolio of counterparty credit risk, most scholars feel

---

7 Douglas J. Lucas, "The Effectiveness of Downgrade Provisions in Reducing Counterparty Credit Risk," *Journal of Fixed Income* 5 (June 1995): 32–41.
8 For the incorporation of credit risk into an overall VAR type of approach, see Ben Iben and Rupert Brotherton-Ratcliffe, "Credit Loss Distributions and Required Capital for Derivatives Portfolios," *Journal of Fixed Income* 4 (June 1994): 6–14.

that the risk exposure is less than 1 percent of the total notional amount of swaps outstanding. Potential default losses would be a fraction of this percent.

In studying the effect of default risk on swap values using typical parameters for interest-rate processes, Darrell Duffie and Ming Huang looked at what happens when you replace a fixed-rate counterparty with a lower-quality counterparty. If the lower quality counterparty's bond yield were 100 basis points higher than the replaced counterparty, this results in a 1-basis-point-higher spread for a 5-year swap.[9] One reason the swap differential is so small is that the 100-basis-point differential on bond financings embraces the possibility of default on payment of principal. With a swap, only interest payments are involved.

SWAPTIONS

Various options exist for swap transactions, and these are known as **swaptions.** One is to *enter into a swap* at a future date. The terms of the swap are set at the time of the option, and they give the holder the right, but not the obligation, to take a swap position. A **call swaption,** if exercised, involves paying floating rate and receiving fixed rate in the swap. With a **put swaption,** assuming exercise, you would pay fixed rate and receive floating rate. A 5/2 put swaption, for example, allows you to pay fixed rate and receive floating rate in a 3-year swap that begins 2 years hence.

Suppose the term structure of interest rates is steeply upward-sloping. As a financial institution, you wish to fund your assets through floating-rate debt for the time being. However, you are concerned that the yield curve will flatten. To protect yourself, you buy a put swaption to swap into fixed-rate debt at a contracted interest rate. If short-term interest rates rise relative to long-term rates, and the latter remain at present levels, your swaption will be a thing of value.

While the swaption to enter into a swap is the most common type of option, others exist. One option is to *cancel a swap* contract. Another type of option allows you to *extend an existing swap* contract. In addition, there are futures and forward contracts on swaps. Being long in such a contract is like holding a call swaption to pay floating rate and receive fixed rate in the swap. A short swap futures or forward contract is like a put swaption to pay fixed rate and receive floating rate in the swap.

CREDIT DERIVATIVES

During the past half-dozen years, markets have developed for **credit derivatives.** The idea is to unbundle the default risk of a loan or security from its other attributes. The original lender no longer needs to bear this risk; it can be transferred to others, for a

---

[9] Darrell Duffie and Ming Huang, "Swap Rates and Credit Quality," *Journal of Finance* 51 (July 1996): 597–620.

price of course. The party who wishes to transfer is known as the **protection buyer.** The **protection seller** assumes the credit risk, and he or she receives a premium for providing this insurance. The premium is based on the probability and likely severity of default, which are concepts taken up in chapter 8.

TOTAL RETURN SWAPS

Cash flows for a **total return swap** are illustrated in the upper panel of Figure 11-2. The protection buyer is assumed to hold a risky debt instrument and agrees to pay out its total return to the protection seller. This return consists of the stream of interest payments together with the change in the instrument's market value. The protection seller agrees to pay some reference rate, and perhaps a negative or positive spread from this rate. In the case of a floating-rate instrument, the reference rate might be LIBOR or the Treasury bill rate; for a fixed-rate instrument, it might be a constant-maturity Treasury rate. The protection buyer receives a cash-flow stream commensurate with a default-free obligation, and the protection seller receives a stream commensurate with a risky debt instrument. The difference between the two streams represents the premium for protection.

Like other swaps, the counterparties do not exchange ownership of the underlying debt obligation. The differential in cash flows is established contractually. While the protection seller participates in the cash-flow stream of the risky debt instrument, he or she does not have to book the loan or investment. However, the protection seller bears the economic risk of default. Should actual default occur, he or she receives only the recovery amount and is out the shortfall from the instrument's face value. The protection buyer receives the full face value. If a debt instrument is downgraded, the protection seller also bears the market-value decline. Suppose that the risky debt obligation has an 8 percent coupon, but that it is downgraded from single-A to triple-B, causing its market value to decline by 3 percent. For a 6-month reset period, the protection seller would

FIGURE 11-2 TOTAL RETURN AND CREDIT SWAPS

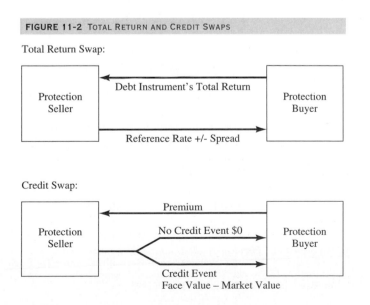

Total Return Swap:

Credit Swap:

receive from the protection buyer only 1 percent, not the full 4 percent semiannual coupon payment.

An advantage of a total-return swap is that credit deterioration is largely based on market-price changes, and not on the legality of whether or not default occurs. While problems occur in getting quotations on certain bonds and floating-rate instruments, an underlying market discipline still prevails.

CREDIT SWAPS

A **credit swap,** sometimes known as a default swap, is similar in concept to the total-return swap, but different in the detail. Together these two types of swaps account for the majority of credit derivatives. Cash flows for a credit swap are illustrated in the lower panel of Figure 11-2. The protection buyer pays a periodic premium to the protection seller, insurance against a risky debt instrument deteriorating in quality. This annuity premium is paid each period until the earlier of: (1) the maturity of the credit swap agreement, or (2) a specific **credit event** occurring, usually default. If the credit event occurs, the protection seller pays the protection buyer a **contingent amount.** This often takes the form of physical settlement, where the protection buyer "puts" the defaulted obligation to the protection seller at its face value. The economic cash flow then is the difference between the face value of the instrument and its market value. Thus, the protection buyer receives payment only when a specific credit event occurs; otherwise the cash flow from the protection seller is zero.

The credit event need not be default, though that is the thing most commonly specified. It could be a credit downgrade, a merger, a corporate restructuring, or some other event that impacts the creditworthiness of the underlying debt instrument. The periodic premium paid, usually quarterly, often is called the **credit-swap spread.** This cost of protection depends on the credit rating of the company, risk migration, and likely recovery should default occur. (See chapter 8.) The pricing of credit swaps and other credit derivatives has been modeled by academic scholars and practitioners.[10] At the time of this writing, a single-A industrial note had a premium, or spread, of roughly 50 basis points (1/2 percent) per annum.

DEFINING DEFAULT AND LIQUIDITY IN THE MARKET

One difficulty with credit swaps is legally defining default. Failure to pay interest and/or principal on time, bankruptcy, receivership, and things of this sort usually are specified. However, legal wrangling being what it is, economic default may occur well before the situation is finally put in legal default. This is particularly true for emerging market debt. (See chapter 14.) Market-price triggers do not have this problem.

An over-the-counter secondary market of sorts exists for credit derivatives of a plain vanilla sort. Unlike an interest-rate swap, where only the difference in fixed/floating interest payments is at risk, the entire face value is usually at risk with a credit

---

[10] See Darrell Duffie, "Credit Swap Valuation," *Financial Analysts Journal* 55 (January/February, 1999): 73–87; Francis A. Longstaff and Eduardo S. Schwartz, "Valuing Credit Derivatives," *Journal of Fixed Income* 5 (June 1995): 6–12; and Robert A. Jarrow and Stuart M. Turnbull, "Pricing Derivatives on Financial Securities Subject to Credit Risk," *Journal of Finance* 50 (March 1995): 53–85.

derivative. Liquidity in the market is spotty. In the "flight to quality" of late 1998, liquidity dried up for all practical purposes. For sovereign credit derivatives in particular, no trades occurred for a number of weeks. Thus, liquidity in credit derivatives is limited.

OTHER CREDIT DERIVATIVES

There are credit derivatives other than the two described, which are the most common. **Spread-adjusted notes** involve resets based on the spread of a particular grade of security over Treasuries. An index is specified, and quarterly or semiannual resets occur where one counterparty must pay the other depending on whether the quality yield spread widens or narrows. Usually the spread is collared with a floor and cap. **Credit options** involve puts and calls based on a basket of corporate fixed-income securities. The strike price often is a specified spread over Treasuries. With **credit-sensitive notes,** the coupon rate changes with the credit rating of the company involved. If the company is downgraded, the investor receives more interest income; if upgraded, less interest income is received. Various other types of credit derivatives have been tried, but the descriptions above should give some flavor of the breadth of products.

❖ SUMMARY

In interest-rate swaps, the obligation to pay interest, but not principal, is exchanged. The most common swap is floating-for-fixed rate, though floating-for-floating (basis) swaps also occur. Often an intermediary is interposed between the two counterparties. Many swaps seem to offer net savings to all parties. Various arguments for the existence of such were examined. Comparative advantage, based on imperfections and information disparity, is suspect because of arbitrage. However, swaps appear to make the market for risk-shifting devices more complete. Differences in default risk and prepayment also may explain the appearance of net savings.

Swap contracts usually are priced on the basis of forward interest rates. If the floating rate is "flat," that is to say no premium, the price quotation is the fixed rate paid. This usually is expressed in terms of a spread over Treasuries, hence the name "swap spread." By viewing the fixed-rate/floating-rate swap as a series of forward contracts, we are able to calculate the present values of the fixed-payment cash flows and the floating-payment cash flows. The equilibrium swap rate is that which results in the two present values being approximately the same. The pricing procedure illustrated also can be used to determine the market value of an existing, standardized swap. The fixed-rate payer suffers a loss when interest rates decline and a gain when they rise. The opposite occurs for the floating-rate payer.

Intermediaries have tried to exploit differences in quality yield spreads between the short-term, floating-rate market and the longer-term, fixed-rate market. In reality, such "credit arbitrage" is an illusion and risk is assumed. Systemic risk is that of a single or small group of swap defaults triggering a meltdown of the market overall. While possible, this occurrence seems remote in today's market. Regulation and self-discipline have come about, and many use value-at-risk (VAR) analyses to judge whether risk exposure is excessive. Increasingly, credit downgrade triggers are being placed in swap contracts that reduce the possibility of default losses being incurred. Risk exposure is substantially less than the total notional amount of swaps outstanding—probably less than 1 percent of such.

Several options exist for swap contracts, and they are known as swaptions. Types include swaptions to enter into a swap at a future date, swaptions to cancel an existing contract, and swaptions to extend a contract.

Credit derivatives, a rapidly changing and evolving market, are designed to unbundle credit risk and sell it separate from the other attributes of a fixed-income security. The protection buyer wishes to insulate himself or herself from the credit risk of a risky debt instrument, and the protection seller provides, for a premium, the insurance. The two most widely used credit-derivative products are the total return swap and the credit, or default, swap. The features of both were explored. One difficulty is defining legally the credit event, like default, that triggers a payment from the protection seller. Liquidity is limited for credit-derivative products.

❖ SELECTED REFERENCES

Arditti, Fred D., *Derivatives.* Boston: Harvard Business School Press, 1996.

Bicksler, James, and Andrew H. Chen, "An Economic Analysis of Interest Rate Swaps," *Journal of Finance* 41 (July 1986): 645–55.

Brown, Keith C., W. V. Harlow, and Donald J. Smith, "An Empirical Analysis of Interest Rate Swap Spreads," *Journal of Fixed Income* 3 (March 1994): 61–78.

Cooper, Ian A., and Antonio S. Mello, "The Default Risk of Swaps," *Journal of Finance* 46 (June 1991): 597–620.

Duffie, Darrell, "Credit Swap Valuation," *Financial Analysts Journal* 55 (January/February 1999): 73–87.

Duffie, Darrell, and Ming Huang, "Swap Rates and Credit Quality," *Journal of Finance* 51 (July 1996): 921–49.

Duffie, Darrell, and Kenneth J. Singleton, "An Econometric Model of the Term Structure of Interest-Rate Swap Yields," *Journal of Finance* 52 (September 1997): 1287–1321.

———, "Modeling Term Structures of Defaultable Bonds," *Review of Financial Studies* 12 (No. 4, 1999): 687–720.

Fabozzi, Frank J., *Bond Markets, Analysis and Strategies,* 4th ed., chapter 23. Upper Saddle River, NJ: Prentice Hall, 2000.

Hull, John C., *Options, Futures and Other Derivatives,* 4th ed. Upper Saddle River, NJ: Prentice Hall, 2000.

Jarrow, Robert, and Stuart Turnbull, *Derivative Securities,* 2nd ed. Cincinnati: South-Western, 2000.

Jarrow, Robert A., and Stuart M. Turnbull, "Pricing Derivatives on Financial Securities Subject to Credit Risk," *Journal of Finance* 50 (March 1995): 53–85.

Litzenberger, Robert H., "Swaps: Plain and Fanciful," *Journal of Finance* 47 (July 1992): 831–50.

Longstaff, Francis A., and Eduardo S. Schwartz, "Valuing Credit Derivatives," *Journal of Fixed Income* 5 (June 1995): 6–12.

Lucas, Douglas J., "The Effectiveness of Downgrade Provisions in Reducing Counterparty Risk," *Journal of Fixed Income* 5 (June 1995): 32–41.

Minton, Bernadette A., "An Empirical Examination of Basic Valuation Models for Plain Vanilla U.S. Interest Rate Swaps," *Journal of Financial Economics* 44 (May 1997): 251–77.

Schumacher, Michael, "Swap Spreads Do Matter," *Journal of Fixed Income* 8 (June 1998): 59–64.

Smith, Clifford W., Jr., Charles W. Smithson, and D. Sykes Wilford, *Managing Financial Risk,* chapters 9–12. New York: Harper & Row, 1990.

Smith, Clifford W., Jr., Charles W. Smithson, and Lee Macdonald Wakeman, "The Evolving Market for Swaps," *Midland Corporate Finance Journal* 3 (Winter 1986): 20–32.

———, "The Market for Interest Rate Swaps," Research paper, University of Rochester, 1987.

Turnbull, Stuart M., "Swaps: A Zero Sum Game?" *Financial Management* 16 (Spring 1987): 15–21.

CHAPTER 12

EMBEDDED OPTIONS AND OPTION-ADJUSTED SPREADS

Often with fixed-income securities, either the issuer or the investor has an option to take action that affects the other party. This option is specified in the **indenture,** a legal document spelling out the conditions of the loan and the covenants under which default occurs. When the option rests with the issuer, market equilibration usually requires a higher interest rate than otherwise would occur. When with the investor, the issuer typically is able to extract a lower interest cost than otherwise would be the case. In this chapter, we examine the valuation of the call feature, the put option, and the sinking fund provision. In the subsequent chapter, we investigate the prepayment risk associated with mortgages. Effectively, the prepayment option is a call feature. The notion of option-adjusted spreads permeates both chapters.

OPTION-ADJUSTED SPREADS

Depending on the option embedded in the contract, two debt instruments alike in all other respects will be valued differently in the market and have different yields. One way to measure the difference is simply to look at the reported **yield spread** between the two instruments. We saw this illustrated when we considered default risk premiums in chapter 8.

A variation of this theme is a **static spread,** which is the spread over the Treasury spot yield curve of one-period rates that an investor would earn if the option-embedded security were held to maturity.[1] A constant spread is added to each Treasury spot rate on the curve, and these spot rates then are used to discount the promised cash flows. The present value obtained should equal the market price of the option-free security. If not, trial and error with different spreads is used until an equality is achieved.

The **option-adjusted spread** (OAS) is different. Whereas the static spread is based on the present Treasury yield curve as a forecast of future one-period rates of interest,

---

[1] See Frank J. Fabozzi, *Bond Markets, Analysis and Strategies,* 4th ed., chapter 14. Upper Saddle River, NJ: Prentice Hall, 2000.

the OAS considers the full range of possible future rates of interest. Therefore, it allows for future interest-rate volatility as opposed to static single-point estimates.

THE BASIC METHODOLOGY

The idea is to map the price of an option-embedded security, like one having a call feature, under different interest-rate scenarios. These scenarios embrace the full spectrum of one-period, interest-rate possibilities. Often a lattice-type, binomial-tree model of the sort described in chapter 6 is used to model the cash flows. Along each interest-rate path, a set of cash flows is generated for the various payments. For the security with an embedded option, price behavior is constrained under certain interest-rate paths. It may be that the security will be called if interest rates decline by 1 percent or more. At this point, the investor receives back the face value together with perhaps a call premium (to be described shortly). Future cash flows beyond this point cease.

For each interest-rate path, the present value of cash flows is calculated using as discount rates one-period Treasury interest rates along the path *plus* a constant spread. These present values then are weighted by the probabilities of occurrence of each path and summed across all paths to obtain the *theoretical present value* of the security. This value is then compared with the security's actual price. If the two are the same, the spread used in the calculations is by definition the option-adjusted spread (OAS). If equality does not prevail, a different spread is employed and a new theoretical present value for the security is generated. Trial and error with different spreads continues until the theoretical present value equals the actual price, at which point the OAS is determined.

AN ILLUSTRATION

Figure 12-1 shows a two-period model with an embedded-option security that promises to pay $57 at the end of each of the next two periods. At time 0, the one-period Treasury rate is 8 percent. At time 1, the one-period rate can go to 9 percent or to 7 percent with equal probability. If the interest rate goes to 9 percent, the option is not exercised by the issuer; the investor receives $57 at the end of period 1, and the promise to pay $57 at the end of period 2 continues. If the Treasury rate goes to 7 percent, the option is exercised, in which case the investor receives $108 at the end of period 1 and there is no further payment.

The theoretical present value of this security is the combination of the two paths as follows:

$$\text{TPV} = 0.50\left[\frac{\$57}{(1.08)} + \frac{\$57}{(1.08)(1.09)}\right] + 0.50\left[\frac{\$108}{(1.08)}\right] = \$100.60$$

However, the market price of the security is $99.50. By an iterative process, we can determine that if we add a constant spread of 96 basis points to all one-period rates, the theoretical value equals the security's market price.

$$\text{TPV} = 0.50\left[\frac{\$57}{(1.0896)} + \frac{\$57}{(1.0896)(1.0996)}\right] + 0.50\left[\frac{\$108}{(1.0896)}\right] = \$99.50$$

Thus, the option-adjusted spread (OAS) in this example is 96 basis points.

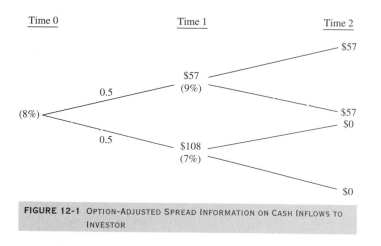

FIGURE 12-1 OPTION-ADJUSTED SPREAD INFORMATION ON CASH INFLOWS TO
INVESTOR

SOME CAVEATS

The OAS calculated for the security is unlikely to be the spread that the investor earns, as that depends on the interest-rate path that actually occurs.[2] The OAS is an average for all paths, and the actual spread earned by an investor may be significantly different from this average. In fact, it may turn out to be negative. The security with the largest OAS is not necessarily the most underpriced. Again, the value depends on the interest-rate path. The point is that the OAS should not be taken as a given outcome but rather as a summary measure of possible outcomes. This analytical tool was developed to come to grips with securities that have complicated embedded-option features.

Recognize that the approach illustrated is but one way that an OAS can be determined. There are other approaches, but most use as a base the simple methodology presented above. In our calculations, we have ignored credit risk, implicitly assuming a Treasury security. The OAS approach can be extended to deal with credit risk by adding a spread for credit risk to that for the embedded-option feature. Obviously a good deal of complication is involved. While the calculation of an OAS for a security is mathematically sophisticated, common sense needs to be applied in interpreting the results. Next in this chapter, we examine two types of embedded option.

THE NATURE OF THE CALL FEATURE

A call provision gives the issuer the option to buy back the instrument at a specified price before maturity. The price at which this occurs is known as the **call price,** and it usually is above the **face value** of the security. In most cases, it declines over time. For example, an 8 percent coupon 20-year corporate bond might be callable at $108 in the first year using the $100-face-value pricing convention. (As we know from chapter 4, each bond has an actual face value of $1,000.) In the second year, the bond is callable at $107.50; in the third, at $107.00; and so forth down to $100 for the 17th through 20th

---

[2] See Robert W. Kopprasch, "Option-Adjusted Spread Analysis: Going Down the Wrong Path?" *Financial Analysts Journal* 49 (May–June 1994): 42–47.

years. For corporate bonds, the call price in the first year often is one year's interest above the face value. For municipal bonds, the call price typically is lower—$102 or $103 being most prevalent, regardless of the level of interest rates.[3]

FORMS OF THE PROVISION

The call feature itself may take several forms. The security may be **immediately callable,** which simply means that the instrument may be bought back by the issuer at the call price at any time. Even here, the investor is partially protected from a call because the initial call price is above the face value of the bond. Moreover, a number of expenses and inconveniences are associated with refunding a bond issue, and these must be factored in by the borrower before a decision to call a bond issue is made. However, should interest rates decline significantly, the issuer may wish to call the bond. Rather than being immediately callable, the call provision may be **deferred** for a period of time. This means that the instrument cannot be called during the deferment period; thus, the investor is protected from a call.

While many corporate bond issues have a call feature, the relative use of the provision varies over time. When interest rates are low and investors demand a premium in yield that corporations regard as too high, the companies will issue noncallable bonds. This was the case in the 1990s, when most bond issues were noncallable. This experience contrasts with that of the 1970s when almost all bonds were callable. When corporate bonds are callable, they usually provide the investor with deferred call protection. For a long-term industrial bond issue, the typical deferment period is 10 years, whereas that for a public utility is 5 years.

Although municipal bonds have a call feature less often than corporate bonds, many issues carry such a provision. The two principal types of municipal securities are general credit obligation and revenue bonds. **General credit obligation bonds** are backed by the "full faith and credit" of the municipality—that is, its full taxing power. **Revenue bonds,** however, are backed only by the revenue of the specific project and not by the taxing power of the municipality. An example of a revenue bond issue is a bond issue to build a toll road. A high percentage of revenue bond issues contain a call feature; this makes sense because it is logical to retire some of the bonds outstanding if any excess cash results from revenues exceeding projections. For general obligation issues, the percentage with a call feature is less. A 10-year deferment period is most common with municipal bonds, though longer and shorter periods are sometimes used. Very few municipal bonds are immediately callable.

While most Treasury securities are noncallable, the call provision for those that are is geared to final maturity. For example, the 11¾ percent bonds of February 2005–2010 have a call feature that enables the Treasury to call the bonds any time between February 2005 and the final maturity five years later, February 2010. The primary purpose of the call privilege is to give the Treasury flexibility in refinancing. By having five years in which to roll over the debt, the Treasury can time its refinancings.[4] When the Treasury

---

[3] See James C. Van Horne, "Call Risk in Municipal Bonds," *Journal of Portfolio Management* 13 (Winter, 1987): 53–57.

[4] For callable Treasury bonds, yield-to-maturity is computed on the basis of final maturity when the market price of the bond is *below* its face value and on the basis of the earliest call date when its market price is *above* face value. When it is below face value, the implication is that the Treasury is unlikely to call the security.

introduced STRIPS (zero-coupon bonds described in chapter 7) in 1985, it ceased issuing callable bonds. Therefore, the relative amount outstanding has declined as new, noncallable bonds are issued.

REDEMPTION VERSUS CALLABILITY

The deferment period protects the investor from early call. However, this protection is not always what it seems. Many issues reserve the right to redeem a bond issue at any time under a set of conditions different from those that govern the call. In most corporate bond indentures, call deferment is restricted to situations in which a refunding takes place. By refunding, we mean refinancing the bond issue with a new bond issue at a lower interest cost.

However, many bond issues can be **redeemed,** provided the source of the redemption is not a refunding. It may be that the issuer has excess liquidity, or it could sell assets. It might issue common stock or be acquired in a merger. With a public utility issue, the flexibility to redeem bonds often emanates from a maintenance and replacement (M&R) fund. In another variation, Texas–New Mexico Power Company claimed that it was forced to sell property because of the threat of eminent domain proceedings by the government and that the proceeds of the sale could be used to redeem bonds. The reality is that numerous loopholes enable a determined issuer to thwart the call protection supposedly afforded an investor in a noncallable or deferred callable bond. As though redemption were not bad enough, the redemption price often is the face value of the bond rather than the higher call price. The line of demarcation between a call and a redemption is blurred. For example, if a company redeems a bond issue out of cash and later issues bonds to restore its liquidity, is it a redemption or a call? Sometimes legal redress is sought, but seldom does the investor win. Investors had best read the fine print before investing to see the conditions under which redemption is possible. Many are surprised.

THE CALL FEATURE'S VALUATION

The call provision gives the borrower flexibility. Should interest rates decline significantly, the borrower can call the debt instrument and refinance at a lower interest cost. However, the decline in interest rates must be sufficient to offset these realities: The call price is above the face value of the instrument and there are flotation, legal, and inconvenience costs. With a call provision, the borrower does not have to wait until final maturity to refinance. In addition to flexibility, the call provision may be advantageous to a corporation with unduly restrictive protective covenants in its existing bond indenture. By calling the bonds before maturity, the company can eliminate these restrictions.

The call privilege works to the benefit of borrowers but to the detriment of investors. If interest rates fall and the bond issue is called, investors can buy other bonds only at a sacrifice in yield-to-maturity. From the standpoint of the investor, the probability distribution of possible returns is different between bonds having a call feature and bonds that have no call feature. To illustrate, suppose an investor had the probabilistic beliefs about a callable bond and a noncallable bond shown in Figure 12-2. We

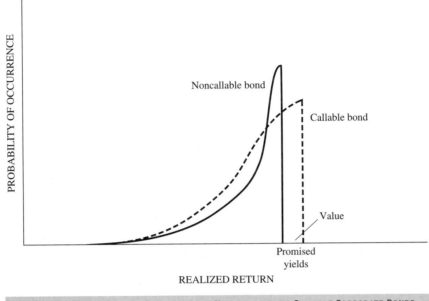

assume that the two bonds are alike in all other respects and both have 20 years to maturity. The distributions are skewed to the left because of the possibility of default, an influence examined in chapter 8. The most favorable outcome is that all principal and interest payments will be met on time so that the realized rate of return equals the promised yield at the time of purchase. Should interest or principal payments not occur as scheduled, the realized yield will be less. (The deviation from promised yield for the noncallable bond depends entirely on the degree of default.)

On the right-hand side of the figure, the likely consequence of the bond's having a call feature is shown. We see that the possibility is still strong that the actual yield will equal the promised yield, although the probability is less. However, there is now a reasonable probability that the bond will be called and that the investor's actual return over the 20 years, including reinvestment, will be less than the promised yield. This negative factor is *in addition* to the possibility of default. As a result, there is a greater probability with the callable bond that the realized return, including reinvestment in a lower-yielding bond, will be less than that of the noncallable bond. This is noticeable in the mid-range of realized returns. The extreme tail of the distribution for the callable bond is not altered materially because it depends on the occurrence of a severe default and not on the bond's being called. It is the intermediate part of the distribution that is altered by the addition of the call feature.

Because of the disadvantage to the investor, the call privilege usually does not come free to the borrower. Its cost, or value, is measured by the difference in yield on the callable bond and the yield that would be necessary if the security were noncallable. In Figure 12-2, it is represented on the horizontal axis by the distance between the two promised yields. In other words, the promised yield of the callable bond should be such that the marginal investor is indifferent between it and a noncallable bond. More fundamentally, this yield is determined by supply-and-demand forces in the market for callable securities. In equilibrium, the value of the call feature will be just sufficient to bring the demand for callable securities by investors into balance with the supply of callable securities by borrowers.

INTEREST-RATE EXPECTATIONS

In the equilibrating process, both borrowers and investors are influenced by expectations regarding the future course of interest rates. When interest rates are high and are expected to fall, the call feature is likely to have significant value. Investors are unwilling to invest in callable bonds unless such bonds yield more than bonds that are noncallable, all other things being the same. In other words, they must be compensated for the risk that the bonds might be called. On the other hand, borrowers are willing to pay a premium in yield for the call privilege in the belief that yields will fall and that it will be advantageous to refund the bonds. In equilibrium, both the marginal borrower and the marginal investor will be indifferent as to whether the bond is callable or noncallable.

When interest rates are low and expected to rise, the call privilege may have negligible value in that the borrower might pay the same yield if there were no call privilege. For the privilege to have value, interest-rate expectations must allow the possibility that the issue will be called. If interest rates are very low and are not expected to fall further, there is little probability that the bonds will be called. The key factor is that the borrower has to be able to refund the issue at a profit. For this to happen, interest rates have to drop significantly, because the issuer must pay the call price, which usually is at a premium above par value, as well as flotation costs involved in the refunding. If there is no probability that the borrower can refund the issue profitably, the call feature is unlikely to have a value.

THE CALL FEATURE AND CONVEXITY

A way to look at the investor call risk of a bond is through the convexity of its price-yield relationship. The mathematical properties and investor desirability of convexity were taken up in chapter 7. In the top panel of Figure 12-3, the price-yield relationship for a bond is shown, assuming no call or early redemption feature. As yield increases, price falls but at a decreasing rate; that is, its second derivative is positive. As a result, the line is convex as opposed to linear. With a callable bond, upside movements in price are limited. This feature is illustrated by the dashed line in the bottom panel of Figure 12-3. The bond is assumed to be alike in every respect but callability to the bond depicted in the top panel. Upside price movements are bounded at the call price, assuming the bond is immediately callable. The price-yield line has negative convexity in the range of lower interest rates, an undesirable property, and positive convexity in the higher range. The greater the difference between the two lines is, the greater the opportunity loss is to the investor should interest rates decline.[5]

---

[5]   For an excellent analysis of the call feature using convexity and duration concepts, see Mark L. Dunetz and James M. Mahoney, "Using Duration and Convexity in the Analysis of Callable Bonds," *Financial Analysts Journal* 44 (May–June 1988): 53–72.

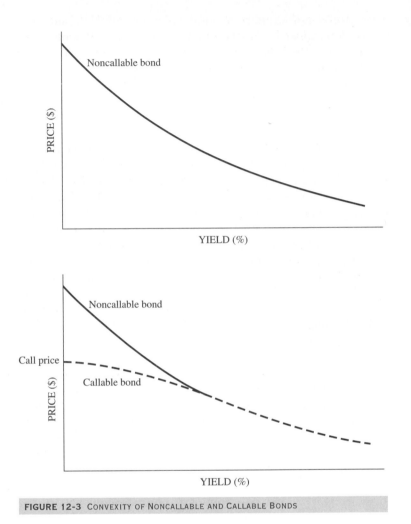

FIGURE 12-3 CONVEXITY OF NONCALLABLE AND CALLABLE BONDS

VALUATION IN AN OPTION PRICING CONTEXT

The call feature, of course, is an option given by investors to the issuer. The equilibration mechanism is

$$\text{callable bond} = \text{noncallable bond} - \text{call option} \qquad \textbf{(12-1)}$$

where the noncallable bond is identical to the callable bond in all respects except the call feature. The greater the value of the call feature is, the lower the value of the callable bond is relative to that of the noncallable one. The level and volatility of interest rates are key factors in giving value to the call feature. A sharp drop in interest rates will cause the option to have more value. In turn, such a drop is related to volatility. In the context of the lower panel of Figure 12-3, we see that the greater the probability of low interest rates, the more valuable the call feature.

More generally, the greater the variance or uncertainty of interest rates, the greater the value of the call option. Once the call option has been valued along the option pricing notions of chapter 10, Equation (12-1) may be used to determine whether the callable bond and the noncallable bond are mispriced. This type of analysis identifies arbitrage opportunities. Working the other way, one can determine the interest-rate variance necessary to bring about an equality (via the value of the call option) in Equation (12-1). This variance is then compared to that of the market. If significantly out of line, indication is given of an arbitrage opportunity.

For example, if the calculation showed that the standard deviation of bond returns necessary to bring about the equality were 28 percent, and you believed 15 percent were more realistic, you would conclude that the two bonds were mispriced. More specifically, the noncallable bond in Equation (12-1) is priced too high in relation to the callable one. This is merely to say that if the "true" standard deviation is 15 percent, then the call option is less valuable than the difference in prices of the two bonds would suggest. To arbitrage, you would buy the callable bond and sell short the noncallable bond. We see then that option pricing notions may be used to determine the equilibration in pricing between callable and noncallable bonds.

Rather than use the option pricing model to value the option component of the callable bond, one can use the option-adjusted spread (OAS) approach discussed earlier in the chapter. By formulating possible interest-rate paths for future one-period rates, the cash flows can be brought back to present values, weighted as to the probabilities of the various paths occurring, and summed to give the theoretical present value. If you assume an OAS and add this to all the one-period rates, the theoretical present value of the callable bond can be determined. The difference between this and the market price of the noncallable bond is the option value expressed in dollar terms. Given our earlier example of an OAS approach to a bond with a call feature, we do not provide an example here.

While the price of the callable bond will always be below that of the noncallable bond, as interest rates increase, the differential narrows. It also narrows as the volatility of interest rates declines. This volatility can be expressed either as a standard deviation of returns or as the dispersion of the paths in the OAS approach.

EMPIRICAL EVIDENCE ON CALL VALUATION

Bond refundings occur in waves. Only when interest rates decline significantly below previous interest-rate peaks, and the bonds are out from under deferred call protection, do large numbers of calls occur. In 1986 and early 1987, interest rates had declined dramatically from the 1981–1982 peak. Bonds issued at the peak with 5-year deferred call protection could be called in 1986–1987, and many were. In the early to mid-1990s, bonds issued at peaks in 1981 and 1984 with 10-year deferred call protection could be called. This, coupled with interest rates touching a 20-year low, resulted in large numbers of calls. Similar waves have occurred in earlier interest-rate cycles, but they were not so pronounced. The incidence of call, then, is highly related to the interest-rate cycle and to the length of time between a trough and previous peak(s).

Empirical evidence, some of which is cited in "Selected References" at the end of this chapter, tells us that the call feature has the most value, and hence cost to the issuer, when interest rates are high and expected to fall. Value typically is measured by the difference in yield between a bond that is callable, or is called, and one that is not. When interest rates are low and expected to rise, the call feature has little value. At this time, the yield curve typically is upward-sloping, whereas it is flat in the former case. Thus, the yield spread between callable and noncallable bonds tends to be greatest when the term structure is flat and narrowest when it is steeply upward-sloping. While this generalization holds for current coupon bonds, a low coupon rate relative to the current coupon rate lessens the probability of a call. Expressed differently, the higher the coupon rate is, the greater the likelihood is of a call should interest rates decline.

The more volatile interest rates are, the greater the spread between callable and noncallable bonds is, all other things the same.[6] As we know from chapter 10, the driving force in valuing any option is volatility, and it holds here for the call option. The combination of high interest rates, a flat yield curve, and substantial interest-rate volatility will result in a high value for the call feature. In contrast, low interest rates, a sharply upward-sloping yield curve, and low interest-rate volatility will result in little or no yield differential between current-coupon callable and noncallable bonds.

For both corporate and municipal bonds, the investor was found to suffer an opportunity loss when a bond was called. That is, the combined yield of this bond together with the refunding bond was less than what could have been obtained with the original bond. Although the realized return to the call date is higher than what could be earned elsewhere, owing to the call premium, the investor suffered an opportunity loss on reinvestment, which more than offset this gain. Because call premiums typically are less with municipal bonds than they are with corporate bonds, the municipal investor suffers more than the corporate investor when a call occurs.

PUTABLE BONDS

Some bond issues involve a put feature. With this feature, after a specified period of time the investor has the option to "put" the security back to the borrower at a specified price. Usually this price is the face value of the instrument. In the majority of cases, the put option can be exercised only in a 30-day window immediately prior to the put date.[7] However, some bonds are putable on more than one occasion. The more often the bond is putable, of course, the more it begins to resemble a floating-rate instrument when it comes to yield. Popular putable-bond structures are 30/10, where the final maturity is 30 years and the put date 10 years from the time of issuance, 10/5, and 20/10. In certain years, there are considerable numbers of putable bonds, with total issues exceeding those for callable bonds. To date, most issuers have been corporations.

---

[6] See Bryan Stanhouse and Duane Stock, "How Changes in Bond Call Features Affect Coupon Rates," *Journal of Applied Corporate Finance* 12 (Spring 1999): 92–99. In a related matter, Gregory R. Duffee, "The Relation between Treasury Yields and Corporate Bond Yield Spreads," *Journal of Finance* 53 (December 1998): 2225–41 finds that when interest rates increase, the yield spread between callable corporate and noncallable Treasury securities narrows. Holding coupon rates constant, the rise in interest rates reduces the probability of call and the value of the call option.

[7] For an excellent discussion of putable bonds, on which my treatment draws, see Leland E. Crabbe and Panos Nickoulis, "The Putable Bond Market: Structure, Historical Experience, and Strategies," *Journal of Fixed Income* 7 (December 1997): 47–60.

THE INVESTOR'S OPTION

The advantage of the put feature to investors is obvious; if interest rates rise, they may put the bonds to the issuer and invest in bonds providing higher yields. The instrument provides considerable positive convexity, which can be valuable in bond portfolio management. When buying a putable bond, yields are quoted in terms of spreads over Treasuries for the final maturity and for the put date. For a 30/10 bond, the spread over 30-year Treasuries might be 24 basis points and over 10-year Treasuries, 50 basis points. To date, the bonds issued have been largely investment grade. Credit quality is important, because the ability to put the bonds back for cash depends on the financial stability of the issuer. The duration of the instrument lies between that for a "bullet" bond with a maturity equal to that of the final maturity and one with a maturity equal to the put date. Where it lies in this range depends on the coupon rate and on the slope of the yield curve.

VALUATION IMPLICATIONS

A putable bond can be viewed in two ways. Suppose we were dealing with a 20/5 bond.

1. We have a 20-year bond with the option to shorten the maturity to 5 years.
2. We also have a 5-year instrument with the option to extend the maturity to 20 years.

If interest rates rise, the first scenario gives us the ability to shorten maturity. In the second case, we have a 5-year instrument with the ability to lengthen its maturity if interest rates fall. As a result of this dual option, the spreads over Treasuries for both dates will be lower, or tighter, than what would prevail if 5-year or 20-year "bullet" bonds were issued. In other words, the options have value and investors are willing to accept a lower yield than they would for investing in bullet bonds.

Crabbe and Nikoulis have found that the issuance of putable bonds varies inversely with the slope of the yield curve. When the yield curve is sharply upward-sloping, there are few issues, whereas when the yield curve is flat many putable bonds are issued. With an upward-sloping yield curve, expectations usually are for interest rates to increase. As a result, the put option is valuable and corporate issuers, mindful of the "cost" to them, refrain from issuing putable bonds as a desirable alternative to issuing a shorter-term bullet bond with a maturity equal to the put date.[8] Because the investor has the option to extend, the putable bond has a lower yield than the bullet. The yield advantage may be as much as 30 basis points. With a positive-sloped yield curve, the final maturity becomes more important in the pricing. As a result, the yield spread of the putable bond over Treasuries will increase, and the advantage over issuing a bullet bond diminishes. If high interest rates accompany the flat yield curve, the option to extend is less likely to be exercised.

In the past, putable bonds have sold at low implied volatilities relative to historical interest-rate volatility. While working to the advantage of investors, the puzzle is why corporations have financed with them. Rational decision making would call for issuing this embedded option when the corporation expects lower interest-rate volatility than do investors.

---

[8] *Ibid.*

THE SINKING FUND

The majority of industrial bond issues and about one quarter of public utility and other corporate bond issues carry a provision for a **sinking fund.** With this provision, the borrower is required to retire a specified face value portion of the issue each year. The idea is to "sink" most of the issue before maturity. Some sinking funds begin not at the time of issuance but after a period of 5 or 10 years. Sinking-fund payments need not retire the entire bond issue; a balloon payment can occur at final maturity. All bonds in an issue have the same maturity, although specific bonds are retired before that date. These bonds differ from **serial** bonds. For example, in a $20 million issue of serial bonds, $1 million of the bonds might mature each year for 20 years. Serial bonds are employed extensively in the municipal bond market but not in the corporate bond market, where the sinking-fund provision is prevalent in the majority of longer-term issues.

CHARACTERISTICS OF THE PROVISION

The sinking-fund retirement of a bond issue can take one of two forms.

1. The corporation can make a cash payment to the trustee, who in turn calls the bonds for redemption at the sinking-fund call price, usually the face value of the bond. Typically, the bonds are called on a lottery basis by their serial numbers, which are published in *The Wall Street Journal* and other papers.
2. The corporation can purchase bonds in the open market and pay the trustee by delivering to it a given number of bonds. If the market price of the bonds is less than the sinking-fund call price, the company will buy bonds in the open market and deliver them to the trustee. If the market price exceeds the call price, the company will make a cash payment to the trustee.

A problem some corporations face in purchasing bonds in the market is the presence of **accumulators.** An accumulator is an institutional or other investor who buys bonds in advance of the corporation's going into the market to acquire them for sinking-fund purposes. If supply is sufficiently restricted, the corporation will be able to purchase bonds only by bidding up the price. In this way, the accumulator hopes to sell the bonds at an inflated price, knowing the corporation must purchase them to satisfy the sinking-fund requirement. For example, an accumulator might buy bonds at a price of $840 per bond to yield 8.6 percent and sell them to the corporation for $920, which corresponds to a yield of 7.3 percent. Although the price is significantly above the previous going market price, imperfections allow the accumulator to partially corner the market, thereby forcing the corporation to pay the inflated price.

While perfectly legal, accumulators are not looked on with favor by corporate borrowers. Only when the bonds sell at a discount from the sinking-fund call price, of course, does accumulation occur. Otherwise, the corporation will make a cash payment to the trustee, who will purchase bonds at the call price. Consequently, the sinking-fund call price sets an upper limit on the price the accumulator can receive. When interest rates are high and discount bonds are prevalent, the presence of accumulators is common, much to the dismay of corporate borrowers with sinking-fund provisions.

In the aforementioned situations, the sinking fund was assumed to pertain to an individual bond issue. A less-known and much less-used provision is a blanket sinking fund, which pertains to multiple bond issues of a corporation. Known as a **funnel sinking fund,** the provision specifies the amount of periodic payment to the sinking fund that is required to retire outstanding bonds. However, the corporate borrower can funnel its sinking-fund payment to a single issue or to several issues. Put another way, it has the choice of which issue or issues to retire. To reduce its overall interest costs, the corporation will usually focus on high-coupon issues. Public utilities are the principal users of "funnel sinkers," though not of the sinking-fund provision in general.

Finally, most sinking funds allow for **acceleration.** This permits the issuer, through the trustee, to call more bonds than required. For example, an issuer might be permitted to call up to twice the mandatory sinking-fund requirement.

VALUE OF THE SINKING FUND

The sinking fund represents a **delivery option** to the corporation. It can satisfy the provision by paying cash to the trustee or by repurchasing bonds in the market. Expressed differently, it has an option to retire debt at the sinking-fund call price—usually the face value—or at the market price, whichever is lower. If interest rates increase and/or credit quality deteriorates, the bond's price will decline in relation to the sinking-fund call price. As a result, the delivery option can have significant value. As with any option it works to the advantage of the holder—in this case, the corporation and its stockholders—and to the disadvantage of bondholders. The greater the volatility of interest rates and/or volatility of firm value, the more valuable the option to the corporation. In these circumstances, investors should require a yield higher than would be required with a comparable serial bond.

The delivery option has been modeled as an interest-rate, path-dependent process using the option-adjusted spread notions described earlier in the chapter, as well as in other ways.[9] The idea is that the option is a thing of value to the issuer. Therefore, the sinking-fund bond is less valuable to the investor and will need to sell at a lower price than an identical bond without a sinking fund.

However, the sinking-fund provision may benefit the bondholder. By delivering bonds whose cost is lower than the call price, the company conserves cash, which may lower the probability of default. Because of the orderly retirement of sinking-fund debt, known as the **amortization effect,** some feel that it has less default risk than nonsinking-fund debt.[10] This argument supposes that the ability of the corporation to make sinking-fund payments is evidence of solvency and that these payments reduce the possibility of a crisis-at-maturity, discussed in chapter 8. In addition, steady repurchase activity adds liquidity to the market, a quality that may be beneficial to investors. Also, a sinking-fund bond has a shorter duration than a nonsinking-fund bond of the same maturity. This factor also may be attractive to investors, but it will depend on the term structure of interest rates. Finally, the sinking-fund bond may get an added boost on the demand side when accumulators acquire it.

---

[9] Andrew Ho and Michael Zaretsky, "Valuation of Sinking Fund Bonds," *Journal of Fixed Income* 3 (June 1993): 25–31; and Thomas Ho and Ronald F. Singer, "The Value of Corporate Debt with a Sinking-Fund Provision," *Journal of Business* 57 (July 1984): 315–36.

[10] Edward A. Dyl and Michael D. Joehnk, "Sinking Funds and the Cost of Corporate Debt," *Journal of Finance* 36 (September 1979): 887–93.

The factors discussed work in opposite directions. The delivery option works to the disadvantage of bondholders, but amortization and other things that reduce risk and/or increase liquidity work to their advantage. Little empirical testing has been done of the net effect of delivery option and amortization. The limited studies undertaken focus on one or the other, and both effects have been supported.

❖ SUMMARY

A number of options may be embedded in bonds, particularly in corporate bonds. The call feature, put option, sinking-fund provision, and prepayment of a mortgage are the more common. Two otherwise identical bonds may be valued differently when one has an embedded option but not the other. An option-adjusted spread (OAS) approach may help us better understand and value the embedded option. The OAS is that constant spread added to all possible future one-period Treasury rates so that the present value of the cash flows for the option-embedded bond equals the bond's market price. The OAS approach allows for future interest-rate volatility, which usually is mapped with a binomial-tree model.

The call provision gives the issuer the ability to buy back the instrument prior to maturity. Securities can be immediately callable or callable after a deferment period of usually 5 or 10 years. The call option works to the advantage of the issuer but to the detriment of the investor. If a security is called, investors usually suffer an opportunity loss because they can invest in other bonds only at a sacrifice in yield. The call must be distinguished from a redemption, in which bonds can be retired as long as the wherewithal is not a refunding. The call option has more value when interest rates are more volatile, and this can be demonstrated using convexity analysis, the option-pricing model, and option-adjusted spread analysis. A callable bond is equivalent to a noncallable bond minus the call option, and this proposition can be used to determine the equilibration in pricing between the two. Empirical evidence suggests that the call feature has the most value when interest rates are high the yield curve is flat, and there is substantial interest-rate volatility; it has little value when the opposite conditions prevail.

A put feature allows the holder of a bond to sell it back to the issuer at a specified price, usually its face value. In recent years, there have been large numbers of putable bonds. Typically, the option can be exercised only in a 30-day window prior to the put date. The putable bond can be viewed as an option to shorten maturity to the put date, or as an option to extend the put date to the maturity. As a result of this dual option, spreads over Treasuries at the put date and at maturity are lower than "bullet" corporate bonds for the same dates. The issuance of putable bonds varies inversely with the slope of the yield curve, and the valuation of such bonds depends upon this factor.

A sinking-fund provision requires the borrower to retire a specified portion of a bond issue periodically. To do so, the issuer can either make a cash payment to the trustee, who calls certain bonds, or can purchase bonds in the open market. It will choose the former if the market value is at or above the sinking-fund call price and select the latter on other occasions. For the latter, accumulators try to buy the bonds before the corporation does and reap a profit. The issuer has a delivery option and this works to the disadvantage of investors, whereas amortization may benefit them with lower default risk and greater liquidity. Limited empirical evidence on the motion is mixed as to whether the delivery option dominates the amortization effect, or vice versa.

❖ SELECTED REFERENCES

Barth, Mary E., Wayne R. Landsman, and Richard J. Rendleman, Jr., "Option Pricing-Based Bond Value Estimates and a Fundamental Components Approach to Account for Corporate Debt," research paper, Graduate School of Business, Stanford University (1998).

Brennan, Michael J., and Eduardo S. Schwartz, "Savings Bonds, Retractable Bonds and Callable Bonds," *Journal of Financial Economics* 5 (1977): 67–88.

Carow, Kenneth A., Gayle R. Erwin, and John J. McConnell, "A Survey of U.S. Corporate Financing Innovations," *Journal of Applied Corporate Finance* 12 (Spring 1999): 55–69.

Crabbe, Leland E., and Panos Nikoulis, "The Putable Bond Market: Structure, Historical Experience, and Strategies," *Journal of Fixed Income* 7 (December 1997): 47–60.

Duffee, Gregory R., "The Relation between Treasury Yields and Corporate Bond Yield Spreads," *Journal of Finance* 53 (December 1998): 2225–41.

Dunetz, Mark L., and James M. Mahoney, "Using Duration and Convexity in the Analysis of Callable Bonds," *Financial Analysts Journal* 44 (May–June 1988): 53–72.

Dyl, Edward A., and Michael D. Joehnk, "Sinking Funds and the Cost of Corporate Debt," *Journal of Finance* 36 (September 1979): 887–93.

Fabozzi, Frank J., *Valuation of Fixed Income Securities and Derivatives,* chapters 5–6. New Hope, PA: Frank J. Fabozzi Associates, 1998.

Goyal, Vidham K., Neela Gollapudi, and Joseph P. Ogden, "A Corporate Bond Innovation of the 90s: The Clawback Provision in High-Yield Debt," *Journal of Corporate Finance* 4 (December 1998): 301–20.

Ho, Andrew, and Michael Zaretsky, "Valuation of Sinking Fund Bonds," *Journal of Fixed Income* 3 (June 1993): 25–31.

Ho, Thomas, and Ronald F. Singer, "The Value of Corporate Debt with a Sinking-Fund Provision," *Journal of Business* 57 (July 1984): 315–36.

Kalotay, Andrew J., "On the Management of Sinking Funds," *Financial Management* 10 (Summer 1981): 34–40.

Kalotay, Andrew, and Bruce Tuckman, "Sinking Fund Prepurchases and the Designation Option," *Financial Management* 21 (Winter 1992): 110–18.

Kalotay, Andrew J., George O. Williams, and Frank J. Fabozzi, "A Model for Valuing Bonds and Embedded Options," *Financial Analysts Journal* 49 (May–June 1993): 35–46.

Kalotay, Andrew, and Leslie Abreo, "Ratchet Bonds: Maximum Refunding Efficiency at Minimum Transaction Cost," *Journal of Applied Corporate Finance* 12 (Spring 1999): 40–47.

Kopprasch, Robert W., "Option-Adjusted Spread Analysis: Going Down the Wrong Path?" *Financial Analysts Journal* 49 (May–June 1994): 42–47.

Pye, Gordon, "The Value of the Call Option on a Bond," *Journal of Political Economy* 74 (April 1966): 200–205.

Stanhouse, Bryan, and Duane Stock, "How Changes in Bond Call Features Affect Coupon Rates," *Journal of Applied Corporate Finance* 12 (Spring 1999): 92–99.

———, "The Impact of Volatility on Duration of Amortizing Debt with Embedded Call Options," *Journal of Fixed Income* 8 (September 1998): 87–94.

Van Horne, James C., "Called Bonds: How Did the Investor Fare?" *Journal of Portfolio Management* 6 (Summer 1980): 58–61.

———, "Call Risk in Municipal Bonds," *Journal of Portfolio Management* 13 (Winter 1987): 53–57.

13

MORTGAGE SECURITIES AND PREPAYMENT RISK

A mortgage is a secured loan, with the security being a real property. This property could be a house or an office building. The two categories of mortgages are residential and nonresidential, also known as commercial. The borrower, or mortgagor, agrees to make monthly payments to a lender, which can be a commercial bank, a thrift institution, an insurance company, a pension fund, or some other lender. Often the payments are indirect through a **mortgage servicer,** which collects them from the mortgagor and forwards them to the ultimate lender. The mortgage itself is not a security because it cannot be traded in a secondary market. To become a security, individual mortgages must be securitized.

As described in chapter 1, *securitization* involves (1) taking an illiquid asset, such as a 30-year, fixed-rate mortgage; (2) packaging it into a pool of like assets; and then (3) issuing marketable securities backed by the pool. Thus, an illiquid asset is transformed into a liquid one with a secondary market. In recent years, approximately 50 percent of the residential mortgages originated in the United States have been securitized. In fact, mortgage securities have become one of the most important fixed-income security markets. A feature that distinguishes them from other securities is the prepayment option, which rests with the borrower. Before exploring this important option, we take up certain aspects of mortgage securities.

SOME FEATURES OF MORTGAGES

There are two kinds of mortgages. The first is the standard **fixed-rate mortgage** (FRM), where level payments are made monthly. Interest and principal are amortized over a set number of years.[1] Although the most prevalent term is 30 years, 15-year and

---

[1] The monthly payment is determined by solving the following formula for X:

$$P = \sum_{t=1}^{12n} \frac{X}{\left(1 + \dfrac{r}{12}\right)^{12n}}$$

where P is the amount borrowed, n is the final maturity in years, and r is the annualized rate of interest. By determining the present value of an annuity of $1 per month in the denominator, calculations are facilitated.

other term mortgages increasingly are finding favor with home owners. The FRM contrasts with an **adjustable-rate mortgage** (ARM). Here the interest rate is reset periodically, reflecting changes in short-term interest rates. The barometer for change is some index, usually either the one-year constant-maturity Treasury rate (CMT), a Federal Home Loan Bank Board District cost of funds index (COFI), or the London Interbank Offer Rate (LIBOR).

While the ARM shifts interest-rate risk to the borrower from the lender, the magnitude of the semiannual or annual reset usually has limits. Moreover, certain ARMs have an overall cap rate. If an initial loan were made at 7 percent, the maximum increase in any one year might be 1½ percent and the overall cap rate 10 percent. Approximately 15 percent of mortgages originated are ARMs, but the proportion varies over time in keeping with interest-rate expectations and volatility, among other things. While some ARMs are securitized, and mortgage-backed securities are issued against the pool, the majority are held by the financial institution making the loan. Consequently, our focus will be on fixed-rate mortgages.

MORTGAGE PASS-THROUGH SECURITY

When a pool of mortgages is securitized, a **pass-through security** is created. With this security, the investor owns a proportionate share of the mortgage pool. Cash flows from the mortgages (interest and principal payments as well as prepayments) are passed along to investors, after deduction of servicing costs. The servicing contract may reside with the original lender or it may be with a third-party contractor. Servicing involves taking in monthly payments, keeping records, and instigating foreclosure procedures when default occurs. The servicing fee generally is in the 0.3–0.4 percent range, and there is considerable competition among providers. When certain other costs, like guarantee fees, are brought into play, the differential between the rate received on the mortgage collateral pool and what the pass-through security holder receives is approximately ½ percent. Except for this differential, there is a cash-flow matching between mortgage payments and payments to the pass-through security holders. However, there is a processing delay of 15 days or so before the cash flows received by the servicing contractor are passed through to the investor.

AGENCY PASS-THROUGHS

Most pass-through securities are guaranteed by the Government National Mortgage Association (Ginnie Mae), an agency of the U.S. government, or by one of the two government-sponsored enterprises: the Federal National Mortgage Association (Fannie Mae) and the Federal Home Loan Mortgage Corporation (Freddie Mac). To qualify for an agency guarantee, the loan must conform to certain standards, such as a loan-to-value ratio of 80 percent or less and a mortgage size of no more than $257,300 (at the time of this writing). These loans are known as **conforming loans.** The agencies charge a guarantee fee. The most creditworthy of the three is Ginnie Mae, for it is legally backed by the U.S. government. Fannie Mae and Freddie Mac, as government-sponsored enterprises, enjoy the moral backing of the government. As this backing is not as strong as legal backing, securities guaranteed by them tend to provide 5 basis points or more in yield compared with an identical Ginnie Mae security.

When an investor purchases a new agency pass-through security, it usually is done on a **"to-be-announced" (TBA)** basis. While the coupon, price, and other trading attributes are known, the specific mortgage pools underlying the security are not known until two days prior to settlement. At this time, the seller is obligated to provide pool information. Although the pools delivered are at the discretion of the seller, the "cheapest-to-deliver" problem discussed in chapter 9 for interest-rate futures contracts is mitigated by delivery guidelines. Virtually all newly issued agency securities are traded on a TBA basis, and the price quotations assume such. This convention enhances liquidity in the pass-through market, because many mortgage pools are small. For existing pass-through securities, pool-specific information is available and uncertainty is reduced.

NONAGENCY PASS-THROUGHS

Mortgages not conforming to requirements of the agencies are known as **nonconforming loans.** These mortgages tend to be larger, and they also tend to have lower loan-to-value ratios. Because most are not guaranteed by a government-sponsored agency, nonagency pass-through securities must be credit enhanced in other ways. Frequently, this enhancement requires the sponsor to take up to the first 5 percent, or sometimes 10 percent, of any losses. This form of credit enhancement is known as **subordination.** Even with credit enhancement, yields on nonagency pass-through securities tend to be ¼ percent or so higher than yields on agency pass-throughs.

For both types of pass-throughs, a grantor trust is the legal arrangement used. The reason is that the agency or financial institution wants to avoid taxation on the interest payments, serving only as a conduit between borrowers and investors. This arrangement was formalized in the Tax Reform Act of 1986, in which the Real Estate Mortgage Investment Conduit, **REMIC,** entity was established to avoid tax ambiguities that might result in double taxation. The pass-through is the base security, which can be either held as a direct investment or used to reconfigure cash flows into other mortgage security products.

MORTGAGE DERIVATIVES

To satisfy different investor maturity and risk desires, the mortgage payments stream of the basic pass-through security has been reconfigured in many different ways. The securities created are known as **derivative products.** The ultimate source of cash flows, of course, is the various mortgagors in the pool making monthly payments or paying off their loans. To create a derivative, the pass-through security is placed in trust. When security payments are made to the trust, these cash flows are subdivided into payments to two or more derivative securities. The allocation is by formula, established when the derivative security is created. The sum of the parts (payments to derivative-security holders) must equal the whole (payments to the pass-through security holder, the trust). The principle is the same as discussed in chapter 7 for stripping coupon and principal payments from a whole Treasury security. For mortgages, the process is shown in Figure 13-1.

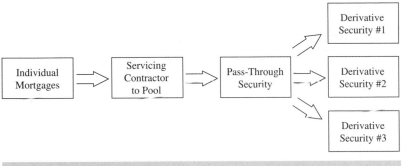

FIGURE 13-1 CASH FLOWS FROM INDIVIDUAL MORTGAGES TO DERIVATIVE SECURITIES

COLLATERALIZED MORTGAGE OBLIGATIONS (CMOs)

One example of the creation of derivative products is the **collateralized mortgage obligation** (CMO), in which the mortgage payments stream is divided into different maturity classes. A standard, "plain vanilla" CMO has four classes, or **tranches.** The first three classes receive cash interest payments. Principal payments are different. The first class receives all principal payments on the underlying mortgages until such securities are entirely paid. At that time, the second class begins to receive principal payments and is entitled to all of them until that class is paid. At this point, the third class receives all principal payments until it is completely repaid.

The last class is an accrual security, known as a "Z bond." Its holders receive no interim interest payments. Rather, interest accrues at a stated coupon rate. Cash payments on a Z bond begin only after the earlier classes have been retired. At that point, its holders receive payments from whatever collateral remains in the pool. Due to mortgage prepayments, the timing and magnitude of payments to the Z-bond holders are uncertain. In Figure 13-2, patterns of cash flows to the various classes are illustrated under the assumption of no change in interest rates. Note in the figure that the first three classes receive interest payments, while the Z bonds do not until all other classes have been retired.

Another security that can be created in a CMO is a **residual class.** As the name implies, this class comes after the Z class. The residual security has no stated interest rate or face value. Rather, it receives any cash flows that are left over after interest and principal payments have been paid on prior classes and all administrative expenses have been paid. Any excess paid at the end is due to (1) overcollateralization of the mortgage pool; (2) interest payments by mortgagees exceeding the coupon payments on the CMO securities; and (3) reinvestment income arising because of the lag between the monthly payments on the pass-through security and the coupon payments to the CMO security holders. Obviously, the residual class bears greater risk than any other class in a CMO. It is like equity.

PLANNED AMORTIZATION CLASS (PAC) AND TARGETED AMORTIZATION CLASS (TAC) SECURITIES

A further derivative product is the **Planned Amortization Class** (PAC). The PAC security, usually the second tranche of a CMO, has scheduled principal payments. Because all

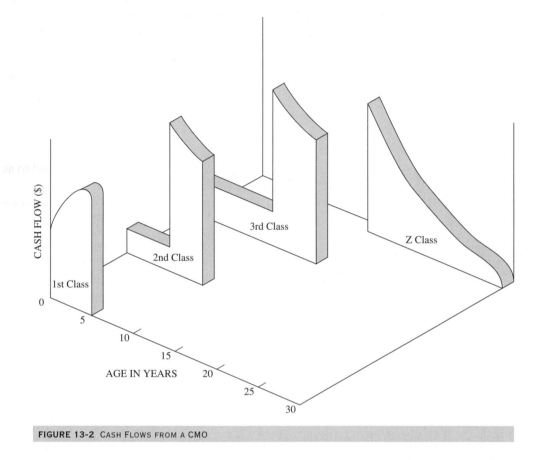

FIGURE 13-2 CASH FLOWS FROM A CMO

principal payments on the underlying mortgages in the pool can be used to make PAC payments, they are highly certain. This high degree of cash-flow certainty comes at the expense of other CMO classes whose cash flows are less certain. The non-PAC classes are known as companion or support classes. They absorb the greater uncertainty occasioned by carving out a PAC class, and their security prices are more volatile. This relationship is illustrated when we discuss the valuation of the prepayment feature. Planned Amortization Class securities are popular and account for about one third of the mortgage derivative products outstanding. A variation of the PAC theme is the **Targeted Amortization Class** (TAC) security. It, too, is designed to provide more certainty as to cash flows than the mortgage pool overall. However, the TAC security does not provide as much cash-flow certainty as does a PAC security, particularly when interest rates increase.[2]

IOs AND POs

With stripped mortgage-backed securities (SMBSs), cash flows from a pool of mortgages are divided along lines of principal and interest. While a number of divisions are

---

[2] For an excellent discussion of PACs and other mortgage derivatives, see Andrew S. Carron, "Understanding CMOs, REMICs, and other Mortgage Derivatives," *Journal of Fixed Income* 2 (June 1992): 25–43.

possible, the predominant form of SMBSs is a complete separation of interest and principal payments. The **interest only (IO)** security holders receive all of the interest payments but none of the principal payments made on the underlying mortgages in the pool. The **principal only (PO)** holders receive all of the principal payments but none of the interest payments. The price behavior of IO and PO securities is illustrated shortly. Because of the extreme nature of the instruments, IOs and POs have a high degree of risk. Accordingly, they can be useful for hedging interest-rate risk.

FLOATERS AND INVERSE FLOATERS

In addition to these repackagings of cash flows, a mortgage pool can be configured so as to have a **floating-rate class.** Here one class receives interest that is reset quarterly with changes in some index, frequently three-month LIBOR. A spread over LIBOR is established, and it remains constant over time. While the floater takes on the characteristics of a short-term security, total interest paid usually is capped. Otherwise, the underlying mortgage pool could not support the other CMO classes if a large increase in interest rates were to occur. Expressed differently, the floater class would draw off too much cash flow from the pool. Whereas the yield on a **straight floater** moves up or down on a one-to-one basis with the index, a **super floater** has a multiple greater than one-to-one.

With an **inverse floater,** the interest rate paid increases when LIBOR declines and decreases when LIBOR rises, if that is the index used. One formula might be $30 - (4 \times \text{LIBOR})$. If LIBOR were 7 percent, the inverse floater's return would be 2 percent, whereas if it were 4 percent the return would be 14 percent. Most formulas are of this variety, with a constant coupon minus some multiple of the index. The return is bounded at zero on the downside. An inverse floater combined with a floater class means that the cash outflows from the mortgage pool are offsetting to some extent. As a result, the other classes are protected. Without an inverse floater class but with a floater class, they are exposed. As a result, payments to the floater class usually are capped.

Each of the security classes can have several subcategories. In fact, there is no end to the way a mortgage pool's cash flows can be segregated. Ultimately the market decides. If investor demand is insufficient, the creation of further mortgage derivative products will abate. This was the case in 1994 when, after a sharp increase in interest rates, investors were badly hurt in POs and certain other mortgage derivatives. As a result of sharply lower demand, the creation of mortgage derivatives from straight pass-throughs was dramatically curtailed in the mid-1990s. The valuation of mortgages and mortgage-backed securities depends on prepayment assumptions, a topic to which we now turn.

PREPAYMENT OPTION AND ITS VALUATION

One of the principal risks with a mortgage security is the uncertainty surrounding prepayment of the underlying mortgages. The borrower may prepay at any time, sometimes subject to penalty but often not. The reasons for prepayment may be relocation, desire for a larger or smaller house, or a decision to refinance because mortgage rates are lower and refinancing is advantageous. A form of prepayment occurs when the mortgagor makes a partial or full loan principal payment ahead of the scheduled amortization of the loan. A person with excess funds may simply decide to "save" through paying down his or her mortgage. This is known as **curtailment,** and while it does not change the amount of subsequent monthly payments, it does shorten the final maturity. Curtailment is usually minor in the total prepayment risk picture.

Prepayments in the mortgage pool greatly affect the timing of cash flows to the mortgage-backed security investor. The more volatile mortgage rates are, of course, the greater the value of the prepayment option is to the borrower and the greater the cost is to the investor.

PREPAYMENT AND CONVEXITY

The risk to the investor can be visualized using the concept of convexity developed in chapter 7 and illustrated in the last chapter for call risk. As we know from that discussion, when interest rates decline sharply, convexity becomes negative. In the case of a mortgage pool, it is not a zero-one situation with the instrument either outstanding or called in its entirety. Rather, as interest rates decline, an increasing portion of the mortgages in the pool prepay. Even when interest rates decline substantially below the coupon rate, not everyone prepays. Still, a high percentage do, and the price-yield relationship has negative convexity in this area. Figure 13-3 illustrates this phenomenon. Unlike Figure 12-3 in chapter 12 for a bond, there is no call price setting an upward boundary on price movements.

For higher interest rates, negative convexity also may prevail, or at least there will be less positive convexity than is the case with bonds. The reason is that people who might move to upgrade their housing or to relocate are discouraged from doing so. They know that they face much higher payments on a new home. As a result, prepayments are below what normally would occur, and this is known as **extension risk.** Put differ-

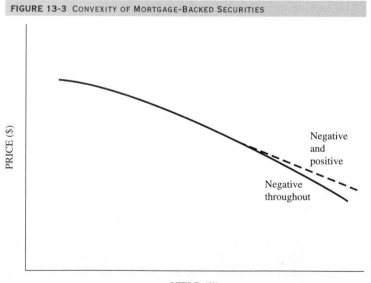

FIGURE 13-3 CONVEXITY OF MORTGAGE-BACKED SECURITIES

ently, the duration of the instrument is increased. If the term structure is upward-sloping, the value decline is more than occurs with a fixed-rate, stated-maturity bond. The solid line in Figure 13-3 reflects negative convexity in the area of higher interest rates. The possibility of negative convexity throughout makes mortgage securities different from a noncallable, fixed-income security for which positive convexity prevails. For substantial interest-rate changes, the mortgage security will perform more poorly, all other things the same.

MEASURES OF PREPAYMENT

Before examining what drives prepayment, we need to know how it is measured. The most common way is with **single monthly mortality** (SMM). The SMM is the percentage of outstanding principal in a mortgage pool that is prepaid during a month. By definition, prepayment is principal paid over and above scheduled amortization payments. Therefore,

$$\text{SMM} = \frac{\begin{array}{c}\text{EOM scheduled principal of pool}\\ \text{minus EOM actual principal}\end{array}}{\text{EOM scheduled principal of pool}} \qquad \textbf{(13-1)}$$

where EOM is the end of the month. The SMM frequently is annualized into what is known as the **conditional prepayment rate** (CPR)

$$\text{CPR} = (1 - \text{SMM})^{12} \qquad \textbf{(13-2)}$$

where SMM is expressed in decimal form. Given the CPR, we can solve for the SMM, which is

$$\text{SMM} = 1 - (1 - \text{CPR})^{1/12} \qquad \textbf{(13-3)}$$

With these two measures in mind, we turn now to factors that best explain prepayment experience.

COUPON RATE AND AGE

This prepayment experience is highly sensitive to the **coupon rate** on the mortgage pool: The higher the coupon on the underlying mortgages is, the more prepayments will occur with a decline in interest rates. This phenomenon is captured in the spread of the coupon rate on the mortgage pool less the current interest rate on mortgages. When the spread goes above 1 percent, prepayments accelerate. By 2 percent, heavy prepayments occur—perhaps one fourth of the pool on an annual basis, as home owners refinance their mortgages. The experience for Fannie Mae 30-year, fixed-rate mortgages is shown in Figure 13-4. On the vertical axis is the percent per month of the pool that prepays—namely, the SMM defined previously. We see that prepayment rates are high when the differential is 2 percent or more. Refinancings of mortgages, called "refis," tend to lag behind changes in interest rates. When interest rates fall, there is inertia on the part of some. Even when they refinance, it takes time to process a new mortgage loan at a financial institution. As rates continue to fall, however, increasing numbers of refis occur. The relative coupon rate is the most important factor explaining mortgage prepayments.

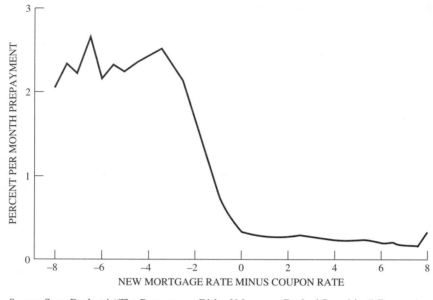

Source: Sean Becketti, "The Prepayment Risk of Mortgage-Backed Securities," *Economic Review of the Federal Reserve Bank of Kansas City* (February 1989): 53.

FIGURE 13-4 PREPAYMENT RATE AND THE COUPON RATE RELATIVE TO NEW MORTGAGE RATES

The **age** of a mortgage pool also affects prepayments. The successor organization to the Public Securities Association (PSA), now known as the Bond Market Association, models prepayment with respect to age in a simple way. The **PSA convention** has prepayments increasing by 0.2 percent per month (on an annualized basis) for 2½ years. At that time, prepayments are assumed to hold steady at 6 percent of the pool for the mortgage's remaining life. At the end of one year, CPR is assumed to be 2.4 percent; at the end of two years, 4.8 percent; and at the end of 2½ years, 6.0 percent. The notion is that in a mortgage's early life, say the first year, the likelihood of prepayment is low. The home owner has just moved or has just refinanced and is unlikely to prepay. As time passes, however, the likelihood of prepayment increases up to a point, after which it levels off. The 6 percent "steady state" corresponds to the average annual turnover of single-family homes in the United States.

The PSA model of prepayment, with respect to age, can be combined with the level of interest rates. When mortgage rates fall significantly below the coupon rate for the pool, prepayments accelerate. They might become 2¼ times the PSA model assumptions, a situation known as 225 percent PSA. If the mortgage pool were more than 2½ years old, this would correspond to prepayments of 2.25 × 6 percent = 13.5 percent of the pool per annum. If new mortgage rates exceed the coupon rate for the pool, prepayments might be only 80 percent PSA. The relationship between CPR and percent PSA is illustrated in Figure 13-5.

The greater the percent PSA, of course, the shorter the life of a pass-through security. The latter often is expressed as the **weighted average life (WAL),** which is the average time that principal is owing, given prepayment assumptions. This measure is to be distinguished from **weighted average maturity (WAM),** which is a weighted average of

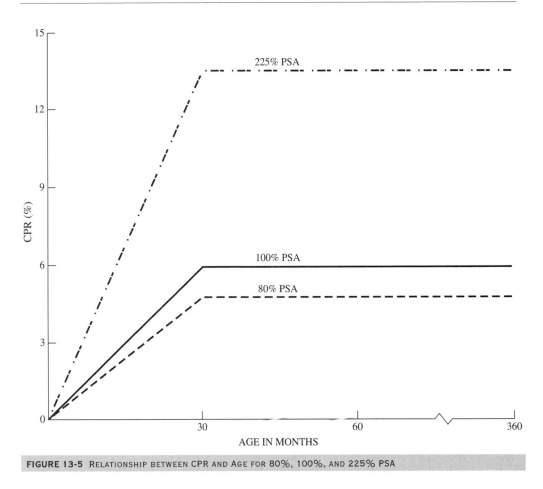

FIGURE 13-5 RELATIONSHIP BETWEEN CPR AND AGE FOR 80%, 100%, AND 225% PSA

final maturities of underlying mortgages in the pool. The relationship between WAL and percent PSA is illustrated in Figure 13-6 for current coupon, 30-year and 15-year, fixed-rate mortgages.

ADDITIONAL FACTORS EXPLAINING PREPAYMENT

Although the relative coupon rate and the age of a mortgage pool are the most important factors explaining prepayment, there are others including a **seasonal** element. Prepayments tend to be higher in the summer than they are at other times of the year. This phenomenon is related to favorable weather for building and the tendency of families to move before the school year begins.

A fourth variable is a **burnout factor.** As employed in the Goldman Sachs prepayment model, this factor relates to the number of times the mortgage pool was in a position to prepay but did not.[3] That is, when mortgage rates fall below the coupon rate, it

---

[3]   See Scott F. Richard and Richard Roll, "Prepayments on Fixed-Rate Mortgage-Backed Securities," *Journal of Portfolio Management* 15 (Spring 1989): 76–82.

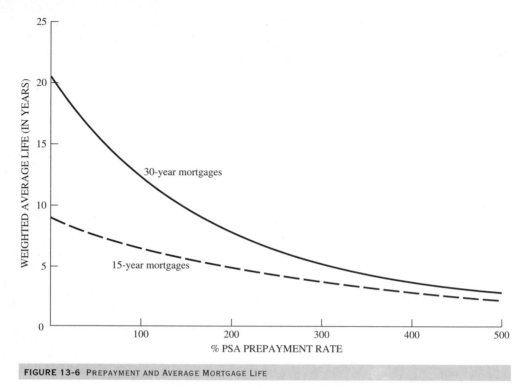

FIGURE 13-6 PREPAYMENT AND AVERAGE MORTGAGE LIFE

makes economic sense to prepay. The more times the prepayment option is "in the money" but is not exercised, the greater the burnout is said to be. In turn, the greater the burnout of a pool is, the less inclination there is to prepay, all other things the same. In the next section we discuss certain borrower-specific information that may be helpful in explaining prepayment.

MODELING PREPAYMENT EXPERIENCE

A lot of work has gone into modeling mortgage prepayments, and a number of studies are referenced at the end of the chapter. Investment banks and scholars have developed econometric models based on the age, coupon rate, and other characteristics of the mortgage pool, together with the term structure of interest rates, likely future interest rates, and volatility. Where a **generic pool** of mortgages is involved, one does not know characteristics of the pool. This is the case for new issues of mortgage-backed securities, where most trade on the TBA (to-be-announced) basis explained earlier. For existing mortgage securities, **pool specific** information is often available concerning the historical payment record.

Ideally, one would like to know demographic characteristics of borrowers in the pool (age, dependents, years of schooling, income, and so on), precise locations of the mortgages, economic and housing market conditions in those areas, and migration patterns. For example, the present price of a house relative to its purchase price may be important. The greater the relative price, the more people tend to rebalance their wealth by trading up or refinancing. As a result, prepayments tend to be higher.[4] Mortgages also are prepaid when they default and an agency or some other guarantor makes good on them. To some extent, defaults are location specific. Because of this and for other reasons, location of the mortgages in a pool is important. A breakdown by state or, if possible, by zip code adds explanatory power to a prepayment model. Among the larger states, California has the highest incidence of prepayment while New York has the lowest, reflecting different mobility. Finally, certain macroeconomic variables can be brought to bear, such as disposable personal income, other measures of economic activity, housing starts, and housing turnover.

One must be mindful that prepayment experience changes over time, making past relationships suspect. In the rapidly changing interest-rate environment of the early through mid-1990s, most prepayment model estimates were rather far off the mark. Despite these difficulties, some models have proved reasonably accurate over the longer run, and certainly they have provided an improved understanding of prepayment risk. Still, significant residual risk may be left unexplained by the factors in the model.

OPTION-ADJUSTED SPREAD APPROACH

As with the call feature in the previous chapter, mortgage-backed securities have been subjected to the option-adjusted spread (OAS) technique. Using a binomial-tree model, possible interest-rate paths are mapped and the cash flows of the mortgage pool for that path estimated. With declining interest rates, increasing portions of the pool will prepay. As a result, the cash flows for that path accelerate. The option-adjusted spread is the constant spread that must be added to all one-period Treasury interest rates so that the weighted average, present value of all the paths equals the security's actual market price. Thus, a large number of interest-rate scenarios are truncated into a simple measure. The greater the OAS of a mortgage security is, the greater the likelihood is that the prepayment option will be exercised by the holder, the mortgagor. As the OAS approach was illustrated in chapter 12 for the call option, we do not repeat that type of example here.

The OAS can be used in judging whether the security is mispriced, assuming one has convictions about the proper pricing of the option. Often, we see plotted over time the OAS spread between a current coupon, mortgage-backed security and a Treasury security of 7 or 10 years to maturity. Judgments are made as to whether the mortgage security is "cheap" when the OAS spread is wide, or "rich" when it is narrow. By buying the mortgage security when it is "cheap," one hopes to show better performance than with Treasuries. Recognize that mortgage-backed securities do well, relative to Treasuries, when interest-rate volatility is low. With volatile interest rates, relative performance suffers. When interest rates decline sharply, prepayment risk hurts relative performance; when they increase sharply, extension risk affects performance adversely. In this sense, investing in mortgage-backed securities, vis-à-vis Treasuries or corporates, is a bet on the volatility of interest rates. Not surprisingly, the OAS spread narrows when volatility declines and widens when volatility increases. When interest rates swing

---

[4] Scott F. Richard, "Housing Prices and Prepayments for Fixed-Rate Mortgage-Backed Securities," *Journal of Fixed Income* 1 (December 1991): 54–58.

significantly, the negative convexity of the mortgage-backed security hurts it relative to securities with positive convexity.

PREPAYMENT BEHAVIOR
OF CERTAIN DERIVATIVES

Prepayment modeling focuses on the experience of the overall mortgage pool. Depending on how the cash flows have been reconfigured, prepayment risk for the derivative securities will vary. Previously, we explored what happens with a CMO.

PLANNED AMORTIZATION CLASS SECURITIES

From earlier discussion we know that with a Planned Amortization Class (PAC) security, the idea is to carve out a class that has a high degree of certainty as to the magnitude and timing of cash flows. All principal payments on mortgages in the pool are dedicated to this purpose. The result is that the cash-flow configuration will be the same over a wide range of prepayment assumptions. The situation is illustrated in Figure 13-7, for the assumptions of 100 percent PSA and 300 percent PSA experience.

As we see, the PAC class receives virtually the same cash flows whether prepayment experience is 100 percent PSA or 300 percent PSA. That is the idea of the PAC security. Within some large boundary, like 75 percent PSA and 400 percent PSA, the cash-flow pattern, and hence the security's weighted average life (WAL), shows little variability with different prepayment rates. This range is known as the **PAC collar.** Of course, the other classes, the companion issues, bear considerable variation in cash flows and WAL under different prepayment assumptions within the range. In setting up a PAC security, the originator picks two extreme prepayment assumptions and then configures the PAC accordingly. As a result, the cash flows are highly certain within this collar range.

Beyond the collar boundaries, the PAC security cash flows are affected. When interest rates decrease or increase dramatically so that the PSA collar is breached, the security becomes known as a **"broken PAC."** The PAC security then trades more like an underlying pass-through security, with significant variation in weighted average life and in price when interest rates change outside the collar. Take a situation where prepayments in the underlying mortgage pool increase substantially. If the companion, or support, bonds in other classes are paid off, no further buffer exists to absorb the unexpected prepayments for the PAC security. Prepayments then affect the PAC security directly.

INTEREST ONLY (IO), PRINCIPAL ONLY (PO),
AND RESIDUAL CLASS SECURITIES

For the interest only (IO)/principal only (PO) classes of securities, price movements tend to be in opposite directions. As interest rates rise, the IO increases in value and the PO decreases, and vice versa. Figure 13-8 illustrates the relationships. With increases in interest rates, fewer prepayments are made. As a result, IO holders receive more total interest, and their security is more valuable. Beyond a point, however, the rate of increase in total cash flows decreases rapidly and present value effects take their toll. Then, the security's value declines with further increases in interest rates. For decreases

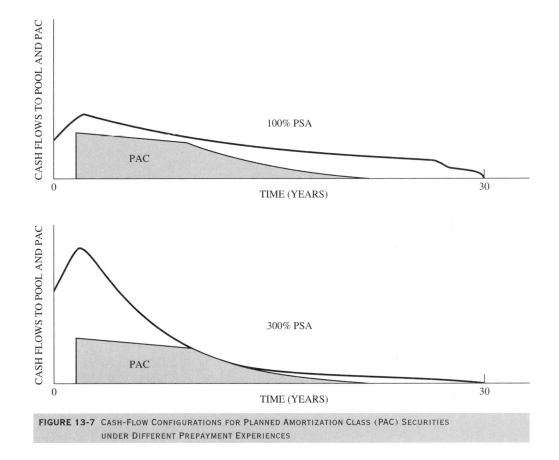

FIGURE 13-7 CASH-FLOW CONFIGURATIONS FOR PLANNED AMORTIZATION CLASS (PAC) SECURITIES UNDER DIFFERENT PREPAYMENT EXPERIENCES

in interest rates, prepayments accelerate and the total interest received diminishes. Thus, the value of the IO declines.

The price behavior for a PO is much like a zero-coupon bond. It shows a decline in price as interest rates increase. This is not only because a higher rate is being used to discount expected cash flows but also because lesser prepayments are increasing the security's effective duration, known as extension risk. When interest rates decline, prepayments accelerate and principal payments move closer in time. As a result, the PO increases in value. The price volatility for IOs and POs is considerably greater than that for the underlying pass-through security. Assuming arbitrage efficiency, the combined market prices of the IO and the PO securities should equal that of the underlying pass-through security. This phenomenon is shown in Figure 13-8.

Finally, the price behavior of the CMO residual class security is interesting. The price of this security tends to be positively correlated with a change in interest rates. When interest rates rise, prepayments decelerate and interim cash flows (after monthly receipt from the pass-through security but lagged payment to the CMO security holders) are reinvested at higher interest rates. As a result, more is left over at the end for the residual class. When interest rates decline, prepayments accelerate. There are fewer excess cash flows to invest, and the reinvestment rate is lower. Consequently, less is left

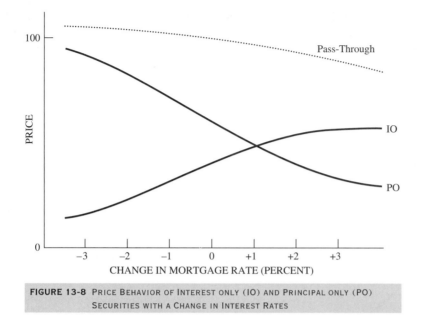

FIGURE 13-8 PRICE BEHAVIOR OF INTEREST ONLY (IO) AND PRINCIPAL ONLY (PO)
SECURITIES WITH A CHANGE IN INTEREST RATES

over at the end and the value of the residual class security declines in price. The direct
relationship of value with mortgage rates makes the residual security useful for hedging purposes. However, the price behavior is very volatile.

Although other mortgage derivatives exist, we have covered the major ones with
respect to their price behavior.

OTHER ASSET-BACKED SECURITIES

Not all asset-backed securities have the prepayment pattern typical for a mortgage
pool. For car loans and credit cards, for example, there is little relationship between prepayments and interest rates. Certificates for Automobile Receivables (CARS) have
stated maturities of three to five years, while Certificates for Amortized Revolving
Debts (CARDS) have stated maturities of four to five years. Both involve monthly payments and can be prepaid. However, there is little sensitivity of prepayments to interest rates. Because of the shorter-term nature of the underlying loan and, perhaps for
other reasons, people tend to make payments in highly predictable ways. Rather than
negative convexity, there is positive convexity throughout the range of interest rates.
This is a desirable property from the standpoint of investors and should find favor in
the market. Thus, prepayment experience varies by the type of underlying asset.

❖ SUMMARY

The securitization of mortgages has created numerous mortgage securities. In the basic
pass-through security, monthly payments and prepayments by borrowers in a mortgage
pool are passed along to security holders, after the deduction of certain expenses. Prepayment risk is a distinguishing characteristic of mortgage-backed and other asset-
backed securities.

Prepayment of the underlying mortgages is highly sensitive to interest rates. As rates decline, more and more mortgages are prepaid, subjecting the investor to the opportunity cost associated with the call feature. Another factor explaining prepayment experience is the age of the mortgage; prepayment rates accelerate initially with seasoning and then level off or decline. The current refinancing rate relative to the coupon rate and the age of the mortgage pool often are combined into the percentage of the PSA prepayment schedule. For 100 percent PSA, the schedule assumes that prepayments increase linearly from $\frac{2}{10}$ of 1 percent of the pool on an annualized basis in the first month to 6 percent in the 30th month and thereafter. For example, 200 percent PSA assumes double these percentages, and 80 percent PSA assumes $\frac{8}{10}$ of them.

Other factors affecting the prepayment behavior of a mortgage pool include seasonality, burnout, location, house prices, and several other pool-specific characteristics. Much effort has gone into modeling prepayment experience, bringing in the factors mentioned together with certain macroeconomic variables. Still, the current refinancing rate, relative to the coupon rate, and the age of the pool are the dominant factors explaining prepayment experience. Option-adjusted spread analysis has proven useful in mapping the cash flows from a mortgage security under different interest-rate scenarios. For mortgages, the convexity of the relationship between price and yield is mostly negative, which is undesirable from the standpoint of the investor. This is not the case for certain other asset-backed securities.

The cash flows of the standard mortgage pass-through security can be reconfigured into a number of derivative securities. With a collateralized mortgage obligation (CMO), the mortgage payments stream is divided into different maturity classes. Mortgage principal payments are initially directed to the first class; when these securities have been extinguished, the payments go to the second class, and so on eventually to the Z class, which is an interest-accrual security. In addition, there may be a residual class that serves as equity and is entitled to any cash that is left over after all other classes have been retired.

With a Planned Amortization Class (PAC) security, the mortgage pool is dedicated to making sure that cash flows to this class are highly certain within a wide range of interest rates. The boundaries are known as the PAC's collar. Because of the greater certainty of cash flows to the PAC class, the cash flows for the companion classes are less certain. A Targeted Amortization Class (TAC) security is like a PAC security, but it has a narrower collar. With an interest-only (IO)/principal-only (PO) arrangement, interest payments are entirely directed to one class while principal payments are directed to the other. Price movements tend to be in opposite directions with a change in interest rates. Finally, a mortgage pool can be configured so as to have a floating-rate class and an inverse-floater class. Here returns vary directly or inversely with some short-term interest-rate index.

❖ SELECTED REFERENCES

Abrahams, Steven W., "The New View in Mortgage Prepayments: Insight from Analysis at the Loan-by-Loan Level," *Journal of Fixed Income* 7 (June 1997): 8–21.

Arditti, Fred D., *Derivatives.* Boston: Harvard Business School Press, 1996.

Becketti, Sean, "The Prepayment Risk of Mortgage-Backed Securities," *Economic Review of the Federal Reserve Bank of Kansas City* (February 1989): 43–57.

Breeden, Douglas T., "Complexities of Hedging Mortgages," *Journal of Fixed Income* 4 (December 1994): 6–41.

Breeden, Douglas T., "Convexity and Empirical Option Costs of Mortgage Securities," *Journal of Fixed Income* 6 (March 1997): 64–87.

Brown, David D., "The Determinants of Expected Returns on Mortgage-Backed Securities: An Empirical Analysis of Option-Adjusted Spreads," *Journal of Fixed Income* 9 (September 1999): 8–19.

Carron, Andrew S., "Understanding CMOs, REMICs, and other Mortgage Derivatives," *Journal of Fixed Income* 2 (June 1992): 25–43.

Carrow, Kenneth A., Gayle R. Erwin, and John J. McConnell, "A Survey of U.S. Financial Innovations," *Journal of Applied Corporate Finance* 12 (Spring 1999): 55–69.

Dunn, Kenneth B., and John J. McConnell, "Valuation of GNMA Mortgage-Backed Securities," *Journal of Finance* 36 (June 1981): 599–616.

Fabozzi, Frank J., *Bond Markets, Analysis and Strategies,* 4th ed., chapters 10–13, 15. Upper Saddle River, NJ: Prentice Hall, 2000.

———,*Valuation of Fixed Income Securities and Derivatives,* 3rd ed. New Hope, PA: Frank J. Fabozzi Associates, 1998.

Fabozzi, Frank J., and David Yuen, *Managing MBS Portfolios.* New Hope, PA: Frank J. Fabozzi Associates, 1998.

Goodman, Laurie, and Jeffrey Ho, "Callable Pass-Throughs: Exercise History," *Journal of Fixed Income* 8 (December 1998): 49–56.

———, "A LIBOR-Based Approach to Modeling the Mortgage Basis," *Journal of Fixed Income* 8 (September 1998): 29–35.

———, "Valuing the Call Option on a Callable Pass-Through," *Journal of Fixed Income* 6 (March 1997): 34–39.

Huang, Charles, and Warren Xia, "Modeling ARM Prepayments," *Journal of Fixed Income* 5 (March 1996): 31–44.

Kon, Stanley J., and Christine Y. Polek, "Time-Varying Empirical Duration and Slope Effects for Mortgage-Backed Securities," *Journal of Fixed Income* 8 (September 1998): 7–28.

Kopprasch, Robert W., "Option-Adjusted Spread Analysis: Going Down the Wrong Path?" *Financial Analysts Journal* 49 (May–June 1994): 42–47.

Richard, Scott F., "Housing Prices and Prepayments for Fixed Rate Mortgage-Backed Securities," *Journal of Fixed Income* 1 (December 1991): 54–58.

Richard, Scott F., and Richard Roll, "Prepayments on Fixed-Rate Mortgage-Backed Securities," *Journal of Portfolio Management* 15 (Spring 1989): 76–82.

Schwartz, Eduardo S., and Walter N. Torous, "Prepayment, Default, and the Valuation of Mortgage Pass-Through Securities," *Journal of Business* 65 (April 1992): 221–40.

Singh, Manoj K., and John J. McConnell, "Implementing an Option-Theoretic CMO Valuation Model with Recent Prepayment Data," *Journal of Fixed Income* 5 (March 1996): 45–55.

14

CONTROLLING CURRENCY RISK

The number and variety of international securities are enormous and growing. As globalization and integration of financial markets gained momentum during the last 15 years, so too did the importance of currency risk. This risk is simply the volatility of the exchange rate of one currency for another. In Figure 14-1, this volatility is illustrated for the U.S. dollar/British pound sterling exchange rate. As shown, the dollar strengthened in value (fewer dollars per pound) from 1981 to 1985, and then weakened in value until 1988, after which it fluctuated until the 1992 European correction when it fell in value. In recent years, it has fluctuated around 1.60. Interest rates and exchange rates are correlated. Consequently, returns on fixed-income securities necessarily are sensitive to currency effects. Currency risk and its relation to interest-rate risk are topics addressed in this chapter.

RISK AND RETURN FROM FOREIGN INVESTMENT

Price volatility for a domestic fixed-income security is a function of domestic interest-rate changes and, if default occurs, the shortfall in return from that which was promised. With a foreign investment, both these factors are involved, together with changes in the value of the foreign currency relative to that of the investor. For a U.S. investor, the single-period rate of return is

$$R = \left(\frac{C_1 + P_1}{P_0} \right)\left(\frac{S_{x,1}}{S_{x,0}} \right) - 1 \qquad \textbf{(14-1)}$$

where C_1 is the coupon payment in period 1, P_1 is the ending price in the foreign currency, P_0 is the beginning price, $S_{x,1}$ is the spot exchange rate at time 1 of dollars per unit of foreign currency, and $S_{x,0}$ is the exchange rate at time 0. Thus, two risks are involved: bond price risk in the local currency and exchange rate risk. The total return from holding a foreign bond can be decomposed into these two parts.

With diversification, both risks can be reduced. This assumes, of course, that diversification is across countries. International diversification usually is more effective in reducing risk than is domestic diversification alone. Because the economic cycles of

FIGURE 14-1 EXCHANGE RATE: U.S. DOLLAR/BRITISH POUND STERLING

different countries are not synchronized and because of possible segmentation effects, it is possible to reduce risk, relative to expected return, simply by investing across countries. The idea is that bond returns tend to be less correlated among countries than they are in any one country.

This idea is illustrated in Figure 14-2. Along the horizontal axis is the number of securities in the portfolio and along the vertical, the standard deviation of portfolio

FIGURE 14-2 DOMESTIC VERSUS INTERNATIONAL BOND DIVERSIFICATION

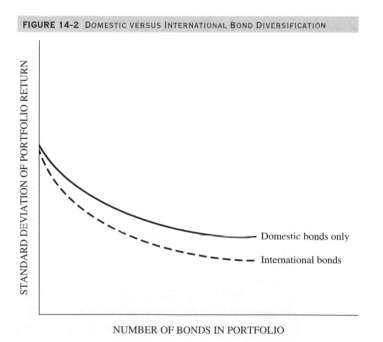

return. As bonds of the same default risk are added to the portfolio, risk is reduced further with international diversification than it is with domestic diversification. Empirical evidence suggests a moderate correlation (0.50 to 0.70) between returns for U.S. bonds and returns for bonds of other advanced industrial countries. This finding argues for risk reduction through international diversification.

EXCHANGE RATE RISK MANAGEMENT

An exchange rate is the number of units of one currency that can be exchanged for another. The currencies of major countries are traded in active markets, in which rates are determined by the forces of supply and demand. The market itself is known as the **spot market,** as currencies are traded currently or on the spot. Foreign exchange risk is the risk that the currency in which an investment is made will decline in value relative to the investor's currency, or that its convertibility will be restricted.

Suppose you are a U.S. investor and you invest in a U.K. bond at a price of £1,000. At the time of investment, the pound is worth $1.60. One year later, the pound declines in value to $1.58. If the bond continues to sell for £1,000 in the U.K. market and has a 6 percent coupon payable annually, the return on investment would be

$$R = \left(\frac{£60 + £1,000}{£1,000} \right) \left(\frac{1.58}{1.60} \right) - 1 = 4.68\%$$

which is less than the coupon payment owing to the strengthening of the dollar (pound weakening) over the year.

Thus, a drop in currency value has a detrimental effect on bond performance. Of course, if the currency in question appreciates, this boosts overall return. If only we knew the way exchange rates would move, we could use currency fluctuations to advantage. But, alas, most of us are not clairvoyant. A foreign bond investment can be hedged in four ways: (1) currency-forward contracts, (2) currency futures, (3) currency options, and (4) currency swaps. In the next several sections, we consider these hedging vehicles.

FORWARD EXCHANGE MARKET

To protect against currency fluctuations, the **forward market** often is used. In this market, one buys a forward contract for the exchange of one currency into another at a specific future date and at a specific exchange ratio. A forward contract provides assurance of being able to convert into a desired currency.

Suppose you wish to hedge a British security transaction. You have bought a security with a single payment of £100,000 to be received 90 days hence. On payment, you intend to convert pounds into dollars. The spot and 90-day forward rates for pounds sterling per dollar are the following:

Spot price (£/$)	0.625
Forward price	0.624

The spot rate is simply the current market-determined exchange rate for the British pound. In our example, $1 is worth £.625, and £1 will buy 1.00/0.625 = $1.60. A foreign currency sells at a **forward premium** if it is worth more in the future (the dollar is worth less). In our example, the British pound sterling sells at a premium because the forward price, expressed in terms of pounds per dollar, is less than the spot price. If the forward price exceeds the spot price, it is said to sell at a **forward discount:** The currency buys fewer dollars for future delivery than it does for present delivery. For example, if the forward price were 0.630, £1 would buy 1.00/0.630 = $1.587 in the forward market as opposed to $1.600 in the spot market.

For stable pairs of currencies, the discount or premium of the forward rate over the spot rate varies from zero to 5 percent on an annualized basis. For somewhat less stable currencies, the discount or premium will be higher. For an unstable currency, the discount may go as high as 20 percent. Much beyond this point of instability, the forward market for the currency ceases to exist. In summary, the forward exchange market allows an investor to insure against devaluation or market-determined declines in value.

ILLUSTRATION OF SPOT AND FORWARD EXCHANGE RATES

Exchange-rate quotations on selected foreign currencies at a moment in time are shown in Table 14-1. The spot rates reported in the first column indicate the conversion rate into dollars. What is quoted in the financial press is the interbank or wholesale rate for large transactions. As a traveler, you cannot buy or sell foreign currency at nearly as good a rate. Often you will pay several percent more when you buy, and receive several percent less when you sell.

In the first column of the table, the conversion rate of one unit of a foreign currency into U.S. dollars is shown. Near the top, we see that the Australian dollar is worth 0.6447 U.S. dollars. To determine how many Australian dollars $1 will buy, we take the reciprocal, 1/0.6447 = A$1.5511. Forward rates are shown for the British pound, the Canadian dollar, the Japanese yen, and the Swiss franc. The relationships between the forward and the spot rates indicate that all of these currencies are at forward rate premiums relative to the U.S. dollar. That is, they are worth more dollars on future delivery than they are now.

THE EURO

The **Euro** appears about halfway down Table 14-1. This is a common currency for the European Monetary Union (**EMU**), which includes such countries as Germany, France, Italy, Netherlands, Belgium, Spain, Austria, Portugal, and Ireland. On January 1, 1999, currency conversion rates between the "legacy" currencies and the Euro were established. For a while, the legacy currencies traded separately from the Euro, but at the previously established conversion ratios with each other. As time went on, most currency hedging transactions for bonds of EMU countries occurred in Euros. The Euro was introduced with much fanfare and began trading January 1, 1999, at $1.17 to the Euro, even getting as high as $1.19. However, there was a steady decline in value until it touched $1.01 in July, 1999. From there, the Euro gained strength and was trading at $1.06 in Table 14-1. It subsequently declined below $1.00 in value.

TABLE 14-1	Foreign Exchange Rates, July 27, 1999	
	U.S. Dollars to Buy 1 Unit	*Units Required to Buy $1*
Argentina (peso)	$1.0005	0.9995
Australia (dollar)	0.6447	1.5511
Brazil (real)	0.5519	1.8120
Britain (pound)	1.5902	0.6289
30-day forward	1.5903	0.6288
90-day forward	1.5910	0.6285
180-day forward	1.5925	0.6279
Canada (dollar)	0.6611	1.5127
30-day forward	0.6613	1.5121
90-day forward	0.6618	1.5111
180-day forward	0.6625	1.5095
Chile (peso)	0.0019	514.7500
China (renminbi)	0.1208	8.2770
Czech. Republic (koruna)	0.0290	34.5290
Euro	1.0624	0.9413
Hong Kong (dollar)	0.1288	7.7615
India (rupee)	0.0231	43.3250
Japan (yen)	0.0086	116.3300
30-day forward	0.0086	115.8100
90-day forward	0.0087	114.7900
180-day forward	0.0088	113.0900
Malaysia (ringgit)	0.2631	3.8005
Mexico (peso)	0.1066	9.3770
Saudi Arabia (riyal)	0.2666	3.7505
Singapore (dollar)	0.5932	1.6859
Switzerland (franc)	0.6635	1.5072
30-day forward	0.6660	1.5016
90-day forward	0.6706	1.4912
180-day forward	0.6777	1.4756
Taiwan (dollar)	0.0310	32.2650
Thailand (baht)	0.0268	37.2800
Venezuela (bolivar)	0.0016	612.7500

UNDERLYING RELATIONSHIPS

Fluctuations in exchange rates are continual and often defy explanation, at least in the short run. In the longer run, however, linkages exist between domestic and foreign inflation, and between interest rates and foreign exchange rates. These relationships provide an underlying theory of international product and financial-market equilibrium. We first present the theory, which assumes free trade and an absence of imperfections, and then touch on the empirical evidence.

THE LAW OF ONE PRICE

Simply put, the **law of one price** says that a commodity will sell for the same price regardless of where it is purchased. More formally, for a single good

$$P^{FC} = P^\$ \times S^{(FC/\$)} \tag{14-2}$$

where P^{FC} is the price of the good in a foreign currency, $P^\$$ is the price of the good in the United States, and $S^{(FC/\$)}$ is the spot exchange rate of the foreign currency per dollar.

If it is cheaper to buy wheat from Argentina than it is from a U.S. producer, after transportation costs and after adjusting the Argentine price for the exchange rate, a rational U.S. buyer will purchase Argentine wheat. This action, together with commodity arbitrage, will cause the Argentine wheat price to rise relative to the U.S. price and, perhaps, for the peso exchange rate to strengthen. The combination of rising Argentine wheat prices and a changing peso value raises the dollar price of Argentine wheat to the U.S. buyer. Theory would have it that these transactions would continue until the dollar cost of wheat was the same for both. At that point, the purchaser would be indifferent between U.S. and Argentine wheat. For that matter, an Argentine buyer of wheat also would be indifferent. For this condition to hold, of course, transportation and transaction costs must be zero, and there must be no impediments to trade.

PURCHASING POWER PARITY

The law of one price is really a way to express **purchasing power parity** (PPP). Invoking the law of one price, PPP says that the rate of exchange between currencies of two countries is directly related to the differential rate of inflation between them. Any change in the differential rate of inflation is offset by an opposite movement in the spot exchange rate. From Equation (14-2), PPP implies

$$1 + P^{\wedge FC} = [1 + P^{\wedge \$}] \times [1 + S^{\wedge (FC/\$)}] \tag{14-3}$$

where the $\wedge$ represents the rate of change in the price level or in the exchange rate. Rearranging,

$$\frac{1 + P^{\wedge FC}}{1 + P^{\wedge \$}} = 1 + S^{\wedge (FC/\$)} \tag{14-4}$$

If the annual rate of inflation is 2 percent in the United States and 3 percent in Canada, the implication is

$$1.03/1.02 = 1.0098$$

or that the Canadian dollar should depreciate in value relative to the U.S. dollar by approximately 1 percent on an annualized basis. If instead the rate of inflation in the United States were 4 percent, we would have

$$1.03/1.04 = 0.9904$$

which means the U.S. dollar should decline in value, relative to the Canadian dollar, by approximately 1 percent per year.

As an approximation to Equation (14-4), many people use

$$P^{\wedge FC} - P^{\wedge \$} = S^{\wedge (FC/\$)} \tag{14-5}$$

in which the exchange rate change is directly related to the inflation differential. In the context of this formula, purchasing power parity is illustrated in Figure 14-3. Equation (14-5) has been used in an expectational sense. For example, suppose we expect inflation in the United States to exceed the average for the European Monetary Union by 2 percent and that the spot exchange rate now is $1.00 to the Euro. At the end of one year, PPP would imply that the exchange rate would be $1.00(1.02) = 1.02 \ \$/\euro$. Again, remember that this is only an approximation. For greater accuracy, we should use Equation (14-4).

How closely a country's exchange rate corresponds to purchasing-power parity depends on the price elasticity of exports and imports. To the extent that exports are traded in world-competitive markets, there usually is close conformity to PPP. Commodities and fabricated products like steel and clothing are highly price sensitive. In general, products in mature industries conform more closely to PPP than products in newer industries with emerging technology. To the extent that a country's inflation is dominated by nontraded goods, like services, there tends to be less conformity to PPP. We know also that PPP does not work well when a country intervenes in the exchange-rate market, either propping up its currency or keeping it artificially low. Before we look at the empirical evidence on PPP, we present the third link to our conceptual framework.

INTEREST-RATE PARITY

The last link concerns the interest-rate differential between two countries. **Interest-rate parity** suggests that if interest rates are higher in one country than they are in another, the former country's currency will sell at a discount in the forward market. Expressed

FIGURE 14-3 ApProximation of Purchasing-Power Parity (PPP) between Two Countries

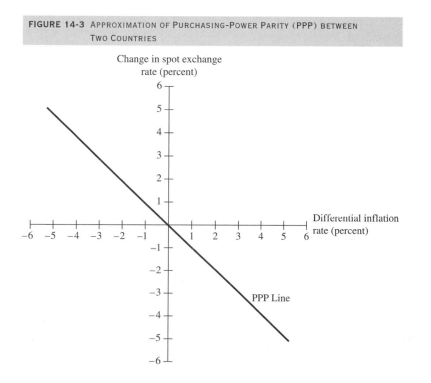

differently, interest-rate differentials and forward-spot exchange rate differentials are offsetting. How does it work? The starting point is the relationship between nominal interest rates and inflation. Recall the Fisher effect from chapter 5: It implies that the nominal rate of interest comprises the real rate plus the rate of inflation expected to prevail over the life of the instrument. Thus,

$$r = R + P^{\wedge} \tag{14-6}$$

where r is the nominal rate, R is the inflation-adjusted real rate of interest, and $P^{\wedge}$ is rate of inflation per annum expected over the life of the instrument.[1]

In an international context, sometimes called the **international Fisher effect,** the equation suggests that differences in interest rates between two countries serve as a proxy for differences in expected inflation. For example, if the nominal interest rate were 6 percent in the United States but 8 percent in Australia, the expected differential in inflation would be 2 percent. That is, inflation in Australia is expected to be 2 percent higher than in the United States. Does this hold exactly? While disagreements arise as to the precise relationship between nominal interest rates and inflation, most people feel that expected inflation for a country has an important effect on interest rates in that country. The more open the capital markets are, the closer the conformity is to an international Fisher effect.

Remember from purchasing-power parity that exchange rates were directly tied to the inflation differential between two countries. Through the common link of inflation differentials, exchange-rate differentials should be related to interest-rate differentials. The mechanism by which this manifests itself is the difference between the spot rate of exchange and the forward exchange rate.

To illustrate interest-rate parity, consider the relationship between the U.S. dollar (\$) and the British pound (£), both now and 90 days in the future; the theorem suggests that

$$\frac{F(\pounds/\$)}{S(\pounds/\$)} = \frac{1 + r_{\pounds}}{1 + r_{\$}} \tag{14-7}$$

where

$F(\pounds/\$) =$ current 90-day forward exchange rate in pounds per dollar
$S(\pounds/\$) =$ current spot exchange rate in pounds per dollar
$\quad r_{\pounds} =$ nominal British interbank Euromarket interest rate, expressed in terms of the 90-day return
$\quad r_{\$} =$ nominal U.S. interbank Euromarket interest rate, expressed in terms of the 90-day return

If the nominal interest rate in Britain were 8 percent and nominal U.S. rate were 6 percent, these annualized rates translate into 3-month rates of 2 percent and 1.5 percent, respectively. If the current spot rate were 0.625 pounds per dollar, we would have

$$\frac{F(\pounds/\$)}{0.625} = \frac{1.02}{1.015}$$

---

[1] Mathematically, the correct expression is $r = R + P^{\wedge} + RP^{\wedge}$. Unless the inflation rate is large, most ignore the cross-product term.

Solving for the implied forward rate,

$$1.015(£/\$) = 0.6375$$
$$F(£/\$) = 0.6281$$

Thus, the implied forward rate is 0.6281 British pounds per U.S. dollar. The pound is at a forward rate discount from the spot rate of 0.625 pounds to the dollar. That is, a pound is worth less in terms of dollars in the forward market, $1/0.6281 = \$1.592$, than it is in the spot market, $1/0.625 = \$1.60$. The discount is $(0.6281 - 0.625)/0.625 = 0.005$. With interest-rate parity, the discount must equal the relative difference in interest rates and, indeed, this is the case, for $(1.02 - 1.015)/1.015 = 0.005$. If the interest rate in Britain were less than that in the United States, the implied forward rate in our example would be less than the spot rate. In this case, the British pound is at a forward premium. For example, if the U.S. interest rate (annualized) were 7 percent and the British rate were 5 percent, the implied 3-month forward rate for British pounds would be

$$\frac{F(£/\$)}{0.625} = \frac{1.0125}{1.0175}$$

Solving for $F(£/\$)$, we have

$$1.0175F(£/\$) = 0.6328$$
$$F(£/\$) = 0.6219$$

Therefore, the forward rate is at a premium in the sense that it is worth more in terms of dollars in the forward market than it is in the spot market.

COVERED INTEREST ARBITRAGE

If interest-rate parity did not occur, presumably arbitragers would be alert to the opportunity for profit. In our first example, had the British pound 90-day forward rate been 0.634 instead of 0.6281, an arbitrageur, recognizing this deviation, would borrow in Britain at 8 percent interest for 3 months. If the amount involved were £100,000, the amount due at the end of 3 months would be £100,000(1.02) = £102,000. Upon receipt of the pound loan, the arbitrageur should convert the £100,000 into dollars in the spot market. At an exchange rate of 0.625, he or she would have $160,000. This amount should be invested at 6 percent interest for 3 months. At the end of 3 months, the arbitrageur would have $160,000(1.015) = $162,400. To cover the loan's repayment in pounds, the arbitrageur should buy British pounds 3 months forward. He or she would need £102,000 to repay the loan. At a 3-month forward rate of 0.634 pounds per U.S. dollar, it would require £102,000/0.634 = $160,883.

In this series of transactions, which is known as **covered interest arbitrage,** the profit is equal to the receipt of funds from investment less the repayment of the loan. For our example

$$\text{Arbitrage profit} = \$162,400 - \$160,883 = \$1,517$$

Arbitrage actions of this sort increase the demand for British pounds in the forward market and increase the supply of dollars. Moreover, borrowing in Britain will tend to increase interest rates there, while lending in the United States will lower American rates. The combination of these forces will work to reduce the interest-rate differential as well as to reduce the discount for the British pound forward exchange rate. Arbitrage actions will continue until interest-rate parity is established and there is zero profit potential on covered interest arbitrage.

INTEREST-RATE PARITY APPROXIMATION

On an annualized basis, interest-rate parity can be expressed as

$$\frac{F^{(FC/\$)} - S^{(FC/\$)}}{S^{(FC/\$)}} = r_{FC} - r_{\$} \tag{14-8}$$

where the forward rate and the two interest rates are for one-year contracts/instruments. Using our earlier example for British pounds, where the current spot exchange rate is 0.625 and U.K. and U.S. interest rates are 8 percent and 6 percent, respectively, the implied discount in the one-year forward market is 2 percent of the spot rate. This means that the forward rate is greater than the spot rate by 2 percent; more pounds per dollar in the future implies a weaker pound over time. The absolute, as opposed to the percentage, discount using Equation (14-8) is

$$R^{(\pounds/\$)} - S^{(\pounds/\$)} = (0.08 - 0.06).625 = 0.0125$$

Thus, the implied forward rate of pounds per dollar one year hence is $0.625 + 0.0125 = 0.6375$.

This simple formula tells us that interest-rate differentials are a proxy for forward exchange rate/spot exchange rate differentials, and vice versa. Equation 14-8 is expressed graphically in Figure 14-4. The upper right-hand quadrant represents a foreign

FIGURE 14-4 APPROXIMATION OF INTEREST-RATE PARITY BETWEEN TWO COUNTRIES (IRP)

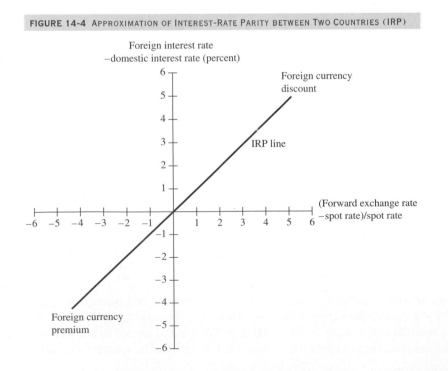

currency discount because the forward exchange rate of the foreign currency per dollar exceeds the spot rate. That is, the foreign currency is expected to depreciate in terms of dollars. In contrast, the lower left-hand quadrant represents a foreign currency premium because the forward exchange rate is less than the spot rate.

At a moment in time, **covered interest-rate parity** tends to prevail for the United States, the European Monetary Union, Britain, Switzerland, Japan, and a few other advanced industrial countries. That is, a precise offsetting relationship exists between differences in interest rates between two countries and the forward exchange rate relative to the spot rate. The difference between the forward and spot exchange rates, and whether one country's currency is at a premium or a discount relative to the other, is driven by differences in short-term interest rates. In turn, these differences are determined primarily by actions of central banks. The currency of whichever country has the lower interest rate will trade at a forward-rate premium relative to the other country's currency.

EMPIRICAL EVIDENCE CONCERNING INTEREST-RATE PARITY

Does this mean that interest-rate parity (IRP) prevails between all sets of currencies at all times? As we have said, for major European currencies and the Japanese yen, where there is largely an absence of imperfections, IRP generally holds within the limits of transaction costs. While the relationship is strong for short-term interest rates, it weakens for longer maturities. For countries with restrictions on exchange as well as tax and other imperfections, IRP is not expected because covered interest arbitrage is not possible.

Looking at IRP another way, known as **uncovered interest-rate parity,** the question is whether the change in the actual exchange rate between two countries equals that previously implied by the interest-rate differential. In other words, does an unbiased expectations hypothesis hold? Evidence through the early 1990s rejected this equality. High-interest-rate countries provided a higher net return, taking account of exchange-rate changes, than did low-interest-rate countries.[2] Although the currency of a high-interest-rate country may depreciate over time, the decline was not sufficient to offset its yield advantage over the low-interest-rate country. However, the evidence from the mid-1990s on was not so clear. During this time frame, equality more nearly prevailed.

OTHER WAYS TO SHIFT RISK

The forward exchange market permits an investor or security issuer to shift currency risk. This protection carries a cost, determined by the relationship between the forward rate and the future spot rate. Whether one wishes to use the forward market depends on one's view of the future and on one's risk aversion. It also depends on whether this

---

[2] Geert Bekaert and Robert J. Hodrick, "On Biases in the Measurement of Foreign Exchange Risk Premiums," *Journal of International Money and Finance* 12 (1993): 115–38; and Piet Sercu and Raman Uppal, *International Financial Markets and the Firm* (Cincinnati: South-Western College Publishing, 1995), chapter 14. For a review of the evidence, see Charles Engel, "The Forward Discount Anomaly and the Risk Premium: A Survey of Recent Evidence," working paper, National Bureau of Economic Research (October 1995).

device is the best of the alternatives available. Currency risk can be shifted in other ways, and our purpose is to explore them.

CURRENCY FUTURES

Closely related to the use of a forward contract is a **futures** contract. Currency futures markets exist for the major currencies of the world—the Australian dollar, the Canadian dollar, the British pound, the Euro, the Swiss franc, the Japanese yen, the Mexican peso, and, of course, the U.S. dollar. A futures contract is a standardized agreement that calls for delivery of a currency at some specified future date—the third Wednesday of March, June, September, or December. Many contracts are traded on an exchange, the major one in the United States being the Chicago Mercantile Exchange.

     The mechanical differences between a forward currency contract and a futures contract are mostly the same as explained in chapter 9 for interest-rate contracts. Currency futures come only in multiples of standard-size contracts—for example, multiples of 12.5 million yen. Forward contracts can be for almost any size. Conceptually, both currency futures and forward markets enable the investor and the security issuer to shift risk in desired ways. However, exchange-traded futures contracts are not sufficiently liquid for large currency traders. They resort to the over-the-counter market, where a contract is tailored to their needs by an investment bank. The vehicle is a forward contract. Thus, most currency transactions involving two-sided hedges are with forward and not futures contracts. Viable over-the-counter markets extend out only several years. For longer-term risk shifting and speculation, one must resort to other devices.

CURRENCY OPTIONS

Forward and futures contracts provide a "two-sided" hedge against currency movements: If the currency involved moves in one direction, the forward or futures position offsets it. **Currency options,** in contrast, enable the hedging of "one-sided" risk. Only adverse currency movements are hedged, either with a call option to buy the foreign currency or with a put option to sell it. The holder has the right, but not the obligation, to buy or sell the currency over the life of the contract. If not exercised, of course, the option expires. For this protection, one pays a premium.

     Exchange-traded options are on spot market currencies and, more prevalently, on currency futures. However, as with currency futures contracts, most currency option transactions are over-the-counter. This market simply is deeper, broader, and often quicker than the exchange market.

     The valuation principles are largely the same as those described in chapter 10, with value depending on exchange-rate volatility. The main difference between a currency and either a debt or a stock option is that the discount rate is not the short-term domestic interest rate. Rather, the appropriate opportunity cost is the domestic interest rate minus the foreign interest rate.[3] If one were to invest directly in a foreign currency, the transaction would be financed domestically using the domestic interest rate. However, it will earn at the foreign interest rate. Therefore, the differential between the two

---

[3] For a detailed examination of currency option valuation and this argument, see Bruno Solnik, *International Investments,* 2nd ed., chapter 9 appendix. (Reading, MA: Addison-Wesley, 1991).

is the appropriate opportunity cost. With this exception, standard option pricing formulas described in chapter 10 may be used to value currency options.

CURRENCY SWAPS

In a currency swap, two parties exchange debt obligations denominated in different currencies. Each party agrees to pay the other's interest obligation. At maturity, principal amounts are exchanged, usually at a rate of exchange agreed on in advance. An illustration is shown in Figure 14-5, involving a British company and a U.S. company. The annual interest obligations are 9 percent in British pounds and 8 percent in U.S. dollars. Maturity is three years, the exchange rate fixed in the swap is $1.60 to the pound, and the amount of debt involved is £1 million. On an annual basis, the U.S. company pays the British company £90,000 in interest (£1 million $\times$ 0.09), while the British company pays the U.S. company $128,000 (£1 million $\times$ 1.60 $\times$ 0.08). At the end of three years, the principal amounts of $1.6 million and £1 million are exchanged back.

The exchanges themselves are *notional* in that only cash-flow differences are paid. If the exchange rate in the first year stays at $1.60 to the pound, the British company owes the U.S. company $128,000 in interest, which translates into £80,000. The U.S. company owes the British company £90,000 in interest, but it pays only the difference of £10,000. In the second year, suppose the pound appreciates to $1.70 to the pound. In this situation, the British company owes the U.S. company the equivalent of £75,294 ($128,000/1.70) in interest. The differential the U.S. company now pays is £90,000 − £75,294 = £14,706. If at the end of three years the exchange rate were again $1.70 to the pound, the interest differential owed by the U.S. company would again be £14,706. With respect to principal, the British company owes the U.S. company the equivalent of £941,176 ($1.6 million/1.70). As the U.S. company owes £1 million in principal, the principal differential payment it must make is £58,824.

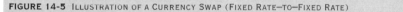

FIGURE 14-5 ILLUSTRATION OF A CURRENCY SWAP (FIXED RATE–TO–FIXED RATE)

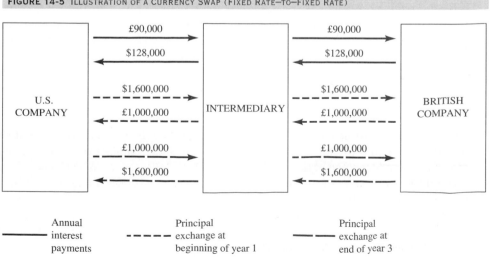

As with an interest-rate swap, no actual principal is exchanged. If one party defaults, no loss of principal occurs per se. There is, however, the opportunity cost associated with currency movements after the swap's initiation. These movements affect both interest and principal payments, as we have seen. In this respect, currency swaps are more risky than interest-rate swaps, where the exposure is only to interest. The example just cited is a fixed rate–to–fixed rate exchange of borrowings.

CURRENCY/INTEREST-RATE SWAPS

Currency swaps can be, and often are, combined with interest-rate swaps. In chapter 11 we examined the mechanics and valuation of interest-rate swaps. With a combined swap, there is an exchange of fixed-rate for floating-rate payments when the two payments are in different currencies. For example, a Japanese company might swap a three-year, fixed-rate Euro-currency-denominated liability for a three-year British pound liability with the floating rate tied to LIBOR. From the standpoint of the Japanese company, there is a combination Euro/British pound currency swap, together with a fixed/floating interest-rate swap. A number of extensions are possible: more than two currencies, options, and other features. As can be imagined, things get complicated rather quickly.

VALUATION IMPLICATIONS

In effect, the currency swap is a simultaneous spot transaction and a series of forward transactions. For our straight currency swap (fixed rate–to–fixed rate) example, there were three forward contracts—corresponding to two interest payments at the ends of years 1 and 2, and a combined interest and principal payment at the end of year 3. If the exchange rate fixed in the swap is identical to the actual exchange rate at the time, the swap's value is zero. As interest rates and exchange rates change over time, however, the value of the swap also changes, being positive for one party and negative for the other.

We can approximate the value of a swap by (1) establishing the market values of the two debt instruments and (2) making an adjustment for the exchange rate. To determine the market values of the debt instruments in their own currencies, we discount to present value future coupon and principal payments by appropriate local interest rates. For our earlier straight-currency swap example, we would determine the market value of a 9 percent British bond, using the current interest rate on like borrowings by comparable-risk British companies, and the value of an 8 percent U.S. bond, using comparable-risk U.S. companies as a basis. The value of the swap in dollar terms is as follows.

$$\text{swap value} = P_{\text{U.S.}} - P_{\text{U.K.}}(\text{Ex.R.}\$/\pounds) \tag{14-9}$$

where $P_{\text{U.S.}}$ is the value of the U.S. corporate bond, $P_{\text{U.K.}}$ is the value of the British corporate bond, and Ex.R. $\$/\pounds$ is the current exchange rate in dollars per pound. Equation (14-9) portrays the value of the swap to receive U.S. dollars and pay U.K. pounds. In our example, it is the value of the swap to the U.S. company. By reversing signs, it becomes the swap's value to the British company.

The value of the swap can be positive or negative. It will increase (in dollar terms) with (1) a decline in U.S. interest rates relative to U.K. rates and (2) appreciation of the U.S. dollar relative to the U.K. pound.

Yet another way to value swaps is to price each of the forward contracts implicit in the swap and then total these components. The limitation to this approach is that the swap often has a longer maturity than the longest forward contract that is traded. Therefore, market information is not available to value all the forward contracts implicit in the swap arrangement.

As with interest-rate swaps, an argument made often is that both parties are able to borrow more advantageously via a swap than they can directly. Again, the argument of comparative advantage in borrowing in local debt markets is invoked; this argument depends on segmentation and/or asymmetric information effects. The argument was examined in chapter 11, where we showed that arbitrage should eliminate any significant and persistent cost advantage. As we know from that chapter, often what appears to be an advantage is due to differences in default risk. However, with cross-border counterparties, the case for market imperfections and segmentation effects is much stronger than it is when the counterparties are both domestic.

Also, the swap market serves to complete the market for risk-shifting devices. Forward, futures, and options contracts are not available beyond several years, except on a negotiated, over-the-counter basis. The swap market permits risk shifting in the longer-term area. From time to time, arbitrage opportunities develop that can be exploited through currency/interest-rate swaps. We would not expect them to persist, for exploitation of arbitrage opportunities makes the market more efficient. Currency swaps provide an essential link to risk shifting across global financial markets. This linkage supplements our discussion of the topic in chapter 11.

THE AMOUNT TO HEDGE

We have examined the various ways to hedge foreign bond investments, saving for now the question of whether it is worthwhile to hedge at all. If the answer to this question is yes, a further question arises as to how much of the portfolio should be hedged. All? Half? Some other percentage? Ideally, a U.S. investor in foreign bonds would like to be 100 percent hedged when the dollar strengthens in value, and 0 percent hedged when it weakens. But this is not hedging. Rather, it is making an active bet on currency movements. Few international bond managers behave in this manner.

A FREE LUNCH?

Andre F. Perold and Evan C. Schulman argue that bond managers should always hedge their currency exposure.[4] The idea is that one can achieve substantial reductions in risk (variance of home-currency returns) with no significant loss in expected return. The average expected return on a currency hedge is zero, and transaction costs are said to be minimal. As currency hedging reduces risk with little or no cost, the authors claim that it's as good as a "free lunch." Of course, if the home currency weakens, you will lose with a hedge, but the authors assume no underlying trend in currency price. They recognize

---

4   Andre Perold and Evan C. Schulman, "The Free Lunch in Currency Hedging: Implications for Investment Policy and Performance Standards," *Financial Analysts Journal* 44 (May–June 1988): 45–50.

that the cost of hedging may be nonzero in the short run, but over the longer run they claim it is essentially zero—that is, currency premiums and discounts are offsetting. The "free-lunch" argument establishes one boundary for currency hedging—namely, 100 percent or full hedging.

THE COST OF CURRENCY HEDGING

One factor affecting a decision is the cost of hedging. Obviously, the greater the cost, the less desirable hedging becomes. For the most part, the cost of hedging is low. For forward contracts, futures, and options among major currencies, the cost is usually less than 1 percent on an annualized basis. To this cost, we must add accounting costs associated with recording transactions and certain other costs. While minor, they contribute to the overall cost of hedging.

Although this cost usually is low, it changes over time. In 1992, short-term interest rates were low in the United States and high in Germany and the rest of Europe. We know from our examination of interest-rate parity that under these conditions, the cost of hedging for a U.S. investor should be high. Indeed it was, being in excess of 6 percent. It makes a great deal of difference if the cost of hedging is less than 1 percent, as is usually the case, or in excess of 6 percent. Therefore, we cannot always assume that currency hedging is cheap. If the cost is significant, the portfolio manager may elect not to hedge. This tendency, coupled with the notion that currency movements generally wash out over the long run, establishes a second boundary for currency hedging—namely, zero or no hedging.

BLACK'S UNIVERSAL HEDGING

Fischer Black makes a rather compelling case for bearing some unhedged currency risk.[5] Using a gains-in-trade theoretic construct, Black found that investors with different consumption baskets can increase their expected utility by taking on some currency risk. He employs a consumption-based equilibrium model and assumes no restrictions or costs to international trade and capital movements, and no governments to foul things up with money creation and things of this sort. Transaction costs are assumed to be zero.

The optimal hedge ratio that results from Black's idealized world is

$$\frac{\mu_m - \sigma_m^2}{\mu_m - \frac{1}{2}\sigma_e^2} \qquad (14\text{-}10)$$

where μ_m is the average expected return on the world market portfolio less each investor's risk-free rate; σ_m^2 is the average (across all investors) of the market portfolio's return variance; and σ_e^2 is the average exchange-rate return variance across all pairs of currencies. The formula is said to be universal in the sense that it applies to all investors regardless of nationality.

Using historical averages for the variables over two sample periods, Black calculated the hedge ratios, finding them to be 0.30 and 0.73 for the two periods. These ratios represent the fraction of a fully diversified international portfolio that should be hedged. Although the empirical results were meant as examples using rather unrefined data, many interpret Black's work as suggesting a 50 percent hedge ratio. This implication

---

[5] Fischer Black, "Equilibrium Exchange Rate Hedging," *Journal of Finance* 45 (July 1990): 899–908.

comes from a rough average of the results for the two sample periods. While this is not what was intended, it nonetheless has developed among casual interpreters of the model.

CLOSING THOUGHTS

Where does this leave us? Zero, 50, 100 percent, or some other percentage hedge? Empirical evidence suggests that complete, 100 percent hedging does not produce superior investment results. In one study, Kenneth A. Froot finds that in the short run hedging reduces volatility, but in the longer run it does not.[6] The reason, Froot argues, is that hedging undoes the natural hedge associated with purchasing-power parity. By overlaying a currency hedge on the PPP natural hedge, bond and stock portfolio return variance actually increases over the long run. In a related study, Bruno Solnik studied unhedged and hedged dollar bond returns for Germany, France, Italy, Netherlands, the United Kingdom, Switzerland, Japan, and the United States.[7] For the long run, he found currency risk of a bond portfolio to be low. Like Froot, he concluded that exchange rates revert to the fundamentals of PPP and largely, but not entirely, wash out over time. For a shorter-term horizon, several years or less, Solnik found that currency effects have a large effect on performance. Hedging reduces volatility in the short run. However, a pension fund with a 20-year horizon need not hedge.

Many international bond portfolio managers are judged against a standard that assumes that part or all of the portfolio is hedged. If a manager were to make active currency bets, he or she would be fully hedged, or nearly so, some of the time and unhedged, or nearly so, other times. Across an extended time horizon, the manager on average would be about one-half hedged. Hence, a standard of a 50 percent hedge ratio has developed for judging at least some international bond managers. Hedging often takes the form of selling forward contracts in the foreign currency to protect against the dollar strengthening in value.

Such standards are far from scientific. Most do not factor in the cost of hedging. As more empirical testing involving different time frames unfolds, the international bond portfolio manager may be better guided. Few unrestricted managers are willing to go unhedged all the time, nor are they willing to hedge completely.

INSTITUTIONAL CHARACTERISTICS AND PORTFOLIO MANAGEMENT

We have looked at a number of currency exposure issues. Before closing the chapter, we touch on some institutional aspects of international bond markets, as well as portfolio management in such markets.

EURO AND FOREIGN BONDS

The **Euro bond market** is a traditional one, with underwriters placing securities in the usual fashion. While a bond issue is dominated in a single currency, it is placed in

---

[6] Kenneth A. Froot, "Currency Hedging over Long Horizons," working paper, National Bureau of Economic Research (May 1993).

[7] Bruno Solnik, "Global Asset Management," *Journal of Portfolio Management* 24 (Summer 1998): 43–51.

multiple countries. Once issued, it is traded over the counter in multiple countries and by a number of security dealers. A Euro bond is different from a **foreign bond,** which is a bond issued by a foreign government or corporation in a local market. Such a bond is sold in a single country and falls under the security regulations of that country. *Yankee bonds* are issued by non-Americans in the U.S. market; *Samurai bonds* are issued by non-Japanese in the Japanese market. Similarly, there are British *Bulldog bonds,* Spanish *Matador bonds,* and Dutch *Rembrandt bonds,* all issued by nondomestics in those countries.

Euro bonds, foreign bonds, and domestic bonds of different countries feature numerous differences in terminology, in the way interest is computed, and in features. We do not address these differences, as that would require a separate book. Fortunately, transaction settlements are standardized for global bond trades and occur through one of two clearinghouses, *Euroclear* or *Cedel.*

Many debt issues in the international arena are floating-rate notes (FRNs). These instruments have a variety of features, often involving multiple currencies. Some instruments are indexed to price levels or to commodity prices. Others are linked to an interest rate, such as the LIBOR. The reset interval may be annual, semiannual, quarterly, or even more frequent. Still other instruments have option features.

PORTFOLIO MANAGEMENT

Management of an international portfolio of developed country bonds is like that of a domestic portfolio when it comes to duration management. However, other aspects are different. Investment in nongovernment foreign bonds is difficult, as approximately two-thirds of bonds that are traded are governments. Therefore, sector selection is much more constrained than it is with a U.S. domestic bond portfolio. Corporate bonds are limited in supply, and mortgage securities for the most part are not issued. As a result, credit risk management usually is not an active decision variable. Most international bond portfolio managers are unwilling to take on significant credit or liquidity risk. This leaves country selection, the degree of currency exposure borne, and duration as the principal levers by which to generate excess returns. Widely used indices for benchmarking performance are Salomon Brothers Non-U.S. World Government Bond Index and J. P. Morgan Global Government Bond Index. Performance attribution according to country selection, currency, duration, and individual bond selection within a country decomposes a portfolio's overall return into these components.

One school of thought believes that investors should invest in countries providing the highest real yields. A **real yield** is the nominal bond yield less expected inflation. As we know from chapter 5, the difficulty is in determining expected inflation. The United States, United Kingdom, Australia, Canada, and a few other countries have inflation-indexed bonds. Such bonds trade on the basis of real yield. Without inflation-indexed bonds, a real yield must be derived. Apart from this measurement problem, the notion is that developed countries with high real yields provide higher currency-adjusted returns than do low real-yield countries. In other words, the exchange-rate change does not offset all of the higher real yield. While excess returns have been demonstrated using this real-yield strategy in the past, the case for such in recent years is unclear. Some of the success of the strategy had to do with the convergence of European currencies into the Euro in the late 1990s—a "play" that now is over.

EMERGING MARKET DEBT

The name "emerging market" for debt instruments implies countries with a speculative-grade or low investment-grade credit rating when it comes to sovereign risk. While there is no agreed-upon definition, it includes Mexico, South America, a number of East Asian countries, and countries in Eastern Europe, as well as Russia and Turkey. The total market approximates in size that of the high-yield (junk bond) market in the United States. Emerging market debt has two segments. The first involves bonds denominated in dollars or in some other nonlocal "hard currency." Bonds in this market are traded according to their spreads over governments, say U.S. Treasuries. The second segment involves bonds denominated in the local currency. Here the investor is exposed directly to currency risk. The most widely used indices to measure performance are those of J. P. Morgan. Their EMLI+ index consists of U.S. dollar and other external currency bonds. EMLI is comprised of bonds denominated in local currencies.

Emerging market returns are more volatile than developed-country bond returns, with a standard deviation in the 1990s roughly twice as large. This volatility is affected by changes in perceived political risk and runs on countries by hedge funds and other "in-and-out" investors. There was the Mexican "peso" problem in 1995 and Asian "contagion" in 1998, which began in Thailand and spread to other Asian countries. During the 1998 crisis, the EMLI+ spread over Treasuries mushroomed to 1600 basis points, compared with 500 basis points earlier in the year and less than 400 basis points in mid-1997. By 2000, spreads had narrowed to 600 basis points. In mid- and late-1998, however, liquidity all but dried up. Thus, investing in emerging market debt can be profitable when spreads narrow, or it can be enormously depressing. On average, the returns have been somewhat higher than those on developed-country bonds. However, the aftermath of 1998 has lingered on.

CURRENCY-OPTION AND MULTIPLE-CURRENCY BONDS

Certain bonds provide the holder with the right to choose the currency in which payment is received, usually prior to each coupon or principal payment. Typically, this option is confined to two currencies, though more may be involved. For example, a 6 percent bond might be issued in Euros with semiannual coupons of 30 Euros per bond. The bond might have the option to receive payment in either Euros or in pounds sterling. The exchange rate is fixed at the time of issue.

As we know from the previous two chapters, the value of such a bond can be viewed as

$$\text{value of bond} = \text{value as 6\% Euro-denominated bond} \atop + \text{ value of option to swap to £} \qquad \textbf{(14-11)}$$

With the option feature, the bond has a higher value, or lower coupon if we hold value constant, than would be the case with a straight Euro-denominated bond. The volatility of exchange rates largely determines the value of the currency option. The greater the volatility is, the greater the value of the option is and the more valuable the bond is in Equation (14-11).

Another option feature is a **conversion option,** which permits an instrument denominated in one currency to be converted into an instrument denominated in another.

A Japanese company might issue a U.S. dollar bond, which is convertible into shares of stock quoted in yen. The exchange rate of yen into dollars is fixed at the time of issuance (via the combined conversion/exchange ratio). Thus, two options are involved: (1) a conversion option of the bond into so many shares of common stock (see chapter 10) and (2) a currency option. If the yen rises in value relative to the U.S. dollar, the investor benefits in being able to exchange a dollar asset, the bond, into a yen asset, common stock.

Bond issues sometimes are floated in multiple currencies. Known as a "currency cocktail," the market value of the bond is less volatile than that of a bond denominated in a single currency. With a **dual currency bond,** interest and principal payments are linked to different currencies. One such product is a Principal Exchange Rate Linked Securities (PERLS) issue. For example, a PERLS might call for interest payments in U.S. dollars at a specified coupon rate and a final principal payment of $1,000 multiplied by the pound sterling/dollar exchange rate at the time of issuance. If this rate were 0.625, the final principal payment would be £625. If the pound strengthens—that is, the £/$ ratio decreases—the investor gains in receiving more than $1,000 at maturity while the issuer loses in the sense of having to pay more. We see, then, that a variety of currency features are possible.

❖ SUMMARY

Currency risk is yet another risk an investor must consider when entering the ever-expanding international arena. Return on investment is a function not only of interest-rate changes but also of exchange-rate movements. Risk can be reduced further with international diversification than with domestic diversification. To protect against a drop in currency value, the forward exchange market may be used. A forward contract enables one to sell a currency at a specific future date and at a price set in advance. The cost for this protection is determined by the difference in the forward and spot exchange rates.

Certain underlying theories provide a better understanding of the relationship between inflation, interest rates, and exchange rates. Purchasing power parity is the idea that a basket of goods should sell at the same price internationally, after factoring into account exchange rates. Relative inflation has an important influence on exchange rates and on relative interest rates. Interest-rate parity suggests that the difference between forward and spot currency exchange rates can be explained by differences in nominal interest rates between two countries. For advanced industrial countries, covered interest arbitrage causes interest-rate parity to hold at a moment in time. Empirical evidence is consistent with the theory of purchasing power parity in the long run but not in the short run.

In addition to forward contracts, an investor can hedge with currency futures. These contracts serve the same economic purpose as forward contracts. Whereas both permit "two-sided" hedges, the option is a "one-sided" hedge for which a premium is paid. Exchange-traded currency contracts are used much less than the over-the-counter market with investment banks. For currencies of advanced industrial countries, viable markets for forward and option contracts extend out several years. Finally, currency swaps are an important longer-term, risk-shifting device. Here, two parties exchange debt obligations in different currencies. Often currency swaps are combined with interest-rate swaps, involving fixed- for floating-rate exchanges. A method for valuing a currency swap was presented.

The amount to hedge is a subject of controversy. Although transaction costs usually arc low, on occasion they are sizable; this uncertainty tends to reduce or eliminate hedging. Others argue for complete, 100 percent hedging because the variance of home country returns can be substantially reduced. Black's universal hedging model suggests that some currency risk exposure should be borne, and a formula is derived for determining the optimal hedge ratio. This ratio is applicable to all investors, regardless of nationality. Many portfolio managers are judged against a standard of some currency hedging, often one half.

International bond markets differ in a number of ways from domestic markets, and certain institutional aspects were explored, as were aspects of international bond-portfolio management. Portfolios can consist of developed country bonds or emerging market debt. Most portfolios consist of one or the other category, but some are mixed. For both markets, indices exist for benchmarking and judging performance. Currency risk can be shifted by use of currency-option bonds, bonds that are convertible into an asset of a different currency, multiple-currency bonds, currency futures contracts, and options contracts, either on spot currencies or on currency futures.

❖ SELECTED REFERENCES

Adler, Michael, and Philippe Jorion, "Universal Currency Hedges for Global Portfolios," *Journal of Portfolio Management* 18 (Summer 1992): 28–35.

Bekaert, Geert, and Robert J. Hodrick, "On Biases in the Measurement of Foreign Exchange Risk Premiums," *Journal of International Money and Finance* 12 (1993): 115–38.

Black, Fischer, "Equilibrium Exchange Rate Hedging," *Journal of Finance* 45 (July 1990): 899–908.

Clarke, Roger G., and Mark P. Kritzman, *Currency Management: Concepts and Practices.* Charlottesville, VA: Research Foundation of the Institute of Chartered Financial Analysts, 1996.

Eaker, Mark R., and Dwight M. Grant, "Currency Risk Management in International Fixed-Income Portfolios," *Journal of Fixed Income* 1 (December 1991): 31–37.

Fabozzi, Frank J., ed., *Perspectives on International Fixed-Income Investing.* New Hope, PA: Frank J. Fabozzi Associates, 1998.

Filatov, Victor S., and Peter Rappoport, "Is Complete Hedging Optimal for International Bond Portfolios," *Financial Analysts Journal* 48 (July–August 1992): 37–47.

Glen, Jack, and Philippe Jorion, "Currency Hedging for International Portfolios," *Journal of Finance* 48 (December 1993): 1865–86.

Grabbe, J. Orlin, *International Financial Markets,* 3rd ed. Upper Saddle River, NJ: Prentice Hall, 1996.

Jarrow, Robert, and Stuart Turnbull, *Derivative Securities,* 2nd ed. Cincinnati: South-Western, 2000, chapter 11.

Levich, Richard M., and Lee R. Thomas, "The Merits of Active Currency Risk Management: Evidence from International Bond Portfolios," *Financial Analysts Journal* 49 (September–October 1993): 63–70.

Perold, Andre, and Evan C. Schulman, "The Free Lunch in Currency Hedging: Implications for Investment Policy and Performance Standards," *Financial Analysts Journal* 44 (May–June 1988): 45–50.

Smith, Clifford W., Charles W. Smithson, and Lee Macdonald Wakeman, "The Evolving Market for Swaps," *Midland Corporate Finance Journal* 3 (Winter 1986): 20–32.

Solnik, Bruno. "Global Asset Management," *Journal of Portfolio Management* 24 (Summer 1998): 43–51.

THE INFLUENCE OF TAXES

Another influence that we observe on the market yields is that of taxes. Up until now, this effect has been ignored as we tried to explain such influences as duration, default risk, and callability on yields. In this chapter, we remedy this deficiency by extending our analysis to consider the consequences of a taxable world on yields and on yield differentials.

In the absence of taxes, the yield of a fixed-income security with a $100 face value and semiannual interest payments is found by solving the following equation for r.

$$P = \sum_{t=1}^{2n} \frac{C/2}{(1 + \frac{r}{2})^t} + \frac{\$100}{(1 + \frac{r}{2})^{2n}} \tag{15-1}$$

where

P = bond's current market price
C = annual coupon payment
n = number of years to final maturity

The yield, r, represents the promised rate of return applicable to all investors.

With taxes, r no longer represents the relevant return for all investors. The reason is that Equation (15-1) does not take into account whether interest income is taxed and whether part of the yield-to-maturity is capital gains, which may be taxed at a rate different from that for interest income. Therefore, the equation does not allow us to determine the effective after-tax rate of return, which, for the taxable investor, is a relevant consideration. We would expect financial markets to equilibrate in terms of after-tax rates of return. Because of different tax situations, a financial instrument will imply different after-tax yields for different investors even though the before-tax yield (r in Equation [15-1]) is the same for all of them.

The after-tax yield for a financial instrument held to maturity can be expressed as the discount rate $\bar{r}$, which equates its current market price with the present value of after-tax returns. Thus,

$$P = \sum_{t=1}^{2n} \frac{C/2(1 - T)}{(1 + \frac{\bar{r}}{2})^t} + \frac{(\$100 - P)(1 - G)}{(1 + \frac{\bar{r}}{2})^{2n}} + \frac{P}{(1 + \frac{\bar{r}}{2})^{2n}} \tag{15-2}$$

where T is the marginal tax rate on ordinary income for the investor and G is the marginal tax rate on capital gains.

We see that interest payments are taxed as ordinary income, while any capital gain that occurs at final maturity, denoted by ($100 - P$), is taxed at a capital gains rate, which usually is less than that for interest income. Equation (15-2) will serve as a focal point for discussion of tax issues.

TAX TREATMENT OF CAPITAL GAINS

If G is less than T in Equation (15-2), bonds trading at a discount will be attractive to some taxable investors, compared with bonds that trade at par or at a premium. As a result, their pretax yield-to-maturity may be lower. In other words, a dollar of capital gains, on a discounted present-value basis, may be more valuable than a dollar of interest income, again on a discounted present-value basis. While this once was unequivocal, tax acts in 1984 and in 1993 substantially reduced the capital gains attraction of discount bonds. Let us examine the tax treatment for various discount bonds.

ORIGINAL ISSUE DISCOUNT (OID) BONDS

For zero-coupon and low-coupon bonds that are sold at a steep discount from face value, the discount must be amortized over the life of the bond and reported as interest income. Moreover, all subsequent purchasers of the bond in the secondary market are subject to the original amortization schedule in reporting interest income. For the issuer, the annual amortization of the discount is treated as an interest expense.

The amortization schedule is not linear, in the sense of dividing the discount by the number of years to maturity to determine annual interest. Rather, the **constant interest method** is used, which embraces present value. As a result, computed annual interest increases at an increasing rate. For a specific period, the amount of amortized discount is (1) the bond's accreted value up to that point, multiplied by (2) the yield for the period, minus (3) the coupon payment, if any, paid during the period. The **accreted value** of the bond is the original issue price plus the cumulative amortization of the discount.

To illustrate, suppose a zero-coupon bond of 10 years were sold for $41.46 to yield 9 percent, using the semiannual compounding convention (see chapter 4). In the first six-month period, the amount of imputed interest is $41.46 \times 0.045 = \$1.87$. In the second six-month period, it is $(\$41.46 + \$1.87) \times 0.045 = \$1.95$. For all 10 years, the semiannual amortization is as follows.

Period	Discount Amortization	Period	Discount Amortization
½	$1.87	5½	$2.90
1	1.95	6	3.03
1½	2.04	6½	3.16
2	2.13	7	3.31
2½	2.23	7½	3.46
3	2.33	8	3.61
3½	2.43	8½	3.77
4	2.54	9	3.94
4½	2.65	9½	4.12
5	2.77	10	4.30
			$58.54

The total of $58.54 is equal to the original discount of $100.00 − $41.46 = $58.54. Both the taxable investor and the issuer are required to use the foregoing interest amounts for tax purposes.

CAPITAL GAINS TREATMENT FOR TAXABLE COUPON BONDS

Since 1984, any capital gain associated with discount amortization of a bond bought in the secondary market is subject to taxation at the ordinary income tax rate. Most investors elect to accrue the discount under the constant interest method illustrated for original issue discount (OID) bonds. Without such an election, straight-line accrual is required by the Internal Revenue Service.

To illustrate the accrual calculations, suppose you bought a 6 percent bond with 4 years to maturity priced at $97.24 to yield 6.80 percent. If you hold the bond to maturity, the accrual each six months will be that shown in Table 15-1. With the constant interest method, the beginning purchase price is multiplied by the semiannual yield, 6.80%/2 = 3.40%, to give the interest earned in the first half year: $3.31. This, minus the coupon payment of $3.00, gives the accrual of $0.31. When this is added to the purchase price, the ending accreted value becomes $97.55. The beginning value in the second column is always multiplied by 3.40 percent to give the interest earned in the third column. Each year, the taxable investor must pay taxes on the coupon payment of $3.00 per semiannual period. For the accrual of the discount, he or she has an option. The tax can be paid on an ongoing basis, or it can be deferred to the time the bond is sold or to maturity. With the first option, the tax basis is increased by the amount of cumulative accrual. If held to maturity, the full discount of $2.76 is subject to taxation at the ordinary income tax rate.

Suppose the investor sells the bond prior to maturity—say at $99.60 at the beginning of year 3. At this juncture, we see in the table that the accreted value is $98.89. The total gain on the sale of the bond is $99.60 − $97.24 = $2.36. Of this gain, the cumulative accrual of the discount is $98.89 − $97.24 = $1.65. This amount is subject to taxation at the ordinary income tax rate, either at the time of sale or before if the investor

TABLE 15-1   Accrual of Discount for a 6% Bond Bought at a Yield of 6.8%

(1) *Period*	*(2)* *Beginning* *Accreted* *Value*	*(3)* *Total* *Interest* *Earned*	*(4)* *Coupon* *Payment*	*(5)* *Accrual* *of Discount*	*(6)* *Ending* *Accreted* *Value*
½	$97.24	$3.31	$3.00	$0.31	$97.55
1	97.55	3.32	3.00	0.32	97.87
1½	97.87	3.33	3.00	0.33	98.20
2	98.20	3.34	3.00	0.34	98.54
2½	98.54	3.35	3.00	0.35	98.89
3	98.89	3.36	3.00	0.36	99.25
3½	99.25	3.37	3.00	0.37	99.62
4	99.62	3.38	3.00	0.38	100.00

elects to pay taxes each year. The difference between the sale price of $99.60 and the accreted value of $98.89, or $0.71, is treated as a long-term capital gain and subject to the generally more favorable capital gains tax rate.

THE DE MINIMIS RULE

The accrual of a discount must be treated in the above manner if the discount from face value is significant. Small discounts are excluded. The IRS regards a discount as *de minimis* if at the time of purchase the discount is less than ¼ of 1 percent multiplied by the number of years that remain to final maturity. For our example, the discount would have been de minimis if it were $0.25 \times 4 = \$1.00$ or less. As it is $2.76, it has to be accrued. De minimis discounts do not need to be accrued. When the bond is sold or when it matures, any gain is treated like a capital gain and is subject to the generally more favorable capital gains tax rate. As a result, bonds with a discount that is de minimis tend to trade at a slightly higher price than other, comparable discount bonds.

CAPITAL GAINS TREATMENT FOR MUNICIPAL BONDS

Since 1993, the tax treatment of municipal bonds has been the same as for taxable bonds. As interest income is tax exempt, however, the relative impact is more pronounced. Any discount from face value is subject to taxation, either at the ordinary income tax rate or at the capital gains tax rate if the discount is de minimis. As a result, municipal bonds selling at a discount typically provide a yield higher than comparable bonds selling at par. In other words, bonds selling at par are more attractive than discount bonds because their return is made up entirely of interest and the final principal payment, neither of which is subject to taxation. Referring to our basic valuation formula for determining the after-tax rate of return, Equation (15-2), if $T = 0$ and G is positive, the discount bond will clearly provide a lower after-tax return for the taxable investor than will a bond whose market price is $100, all other things the same. If market equilibration occurs in terms of after-tax rates of return, the discount municipal bond must provide a higher yield than a bond selling at par.

TAX TIMING OPTIONS

Let us return to taxable bonds. Assume that the price of a bond purchased at a discount is now in excess of its accreted value or its purchase price if the discount is de minimis. Realization of the favorable capital gains tax rate depends on the bond's being held some minimum period, say six months. If it is held for this time and then sold, the gain or loss is considered to be long term and subject to the lower capital gains tax rate. If it is sold prior to the end of the minimum period, the gain or loss is short term and subject to the ordinary income tax rate, the same as that on interest income. Therefore, the desirable course is for a bondholder to take capital losses short term and defer capital gains until they become long term. This strategy constitutes a valuable timing option. Another timing option has to do with the premium amortization of a bond purchased above par. The premium is amortized to maturity, and the annual amortized amount is deductible against ordinary income for tax purposes. At times, it makes sense to sell a bond bought at or below par, which subsequently goes to a premium, and then repurchase the bond (or buy a like bond) in the market. By so doing, you raise your basis in the bond and are able to deduct the amortized premium, thereby reducing the present value of tax payments. This, too, is a valuable timing option.

Various scholars have tested empirically for tax-timing options being embedded in the prices of securities having different coupon rates.[1] While there is evidence of tax-driven clienteles impacting bond prices, the effect is small. Put another way, tax-timing options appear to be only a minor factor in the market equilibration process by which bonds are valued, one relative to another.

MUNICIPAL BONDS AND THE TAXATION OF INTEREST INCOME

The tax treatment of interest income is different for different financial instruments. As a result, the after-tax rate of return computed with Equation (15-2) is affected. Interest on certain state and local government securities is exempt from federal income taxes, while that for other bonds is taxed at the ordinary income tax rate. For such public purposes as schools, parks, sewers, and buildings, interest income on municipal debt is fully tax exempt. In addition, the interest income for such securities usually is not subject to state income taxes if the security is an obligation of the state involved or an obligation of a local government within the state. However, if the security is of another state, the interest usually is taxable at the state level. Most states tax out-of-state municipal bond interest differently from in-state bond interest, providing an incentive for their own state residents to hold in-state bonds.[2] Finally, the interest on Treasury securities is subject to federal income taxes but is exempt from any state or local income tax.

Certain "private purpose" bonds, such as mortgage revenue bonds and bonds to finance student loans, are restricted in the amounts that can be issued and still qualify for tax exemption. (In addition, their interest is treated as a preference item when it comes to calculating the alternative minimum tax.) Finally, interest is fully taxable on bonds issued by a municipality not viewed by Congress as essential. This category includes sports stadium bonds, pollution control bonds, and most industrial revenue bonds. The question of which projects qualify for tax-exempt financing and which, by exclusion, do not involves the social allocation of capital, a topic examined in the next chapter. For now, we assume that municipal bonds finance public projects and that their interest is entirely tax exempt.

---

[1] George M. Constantinides and Jonathan E. Ingersoll, Jr., "Optimal Bond Trading with Personal Taxes," *Journal of Financial Economics* 13 (September 1984): 299–335; Robert H. Litzenberger and Jacques Rolfo, "Arbitrage Pricing, Transactions Costs and Taxation of Capital Gains: A Study of Government Bonds with the Same Maturity Date," *Journal of Financial Economics* 13 (September 1984): 337–51; Bradford D. Jordan and Susan D. Jordan, "Tax Options and the Pricing of Treasury Bond Triplets," *Journal of Financial Economics* 30 (November 1991): 135–64; Richard C. Green and Bernt A. Odegaard, "Are There Tax Effects in the Relative Pricing of U.S. Government Bonds?" *Journal of Finance* 52 (June 1997): 609–33; and Edwin J. Elton and T. Clifton Green, "Tax and Liquidity Effects in Pricing Government Bonds," *Journal of Finance* 53 (October 1998): 1533–62.

[2] For an analysis of this phenomenon and the relative valuation of the two types of municipal bonds, see C. Steven Cole, Pu Liu, and Stanley D. Smith, "The Capitalization of the State Tax Exemption Benefit in Municipal Bond Yields," *Journal of Financial and Strategic Decisions* 7 (Summer 1994): 67–77.

Municipal bonds usually are issued as **serial bonds,** where a given amount matures each year. For a $50 million municipal bond issue, $2 million might mature every year for 25 years. Each maturity involves a separate bond with a coupon rate that can, and usually does, differ from coupon rates for the other maturities. There are two basic types of municipal bond. **General obligation bonds** are backed by the *full faith and credit* of the issuing municipality. This means the general taxing power of the issuer, as well as its ability to generate fees and other charges. The second category of municipal security is the **revenue bond.** Revenue bonds are issued to finance projects, such as a parking garage or a municipal hospital. Revenues from the project are dedicated to service the debt. The bondholder has claim only to the project; the bonds do not enjoy the general backing of the municipality. All other things the same, general obligation bonds usually are of higher credit quality than revenue bonds.

In addition to bonds, municipalities also issue shorter-term securities. Municipal notes, frequently of a tax anticipation nature, typically are for 12 or fewer months. Floating rate paper has been popular in recent years, given the demand for such by municipal money market funds and by corporations. Such paper is known as **variable rate demand notes (VRDN),** and the rate is reset either daily or every 7 days. At the time of this writing, total debt outstanding of state and local governments was $1.2 trillion. This amount compares with $3.7 trillion for the federal government, $3.8 trillion for corporations, and $4.2 trillion for home mortgages. Due to budget surpluses during the 1990s, the net supply of municipal securities outstanding increased only slowly over time.

THE NATURE OF THE MUNICIPAL MARKET

Because of the tax-exempt feature, eligible municipal securities are of interest mainly to individuals in high tax brackets and to financial institutions paying taxes at or nearly at the full corporate tax rate. A nonprofit organization that pays no taxes would have little reason to invest in municipal securities, considering that yields on default-free Treasury securities are higher. The market for municipals consists mainly of high-income individuals either directly or through municipal security mutual funds, property and casualty insurance companies, and bank personal trusts and estates. The latter is a conduit for individuals. Before the Tax Reform Act of 1986, commercial banks were important investors in municipal securities, particularly short-term ones. However, the Tax Act changed that, effectively making interest on such bonds taxable for the commercial bank investor. As a result, banks no longer are important purchasers of new municipal bonds. They still hold some older municipal bonds and, from time to time, invest in special situations.

The demand for municipal securities by property and casualty insurance companies varies with their underwriting cycle, which is subject to dramatic swings over time. When the underwriting cycle is favorable to insurers, they are able to charge good premiums and profitability is high. During these times, appetite is strong for tax-exempt securities. For the downside in the cycle, however, competition erodes profitability and the marginal tax rate plummets. Their demand for new municipal securities dries up. Over cycles, property and casualty companies account for about 15 percent of the total holdings of municipal securities. The bulk of demand for municipal securities comes from individuals, either directly (about 35 percent of total municipal securities outstanding) or indirectly through mutual funds and trusts and estates (about 40 percent).

TAXABLE VERSUS TAX-EXEMPT YIELDS

Because of differential taxation of interest income, before-tax yields are lower for municipal securities than they are for other bonds of equivalent risk. One comparison is with corporate bonds. In Figure 15-1, the yield differential between Aaa corporate bonds and Aaa municipal bonds is shown for 1960–1999. We see that the differential is always positive and has fluctuated around 1¾ percent in recent years. However, it was much higher in the early 1980s when interest rates also were much higher.

The tax benefit is proportional to the level of interest rates. Suppose the marginal tax rate for an investor were 30 percent and that the yield on taxable bonds were 8 percent. The yield on the tax-exempt security would then need to be $8\%(1 - 0.3) = 5.6\%$ for the investor to be indifferent between the two securities on an after-tax basis. Under these circumstances, the yield differential would be 2.4%. Suppose now that taxable rates fall to 7 percent. For indifference, the yield on the tax-exempt security would need to be $7\%(1 - 0.3) = 4.9\%$. The yield differential now would be 2.1%. Thus, the yield differential would be expected to vary with the overall level of interest rates, and Figure 15-1 is consistent with this expectation.

Another popular expression of the relationship between taxable and tax-exempt securities is the municipal yield as a percent of the Treasury yield. At July 27, 1999, percentages were as follows for long-term, general-obligation municipal bonds and for Treasury bonds.

Maturity	*Aaa Muni Yield*	*Treasury Yield*	*Muni/Treasury Percent*
15-year	5.03%	6.19%	81.3%
20-year	5.18	6.28	82.5
25-year	5.21	6.24	83.5
30-year	5.23	6.08	86.0

For people active in the municipal bond market, the last column is known as **"the ratio,"** and it conveys much information as to relative pricing. We will say something about the changing percentages with maturity later.

VALUE OF THE TAX-EXEMPTION FEATURE

One of the interesting aspects of the municipal market is the value placed on tax exemption. For an investor to have no preference between a municipal security and, say, a corporate security of equal risk, the following would need to hold for par-value bonds:

$$r_{\text{muni.}} = r_{\text{corp.}}(1 - T) \tag{15-3}$$

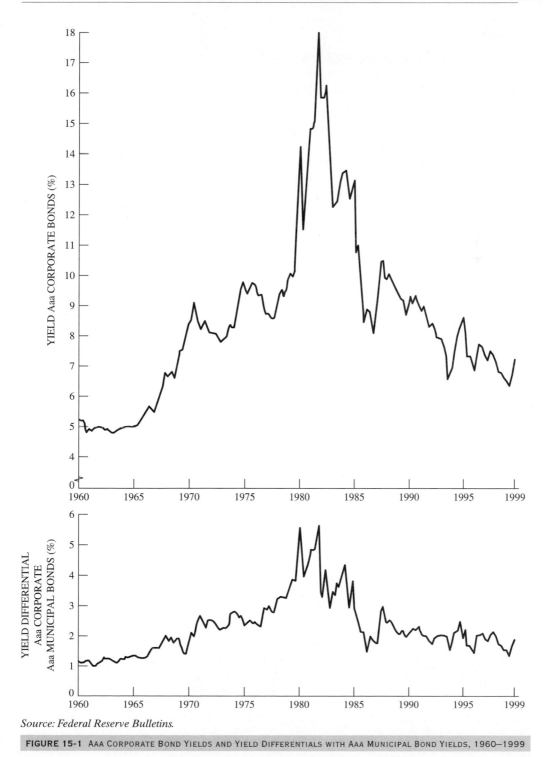

Source: Federal Reserve Bulletins.

FIGURE 15-1 AAA CORPORATE BOND YIELDS AND YIELD DIFFERENTIALS WITH AAA MUNICIPAL BOND YIELDS, 1960–1999

where

$$r_{\text{muni.}} = \text{the yield on the municipal security}$$
$$r_{\text{corp.}} = \text{the yield on the corporate security}$$
$$T = \text{the marginal tax rate of the investor}$$

We assume that the return on both securities is made up solely of interest income, with no capital gains or losses. If $r_{\text{muni.}}$ were greater than $r_{\text{corp.}} (1 - T)$, taxable investors would invest in municipal securities; if it were less, they would invest in corporates. The implied general tax rate in the market can be determined by

$$T_{\text{mkt.}} = 1 - \frac{r_{\text{muni.}}}{r_{\text{corp.}}} \qquad \textbf{(15-4)}$$

If taxable investors had a marginal tax rate (comprising federal, state, and local income taxes) greater than $T_{\text{mkt.}}$, they would invest in municipals; if the marginal tax rate were less, investors would invest in corporates.

   If we regard Aaa municipal long-term bonds and Aaa corporate bonds as comparable from the standpoint of risk, the implied marginal tax rate for long-term bonds would be that shown in Figure 15-2 for the period 1960–1999. As seen in the figure, the implied tax rate ranged from 16 to 43 percent over the period involved.

VARIATION OF IMPLIED TAX RATE

Particularly noticeable is the pattern since 1975. In early 1975, the implied tax rate was around 26 percent. It rose sharply in 1976, stayed at a plateau for several years in the high 30s, and then peaked at 43 percent in 1979. As interest rates in general rose rather dramatically in 1980–1981, the tax rate then declined to the lower 30s. In late 1981 and 1982, the implied tax rate dropped to a low of 22 percent and fluctuated. A partial reason for the sharp drop in 1981 was the Tax Act of 1981, which lowered tax rates in general and the maximum effective rate on interest income in particular. Relative to taxable securities, tax-exempt securities were less attractive than they had been before.

   In the post-1981 period, the implied marginal tax rate fluctuated with no marked trend. Through 1985, it went down or up depending on the need to draw individual investors into the market. When *ex ante* supply was large and institutional demand small,

FIGURE 15-2 IMPLIED MARGINAL TAX RATE USING Aaa CORPORATE AND Aaa MUNICIPAL BONDS, 1960–1999

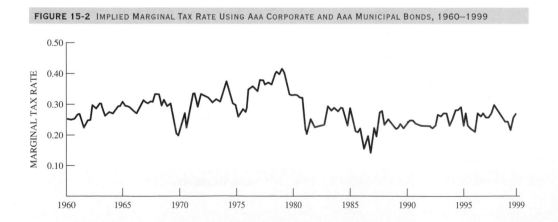

individuals were drawn in with increasing interest rates relative to taxable bonds. As a result, the value of tax exemption declined. The opposite occurred when *ex ante* supply was moderate and institutional demand was high.

The period around the 1986 Tax Act is interesting. As the bill was being discussed in Congress, it became clear that the maximum individual tax rate would be lowered significantly and that commercial banks would no longer find municipal securities attractive. These things made municipals less desirable, relative to taxable bonds, and the implied tax rate dropped to 17 percent by the summer of 1986. When the bill was finally completed, however, things changed. Alternative tax shelter opportunities were sharply curtailed. In addition, as mentioned earlier, private-purpose financing was significantly restricted, thus reducing the future supply of tax-exempt bonds. Once these aspects of the bill came to light, interest rates on municipal bonds rose relative to those on taxable bonds, and the implied tax rate went to 25 percent. Since that time, the implied tax rate has fluctuated around 25 percent with no discernable trend.

However, there have been times recently when the implied tax rate has jumped one way or the other. In late 1998, it declined to 22 percent, indicating less demand for municipals vis-à-vis taxables. At the same time, the ratio of 30-year municipal yields to Treasury yields touched 98 percent, compared with 86 percent earlier in the year. As reflected earlier in the book, this was a time of financial panic and "flight to quality," meaning Treasury securities. By mid 1999, the implied tax rate returned to 25 percent and the "ratio" to 86 percent.

THE EFFECT OF TAX REFORM AND SUPPLY

Major tax reform, particularly as it affects individual investors, is important in explaining changes in the implied tax rate over time.[3] Prior to the 1986 Tax Reform Act, an additional explanatory factor was the segmented nature of the municipal securities market and the demand by institutional investors. Although some evidence still can be found of partial segmentation of the tax-exempt market from the taxable market, it is not nearly as pronounced as before. Nonetheless, supply factors affect the market, causing the implied tax rate to decline (tax-exempt yields rising relative to taxable yields) when net supply increases sharply and vice versa.

Still, tax reform and discussion of it in Congress seem to have the greatest effect on the implied tax rate. Actual changes in tax rates in 1990 and 1993, though only moderate, together with discussion in the mid- and late-1990s of a decrease and flat tax, go a long way toward explaining fluctuations in the implied tax rate in the 1990s. However, none of these events come close to the 1981 and 1986 Tax Acts in their effect on the relative value of the tax-exemption privilege.

Note that the average implied tax for long-term municipal bonds, about 25 percent in recent years, is lower than the highest marginal tax rate for individuals and for other taxable investors. In 1999, for example, the highest marginal tax rate (federal) was 39.6 percent. This rate suggests that state and local governments do not enjoy all the tax

---

[3] See James M. Poterba, "Tax Reform and the Market for Tax-Exempt Debt," *Regional Science and Urban Economics* 19 (September 1989): 537–62. For the impact of fire and casualty insurance companies, see Karlyn Mitchell and Michael D. McDade, "Preferred Habitat, Taxable/Tax-Exempt Yield Spreads, and Cycles in Property/Liability Insurance," *Journal of Money, Credit and Banking* 24 (November 1992): 528–52.

benefits associated with municipal interest tax exemption and that a portion goes to investors. The tax-exemption feature is not fully priced in the marketplace in that the municipalities do not capture all the benefit.

MUNICIPAL VERSUS TAXABLE YIELD CURVES

Apart from fluctuations over time, the implied tax rate varies by maturity. It is lowest in the long-term end of the market. For short- and intermediate-term securities, yields on municipal securities typically are less, relative to taxable yields, than they are for long-term securities. Therefore, the implied tax rate is higher. In the past, this phenomenon may have been largely attributable to the practice of commercial banks in restricting their investment activities to short- and intermediate-term securities. Commercial bank interest in municipal bonds evaporated with the 1986 Tax Reform Act, as we have discussed. Without commercial bank demand in the short end of the yield curve, the yield curve for municipal securities flattened somewhat after 1986.

 While flatter than before, municipal yield curves on average are still more upward-sloping than yield curves for taxable securities. An example is shown in Figure 15-3 for Aaa general obligation municipals and Treasuries. The dips in the Treasury curve for 5 years, 10 years, and 30 years are caused by the excess demand for newly issued, "on the run" securities relative to securities in surrounding maturities. (See chapter 6 for an explanation of this liquidity phenomenon.) In the figure, we observe that the municipal curve is more upward sloped than the Treasury curve. Expressed differently, the relative demand for short-term municipals is greater than for long-term municipals. This is reflected also in the "ratio" of municipal to Treasury yields, which at the time of the graph were 66.0 percent for 1-year maturities, 68.5 percent for 2 years, going up to 83.5 percent for 25 years and 86.0 percent for 30 years. Thus, the tax-exemption feature is more valued in the short end of the yield curve than it is in the long end. This has im-

FIGURE 15-3 TREASURY AND GENERAL OBLIGATION AAA MUNICIPAL YIELD CURVES JULY 27, 1999

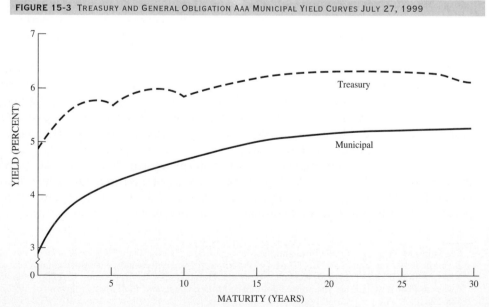

portant implications for the municipal interest-rate swap market. In order to reduce their "all-in" cost of funds, some municipalities borrow directly on a floating-rate basis and swap to pay fixed.

PREFERRED-STOCK TAX EFFECTS

Preferred-stock dividends are tax advantaged to the corporate investor but not to other investors. In most cases, the dividend is 70 percent exempt from federal taxation. (The full dividend is subject to state income taxes.) This means that if Green Shoe Company invests in the 8 percent preferred stock of Allied Transit Corporation and a $4 semi-annual dividend is paid, $2.80 is exempt from taxation. If Green Shoe is in a 35 percent tax bracket, it would pay taxes of ($4.00 − $2.80)0.35 = $0.42 on the dividend. This amounts to $0.42/$4.00 = 10.5 percent on the overall dividend. Certain conditions must be met to qualify for the 70 percent exemption. The corporate investor must hold the stock for more than 45 days. Moreover, the corporation paying the dividend must pay it out of profits.

STRAIGHT PREFERRED-STOCK INVESTMENTS

Because of the favorable intercorporate dividend tax treatment, a preferred stock tends to sell at a lower yield than does a bond of the same corporation. This lower yield occurs despite the lesser claim to income, as preferred-stock dividends are declared at the discretion of the board of directors, and the lesser claim to assets in liquidation, as preferred stockholders come after all debtholders have been paid. The yield differential is a function of relative supplies in the two security markets and the value of tax exemption to corporate investors. Most corporate investors do not hold preferred stock as a long-term investment, but rather as part of their marketable securities portfolio held for liquidity purposes.

One device to take advantage of the 70 percent tax exemption is the hedged dividend capture. The idea is to invest in stocks, usually preferred, right before a dividend is to be paid and, at the same time, write a call option on the stock. This is known as a covered call in the sense that the investor can deliver stock he or she already owns if the option holder exercises his or her call. This will happen if the stock rises significantly in price, and the corporate investor will realize only the premium paid for the call. If the market price fluctuates, the investor will realize the dividend on favorable tax terms, as well as the call premium. Holding the stock for the mandatory 46 days for tax purposes, the position in the stock and the option are reversed, and the firm seeks another stock about to pay a dividend. Finally, if the stock should decline significantly in price, the investor's loss is buffered by the call premium received. Moreover, the position can be reversed before too much damage occurs.

AUCTION-RATE PREFERRED STOCK

A special type of preferred stock whose interest rate floats with money market rates is **auction-rate preferred stock.** Several variations of this security exist, depending on the investment bank promoting the product. With all, the return changes at periodic reset dates with changes in interest rates. One of the more popular securities is money market preferred stock (MMP). With MMP, an auction is held every 49 days. This provides the investor with liquidity and relative price stability as far as interest-rate risk goes. It does not protect the investor against default risk.

The new rate is set by the forces of supply and demand in keeping with interest rates in the money market. A typical rate might be 0.75 times the commercial paper rate, with more creditworthy issuers commanding an even greater discount. As long as enough investors bid at each auction, the effective maturity date is 49 days. As a result, little variation occurs in the market price of the instrument over time, and this represents a substantial advantage. In a failed auction that has insufficient bidders, there is a default dividend rate for one period that is frequently 110 percent of the commercial paper rate. In addition, the holder has the option to redeem the instrument at its face value. These provisions are attractive to the investor as long as the company is able to meet the conditions. If the company should default, however, the investor loses. Only a few instances of failed auctions and default have occurred.

These and a host of similar floating-rate instruments are tax arbitrage devices. They permit the corporate investor to earn a tax-advantaged return and the corporate issuer to raise funds at a cost below what would be paid with commercial paper borrowings. Both parties gain at the expense of the federal government. The exact sharing of the tax benefits by the two parties is market determined, and it depends on the supply of securities coming to market and on demand. The sharing proportions vary over time with market conditions. On average, however, the issuer tends to capture the greater portion of the total tax benefits. The Treasury periodically reviews these instruments and may propose reducing the percentage exemption or eliminating it altogether. So far this has not happened, because there are political constituencies who argue against it.

❖ SUMMARY

Taxes affect yields in a variety of ways. For certain situations, discount bonds enable an investor to enjoy the more favorable capital gains tax treatment on part of the total return. For original issue discount bonds, the discount must be amortized using the constant interest method. This method takes account of present value, so the amortized amount increases over time. Each year, the taxable investor must pay taxes at the ordinary income tax rate on the discount amortized for that year. An exception to this rule occurs if the discount is *de minimis*.

If a bond is sold before maturity, the portion of the capital gain represented by amortization of the discount is subject to taxation at the ordinary income tax rate. Any excess gain is taxed at the capital gains tax rate. All coupon payments are taxed as ordinary income in the year of receipt. Discount municipal and taxable bonds are treated in the same manner, but for municipal bonds only capital gains are subject to taxation. With differential taxation of ordinary income and capital gains, the bondholder has a timing option as to taking losses on a short-term basis and gains on a long-term basis, together with an option as to premium amortization.

Because interest income on eligible municipal securities is tax exempt, yields are lower than they are on other fixed-income securities. The higher the level of interest rates is, the wider the differential should be between yields on the two types of bonds. While the municipal bond market was relatively segmented on the demand side in the past, the 1986 Tax Reform Act reduced this considerably. The market now is dominated by individual investors who invest either directly or through municipal bond and money market mutual funds. The value of the tax-exemption feature is shared by the municipality and the investor. We study it by analyzing over time the implied tax rate. The wider the yield differential is between taxable and tax-exempt bonds, the higher the implied tax rate is, and vice versa. As yield curves for tax-exempt bonds tend to be more upward-sloping than those for taxable bonds, the implied tax rate is higher for shorter-term securities than it is for longer-term ones.

Preferred-stock dividends carry a 70 percent tax exemption for the corporate investor. As a result, preferred stocks tend to sell at lower yields than corporate bonds, holding risk constant. To take advantage of this feature, some corporate investors use a hedged dividend capture. Auction-rate preferred stock has been popular as a marketable security for the corporate investor.

❖ SELECTED REFERENCES

Cole, Steven C., Pu Liu, and Stanley D. Smith, "The Capitalization of the State Tax Exemption Benefit in Municipal Bond Yields," *Journal of Financial and Strategic Decisions* 7 (Summer 1994): 67–77.

Constantinides, George M., and Jonathan E. Ingersoll, Jr., "Optimal Bond Trading and Personal Taxes," *Journal of Financial Economics* 13 (September 1984): 299–335.

Crowder, William J., and Mark E. Wohar, "Are Tax Effects Important in the Long-Run Fisher Relationship? Evidence from the Municipal Bond Market," *Journal of Finance* 54 (February 1999): 307–18.

Elton, Edwin J., and T. Clifton Green, "Tax and Liquidity Effects in Pricing Government Bonds," *Journal of Finance* 53 (October 1998): 1533–62.

Farinella, Joseph A., and Timothy W. Koch, "Who Took the Slope Out of the Municipal Yield Curve?" *Journal of Fixed Income* 4 (September 1994): 59–65.

Green, Richard C., "A Simple Model of the Taxable and Tax-Exempt Yield Curves," *Review of Financial Studies* 6 (No. 2, 1993): 233–64.

Green, Richard C., and Bernt A. Odegaard, "Are There Tax Effects in the Relative Pricing of U.S. Government Bonds?" *Journal of Finance* 52 (June 1997): 609–33.

Green, Richard C., and Kristian Rydqvist, "Ex-Day Behavior with Dividend Preference and Limitations to Short-Term Arbitrage: The Case of Swedish Lottery Bonds," *Journal of Financial Economics* 53 (August 1999): 145–88.

Jordan, Bradford D., and Susan D. Jordan, "Tax Options and the Pricing of Treasury Bond Triplets," *Journal of Financial Economics* 30 (November 1991): 135–64.

Poterba, James M., "Tax Reform and the Market for Tax-Exempt Debt," *Regional Science and Urban Economics* 19 (September 1989): 537–62.

Rumsey, John, "Comparison of Tax Rates Inferred from Zero-Coupon Yield Curves," *Journal of Fixed Income* 5 (March 1996): 75–81.

Scholes, Myron S., and Mark A. Wolfson, *Taxes and Business Strategy: A Planning Approach.* Upper Saddle River, NJ: Prentice Hall, 1992.

Van Horne, James C., "Implied Tax Rates and the Valuation of Discount Bonds," *Journal of Banking and Finance* 6 (June 1982): 145–60.

THE SOCIAL ALLOCATION OF CAPITAL

Early in this book, we stated the proposition that funds flow from savings-surplus economic units to savings-deficit ones *primarily* on the basis of expected return and risk. We then looked at various factors affecting risk and return and analyzed their impact on the yields we observe in the marketplace. We saw that the more efficient the financial markets of a society are, the less will be the cost and inconvenience with which funds flow from ultimate savers to ultimate investors in real assets. The efficient channeling of savings requires competition among financial intermediaries and continual financial innovation.

In this chapter, we examine another influence on the flow of funds and on interest rates—the influence of the government. This influence is one apart from its taxing power and certain other government restrictions already discussed. Our focus will be on attempts by the government to direct the flow of funds in society toward socially desirable goals or to lower the interest-rate cost to socially desirable borrowers. These attempts fall under a broad heading that we shall call the **social allocation of capital.** Because of the nature of the topic, our consideration of it will be somewhat more conceptual in orientation than was true of former topics.

THE ISSUES INVOLVED

By social allocation of capital, we mean any action by the government that attempts to direct the flow of savings in our society toward some specific objective. This objective might be housing (through mortgages), inner cities, low-income families, pollution and environmental control, minority enterprises, consumer cooperatives, small businesses, farmers, a failing corporation, or what have you. The essential thing is that savings flows are directed in ways that would not occur if market forces alone were allowed to prevail. In other words, the "socially desirable" project does not attract the financing that the government would like it to attract at an interest rate that is sufficiently low from a social standpoint. To remedy the perceived deficiency, the government steps into the savings-allocation process to redirect flows toward socially desirable projects at appropriate interest rates (presumably low).

At the time the program is initiated, the perceived social benefits exceed the social costs in the eyes of the initiators—Congress, the executive branch, state legislatures, or others. The benefits are readily apparent; one category or group in society is able to borrow at favorable interest rates whereas before, credit was either unavailable or available only at a higher interest cost. As a result of a program to socially allocate capital, they move to the head, or nearly to the head, of the credit line. However, seldom are the social and economic costs of a program evaluated in their totality. These costs involve not only the *out-of-pocket cost* to the government in administering the subsidy but also the *opportunity cost* of the restrictions imposed on the efficiency of financial markets; the opportunity cost of lessened economic growth, which in turn results from directing savings toward projects on the basis of social return as opposed to economic return; and, in certain cases, the redistributional effects that work to the detriment of low-income individuals. Too often the costs of a method to socially allocate capital are not considered in their entirety, or they are ignored altogether because of their "hidden" nature.

A number of methods have been used to socially allocate capital to a desired cause and/or to lower the interest rate that otherwise would be paid. We endeavor to evaluate these methods with respect to their conceptual underpinnings. The methods examined include (1) a ceiling rate of interest on loans; (2) the use of a government guarantee to enhance a borrower's appeal in the market; (3) a government interest subsidy to the borrower or lender; (4) the government borrowing in the financial markets and relending to the socially desirable project; (5) the imposition of various government regulations, such as deposit rate ceilings, to divert the flow of savings to a social project; and (6) the federal government deciding who and what qualify for tax-exempt financing. We investigate each of these in turn.

CEILINGS ON BORROWING COSTS

Sometimes a government body will have usury laws, which govern the maximum interest rate a lender can charge. The intent of these laws is to lower the cost of borrowing, particularly to lower-income families, and to protect those less educated in the mathematics of compound interest. Whereas once usury laws were religious in conception, this has not been the case since Martin Luther caused lending to be tolerated, if not respected. In the past, the greatest concentration of usury laws occurred in the areas of consumer credit and residential mortgages. The question we wish to address is, What is the effect of interest-rate ceilings on the supply of loans and on noninterest costs?

THE EFFECT OF USURY LAWS

When the equilibrium market rate of interest is below the interest-rate ceiling imposed under a usury law, there is no effect on either the supply of loans or on noninterest costs. Borrowing and lending occur in free and competitive markets. However, when the ceiling is below what otherwise would be a market clearing rate, an adverse effect usually results. The notion that interest rates can be held down by government mandate without an adverse effect on loan flows rests on a proposition of complete segmentation, or unsubstitutability, between markets. In other words, the supply of loans is interest inelastic.

The situation is illustrated in Figure 16-1. At the market clearing rate of r_c, the supply is still d^*, while at the lower rate determined by usury laws, r_u, the supply is still d^*. However, at a rate of interest of r_u, desired demand is d', so there is excess demand of $d' - d^*$. In the face of this excess demand, lenders would be expected (1) to increase the quality of their loan portfolios by raising credit standards and screening out riskier borrowers, frequently low-income families; and/or (2) to seek additional compensation through various noninterest devices such as closing fees, servicing fees, and discounts from the face value of the debt instrument (known as *points*).[1] Thus, even with completely segmented markets and an inelastic supply curve, the presence of excess demand results in some side effects that are adverse from the standpoint of the framers of usury law legislation.

In the case of an interest-elastic supply curve, the amount of loanable funds available will be less if the usury rate is below what would otherwise be the market clearing rate of interest. From all that we know about the competitive nature of financial markets, we would have to say that an assumption of an elastic supply curve is reasonable. The situation is illustrated in Figure 16-2.

We see that at a ceiling rate of interest of r_u, lenders will supply loans in the amount of d'', which of course is less than would occur with a market clearing rate of r_c. The presence of excess loan demand, $d' - d''$, will result in the same incentives as before—namely, for lenders to upgrade the quality of their loans and to seek other compensa-

FIGURE 16-1 ILLUSTRATION OF INTEREST-RATE CEILING WITH AN INELASTIC SUPPLY CURVE

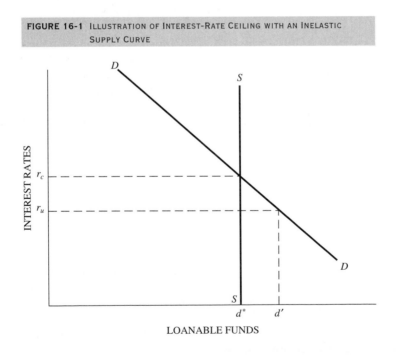

---

[1] A discount from face value enables the lender to obtain a higher effective yield. If the face value were $1,000, the usury rate ceiling were 10 percent, and the lender advanced only $940, the yield would be higher than 10 percent because the borrower would need to repay the full $1,000 plus compound interest of 10 percent.

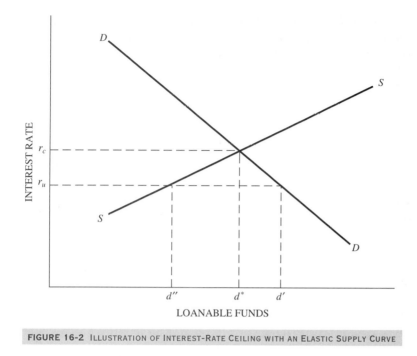

FIGURE 16-2 ILLUSTRATION OF INTEREST-RATE CEILING WITH AN ELASTIC SUPPLY CURVE

tion that falls outside the usury law. To the extent this occurs, the supply of loans at r_u may be greater than d''. What we have done then is to introduce dimensions other than interest payments to the supply of loanable funds. As a result, the supply curve in Figure 16-2 would no longer hold, but in some measure would shift to the right. It is conceivable the shift might be sufficient to provide d^* or even more loanable funds at the lower-than-market clearing rate, r_u. However, this does not mean that the usury law is working for its intended purpose—only that it is being circumvented and the lender is receiving payment by other means.

THE NEGATIVES OF INTEREST-RATE CEILINGS

Are usury laws harmful then? For the most part, the answer is yes. For one thing, they affect the efficiency with which financial markets operate. Inherently, the mechanisms for circumventing usury laws are less efficient than the simple use of interest rates to allocate credit. To the extent that a financial market is less efficient, there is greater cost and/or inconvenience associated with the channeling of savings in society. Moreover, circumvention around usury laws results in less truth in lending. Borrowers may not fully recognize the true costs of a loan. To the extent they are deceived relative to what they would be if interest charges alone were the only cost, this too is counter to the intentions of those advocating social measures to allocate capital.

Finally, and perhaps most important, usury rates below market clearing rates of interest usually result in the rationing of credit. The larger the gap of excess demand is in Figure 16-2, the more lenders will try to increase the quality of their loans and seek alternative forms of compensation. In upgrading quality, riskier loan applicants will be increasingly rejected. To the extent that these applicants are low-income people or the poor, their ability to borrow is foreclosed. As the formulation of most usury laws is with a concern for the cost of borrowing by the poor, ironically the end result may be that there is no cost for them because they are unable to obtain credit at the ceiling rate. Thus, there should be concern not only with the impact of usury laws on the total amount of credit extended but on the composition of borrowers, as well.

In general, empirical studies on consumer credit and mortgages have shown that when interest-rate ceilings were binding, the volume of loans declined, lenders tried to upgrade quality to the detriment of lower-income individuals, and noninterest methods of compensation increasingly were employed. These findings are in accord with our previous conceptual discussion of usury laws in financial markets characterized by elastic supply curves.

GOVERNMENT GUARANTEES AND INSURANCE

The government also can make social allocations of capital through a guarantee of a borrower's obligations to private lenders or through insurance, by which the government insures a loan against default. Virtually every department of the federal government has guaranteed and insured loan programs—hundreds in all. With such a program, of course, the default risk of the loan is reduced to zero. With this risk reduction, the debt obligation is made more attractive to investors. The potential borrower may now be able to attract lenders where before there were none, or he or she may simply pay a lower interest cost. In all cases, the debt instrument becomes a more desirable substitute relative to other financial instruments in the marketplace. As the guarantee and insurance are identical with respect to risk reduction, we analyze only the guarantee.[2]

The situation is illustrated in Figure 16-3. In this case, the demand curves represent those of a single borrower. Without a guarantee, the demand curve DD and supply curve SS intersect at point X, which results in a market clearing rate of interest of r_c. With the guarantee, however, the supply curve shifts to the right—to $S'S'$. This occurs because the financial instrument now is more attractive due to the reduction in risk. If borrowers are unrestricted by the government in the amount they are able to borrow, they will seek d' in financing at an interest rate of r'. Thus, the interest rate will decline and the amount borrowed will increase. If, however, the government restricts the amount that can be borrowed, the effective supply curve shortens. Suppose for purposes of illustration the restriction were set at the amount borrowed before the guarantee, $d*$. Instead of a supply curve of $S'S'$, the supply curve would be $S'd*$ in Figure 16-3. As a result, the interest rate would be r''. Thus, the entire effect of the guarantee would be on interest cost and not on the amount of financing.

---

[2] The cost of insurance may be borne by the government, by the borrower, or by all borrowers in a category based on the default experience of the category. In the first two instances, insurance and the guarantee are similar; in the last they are not, with respect to cost. As exploring this topic would be a digression from the central focus of this chapter, we do not do so.

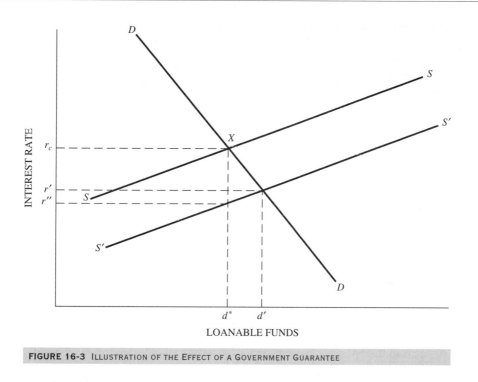

FIGURE 16-3 ILLUSTRATION OF THE EFFECT OF A GOVERNMENT GUARANTEE

THE TRANSFER OF UNDERLYING RISK

The use of a guarantee or insurance has great appeal. Borrowers are able to avail themselves of financing that otherwise might not be available or available only at a significantly high interest cost. In many instances, the government receives a guarantee, or insurance, fee. Proponents of this method of socially allocating capital will argue that everyone gains and no one loses. The apparent implication is *pareto* optimality with no boundaries. However, when one analyzes the situation a little more closely, one finds that there is a cost and that someone must bear this cost.

The crux of this issue is that underlying risk does not go away with a government guarantee or insurance. Borrowers can still default, particularly if the amount of government assistance is limited. The underlying risk is simply shifted from the investor to the federal government and to taxpayers at large. If default occurs, the federal government will need to make good on the obligation. In the final analysis, this will result in foregoing federal programs, increasing taxes, or increasing the federal debt. Therefore, the guarantee or insurance program has a cost, though admittedly it is largely a hidden one. It is a contingent or potential cost to present and future taxpayers. As discussed in chapter 8, which dealt with default risk, the cost is represented by the left-hand side of the probability distribution of possible returns in which the actual returns are less than the promised return. This probabilistic cost is absorbed by the government to make credit available at a lower cost to a socially desirable project.

Thus, the government supplants the marketplace in judging the risk-return trade-off, and return is broadened to include not only the project's economic return but its social return, as well. This supplanting is discussed later in the chapter once we have considered other methods for social allocation of capital.

OPTION-PRICING VALUATION

With a guarantee, effectively an option to the borrower has been written by the government. (See chapter 10 for the principles of option valuation.) The option has an exercise price equal to the face value of debt, and its expiration date is the maturity of the debt. If the value of the associated asset at expiration exceeds this face value, the option is exercised. If below, the option is not exercised and whatever value remains goes to the lender with the guarantor making up the shortfall. As with any option, the principal value driver is the volatility of the associated asset. The option holder, the borrower, has an incentive to increase risk. If a favorable outcome occurs, from the wider distribution of possible outcomes, the borrower can win big. If the outcome is unfavorable, the borrower walks away leaving the guarantor "holding the bag." Thus, a game is played against the guarantor, the most visible manifestation of such being the savings and loan debacle of the 1980s in the United States. The incentive of any option holder to "roll the dice" (increase risk) is adverse to the government guarantor, as a number of scholars have found who have used option-pricing notions to value the guarantee.[3]

INTEREST-RATE SUBSIDIES

A third method for socially allocating capital is for the government to pay an interest-rate subsidy either to the lender or to the borrower. When it goes to the lender, the government typically subsidizes a category of loans—such as mortgages or loans to cities. This approach tends to be "shotgun," in that it benefits all borrowers in a particular category. While this may be appropriate if one is trying to stimulate housing or construction overall, it is not effective if the purpose is to enable low-income families to purchase housing. Here a subsidy to the borrower, or to the lender where the subsidy is tied to a loan to a specific borrower, is better. Note that in either case, the lender receives the market clearing rate of interest on the loan. The borrower pays this rate minus the subsidy.

THE EFFECT OF THE SUBSIDY

With an interest-rate subsidy, the demand for that type of financing presumably will increase. Whether the supply of financing increases, however, depends on the elasticity of supply. In turn, this depends on the substitutability between the type of debt instrument or market involved and other financial instruments. If the supply curve is reasonably interest elastic, the amount of financing will increase. The situation is illustrated in Figure 16-4. Before the subsidy, the demand for financing is depicted by DD. With a supply curve of SS, financing in the amount of d^* will occur at the market clearing rate of r_c. With a subsidy of $R - r_c$, the demand curve shifts to $D'D'$. In turn, this causes the amount

[3] See Robert Merton, "An Analytical Derivation of the Cost of Deposit Insurance and Loan Guarantees," *Journal of Banking and Finance* 1 (June 1977): 3–12; E. Phillips Jones and Scott P. Mason, "Valuation of Loan Guarantees," *Journal of Banking and Finance* 4 (March 1980): 89–107; Howard Sosin, "On the Valuation of Federal Loan Guarantees to Corporations," *Journal of Finance* 35 (December 1980): 1209–21; M. J. P. Selby, J. R. Franks, and J. P. Karki, "Loan Guarantees, Wealth Transfers and Incentives to Invest," *Journal of Industrial Economics* 37 (September 1988): 47–65; and Robert C. Merton and Zvi Bodie, "On the Management of Financial Guarantees," *Financial Management* 21 (Winter 1992): 87–109.

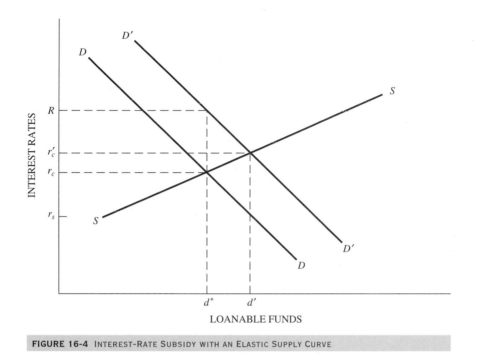

FIGURE 16-4 INTEREST-RATE SUBSIDY WITH AN ELASTIC SUPPLY CURVE

of financing to increase to d', and the market clearing rate to increase to r'_c. However, the interest rate the borrower pays is the new market clearing rate minus the subsidy, or $r'_c - (R - r_c) = r_s$. Thus, the amount of financing increases, and the effective interest rate paid by the borrower declines.

If the supply curve were inelastic, however, there would be no increase in the amount of financing. This situation is illustrated in Figure 16-5. Here a subsidy of $R - r_c$ shifts the demand curve to $D'D'$. However, because of the inelastic supply curve, the amount of financing does not increase. The shift in the demand curve is reflected entirely in an increase in the market clearing rate—namely, from r_c to R. Thus, this increase exactly offsets the subsidy, so the effective rate of interest to the borrower is the same as before. Put another way, the entire subsidy goes to the lender.

EFFECTIVENESS OF THE SUBSIDY

Therefore, the degree of substitutability between the financial instrument or market involved in the subsidy arrangement and other financial instruments and markets determines the success of the arrangement. With an inelastic supply curve, neither is the amount of financing raised nor is the effective rate paid by the borrower lowered. Given all we know about financial markets, however, the case seems weak for a completely inelastic supply curve of loanable funds. We would expect supply curves to be reasonably elastic and the situation to resemble that depicted in Figure 16-4.

One important feature of the interest-rate subsidy approach to the social allocation of capital is that the government does not intercede directly in the marketplace. It pays a subsidy, but financial markets then equilibrate on the basis of expected return and risk. Therefore, there is a minimum of interference in the workings of financial markets.

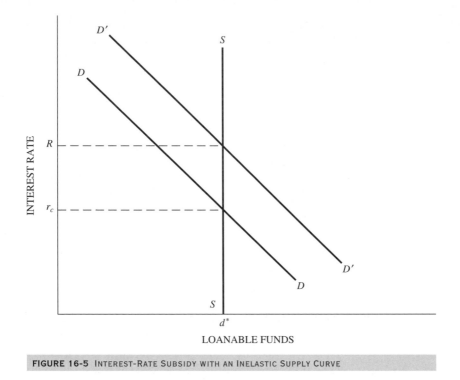

FIGURE 16-5 INTEREST-RATE SUBSIDY WITH AN INELASTIC SUPPLY CURVE

However, indirect pressure on financial markets can result if the subsidy is raised by increasing the amount of government debt. If the government issued securities in the Treasury or municipal markets, this action could adversely affect the supply curve for the particular market to which the government was trying to allocate capital socially if substitutability existed between the markets. Put another way, final general equilibrium in financial markets is the important criterion in judging the success of a plan to socially allocate capital. If the secondary effects offset the initial action, this result must be considered before a decision can be made.

Instead of an increase in government debt to pay for the subsidy, the capital may be raised by an increase in general taxes. In this case, there is little effect on other financial markets, and this offsetting factor can be safely ignored when the merits of the subsidy arrangement are judged. Once we have considered all the methods for the social allocation of capital, we will discuss further the relative merits of an interest-rate subsidy approach.

FINANCIAL INTERMEDIATION THROUGH BORROWING AND RELENDING

Another way to socially allocate capital is for the government, or an agency thereof, to borrow in the financial markets and then to relend to a financial institution, a corporation, a housing authority, a municipality, a farm cooperative, or what have you—either at the same rate at which it borrows or at a higher rate. In either case, the rate charged is lower than the rate the ultimate borrower would pay in the market.

THE SITUATION ILLUSTRATED

In all of these cases, the government becomes a financial intermediary for redirecting the flow of savings toward socially desirable projects. In so doing, the creditworthiness of the government or its agency is substituted for that of the party involved. Because of the creditworthiness of the government, the rate the borrower pays is lower. The situation is illustrated in Figure 16-6. Before the government program to borrow and relend to the socially desirable project, the intersection of the supply, SS, and demand, DD, curves results in a market clearing rate of r_c and in a total amount borrowed of d^*. When the government steps in, it replaces the previous supply curve with a new supply curve, $S'S'$. We assume that the interest rate charged, r_s, is the same regardless of the amount borrowed, although this need not be the case.

It is possible that part of the funding of the project will be fulfilled by private sources if a discriminating auction takes place. In the case of Figure 16-6, this condition would result in a kinked supply curve of SXS', with the former portion coming from private sources. If the subsidy rate charged is low enough, however, the government will end up entirely displacing the financing of the project through private sources. Another qualification to Figure 16-6 is that the government may not wish to provide unlimited amounts of financing at a rate of r_s. Rather, it may simply agree to provide up to so much financing, in which case the supply curve $S'S'$ in Figure 16-6 would be a horizontal line that would stop abruptly at some point.

FIGURE 16-6 THE EFFECT OF BORROWING AND RELENDING

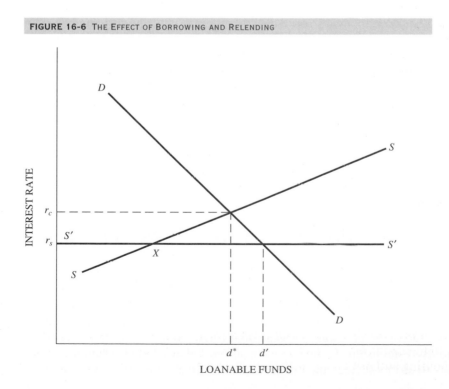

LOANABLE FUNDS

THE EFFECT OF GOVERNMENT INTERMEDIATION

The effect of this method of socially allocating capital is similar to the effect of a government guarantee or insurance. In whole or in part, the government absorbs the risk of default. As before, the underlying risk of the project does not go away; it is merely shifted from private investors to the government and, ultimately, to taxpayers at large. In addition, the amount borrowed will be larger than would occur under free market conditions unless the government limits the amount it is willing to lend. In Figure 16-6, equilibrium borrowings occur at d', where before they were at the lower d^*.

    What happens, of course, is that the government borrows at a favorable interest rate and then relends to the project involved. Again, the equilibrating mechanism in financial markets is distorted. Funds no longer flow on the basis of expected return and risk. One set of potential borrowers moves to the head of the credit line and capital is allocated to those borrowers on the basis of government decree, not by the marketplace. To the extent that substitutability exists between the financial instrument or market involved in the social allocation process and other financial markets, and to the extent that the amount of financing for the social project is larger than would otherwise be the case, the supply function for the other markets is adversely affected from the standpoint of borrowers. In other words, the supply curves for the other markets shift to the left. In general equilibrium, then, other borrowers may pay somewhat higher interest rates as a result of the government's borrowing and relending for the social project.

    From another viewpoint, as long as a project can obtain a social allocation of capital from the government while relatively few others are able to do so, it enjoys a significant advantage. However, if a large number of other borrowers have similar access to the government, the advantage diminishes. Beyond a point, essentially all financial flows would be determined by social criteria rather than economic criteria, and no private financial markets would exist as we know them. Savings would not flow to investment projects that appear to be most productive from an economic standpoint. They would flow on the basis of government-determined priorities. To the extent that these priorities differed significantly from economic priorities, the economic growth of the country would lessen and the wherewithal to address social problems would be reduced. The point of all this is simply to show that while some borrowing and relending by the government for social purposes may be beneficial to the favored parties and not significantly detrimental to other borrowers, as more and more of this type of action takes place, the advantage quickly disappears.

REGULATIONS AFFECTING INVESTOR AND BORROWER BEHAVIOR

The fifth method for socially allocating capital is the use of government regulations to divert the flow of savings toward socially desirable projects. In this case, artificial restraints are established to affect the flows. The best-known and most important example of this method in the past was mortgage financing, so our discussion will center on this example. By establishing ceiling rates of interest that mortgage lending institutions could pay to attract savings and by creating certain barriers to the saver with respect to investing elsewhere—that is, by restricting competition—the government hoped to increase mortgage financing at rates of interest lower than would otherwise be the market clearing rates. Unlike other approaches for socially allocating capital, the government's role is indirect, sometimes bordering on the obscure, but nonetheless may be powerful.

THE EFFECTIVENESS OF THIS APPROACH

The success of this approach depends on the degree of substitutability between markets. The more isolated the mortgage market is relative to other markets and the less substitutability there is between mortgages and other financial instruments, the greater the flow of savings to mortgages will be and the lower the rate of interest, all other things remaining the same. However, if mortgages and other financial instruments are perfect substitutes, lenders who are unrestricted by the government will simply substitute other securities for mortgages whenever the risk-adjusted rate of return falls below that available in other financial markets. The actions of these unrestricted investors will offset actions by financial institutions, which are restricted in their investment behavior to mortgages. That is, increases in mortgage purchases by restricted lenders will merely fill the gap created when unrestricted lenders leave the mortgage market. There will be no net increase in mortgage loans.

Let us turn now to the situation in which mortgages and other securities are less-than-perfect substitutes, and unrestricted lenders are present in the mortgage market. Here there would be a less than one-for-one offset by unrestricted lenders in selling mortgages for other securities when the risk-adjusted return was forced below that available in other markets. In the extreme case of zero substitutability between markets, there would be no offset. As long as the degree of substitutability is less than perfect, there will be a "stickiness" on the part of unrestricted lenders in selling mortgages, even though risk-adjusted rates may be more attractive elsewhere. As a result, this approach to allocating capital socially will be only partially successful. In summary, this approach is essentially one in which the government imposes restrictions to thwart competition so the flow of savings to mortgage lending institutions can be enhanced.

THE COSTS TO SOCIETY

This approach places no direct cost on the government and on taxpayers, apart from the cost associated with administering the program. There are, however, a number of hidden costs. For one thing, artificial restrictions result in a less efficient functioning of financial markets. Certain savers must accept lower interest rates on their savings than otherwise would prevail. The opportunity cost falls unevenly on different savers. Higher-income individuals with larger amounts of savings typically are able to avail themselves of alternative investment opportunities, like money market instruments that pay higher rates of interest. Meanwhile, low- to moderate-income individuals must accept the lower savings rates because these investors do not have such alternatives. The adverse distributional impact of deposit rate ceilings on the small saver has been supported empirically.

Deposit rate ceilings no longer exist in the United States. With the deregulation of the financial services industry, they were phased out in the 1980s. However, this method of social allocation of capital is not only of historical interest to Americans but is still used in certain countries. Therefore, an understanding of it remains important.

QUALIFICATION FOR TAX-EXEMPT FINANCING

The last method we examine for socially allocating capital is the designation of certain projects for tax-exempt financing. The advantage to the borrower is obvious—the interest cost is significantly less than it would be if taxable bonds were issued. While we usually think of municipal debt as financing schools, sewers, public buildings, parks, and highways, private purposes have qualified as well. Corporations through industrial revenue and pollution control bonds, home owners through mortgage revenue bonds, farmers, students, and a number of others all now or in the past have qualified for tax-exempt financing. Although such access had been widespread in the 1970s, it was reduced significantly by Congress in the 1980s. Still, some projects continue to qualify, so it is important to understand the concepts behind the use of this method of social allocation of capital.

If we ignore second-order effects for the moment, the situation is illustrated in Figure 16-7. In the absence of financing "qualified" private projects on a tax-exempt basis, the intersection of the supply, SS, and demand, DD, curves results in a market clearing rate of r_c and in a total amount borrowed of d^*. The availability of lower-cost tax-exempt financing shifts the supply curve to the right in the figure. Qualified borrowers now seek

FIGURE 16-7 TAX-EXEMPT FINANCING OF PRIVATE PROJECTS

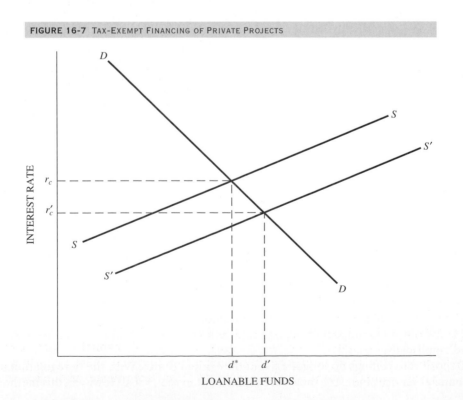

LOANABLE FUNDS

d' in financing at the lower market clearing rate of r_c'. Thus, additional less-productive projects are undertaken, which would not be the case if they had to be financed in the taxable bond market. The magnitude is depicted by $d' - d^*$ on the horizontal axis in Figure 16-7. Obviously, an investor has great incentives to get his or her project qualified for tax-exempt financing. Given rational behavior, it is little wonder that such financing of essentially private projects flourished. The limiting factors are only the demand for such projects and the legality of whether a project qualifies for tax exemption.

BENEFITS, COSTS, AND EXTERNALITIES

Certain second-order effects cloud the picture presented in Figure 16-7. Certainly society gains with some of the projects: Employment in a depressed area is stimulated; pollution is reduced; housing may be enhanced; hospitals are built or improved; or energy production is increased. These benefits are an inducement to those in government to continue to allow the municipal interest subsidy to be spent for these purposes. However, obvious issues of equity and redistribution of income arise regarding who qualifies and who does not. Moreover, there are costs. For one thing, the federal government loses revenue, as tax-exempt bonds are substituted for taxable bonds. In essence, the government subsidizes those private projects that qualify. Owing to certain offsets, the revenue loss is less than one-for-one. Still, the loss to the government is significant; it results in federal programs being delayed or abandoned, higher taxes for others, or increases in the federal debt.

As discussed before for other methods, at the margin, less-productive projects are favored over those that can be financed only with taxable bonds. Consequently, society bears an opportunity cost in lower productivity than is possible if all private projects competed for capital on the same basis. As the overall supply of municipal securities increases, municipalities may have to appeal for funds from investors in lower and lower tax brackets. As discussed in the previous chapter, this will occur if the municipal securities market is partially segmented. As a result, municipalities financing public projects may need to pay a higher interest cost than would be true if there were no tax-exempt financing of private projects. Thus, the capital costs associated with providing such traditional facilities as schools, sewers, recreational areas, and highways may increase.

POLICY IMPLICATIONS

In this chapter, we have examined a number of means by which the government can influence the flow of savings to a desired cause and/or reduce the rate of interest paid by a designated borrower. In all cases, there is intervention in the marketplace; hence we have in whole or in part a social allocation of capital as opposed to a pure market allocation. The political appeal is irresistible—there appear to be enormous benefits and, on the surface at least, few costs.

However, we know from our previous discussion that there are costs. For one thing, the function of financial markets is altered. This function is to channel savings in society efficiently to the most productive investment opportunities. These opportunities may be private sector investments, where rates of return are private, or public sector investments with social rates of return. The mechanism by which funds are channeled is the trade-off between expected return and risk. When the government explicitly directs funds to certain investments that either would not be able to attract funds on their own or would attract them only at a higher rate of interest, it tampers with the workings of the marketplace. This tampering can lead to less efficient financial markets with the result that savings are allocated at higher costs and/or with greater inconvenience.

Funds no longer flow on the basis of expected return and risk. Certain borrowers—namely, those whom the government decides are socially deserving—no longer must justify their investment's private or social rate of return in relation to a market-determined standard of efficiency. The result is that some investments are undertaken that would be rejected if the borrower had to compete directly in the financial markets for funds. Put another way, in society as a whole investments are undertaken that are not optimal in the sense of economic efficiency. As a result, real economic growth may be adversely affected. The capital market discipline of who gets what on a risk-return basis is supplanted.

What we have is the social allocation of capital to selected projects, some by choice and others by default. As we have discussed repeatedly, a serious question of equity arises as to who should benefit from the social allocation of capital. In a number of instances, income is redistributed, not always with the intended or desired results. Moreover, the loss of tax revenue to the federal government that is associated with certain of the methods requires new taxes, expenditure reductions, or more Treasury borrowings. These second-order effects are seldom considered but are factors of concern nonetheless.

This is not to say that savings flows should be allocated on the basis of economic considerations alone. Without question, certain social needs go unmet, and some of these needs may be satisfied by the social allocation of capital. The problem is that methods for socially allocating capital are seldom evaluated in their totality. Usually, the benefits are readily apparent and always cited. However, the "true costs" are seldom considered. As a result, the idea is often given that the social allocation of capital is either without cost or that the costs are unimportant. As we have shown, however, there is a cost, not only to the government and to taxpayers but also to society as a whole, in having less efficient financial markets and lower-than-possible economic growth. Unfortunately, the deeper the cost is hidden, the more tempting the decision is to allocate capital socially. Even more disturbing is that usually the more hidden the cost of a method is, the less efficient the process is by which capital is allocated socially.

The benefits of a plan to allocate capital socially must be judged in relation to the opportunity cost to taxpayers, to other borrowers, to savers, to the efficiency of financial markets, and to the economic and/or social contribution forgone by the rejection of other projects. While the decision-making process is easier if these costs can somehow be ignored, they represent the very crux of the issue. As they ultimately must be borne by society in one way or another, these costs should be analyzed when a decision is made.

In those cases where Congress or some other part of government deems it appropriate on the basis of a cost-benefit type of analysis to allocate capital socially, a strong case can be made that the allocation should be in the form of an interest-rate subsidy to the borrower. Assuming a high degree of substitutability and competition between various financial instruments—and most evidence seems to confirm this—the subsidy is likely to be the most effective way to allocate capital socially, provided it comes from general tax revenues. With an interest-rate subsidy, financial markets are able to perform their function in terms of market clearing rates of interest. With an absence of restrictions, we would expect financial markets to perform as efficiently as possible under the circumstances. The subsidy would come from the federal government at the expense of taxpayers in general rather than a subset of them. The advantage of such an arrangement would be that savings would be more efficiently channeled in society. While there is still the question of social priorities versus economic priorities,[4] once this is resolved, a free-market mechanism would allocate savings in a competitive environment on the basis of risk and return.

❖ SUMMARY

The social allocation of capital involves efforts by the government to direct the flow of savings in society toward socially desirable projects and/or to lower the interest cost for these projects. A number of methods for allocating capital socially were analyzed. These include (1) a ceiling or usury rate of interest on loans, (2) the use of a government guarantee or insurance, (3) an interest-rate subsidy, (4) the government's borrowing in the financial markets and relending to the socially desirable project, (5) the use of regulations to divert the flow of savings toward socially desirable projects, and (6) the specification of who and what projects qualify for tax-exempt financing. Each of these methods was examined in regard to its effect in increasing the flow of financing and in lowering interest costs. A key ingredient was found to be the substitutability of the financial instrument in question with other financial instruments.

In most cases, the costs of allocating capital socially are not understood. These costs include such things as the probabilistic cost of making good on a guarantee or insurance by the government, the less-efficient functioning of financial markets, the lessened allocative efficiency of real resources, the loss of tax revenue to the federal government, and the consequences of how it is made up. It is critical that these costs be considered in relation to their benefits before a decision to socially allocate capital is made. Too often this analysis does not occur, due to the "hidden" nature of many of the costs. When it is deemed appropriate to socially allocate capital, a strong case can be made for the use of an interest-rate subsidy because it has the least disruptive influence on the functioning of financial markets. Use of this method implicitly assumes a reasonably high degree of substitutability among financial instruments.

❖ SELECTED REFERENCES

Crafton, Steven M., "An Empirical Test of the Effect of Usury Laws," *Journal of Law and Economics* 23 (April 1980): 135–45.

Gale, William G., "Economic Effects of Federal Credit Programs," *American Economic Review* 81 (March 1991): 132–52.

Innes, Robert, "Investment and Government Intervention in Credit Markets When There Is

Asymmetric Information," *Journal of Public Economics* 46 (December 1991): 147–81.

Kaufman, George G., ed., *Efficiency of the Municipal Bond Market: The Use of Tax Exempt Financing for "Private" Purposes.* Greenwich, CT: JAI Press, 1981.

Li, Wenli, "Government Loan, Guarantee, and Grant Programs: An Evaluation," *Economic*

---

[4] The use of a subsidy may result in overconsumption of certain commodities relative to others. Consideration of this issue in an overall framework of public choice is beyond the scope of this book.

Quarterly of the Federal Reserve Bank of Richmond 84 (Fall 1998): 25–51.

Merton, Robert C., and Zvi Bodie, "On the Management of Financial Guarantees," *Financial Management* 21 (Winter 1992): 87–109.

Mester, Loretta J., "Why Are Credit Card Rates Sticky?" working paper, Federal Reserve Bank of Philadelphia (June 1993).

Penner, Rudolph G., and William L. Silber, "The Interaction between Federal Credit Programs and the Impact on the Allocation of Credit," *American Economic Review* 63 (December 1973): 838–52.

Pyle, David H., "The Losses on Savings Deposits from Interest Rate Regulation," *Bell Journal of Economics and Management Science* 5 (Autumn 1974): 614–22.

Selby, M. J. P., J. R. Franks, and J. P. Karki, "Loan Guarantees, Wealth Transfers and Incentives to Invest," *Journal of Industrial Economics* 37 (September 1988): 47–65.

Sosin, Howard, "On the Valuation of Federal Loan Guarantees to Corporations," *Journal of Finance* 35 (December 1980): 1209–21.

Van Horne, James C., "The Withering of Capital," *Journal of the Midwest Finance Association* 10 (1981): 83–91.

In this index, page numbers in *italics* designate figures; page numbers followed by "t" designate tables; *See also* cross-references designate related topics or more detailed topic breakdowns.

benefits, costs, and externalities, 287
method, 286–287
by regulations affecting borrowing and lending, 284–286
costs to society, 285–286
effectiveness, 285
Source and use statements, 18t, 18–19
Speculation, in futures, 147–153. *See also* Futures contracts; Hedging and speculation
Speculator, defined, 147
Spot currency rates, 242
Spot market, 241
Spot prices, 150–151, *151*
Spread
bid-ask, 125
credit-swap, 204
option-adjusted, 207–209, *209,* 215. *See also* Call feature; Option-adjusted spreads
static, 207
swap, 196–197
Spread-adjusted notes, 205
Spread strategy, 107
Stock, preferred, taxes and, 271–273
Straight floaters, 228
Strategies for portfolio management, 106–108
Strike (exercise) price, 162
Stripped mortgage-backed securities (SMBs), 226–227, 233–236
Stripping, coupon, 113–114
Subordination, 224
Subsidies, interest-rate, 280–283, *281, 282*
Substitutability, of maturities, 80–82
Super floaters, 228
Swap reversal, 198
Swaps
basis, 192
credit (default), 204
currency, *251,* 251–253

currency/interest-rate, 252
valuation implications, 253–254
floating/fixed, 191–192
interest-rate, 191–204
credit derivatives, 202–205, *203*
credit risk, maturity, and systemic risk, 199–202
features of, 191–192, *193*
pricing, 196–198, 197t
secondary market values, 198–199
swaptions, 202
valuation issues, 192–196
total return, 203–204
Swap sale, 198
Swaptions
call, 201, 202
put, 201, 202
SYCURVE (slope of the yield curve) options, 177–178
Systemic risk, 201

T

Targeted amortization class (TAC) securities, 226
Taxes, 260–273
on capital gains, 261–264
de minimis rule, 263
municipal bonds, 263
original issue discount (OID) bonds, 261–262
taxable coupon bonds, 262–263
tax timing options, 263–264
municipal bonds and interest income, 264–265
preferred stock and, 271–273
auction-rate preferred stock, 271–272
straight preferred stock, 271

taxable versus tax-exempt yields, 266, *267*
value of tax-exemption feature, 266–271
effect of tax reform and supply, 269–270
municipal versus taxable yield curves, *270,* 270–271
variation of implied tax rate, 268–269
Tax-exempt financing, 286–287
Tax exemption, value of, 266–271
effect of tax reform and supply, 269–270
municipal versus taxable yield curves, *270,* 270–271
variation of implied tax rate, 268–269
Tax laws, swap value and, 195–197
Tax Reform Act of 1986, 269
TBA (to-be-announced) basis, 224, 232
Term, risk and, 138–141
Term premiums, 84, *84*
Term structure, 77–94
Cox-Ingersoll-Ross (CIR) theory, 88–89
general equilibrium notions, 86–87
term structure implications, 87–89, *88*
definition of, 77–79, *78*
empirical evidence of, 91–92
lattice models of, 90–91, *91*
market segmentation and, 85–87
multifactor models of, 89–90
of pure discount bonds, 114, *115*
pure expectations theory, 79–83
arbitrage and market efficiency, 83